Deaf People in the Criminal Justice System

Deaf People in the Criminal Justice System

Selected Topics on Advocacy, Incarceration, and Social Justice

Edited by
Debra Guthmann,
Gabriel I. Lomas,
Damara Goff Paris,
and Gabriel A. "Tony" Martin

Gallaudet University Press
Washington, DC

Gallaudet University Press
Washington, DC 20002
gupress.gallaudet.edu

Printed in the United States of America

ISBN 978-1-944838-81-2 (casebound)
ISBN 978-944838-83-6 (paperback)
ISBN 978-1-944838-82-9 (ebook)

Complete Cataloging-in-Publication Data for this title is available from the Library of Congress.

∞ This paper meets the requirements of ANSI/NISO Z39.48–1992 (Permanence of Paper).

Cover design by Tracy Cox.

Signed chapter summaries for this book are available on the Gallaudet University Press YouTube channel:
www.youtube.com/GallaudetUniversityPress

Contents

Introduction vii
Deaf People in the Criminal Justice System:
Selected Topics on Advocacy, Incarceration, and Social Justice
Debra Guthmann, Gabriel I. Lomas,
and Damara Goff Paris

Part I | Research and Evaluation

1 Demographics and Etiology in Deafness: Sociocultural Elements of Relevance to the Criminal Justice System 3
Damara Goff Paris, E. Basil Kessler,
and Gabriel A. "Tony" Martin

2 Assessing Linguistic Incompetence in the Criminal Justice and Mental Health Systems 22
Roger C. Williams

3 Research Methods With Deaf People in the Justice System 40
Raychelle L. Harris and Donna M. Mertens

Part II | Theory, Practice, and Specialized Services

4 School-to-Prison Nexus: Deaf Youth and the Juvenile Justice System 63
Gabriel I. Lomas

5 Substance Use Disorders Among Deaf Offenders 82
Debra Guthmann and Marcia Kolvitz

6 Deaf People Within the Justice System: Insights From the United Kingdom 115
Susan O'Rourke, Sally Austen,
and Elizabeth Wakeland

7 Discourse, Sign Language Interpreters, and the Criminal Justice System: Implications for Communicating With Deaf People 131
Theresa B. Smith

Part III | Legal Aspects

8 Deafness, the Individuals With Disabilities Education Act, and the Juvenile Delinquency System 167
Daniel Shaw

9 Nondiscrimination in the Criminal Justice System: An Examination of the Americans With Disabilities Act and Section 504 of the Rehabilitation Act 181
Barry C. Taylor and Rachel M. Weisberg

10 The Attorney–Client Relationship 212
Amber D. Farrelly

11 Disability Justice in the Age of Mass Incarceration 229
Talila A. Lewis

12 Deaf People in the Criminal Justice System: Concluding Thoughts 304
Debra Guthmann and Gabriel I. Lomas

Contributors 317

Index 325

Introduction
Deaf People in the Criminal Justice System: Selected Topics on Advocacy, Incarceration, and Social Justice

Debra Guthmann,
Gabriel I. Lomas, and
Damara Goff Paris

We are pleased to bring you this collection of writings on deaf people in the criminal justice system. Our goal is to educate more people on this often-neglected topic. When reviewing the literature, we found very few scholarly references to the deaf experience when it came to arrests, incarceration, or the court system. We also found that very few police officers, lawyers, advocates, judges, and juries were familiar with the language and culture of the Deaf community. The concept for this book evolved because of the urgent need to have materials available that help professionals who work in a wide range of settings better understand the criminal justice experience for deaf individuals.

When thinking of a title for this book, some of the authors expressed concern about the use of the words "criminal justice." Unfortunately, our legal system does not always provide "justice" for all deaf people. In the book, several authors share stories and examples of deaf inmates, illustrating a variety of experiences and injustices that happened to them. In reviewing the literature, we discovered that there are few published journal articles or book chapters related to deaf people and the criminal justice system. To address the lack of scholarly material on this topic, we have brought together an interdisciplinary group of authors to share their professional and personal experiences related to deaf people and the criminal justice system. We have included attorneys, clinicians, interpreters, administrators, researchers, and advocates to provide the reader with a broader perspective regarding this largely unexplored topic.

In this book, we focus primarily on the U.S. criminal justice system but have included several authors from Great Britain who have published extensively and have had experience with deaf people and the justice system in their country. The legal systems in Great Britain and the United States have some similarities as well as some differences, and the challenges faced by deaf people in the criminal justice system are global. Readers will find these parallels interesting and may uncover resources that could be helpful in the United States or in other legal systems throughout the world.

The legal system is a complex one to maneuver, and without appropriate access, many injustices can occur. Deaf people in prison may not be given the same access as hearing individuals, and each step leading to and including incarceration has potential barriers. Deaf people in the criminal justice system are routinely denied sign language interpreters, video access, and other accommodations not only while in prison but at each stage of the legal process. The lack of advocates who are qualified to work with deaf people in prison further exacerbates the marginalization of this population.

There is insufficient data regarding the number of deaf individuals who are incarcerated or involved in other aspects of the legal system. The research and data available related to the criminal justice system and deaf individuals are also sparse when it comes to what happens when a deaf person enters the legal system. While working on the book, the editors contacted different states to try to get a sense of the number of deaf individuals who were incarcerated. The information is not publicly available, and most of the states do not keep track of which inmates are deaf. Additionally, in some states the majority of deaf inmates are in one facility, whereas in other locations they are spread out throughout the state system.

There is a lack of prevention, assessment, and treatment available to deaf individuals with mental health and substance use disorders. This absence can lead to deaf individuals being in the legal system without access to therapeutic interventions that could assist in preventing recidivism. There are situations where deaf people are unable to go to treatment in their home community, which a hearing person would have the ability to do on release, and this lack of access exacerbates challenges and increases the risk of relapse for deaf individuals. This is precisely the kind of subject that is addressed in this book because it has been largely overlooked in the academic arena. This book aims to bring interdisciplinary contributors together to shed light on both problems and solutions for deaf people who interact with the legal system. Readers will find such topics and more discussed in greater depth in this book.

DEFINITIONS

Throughout this book, we use the word "deaf" to refer to all people who may identify as deaf, deafblind, deaf disabled, hard of hearing, late-deafened, and hearing impaired. This definition is consistent with the one offered by the National Deaf Center (2020) and recognizes that many people have an identity that is fluid, changes over time, and fluctuates with the setting. Historically, one of the more dominant views of deaf people has been a medical model in which hearing loss is viewed as a health deficit in need of medical intervention. When referring to the medical model, deaf people are sometimes referred to as deaf, hearing impaired, or people with hearing loss. The term "hearing impaired," although at one time considered to be appropriate to use, is no longer the preferred terminology. Members of the Deaf community identify as a linguistic and cultural minority group and designate this by capitalizing the "D" in "Deaf." The Deaf community in the United States uses American Sign Language (ASL) as the shared language. Culturally Deaf people are included in our use of "deaf" throughout this book.

Deaf people typically develop visual language (ASL) naturally, much like the experience of spoken language development of hearing children born to hearing parents. The majority of deaf children are born to hearing parents, and many may not be exposed to ASL during early childhood. Some deaf people may have language development challenges, including language deprivation, cognitive impairment, neuroatypical features, the presence of disabilities, and sometimes exposure to multiple languages with no clear and consistent language for use at home, at school, and in the community.

Typically, prisoners have some access to communication with people outside of prison, although it may be limited owing to the level of security where one is being held. Hearing eligible prisoners may make telephone calls or visit with friends and family members. Deaf people who cannot effectively use the phone rely on other means of telecommunication. In the past, deaf people used a digital teletype device called a telecommunication device for the deaf (TTY or TDD). The device was slow and cumbersome because users were required to type English words to communicate, and the person on the other end had to wait to reply until the user was finished. However, advances in technology and the widespread availability of high-speed internet in most communities have eliminated the TTY. Today, most deaf people prefer to use a videophone (VP), a device that transmits both sound and video, much like Skype. Because deaf people can see each other when using a VP, communication happens in real time. Furthermore, relay services (an operator service that allows a hearing party and a deaf party to call one another) now use video relay services in which interpreters voice and sign in real time, making conversations feel natural and smooth.

There are prisons that do not have VPs for inmates, and because of that, even though they are outdated and cumbersome, TTYs may be used. Even in prisons that have VPs, because of the demand for their use, inmates may revert to using TTYs because they are more available than VPs. Until recently, deaf people have not had access to VPs in prisons. However, lawsuits filed in some states have enabled inmates located in those areas to use VPs to make calls and reconnect with family members. These issues are addressed in several chapters of this book but covered more in depth in Chapter 9 by Barry Taylor and Rachel Weisberg, disability attorneys who have won cases that have increased communication access for some deaf inmates.

HOW THIS BOOK IS ORGANIZED

The book uses a combination of research, clinical, anecdotal, and legal case examples to illustrate key points. All case examples have identifying information changed to protect the confidentiality of the deaf individual. This format helps readers build a greater understanding of the topics. One anecdote that was shared by one of our editors was from John Smith (pseudonym) and illustrates the isolation and communication frustrations experienced by deaf individuals who are incarcerated (Smith, personal communication, May 15, 2018).

There are about 80 deaf prisoners at the Estelle Unit in Huntsville, Texas. Most of them are nicknamed the "Sitting Stones" because they sit and watch TV in the recreational dayroom all day long. Some have longer sentences than others and will be in prison for many years. There was one deaf inmate who refused to become one of the sitting stones. While in school and as an adult, he struggled with his reading and writing skills, and that was a barrier for him. There was also a major shift in his life when he used a VP for the first time. He became reconnected with his deaf nieces and nephews, whom he had not seen for a long time. After chatting with them on the VP, he would feel somewhat inferior because he struggled to understand what they were discussing. He knew what he needed to do and was determined to do it himself. He obtained a dictionary and began reading the newspaper daily. He used the dictionary frequently because there were so many words that he did not understand. He collected piles of magazines, newspapers, and books in his cell. He would look up words from the dictionary and write down the definitions of the new vocabulary on paper. He became motivated to have conversations with his nieces and nephews and discuss the new vocabulary words he was learning.

Being an incarcerated deaf individual can result in significant isolation. This case underscores the importance of having VPs in prisons. VPs ensure that deaf inmates have the same access as hearing inmates. They also help to build a bridge with the outside world and give hope to isolated inmates. Although this example refers to communication with those outside of prison, the inability to interact with hearing inmates and prison personnel may exacerbate the deaf inmates' feeling of isolation and could impact their mental health.

STRUCTURE OF THE BOOK

The editors reached out to experts in the field who could contribute to key areas related to criminal justice and deaf people. These areas include juvenile and adult justice, language and communication, interpreter issues, substance abuse and mental health, research considerations, and the legal system. The book is divided into three sections, which include: 1. Research and Evaluation; 2. Theory, Practice, and Specialized Services; and 3. Legal Aspects.

In Chapter 1, "Demographics and Etiology in Deafness: Sociocultural Elements of Relevance to the Criminal Justice System," Damara Goff Paris, E. Basil Kessler, and Gabriel A. "Tony" Martin focus on the issues surrounding concrete data collection of demographic information pertinent to deaf individuals. Part of the difficulty in identifying accurate numbers has to do with the lack of questions regarding the use of ASL on self-reporting surveys, which can skew the results toward the number of people participating in the surveys who are not cultural representatives of the Deaf community. Additionally, the U.S. Census states on their website that questions regarding languages spoken and English-speaking ability were not designed to collect information about sign language users and that they count ASL users as those who speak English. This lack of data collection on a national level further impacts researchers' ability to determine the number of ASL users in the United States.

In Chapter 2, "Assessing Linguistic Incompetence in the Criminal Justice and Mental Health Systems," Roger C. Williams addresses critical elements related to the court system and linguistic incompetence with deaf people. Williams offers procedures for assessing linguistic incompetence. Linguistic competence is crucial in all cases. Defendants must be able to understand the charges against them. Linguistic incompetence is usually something long-standing, meaning that the individual charged with a crime has struggled with language for most or all of their lives. In some cases, defendants might be linguistically incompetent, resulting in many challenges. At the same time, zealous prosecutors may fail to consider that the deaf person may be innocent of charges brought against them.

In Chapter 3, "Research Methods With Deaf People in the Justice System," Raychelle L. Harris and Donna M. Mertens explore the world of research with deaf people in the criminal justice system and give readers examples of how research with small populations can be done. While research is abundant in the world of criminal justice for hearing people, little research has been done involving deaf people. There are a number of reasons for this, many of which this chapter addresses.

In Chapter 4, "School-to-Prison Nexus: Deaf Youth and the Juvenile Justice System," Gabriel I. Lomas shares his experiences with the school-to-prison nexus for deaf students. He explains how school policies frequently drive deaf students away from treatment and toward the criminal justice system. Examples in the chapter illustrate how multiple systemic challenges may result in deaf students experiencing a nexus that leads to a prison pipeline. Lomas makes recommendations on how to disrupt the school-to-prison nexus for deaf students.

In Chapter 5, "Substance Use Disorders Among Deaf Offenders," Debra Guthmann and Marcia Kolvitz address the presence of co-occurring disorders related to deaf offenders who may have substance abuse and/or mental health conditions. Throughout the chapter, the experiences of two deaf men are included to give the reader insight into what may happen when deaf offenders are incarcerated for substance abuse-related infractions. The intersection of substance abuse, mental health, and criminal behavior among deaf people is explored in greater depth in this chapter.

In Chapter 6, "Deaf People Within the Justice System: Insights From the United Kingdom," Susan O'Rourke, Sally Austen, and Elizabeth Wakeland, all

British, share scholarship and offer insights on the factors that contribute to crimes committed by deaf people. They explore theories of criminal behavior and evaluate it in the context of the deaf experience. They include both challenges and successes experienced with deaf people and the criminal justice system.

In Chapter 7, "Discourse, Sign Language Interpreters, and the Criminal Justice System: Implications for Communicating With Deaf People," Theresa B. Smith explores the complexity of what it means to interpret for people who are deaf within the criminal justice system. Smith discusses why certified and qualified interpreters are essential to this arena. Summaries of actual cases are used to analyze, highlight, and explain some of the issues and implications, concluding with some recommendations for establishing policies and procedures for the use of interpreters within this kind of system.

In Chapter 8, "Deafness, the Individuals With Disabilities Education Act, and the Juvenile Delinquency System," Daniel Shaw reviews special education law, including the Individuals With Disabilities Education Act, and the intersection of these laws with the juvenile corrections system. IDEA is the primary law that allows for communication access for deaf youth in schools. The child's right to a free, appropriate, publicly funded education does not terminate when a deaf youth becomes incarcerated, so IDEA continues to be the primary law of reference for incarcerated deaf children.

In Chapter 9, "Nondiscrimination in the Criminal Justice System: An Examination of the Americans With Disabilities Act and Section 504 of the Rehabilitation Act," Barry C. Taylor and Rachel M. Weisberg address key elements of these laws as well as case law that supports access for deaf clients and inmates. The authors look at a number of issues, including those related to interpreters, videophone access, accessible alerts, and assessments of needs. Taylor and Weisberg also share an overview of the type of defense that law enforcement, corrections, or a criminal court can make when defending ADA cases and touch briefly on the issue of remedies.

In Chapter 10, "The Attorney–Client Relationship," Amber D. Farrelly discusses the role of the attorney when representing deaf clients, and the importance of trust and diligent representation. She emphasizes the importance of ensuring the right to due process and access to counsel through direct communication or sign language interpreters. Finally, Farrelly discusses both mental and linguistic competency and the implications of these situations under the law.

In Chapter 11, "Disability Justice in the Age of Mass Incarceration," Talila A. Lewis comprehensively examines the challenges faced by deaf people navigating the criminal justice system. As the director of the nonprofit Helping Educate to Advance the Rights of the Deaf, and an attorney with a passion for advocacy, Lewis has been successful in advocating on numerous cases in which deaf people have been incarcerated unfairly or are denied access behind bars. Lewis offers readers strategies for advocacy through case examples and case law citations related to deaf people.

Chapter 12, "Deaf People in the Criminal Justice System: Concluding Thoughts," by Debra Guthmann and Gabriel I. Lomas, brings together the collective viewpoints of all contributors. The chapter expands on some of the key points that have been discussed throughout the book and emphasizes the need for additional advocacy, education, and action in the field. The concluding chapter also offers recommendations for future work.

CLOSING COMMENTS

We have written this book for a broad audience of readers. Of course, those who work in justice and law are a primary audience. Attorneys preparing for cases with deaf people will now have a resource to assist them in their work. Additionally, mental health professionals who work with deaf people will likely find many chapters of this text helpful in their practice and preparations for forensic services. Sign language interpreters have had few resources to turn to when preparing for their role in court. We hope that they, in addition to education professionals, family members, and advocates, will also find the materials in these pages useful in understanding deaf people and the criminal justice system.

Whatever your area of interest, we hope you enjoy reading this book and find the materials in this text beneficial and informative.

REFERENCE

National Deaf Center. (2020). *Defining deaf.* https://www.nationaldeafcenter.org/defining-deaf

Part 1

Research and Evaluation

1

Demographics and Etiology in Deafness: Sociocultural Elements of Relevance to the Criminal Justice System

Damara Goff Paris, E. Basil Kessler,
and Gabriel A. "Tony" Martin

This chapter addresses the lack of specific statistics relevant to deaf individuals who have experienced the criminal justice system. We note the scarcity of comprehensive data relating to the number of deaf individuals who identify culturally as members of the Deaf community in the United States and who have also been involved in the criminal justice system. The few available sources of data are insufficient and incomplete and often focus on people who identify themselves from a medical model of deafness.

In this chapter, we include information about etiology and sociocultural factors of the Deaf community; varying degrees of hearing loss; Deaf cultural identity; and information on both disability and deaf populations relevant to court cases, incarceration, and interaction with law enforcement. Such information is important for professionals who are largely unfamiliar with and rarely interact with deaf individuals.

ADDRESSING ETIOLOGY AND SOCIOCULTURAL REALITIES

In any study on individuals who are deaf, it is imperative that readers understand that there is little homogeneity in the population. As noted throughout this chapter, the Deaf community is made up of diverse individuals with multiple etiologies.

The etiology of one's deafness is central to understanding the experience of being a person who is deaf. It is not uncommon for those unfamiliar with members of the Deaf community to consider etiology from within an audiological framework. That framework focuses on whether the loss occurred prenatally, perinatally, or postnatally. An exclusively audiological understanding also includes the configuration of the loss, conductive or sensorineural, as well as the severity of the loss.

When the term "deaf" is used, many professionals unfamiliar with the diversity within the Deaf community likely default to what is frequently referenced as the medical model of deafness, that is, one's lack of auditory acuity. This model, also referred to as a model of pathology, is easily defaulted to because nondeaf people believe they know what it might be like not to hear. Additionally, individuals who are not deaf often view the experience of being deaf as a significant loss, whereas deaf people do not. Jaspers and Hewstone (1982) maintained that attribution assignments are more easily justified by those who are not members of the group being defined. Such definitions are often ascriptions of assumed universal characteristics that hold hostage the reality and importance of diversity within Deaf communities and interfere with the possibility of individual agency.

It is therefore incumbent on anyone working with people who are deaf to set aside the medical/pathological model and replace it with the sociocultural model of and by deaf people. Although we briefly mention the medical/pathological models, we do so only to provide information about past (and still current) perspectives relating to deaf individuals. Ladd (2005) stated very clearly that the sociocultural model is a strengths-based model emphasizing capabilities and possibilities, not deficits. This model punctuates the linguistic and cultural realities of deaf people that rely not on one's ability to hear but on shared membership with elements that include preferred language (American Sign Language [ASL]), educational experiences (residential school or mainstream programs with sign language interpreters), familial experiences (many deaf people having parents who can hear), arts, customs, athletics, political issues and activism, and specially modified communication devices. Each provides opportunities for unique experiences of human engagement. All are derived from a communal experience of being deaf that transcends the severity of a hearing loss and replaces it with a sense of membership and identity that must be addressed, purposefully and specifically, when working with deaf citizens in the criminal justice system.

BRIEF OVERVIEW OF TYPES AND CAUSES OF HEARING LOSS

Before discussing the demographics relevant to deaf individuals, it is important to touch on how hearing loss is defined as well as some of the more common causes of hearing loss. We provide this information only for the reader to understand how prevalent the medical model of deafness is when hearing loss is discussed in the literature or statistics, without reference to cultural aspects of the community.

The World Health Organization (WHO, 2016, p. 3) defines four categories of hearing loss:

- **Slight or mild hearing loss (26–40 dB):** trouble hearing speech from a distance, soft speech, or around background noise.

- **Moderate (41–60 dB):** Difficulty hearing normal speech even in close encounters.
- **Severe (61–80 dB):** Ability to hear only very loud speech or loud sounds in the environment (i.e., truck sirens). Conversational speech is normally not heard.
- **Profound (over 81 dB):** Loud sounds are usually perceived through vibrations.

There are three basic types of hearing loss. **Conductive hearing loss** relates to the outer and middle ear and its physiology, which can frequently be corrected through surgery. **Sensorineural hearing loss** is damage to the inner ear or the nerve pathways from the inner ear to the brain. Most frequently, the cause of hearing loss, it is often permanent and not surgically corrected (although this hearing loss sometimes benefits from cochlear implants). **Mixed hearing loss** is caused by the combination of conductive and sensorineural hearing loss.

We have briefly mentioned auditory information for those who are unfamiliar with decibel loss and types of hearing loss. However, this chapter focuses on issues regarding the demographics for culturally deaf populations who use ASL as their primary means of communication and often do not identify with medical models of hearing loss. The degree to which deaf individuals self-identify as culturally deaf or as individuals who have a hearing loss depends on many variables, including the age of onset, degree of loss, their parentage, their exposure to and use of ASL, and whether they identify culturally with other members who use ASL as their mode of communication.

GENERAL STATISTICS FROM VARIOUS ASSESSMENTS

According to Lin, Niparko, and Ferucci (2011), it is estimated that 12.7% of Americans 12 years and older have bilateral (loss in both ears) hearing loss and that the percentage increases to 20.3% if individuals with unilateral hearing loss (loss of hearing in one ear) are included. These percentages are based on a review of data from the National Health and Nutritional Examination Surveys from 2001 through 2008, as well as a definition of hearing loss provided by the WHO (2018). According to the most recent information from the WHO website, disabling hearing loss is defined as a hearing loss "greater than 40 decibels (dB) in the better hearing ear in adults and a hearing loss greater than 30 dB in the better hearing ear in children" (WHO, 2018, para. 3).

The American Community Survey is an annual demographics survey that provides population estimates for the U.S. Census. The 2019 Disability Characteristics Survey (U.S. Census Bureau, 2019) states that 2% of the survey respondents between the ages of 18 and 64 report a hearing loss, and 13.7% over the age of 65 report hearing loss. Although the survey breaks down ethnic identity by overall percentages reported, these numbers are not separated by specific disability. The survey discusses the percentage of hearing loss by age categories (i.e., under 5 and 5–17 years old) but does not include categories that identify communication methods such as whether the participants use ASL, signed English systems (which provide one sign for one English word regardless of the meaning of the word beings used) (Holcomb, 2013), or spoken languages.

The National Health Interview Survey, through the Centers for Disease Control and Prevention (2017), provides a different statistical analysis. According to their report, between 2014 and 2016, 15.9% of the population over the age of eighteen report hearing difficulty.

Several data collection efforts focus on children in K–12 settings. The National Center on Deaf-Blindness (NCDB, 2016) developed an annual National Child Count of Children and Youth Who Are DeafBlind report in 1986. According to their 2016 report, a total of 9,574 children were identified as DeafBlind through their data collection efforts in 2015.

Until 2013 to 2014, Gallaudet University collected statistics annually on the national and regional number of deaf children and youth in K–12. According to their most recent report, a total of 6,804 students were reported, 53% of whom were male and 47% female (Office of Research Support and International Affairs, 2014).

RACIAL/ETHNIC GROUPS AND DEAFNESS

Those who work in the criminal justice field are faced on a day-to-day basis with issues of the intersectionality of their own racial and ethnic affiliation with those of men and women in the criminal justice system. When working with a deaf person, criminal justice personnel must determine what intersectional dynamics might be of particular import to those with whom they work. A number of researchers have identified some important findings concerning certain group membership within the larger Deaf community.

Hoffman and colleagues (2017) found that non-Hispanic White adults are more likely to have hearing loss compared with adults in other ethnic groups. Non-Hispanic Black adults have the lowest prevalence of hearing loss between ages 20 and 69. American Indians/Alaska Natives and White individuals had the highest numbers of hearing loss, whereas Black/African Americans had the lowest prevalence for those ages 65 and older (McKee et al., 2018). Research addressing hearing loss in the Hispanic/Latino community found that 1 in 7 people (15%) identified as having hearing problems (Cruikshanks et al., 2015).

IMPACT OF SPECIFIC ETIOLOGY ON STATISTICS

Other factors also may impact the collection of data and, subsequently, our understanding of deaf people in the United States. These include periodic epidemics of disease, genetic factors, infant screening for hearing loss, noise pollution, and hearing loss relevant to returning veterans of war. As a result of these factors, reported numbers on hearing loss and deafness will rise or fall accordingly or be skewed in one area of the country compared with the rest of the population.

The Rubella Epidemic

Research that began in the 1940s and continued into the 1960s in Australia, the United Kingdom, and the United States cleared the way for recategorizing congenital rubella syndrome (CRS), once considered a minor rash, to a major health threat during pregnancy (Plotkin, 2006). The rubella epidemic struck the United States in 1964 and 1965, having migrated from Europe. An estimated 12.5 million people contracted the rubella virus between 1964 and 1965 (CDC, 2017). As infants were born, medical research recognized the systemic impact of CRS that lead to possible multiple pathologies affecting the brain, eyes, ears, lungs, liver, and spleen, to name but a few (Plotkin, 2006).

Doctor and Davis (1972) noted that the 1970 *Directory of Services for the Deaf* reported the greatest number of deaf students in preschool and regular classes in the country's history. Specifically, residential schools had waiting lists of students looking to enter their doors. The numbers of students and schools for the deaf have decreased dramatically over the years as a result of vaccination that has reduced the prevalence of rubella. By 2004, rubella and CRS had been declared eradicated in the United States (CDC, 2017). Currently in the United States, fewer than 10 people are reported to have contracted rubella annually (CDC, 2017).

Usher Syndrome

Usher syndrome is a genetic disease that combines deafness or hearing loss with an eye disease called retinitis pigmentosa (RP). In some cases, balance is also impacted. There are three types of Usher syndrome. Type 1 refers to individuals who are born with profound hearing loss at birth and have balance problems. Visual problems usually occur by age 10, beginning with night vision difficulties and progress to significant vision loss over several decades. Often, children with type 1 Usher syndrome do not benefit from hearing devices (although they may be candidates for cochlear implants) and may be introduced to a signed English system or ASL. Type 2 refers to children born with moderate to severe hearing loss and may often communicate orally and benefit from assistive hearing devices. RP often occurs in late adolescence. Children with type 3 are often born with normal hearing at birth and a near-normal balance, but with age, a progressive hearing loss occurs with accompanying balance difficulties in some children (Malm et al., 2011). The decline in both hearing and vision varies, with hearing loss being developed by adolescence, and the individual may need hearing aids by mid- to late adulthood. Night blindness may develop during adolescence; vision loss increases to legal blindness by midlife.

According to the National Institute on Deafness and other Communication Disorders (2017), Usher syndrome accounts for about 50% of all hereditary DeafBlind cases, impacting 3% to 6% of all children who are deaf and another 3% to 6% of children who are hard of hearing.

Some populations demonstrate a higher incidence of Usher syndrome. For example, in the United States, a larger proportion of the Louisiana Acadians have type 1, which is the most severe (Umrigar et al., 2017). As a result, hearing loss-related population statistics might be disproportionate in this geographical area.

Noise-Induced/Acquired Hearing Loss

Noise-induced hearing loss (NIHL) is cited as one of the most common forms of sensorineural hearing loss (Le et al., 2017). A 2011 to 2012 CDC study involving hearing tests and interviews with participants cited that at least 10 million adults (6%) in the United States under the age of 70 demonstrate hearing loss in one or both ears from exposure to loud noise. The WHO estimated that one-third of all cases of hearing loss could be attributed to noise exposure.

Recent studies show an increase in hearing loss in adolescents and young adults. Evidence suggests that loud rock music along with increased use of portable music players, frequently used with wired or wireless earphones, may be responsible for this phenomenon. Researchers have also estimated that in as many as 17% of teens (ages 12–19) features of their hearing test are suggestive of NIHL in one or both ears, with a prevalence of increased NIHL among female youth (Henderson et al., 2011).

Veterans and Hearing Loss

Currently, more than 445,000 veterans are receiving compensation for hearing loss associated with military service, and 395,000 are receiving compensation for service-related tinnitus (Saunders & Griest, 2009). These conditions are the top two service-connected disabilities for U.S. veterans who have received a disability award from the U.S. Department of Veterans Affairs (Frayne et al., 2011).

A study (Oleksiak et al., 2012) conducted on hearing loss among veterans with mild traumatic brain injury found that the participating veterans reported tinnitus (75.7%) and hearing loss (59.8%). Nearly half (48.6%) of the veterans were diagnosed with conductive hearing loss, sensorineural hearing loss, or central auditory dysfunction. An additional 24.3% of the veterans had subclinical levels of auditory dysfunction.

DEMOGRAPHICS RELEVANT TO CRIMINAL JUSTICE AND PEOPLE WITH DISABILITIES

Before discussing data pertinent to deaf individuals, general information about people with disabilities and criminal justice incidents should be shared. Although deaf individuals often do not consider themselves disabled and identify more as a cultural minority, they are regarded by government agencies and medical professionals to be part of the disability group. When reviewing statistics—regarding people with disabilities, it is helpful for us to understand that although the statistics may not include deaf people, similarities in the data may be found.

In a report released by RespectAbility (Mizrahi et al., 2016), it was estimated that more than 750,000 incarcerated individuals have a disability and that 32% of those in federal prisons and 40% of individuals incarcerated in jails have at least one disability. Bronson et al. (2015) reported that between 2011 and 2012, approximately 30% of state and federal prisoners and 40% of jail inmates have at least one disability. Women were more likely than men to report a disability. In addition, incarcerated individuals with a disability were more likely than nondisabled individuals to report serious psychological distress lasting more than 30 days. Individuals in prison were four times more likely to report psychological distress, whereas jail inmates were more than 2.5 times likely to report psychological distress.

According to House et al. (2018), youth with disabilities are disproportionately represented in correctional facilities and estimated to form up to 80% of incarcerated youth, according to their statistical analysis of various reports. Their analysis also posits that youth with disabilities are more likely to be incarcerated at an earlier age and be repeat offenders. Additionally, youth with disabilities have a high risk of recidivism, averaging 2.75 years, compared with 7 years for youth who are not disabled. McCauley (2017) estimated that Black individuals with disabilities are at particularly high risk for arrest, with 55% being arrested by age 28. McCauley also looked at other disparities regarding arrests.

> This disability gap in the cumulative probability of arrest persists when one looks at racial/ethnic groups by gender—with a gap of approximately 11.0 between those with disabilities and those without for White males and White females, a disability gap that is larger for males (13.94) than females (10.61) for Hispanics, and a disability gap that is larger for females (18.92) than males (12.51) for Blacks. (McCauley, 2017, p. 1980)

VanderPyl (2018) referred to the Department of Education Office of Civil Rights' report that indicated students with disabilities made up 12% of school populations, yet 25% of these students are arrested and referred to law enforcement. The National Council on Disability (NCD, 2015) reported that 85% of incarcerated youth have learning and/or emotional disabilities. Yet only 37% receive special education in school programs, with many going undiagnosed until adulthood.

CRIMINAL JUSTICE DEMOGRAPHICS AND THE DEAF POPULATION

Although data on the number of deaf individuals who experience the criminal justice system remains scarce, a few reports have emerged recently. RespectAbility (Mizrahi et al., 2016) estimated that 153,000 deaf individuals are incarcerated in jails or state and federal prisons. Their statistics were based on a special report by the U.S. Department of Justice (Bronson, Maruschak, & Berzofsky, 2015), which stated that 6.5% of all prisoners are deaf or have a serious hearing difficulty and that of these 8% were White, 3.1% Black/African American, 6.9% Hispanic/Latino, 8.4% two or more races, and 7.9% Other (including American Indian and Alaska Natives, Asian, Native Hawaiian, and other Pacific Islanders; U.S. Department of Justice, 2015). The report also stated that prisoners often had more than one disability.

In an article for *Mother Jones*, titled "The Secret World of Deaf Prisoners," Ridgeway (2009) referred to an estimated one-third of the population in prison having "difficulty hearing." Ridgeway also stated that there appeared to be no comprehensive collection of data on the number of deaf individuals who are incarcerated. Neave-DiToro et al. (2018) referenced several studies that indicated that the number of incarcerated individuals with "communication disorders" is significantly higher than that in the general population. The data included individuals with autism, speech disorders, and hearing loss without specific statistics relevant to each type of disability.

A publication issued by the Ruderman Family Foundation (Perry & Carter-Long, 2016) stated that between one-third and one-half of people killed by law enforcement officers have a disability. The report further explains that comprehensive data is not collected in regard to fatalities resulting from interactions between people with disabilities and law enforcement. Their estimation of the number of disabled people impacted results from reviewing a collection of studies. Although the report did not provide specific data on the number of deaf people killed by law enforcement officers between 2013 and 2015, it cited the case of John Williams. Williams, a severely hard of hearing First Nations woodcarver, was walking down the street with his carving knife when law enforcement spotted him and ordered him from behind his range of view to drop his knife. He was fatally shot five times.

Vallas (2016) reported two incidents in which a deaf person was incarcerated because of communication issues between law enforcement and a deaf person. The first case involved Christine Stein, from North Dakota, who had called 911 through video relay services to receive assistance with a man who was suicidal in her home. Unable to understand her, the responding officers arrested her because they thought she had harmed the individual. She was denied an interpreter during questioning, booking, and her court appearance. The charges were dropped when she finally had access to a sign language interpreter.

The second case involved Abreham Zemedagegehu, a deaf Ethiopian immigrant whose first language was Ethiopian Sign Language. He was arrested at an airport on suspicion that he had stolen an iPad that had been given to him by The New York Times Neediest Cases Fund to help with his communication needs. He was denied a sign language interpreter and given only a teletypewriter (TTY) to communicate over the phone. Owing to his difficulty understanding English, the device was not helpful, and access to a videophone using sign language services was denied.

Although scarce, there are more statistical reports bearing on the number of deaf individuals who are incarcerated or arrested than on the number of those who go through court systems.

ISSUES AROUND COLLECTION OF DATA

Historically, researchers who work with issues around deaf individuals have generally found an absence of valid data that well represent the population of culturally deaf citizens. Universally, problems exist in how hearing loss is defined across a diverse spectrum of people as well as how such data is collected.

In trying to understand hearing loss, we are struck with the phenomenon that hearing loss may be understood differently across one's life span. For example, deaf children of deaf parents are typically enculturated in the Deaf community and align closely with ASL and cultural mores and values of the community. Deaf children of hearing parents typically do not have such an enculturation process early on in their lives. They may, however, elect to align themselves with the Deaf community as they mature and have shared experiences with the culturally deaf.

Hearing adults who acquire a hearing loss either through the aging process or by some specific experience, for example, serving in the military, rarely identify as deaf, and most do not identify as culturally deaf. They typically accept that they have a hearing loss but would not posit that such a loss carries with it a label of disability or, even worse, a handicap. In this case, a hearing loss of any etiology or time of onset is not a self-identifying, subjective experience. It is merely an inconvenience.

In the three preceding examples, the universally accepted categories of deafness, that is, medical descriptions of hearing loss (WHO, 2018) appear to meet the needs of medical personnel, epidemiologists, and special educators. These categories do little to inform individuals or parents what the diagnosis of a hearing loss means at the subjective level.

Earlier, we discussed the audiological variables of hearing loss. There is also an environmental framework that addresses some of the day-to-day experiences of deaf people. We have the family context that includes how they respond to the diagnosis of a hearing loss as well as the role the identified child plays within the family. We must attend to the communication preferences and expectations within the home that encompass the quality of that language, the amount and type of linguistic interactions, and how deaf children are enculturated. Finally, there is a strong likelihood that numerous early interventionists, medical personnel, and educators are involved in the child and family's life.

As can be seen, the categories of deafness have little utility aside from noting the type and severity of a hearing loss. When we work with deaf individuals, we must transcend those simple metrics and be earnest in our understanding of the subjective response of the loss, if it is indeed experienced as a loss, and how that understanding impacts those with whom we work.

Instruments Omitting Sign Language Use and Cultural Identity

A common theme that seems to be prevalent when analyzing surveys and survey questions directed toward deaf individuals is the lack of questions concerning sign language use and cultural identity.

According to the U.S. Census Bureau (2019), under frequently asked questions, there is a statement that addresses ASL users. The census questions regarding languages spoken apart from English did not include ASL usage. The website states:

> The three questions used to capture languages spoken and English-speaking ability are not designed to identify American Sign Language users. The current question design supports the 1975 amendment to the Voting Rights Act, which prohibits discrimination against non-English language minorities when voting. The enforcement of the Voting Rights Act is focused on non-English languages that are spoken by members of racial minority groups. The law does not address or provide for sign languages used by hearing disabled population. Thus, the Census Bureau counts ASL speakers among those who speak English. (U.S. Census Bureau, 2019)

A petition was available at change.org encouraging people to support the inclusion of ASL among the questions regarding language use in the 2020 Census. In a memo issued on February 27, 2018, by the director of the Decennial Census Programs, support materials will be provided in ASL (among other languages) for the census questionnaire, but no mention of questions relevant to ASL usage was addressed.

Mitchell (2006) addressed some of the problems prevalent in instruments that collect data about hearing loss. Part of the problem, he stated, is that "at the definitional level, however, the demography of deafness becomes problematic when it is recognized that deafness is not only an audiological condition but also a social label" (p. 113). In other words, the focus appears to be on the medical aspect of hearing loss but not the cultural and language relevancy of self-identification. Hard of hearing people who do not culturally identify as members of the Deaf community would focus on the degree to which they understand speech, whereas deaf people who are part of the signing community would consider the aspect of sign language usage as their identification.

Some of the national surveys conducted to collect data on deaf individuals, such as the Survey of Income and Program Participation (SIPP), may focus on the degree of difficulty individuals may have in hearing human speech. Rarely do such data collection instruments focus on the preference of using sign language or preference of signed communication over assistive listening devices.

Accessibility of Surveys

We concur that some of the difficulty in collecting data specifically relevant to the culturally deaf members of the community has to do with researchers' lack of understanding of the complexity of the Deaf community (Harris et al., 2009) and accessibility of traditional survey methodologies. Most demographic surveys are conducted online or are written in English. Members of the Deaf community who use ASL as their first and/or primary language may be similar to other individuals who are not English-as-first-language users. In this circumstance, survey questions may not be readily accessible. Survey materials translated into visual modes of communication are rarely encountered and, if available, might encourage more ASL users to participate in surveys. In addition, there are likely groups representing differing priorities and experiences of being deaf that may not receive notice by survey conductors or researchers. As a result, it is understood that lower numbers of ASL users actually participate in the surveys.

Lack of Consistent Data

As mentioned previously, there is a lack of consistency among demographic reports for some of the larger survey statistics; that is, SIPP, the National Health Interview Survey, through the Centers for Disease Control and Prevention, WHO, and other survey results vary. This is largely because of the focus of their survey as well as the way they target respondents. According to the NCDB (2017), part of the problem of data collection compilations is how DeafBlind children are documented per their disability. The report, for example, stated that the Office of Special Education Programs had disclosed that there were a total of 1,443 students who were identified as DeafBlind from 2014 to 2015, but the NCDB reported findings of more than three times that number. Part of the discrepancy was attributable to the fact that often DeafBlind children with additional disabilities are documented as having developmental delays or included in other disability categories instead of DeafBlind.

Lack of Cohesive Data on Incarcerated Deaf People Who Use ASL

It is clear that the experience of being deaf (or identifying as a person who has a hearing loss) is a very subjective, personal experience. At one end of the experiential spectrum, some people embrace not the loss but the identity and rich culture of a linguistically unique population, users of ASL and other signed languages. At the opposite end of the spectrum is the factory worker or farmer with an acquired hearing loss who equates the loss to that of a vision problem, corrected by a pair of glasses. In the case of the factory worker or farmer, their hearing loss may be corrected by a set of hearing aids that are used or not used as they may see fit. It is no wonder that our reliance on the categories of deafness alone, that is, type and severity of a hearing loss, does little to capture the diverse tapestry of a deaf individual and their deaf experience. Therefore, what data we have are incomplete and represent challenges for scholars who aim to research this population.

If the data are in fact incomplete and inadequate, it is likely that we are collecting data for the sake of it. A far worse reality is that we have no questions that we believe need to be answered. This might explain why we have no comprehensive data set that helps us understand the deaf prison population. If such a data set existed, we would be able to answer the following questions.

- The age of onset and severity of hearing loss
- The primary mode of communication for deaf prisoners
- The number of ASL users in our prisons
- The number of interpreters hired by the penal system to accommodate deaf inmates
- The number and type of assistive listening devices purchased and used by the penal system
- Where our deaf prisoners were educated, and the highest level of education attained
- The number of deaf prisoners with secondary and tertiary disabilities significant enough to question their placement in specific penal environments

This information may not seem relevant to those in the criminal justice system, but such data would help us identify barriers and deficiencies in the system and consider solutions for the future needs of deaf prisoners by understanding the prevalence of support needed to increase accessibility for those who are incarcerated.

RECOMMENDATIONS

We have attempted to portray the complexities involved in attempting to understand how deafness impacts one's life. We have shown that the physiological loss of hearing goes only so far in explaining the important differences among those who are deaf.

We believe we have made the case that current data sets, data collection methods, and research questions are inadequate to understand deaf people and the lives they lead. We understand that membership of any specific subcommunity within the larger Deaf community necessitates that we purposefully begin to measure the differences and similarities between groups. We further recognize that at the national level no single group can or should speak on behalf of those who identify as deaf. However, those groups should be consulted as we seek a more comprehensive and representative understanding of deaf individuals in America. Our recommendations scratch the surface of the need for data collection efforts. It is our hope that on the basis of this discussion, government agencies, researchers, and school personnel further examine and consider additional ways to ensure current and future instruments are accessible, comprehensive, and relevant to deaf individuals who experience the criminal justice system.

Data Collected by the Department of Justice, Prisons, and Jails

More instruments should be developed that specifically address accessibility of deaf prisoners and that aim to collect data about deaf people during and after incarceration. Blanck (2017) recommends that jails and prisons develop and enforce the Americans With Disabilities Act self-evaluation plans and the establishment of nationwide identification and monitoring of inmates with disabilities. To expand on this recommendation, we believe that jails and prisons should undertake the following:

- Document whether a prisoner is deaf and all relevant medical information
- Note communication preferences and hearing assistive devices
- Document whether the deaf prisoner needs videophones, captioned telephones, or amplification of telephone equipment, as well as captioned or signed educational material
- Examine policies that impact notification systems for prisoners and document whether changes have been addressed to ensure that deaf prisoners are receiving accessible information from guards and prison personnel

In addition, data concerning the efforts of programs to assist deaf prisoners during and after incarceration should be collected on the accessibility requests made by deaf prisoners and their advocates in order to fully participate in opportunities to improve their skill set, mental health, and substance abuse services, and the type of accommodations made should be documented.

Comprehensive Data Collected by Law Enforcement Agencies

Perry and Carter-Long (2016) touched on violent encounters between law enforcement and people with disabilities, often resulting in fatalities. Documenting such incidents and releasing reports about the type of disability and interactions are important. For deaf individuals, it is imperative that law enforcement agencies note the type of accommodations used (or lack of them) during interactions, particularly during questioning and arrests. McCauley (2017) further posited that documentation should include how arrest probabilities vary by disability type and race/ethnicity and encourages policymakers to incorporate data on risk factors of untrained officers who interact with people who have disabilities. We suggest that specific data be collected on how much time is spent training officers on issues pertinent to deaf individuals.

Vallas (2016) recommended specific data collection for police officers interacting with people who have disabilities. Having reviewed her recommendations, we propose specific recommendations that would help increase information concerning law enforcement and contact with deaf individuals, including the following:

- Police encounters with deaf people, circumstances that led to the encounters
- Police shootings and deaths involving deaf individuals

- Whether additional disabilities occurred as a result of custody
- Requests for provision, denial, or removal of reasonable accommodations during the interaction, especially during arrests and while in custody

Comprehensive Data Collected by Court Systems

Accessibility in the courtroom is imperative toward the equivalent due process of deaf individuals. We recommend that courts identify someone to collect data on the requests by individuals who need sign language interpreters, certified deaf interpreters, real-time captioning, and assistive listening devices. Furthermore, data should be collected on such issues as whether the accommodations were provided and the time frame in which services were requested and provided, whether accommodations were denied as well as the rationale used to deny the requests. Finally, when accommodations and services are provided, the quality of those accommodations and services should be assessed.

Data Collection Pertinent to School Personnel

The NCD (2015) issued a report concerning the complexities of the school-to-prison pipeline pertaining to students with disabilities. They made a number of recommendations for a systematic overhaul to ensure that students with disabilities were not unduly targeted, and data were collected to identify and analyze the correlation between lack of educational support and entry into the juvenile justice system.

The suggestions included measures to ensure that the Civil Rights Data Collection (CRDC) enforces its mandatory data collection by public schools. The CRDC collects information, including race/ethnicity, sex, limited English proficiency, and disability. NCD (2015) emphasized that although the report is mandatory, data is underreported "relating to students with disabilities. This is particularly evident in several categories relevant to the school-to-prison pipeline, including retention, bullying and harassment, suspensions and expulsions, incidents of restraints and seclusion, and school-based arrests" (pp. 53–54). Additionally, they stated that "districts and schools currently face no ramifications from the Department for underreporting" (p. 54). The report recommended stricter ramifications for underreporting.

Such information should also be mandated by schools for deaf students, which should include information on expulsions, suspensions, school-based arrests, and types of accommodations provided. Furthermore, there should be additional information resulting from arrests, particularly concerning whether the student was provided accommodations while in custody. NCD (2015) also encourages legislative changes that would expand data collection through reauthorizations of the Individuals With Disabilities Education Act and the Juvenile Justice Delinquency Prevention Act. Such information for deaf students should include the onset of hearing loss, use of auditory devices, preferred modes of communication, and culture identification.

Collection of Data for Transitional and Community-Based Services

In order to examine the potential relationship between recidivism and transitioning or community-based services for deaf youth and adults who move out of jails and prisons into the community, data should be collected to determine the potential impact of accessibility to these services and reoffending. Outpatient treatment for mental health services or substance abuse, peer support, probation officer case management, supportive housing, mobile crisis teams, and court mandate services should document whether an individual is deaf, whether an accommodation was requested, what accommodations are provided, and the rationale for denying accommodations.

Other Recommendations and Conclusions

We suggest that the following steps be taken to remedy the lack of reliable data specific to deaf people in the United States: (1) establish a group of researchers from across the life span to review existing surveys and identify missing and/or inadequate data; (2) this group of researchers should include a representative sample of different subcommunity representatives; (3) this group of researchers should develop a series of instruments and methods to collect at: (a) age of onset, (b) type, (c) severity, (d) communication preference, (e) breakdown of race, (f) education and training (pre-K through adult), (g) employment status, (h) participation in government-supported programs, for example, vocational rehabilitation (SSI, SSDI), (i) marital status, (j) use of assistive technologies (pre-K through adult); (k) medical circumstances including multiple disabilities, and (l) subjective levels of importance of specific life experiences, for example, preferred mode of communication, education experience (quality and type), opportunities to function within both the deaf and hearing worlds, and perhaps others. It may also be worthwhile to collect information from parents of deaf children. Such data could address anticipated or chosen communication, and academic, social, and assistive technologies.

A consortium of institutions of higher education should be given the authority and obligation to pool monies and personnel in order to establish a clearinghouse of data collected in order to present a more accurate and comprehensive picture of the deaf experience in court, during interactions with law enforcement, and during incarceration. VanderPyl (2018) stated that often scholarship is "conducted and written *by* researchers *for* researchers" (p. 14) and that more research is needed that incorporates the actual living experiences of marginalized populations, particularly youth with disabilities. The better we understand their experience, the better we can prepare professionals in the criminal justice system to develop and maintain an accessible environment for deaf people.

In addition, national groups who represent deaf interests should be involved in the development and dissemination of data collection instruments. These organizations are understood to have access to specific populations of deaf people and to have a history of data collection experiences. Although not a comprehensive list, several suggestions offered by organizations for deaf individuals include:

- National Association of the Deaf
- Alexander Graham Bell Association for the Deaf and Hard of Hearing
- American Association for the DeafBlind
- American Deafness and Rehabilitation Association
- American Society for Deaf Children
- American Tinnitus Association
- Association of Late-Deafened Adults
- Boys' Town National Research Hospital
- Cochlear Implant Association
- Council on Education of the Deaf
- Deafness Research Foundation
- Deaf Women United
- Gallaudet University Alumni Association, Regional Centers, and Research Institute
- Starkey Hearing Foundation: Hear Now
- Helen Keller National Center for Deaf-Blind Youths and Adults
- Sacred Circle (Deaf individuals who are American Indian, Alaska Native, and First Nations)
- National Asian Deaf Congress
- National Black Deaf Advocates
- National Center for Accessible Media
- California State University, Northridge/National Center on Deafness
- National Council of Hispano Deaf and Hard of Hearing
- National Cued Speech Association
- National Deaf Education Project
- National Technical Institute for the Deaf at RIT
- Postsecondary Education Programs Network
- Rainbow Alliance of the Deaf
- Telecommunications for the Deaf and Hard of Hearing

The organizations and businesses listed in the foregoing are aligned with the multiple priorities of the American Deaf community. They also include pre-K–12 and postsecondary-related organizations as well as peripheral groups that provide assistive technology and telecommunication services.

We conclude that it is imperative that specific data be collected that address the cultural and language components that make up the Deaf community. Government data collection personnel must work with professionals and organizations by and for deaf individuals and in conjunction with criminal justice personnel (including law enforcement, staff in incarceration settings, court systems, and lawyers). We must ensure that the instruments and procedures used are valid and reliable, thus allowing us to have greater confidence in the data collected and in the conclusions drawn from those data.

REFERENCES

Blanck, P. (2017). *Disability in prison* (Preprint). https://bbi.syr.edu/wp-content/uploads/application/pdf/bio/2017-blanck-disbaility-prison-accessible.pdf

Bronson, J., Maruschak, L., & Berzofsky, M. (2015, December). *Disabilities among prison and jail inmates*. U.S. Department of Justice, Office of Justice Programs. https://www.bjs.gov/content/pub/pdf/dpji1112.pdf

Centers for Disease Control and Prevention. (2017). QuickStats: Percentage of adults aged ≥18 years with any hearing loss, by state—National Health Interview Survey, 2014–2016. *Morbidity and Mortality Weekly Report, 66*(50), 1389. http://dx.doi.org/10.15585/mmwr.mm6650a7

Cruickshanks, K. J., Dhar, S., Dinces, E., Fifer, R. C., Gonzalez, F., 2nd, Heiss, G., Hoffman, H. J., Lee, D. J., Newhoff, M., Tocci, L., Torre, P., 3rd, & Tweed, T. S. (2015). Hearing impairment prevalence and associated risk factors in the Hispanic community health study/Study of Latinos. *JAMA Otolaryngology--Head & Neck Surgery, 141*(7), 641–648. https://doi.org/10.1001/jamaoto.2015.0889

Doctor, P. V., & Davis, F. E. (1972). Educational impact—The 1964–5 rubella epidemic in the United States. *American Annals of the Deaf, 117*(1), 11–13.

Frayne, S. M., Chiu, V. Y., Iqbal, S., Berg, E. A., Laungani, K. J., Cronkite, R. C., Pavao, J., & Kimerling, R. (2011). Medical care needs of returning veterans with PTSD: Their other burden. *Journal of General Internal Medicine, 26*(1), 33–39. https://doi.org/10.1007/s11606-010-1497-4

Harris, R., Holmes, H. M., & Mertens, D. M. (2009). Research ethics in sign language communities. *Sign Language Studies, 9*(2), 104–131. https://doi.org/10.1353/sls.0.0011

Henderson, E., Testa, M. A., & Hartnick, C. (2011). Prevalence of noise-induced hearing-threshold shifts and hearing loss among U.S. youths. *Pediatrics, 127*(1), e39–e46. https://doi.org/10.1542/peds.2010-0926

Hoffman, H. J., Dobie, R. A., Losonczy, K. G., Themann, C. L., & Flamme, G. A. (2017). Declining prevalence of hearing loss in U.S. adults aged 20 to 69 years. *JAMA Otolaryngology—Head & Neck Surgery, 143*(3), 274–285. https://doi.org/10.1001/jamaoto.2016.3527

Holcomb, T. K. (2013). *Introduction to American deaf culture*. Oxford University Press.

House, L., Toste, J., & Austin, C. (2018). An overlooked population: Systematic review of transition programs for youth with disabilities in correctional facilities. *Journal of Correctional Education, 69*(2), 3–32.

Jaspers, J., & Hewstone, M. (1982). Cross cultural interaction: Social attribution and intergroup relations. In S. Bochner (Ed.), *Cultures in contact* (pp. 127–157). Pergamon Press.

Ladd, P. (2005). Deafhood: A concept stressing possibilities, not deficits. *Scandinavian Journal of Public Health, 33*(66), 12–17. https://doi.org/10.1080/14034950510033318

Le, T. N., Straatman, L. V., Lea, J., & Westerberg, B. (2017). Current insights in noise-induced hearing loss: A literature review of the underlying mechanism, pathophysiology, asymmetry, and management options. *Journal of Otolaryngology—Head & Neck Surgery, 46*(41). https://doi.org/10.1186/s40463–017–0219-x

Lin, F. R., Niparko, J. K., & Ferrucci, L. (2011). Hearing loss prevalence in the United States. *Archives of Internal Medicine, 171*(20), 1851–1853. https://doi.org/10.1001/archinternmed.2011.506

Malm, E., Ponjavic, V., Moller, C., Kimberling, W. J., & Andreasson, S. (2011). Phenotypes in defined genotypes including siblings with Usher syndrome. *Ophthalmic Genetics,* 32, 65–74. https://doi.org/10.3109/13816810.2010.536064

McCauley, E. J. (2017). The cumulative probability of arrest by age 28 years in the United States by disability status, race/ethnicity, and gender. *American Journal of Public Health, 107*(12), 1977–1981. https://doi.org/10.2105/AJPH.2017.304095

McKee, M. M., Stranskey, M. L., & Reichard, A. (2018). Hearing loss and associated medical conditions among individuals 65 years and older. *Disability and Health Journal, 11,* 122–125. https://doi.org/10.1016/j.dhjo.2017.05.007

Mitchell, R. (2006). How many deaf people are there in the United States? Estimates from the survey of income and program participation. *Journal of Deaf Studies and Deaf Education, 11*(1), 112–119. https://doi.org/10.1093/deafed/enj004

Mizrahi, J. L., Jeffers, J., Ellis, E. B., & Pauli, P. (2016). Disability and criminal justice reforms. *Respectability.* https://www.respectability.org/2016/06/disability-and-criminal-justice-reform-keys-to-success/

National Center on DeafBlindness (2017). *The 2016 national child count of children and youth who are Deaf-Blind.* https://www.nationaldb.org/media/doc/2016-National-Deaf-Blind-Child-Count-Report-PDF-FINAL.pdf

National Center on Deaf-Blindness. (2016). *The 2015 national child count of children and youth who are Deaf-Blind.* https://www.nationaldb.org/media/doc/2015-National-Deaf-Blind-Child-Count-Report.pdf

National Council on Disability. (2015). *Breaking the school-to-prison pipeline for students with disabilities.* https://www.ncd.gov/publications/2015/06182015

National Institute on Deafness and Other Communication Disorders. (2017). *Usher syndrome.* https://www.nidcd.nih.gov/health/usher-syndrome

Neave-DiToro, D., Fuse, A., & Bergen, M. (2018). Law enforcement interactions: The role of communication sciences and disorders professionals. *Communication Disorders Quarterly, 40*(4). https://doi.org/10.1177/1525740118810898

Office of Research Support and International Affairs. (2014, October). *Regional and national summary report of data from the 2013–14 Annual Survey of Deaf and Hard of Hearing Children and Youth.* RSIA, Gallaudet University.

Oleksiak, M., Smith, B. M., St. Andre, J. R., Caughlan, C. M., & Steiner, M. (2012). Audiological issues and hearing loss among veterans with mild traumatic brain injury. *JRRD, 49*(7), 995–1004. https://doi.org/10.1682/JRRD.2011.01.0001

Perry, D. M., & Carter-Long, L. (2016). *The Ruderman white paper on media coverage of law enforcement use of force and disability: A media study (2013–2015) and overview.* The Ruderman Family Foundation.

Plotkin, S. C. (2006). The history of rubella and rubella vaccination leading to elimination. *Clinical Infectious Diseases, 43* (Suppl. 3), S164–S168. https://doi.org/10.1086/505950

Ridgeway, J. (2009, October 9). The secret world of deaf prisoners. *Mother Jones.* https://www.motherjones.com/crime-justice/2009/10/secret-world-deaf-prisoners-0/

Saunders, G. H., & Griest, S. E. (2009). Hearing loss in veterans and the need for hearing loss prevention programs. *Noise Health, 11,* 14–21. http://www.noiseandhealth.org/text.asp?2009/11/42/14/45308

Umrigar, A., Musso, A., Mercer, D., Glausier, C., Bakeer, M., Marbler, M., Hicks, C., & Tsien, F. (2017). Delayed diagnosis of a patient with Usher syndrome 1C in a Louisiana Acadian family highlights the necessity of timely genetic testing for the diagnosis and management of congenital hearing loss. *Sage Open Medical Case Reports, 5*, 1–7. https://doi.org/10.177/20503i3X17745904

U.S. Census Bureau. (2019). *American community survey 1-year estimates.* https://data.census.gov/cedsci/table?q=S18&d=ACS%201-Year%20Estimates%20Subject%20Tables&tid=ACSST1Y2019.S1810

Vallas, R. (2016, July). Disabled behind bars. The mass incarceration of people with disabilities in America's jails and prisons. *Center for American Progress.* https://www.americanprogress.org/issues/criminal-justice/reports/2016/07/18/141447/disabled-behind-bars/

VanderPyl, T. (2018). Incarcerated DisCrit: The intersection of disproportionality in race, disability, and juvenile justice. *Justice Policy Journal, 15*(1), 1–19.

World Health Organization. (2016, March 3). *Childhood hearing loss: Act now, here's how.* https://www.who.int/docs/default-source/imported2/childhood-hearing-loss--strategies-for-prevention-and-care.pdf?sfvrsn=cbbbb3cc_0

World Health Organization. (2018, August 27). *Deafness and hearing loss.* https://www.who.int/news-room/fact-sheets/detail/deafness-and-hearing-loss

2

Assessing Linguistic Incompetence in the Criminal Justice and Mental Health Systems

Roger C. Williams

Serena (not her real name), a deaf 35-year-old woman, was arrested on charges of larceny. As this was her fourth offense, she was subjected to more severe penalties and a trial in a higher court than for her first three offenses. At her first appearance, the interpreter hired by the court advised the judge that communication was not effective, and the interpreter did not feel the defendant understood the proceedings. Her public defender then requested a hearing to determine fitness to stand trial. Like all states, South Carolina statutes provide a legal mechanism for determining fitness in cases where any party raises a question of competence to continue with court proceedings. South Carolina Code of Laws § 44-23-410 sets forth a procedure for determining fitness in two different situations: (1) mental illness, where the examination is done by the Department of Mental Health, and (2) intellectual disability, where the examination is done by the Department of Disabilities and Special Needs. While the statute defines a lack of fitness to stand trial as "lacks the capacity to understand the proceedings against him or to assist in his own defense as a result of a lack of mental capacity" (S.C. Code Ann. § 44-23-410 (1)A, 2012), no provision is made for an individual who is neither mentally ill nor intellectually disabled, as was Serena. Her public defender successfully argued before the court that she needed an assessment of her communication skills.

Following a communication skills assessment, as will be described later in this chapter, the court determined that she was not competent to stand trial, and the case was nolle prossed, the legal term for the decision by a prosecutor to discontinue proceeding with the case. As no further legal action was sought by the prosecuting attorney, she was released. As previously indicated, this was Serena's fourth appearance in court. In her earlier cases, no interpreter was provided by the court, her comprehension was assumed, and she had pled guilty or, more accurately, had signed a form stating that she was pleading guilty. Thankfully, none of the earlier charges resulted in her being incarcerated.

Serena's case is hardly unique. Vernon and Miller (2005) reported that the great majority of the cases they reviewed in writing their book should have resulted in a finding that the defendant was not competent to stand trial on the basis of linguistic incompetence. For example, in *State v. Burnett* (2005), the Ohio state supreme court affirmed the trial court's finding that a "deaf mute" defendant was incompetent to stand trial. The court held that the defendant's concrete thinking and idiosyncratic method of communication (which involved the use of gestures, American Sign Language (ASL), and a system of "home signing" established among his family members) precluded having interpreters' function as intermediaries between him and legal personnel. No mental health expert ever evaluated the defendant. The trial court based its finding on the testimony of a master's-level social worker who also had an associate's degree in sign language. It is worth noting that serious questions have been raised about the interpreter's performance in this case (Mathers, 2009), which, absent a formal communication assessment, are difficult to resolve. In another case (*U.S. v. Jones*, 2006) involving a deaf defendant who could not understand "standard sign language," a federal district court declared that the defendant was "physically incompetent" to stand trial under the Dusky standard (Mossman et al., 2007).

At other places in this edition, writers describe the legal basis and response to this situation. This chapter looks at the diagnosis of language disorder, the assessment itself, and the key role it can play in determining whether an individual is competent to stand trial or participate in other legal proceedings. This communication skills assessment and the procedure can be found at http://www.mentalhealthinterpreting.net/communication-skills-assessment.html. It is recommended that readers access the communication skills assessment while reading this chapter to provide an easy reference.

Language disorder was first defined in the fifth edition of the *Diagnostic and Statistical Manual of Mental Disorders* (American Psychiatric Association, 2013). For the first time, this diagnosis specifically recognized that individuals who use a sign language could also have a language disorder. It is worth reviewing the criteria because any discussion of linguistic competence almost always requires that the individual in question meet this definition for difficulties that are developmental in nature.

A. Persistent difficulties in the acquisition and use of language across modalities (i.e., spoken, written, sign language, or other) due to deficits in comprehension or production that include the following:
   1. reduced vocabulary (word knowledge and use);
   2. limited sentence structure (ability to put words and word endings together to form sentences based on the rules of grammar and morphology); and
   3. impairments in discourse (ability to use vocabulary and connect sentences to explain or describe a topic or series of events or have a conversation).

B. Language abilities are substantially and quantifiably below those expected for age, resulting in functional limitations in effective communication, social participation, academic achievement, or occupational performance, individually or in any combination.
C. Onset of symptoms in the early developmental period.
D. The difficulties are not attributable to hearing or other sensory impairment, motor dysfunction, or another medical or neurological condition and are not better explained by intellectual disability (intellectual developmental disorder) or global developmental delay. (American Psychiatric Association, 2013, 315.39/F80.9)

As can be seen from this definition, the key elements are the broad nature of the linguistic challenges and the onset being in the early developmental period. Language deprivation in individuals who are deaf has not been the subject of extensive research, although it is increasingly being recognized as a reality and as a source of significant concern (Hall et al., 2017). What we do know is that the first 12 months of life are crucial to language acquisition (Kuhl, 2000) and that the vast majority of parents of deaf children lack the language fluency to foster that early language acquisition (Gallaudet Research Institute, 2011). Miller and Vernon (2002) estimate that 25% of the general Deaf community meets the criteria for language disorder. In a review of prison inmates, Miller (2004) estimates that approximately 40% of individuals who are deaf and incarcerated have a language disorder. For individuals who are hospitalized in a psychiatric setting, the incidence has been estimated to be as high as 75% (Glickman, 2005). The initial descriptions of this problem in the deaf population focused on the behavioral and emotional manifestations of the language delay. "Primitive personality disorder," a label that was used by some of the earliest researchers in the field (Rainer et al., 1963) and was still being used as late as 2005 (Vernon & Miller, 2005), describes a collection of symptoms that fundamentally hinged on the catastrophic failure to develop language. The American Psychiatric Association does not recognize primitive personality disorder as an official diagnosis, and, as noted by Glickman (2009), the label is pejorative and could further stigmatize this population. In hearing adults, estimates are that approximately 5% of the population has a language disorder (Tomblin, 2010; World Health Organization, 1992). It is worth noting that the rate is much higher in individuals who are incarcerated and that hearing individuals with a language disorder are more likely to be unemployed and have more psychiatric disabilities, lower socioeconomic status, and fewer friends (Rost & McGregor, 2012). In about one-third of hearing individuals, the cause can be identified as a known neurological risk factor such as fetal anoxia or cytomegalovirus (CMV). However, in many cases, there is no identifiable cause (Norbury et al., 2016).

Human beings can develop language dysfluency because of a number of medical, psychiatric, and psychological conditions. The term "dysfluency" is used most often to refer to speech articulation difficulties like stuttering. In this chapter, the term "dysfluency" is being used differently. Following Pollard (2013), who in turn based his definitions on Andreasen's (1986) study of language, thought, and communication disorders in psychiatry, the term "dysfluency" is used to refer to two phenomena. The first is specific disruptive errors in language use that are atypical for native users of a language. Examples would be the unnecessary repetition of a sign or word or omission of key parts of speech, which may be a symptom of a psychotic disorder.

The second kind of dysfluent communication refers to a general lack of proficiency that is significant enough to impair communication with someone who is proficient in the language. Our interest is primarily in ongoing patterns; that is, errors repeated reliably for at least a period of time. A hearing person who is intoxicated and who is slurring their speech would be dysfluent, at least until they sober up. The medical cause, alcohol intoxication, would be widely assumed, especially if the person displays other behaviors associated with intoxication. A person who has just had a stroke, and struggles to remember words/signs, and speaks or signs in a slow, hesitant, halting manner shows another form of dysfluency.

The first discussions of sign language dysfluency in recent deaf mental health literature referred to well-known psychiatric causes. Alice Thacker (1994, 1998) was the first person to identify sign language dysfluencies in deaf people who had a severe mental illness that correspond to dysfluencies seen in hearing people, and subsequent authors, including Trumbetta and colleagues (2001), continued this discussion. Pollard (1998) has also made important contributions to the identification of sign language dysfluency related to psychiatric problems (Marschark & Clark, 1998). Poizner and colleagues (1987) studied deaf people who had experienced strokes and identified aphasias in sign language that correspond to aphasias in spoken language. We also know that deaf people with severe levels of autism can engage in behaviors like echolalia (repeating words or phrases) as well as have difficulty with pronouns like "I" or "me." Severe levels of developmental disorder can impair language development in both deaf and hearing people (Morgan et al., 2007). Both groups can also have specific language learning disabilities, although diagnosing these in deaf people is far more complicated (Pollard, 1998). Charlene Crump and Steve Hamerdinger (2017) have identified how common causes of deafness may impact language development in deaf people.

Although all of the medical and psychiatric reasons for language dysfluency in hearing people may also be causal factors for deaf people and although deaf people may have additional medical/neurological bases for language dysfluency, the greatest factor accounting for poor language skills in deaf people, in my experience, is language deprivation. Absent the exposure to natural sign language during the critical period for language development, many deaf children are deprived of the language learning experiences that would result in a full, native language.

When it is alleged that an individual is not competent to stand trial, it is incumbent on the court to demonstrate that the individual is indeed competent to proceed. As noted earlier, this question has traditionally been raised in the presence of a mental disorder or intellectual disability. However, all states have language that is similar to South Carolina's, leaving open the possibility of incompetence because of a language disorder. Although the determination of competence is solely within the court's purview, it is standard practice for the court to request an assessment and report from which the judge will then make a determination. The use of communication assessments is still in the developmental stage, but using some type of formal procedure provides the court with some confidence that it has the information needed to come to a conclusion.

The tool described here was an outgrowth of work done by The Alabama Department of Mental Health and the South Carolina Department of Mental Health, who had developed similar communication assessment instruments (Crump, 2005; Williams & Critchfield, 2003; Williams & Crump, 2018). Their instruments were built on the work of Greg Long, who created a communication assessment tool for individuals in employment settings (Long & Alvares, 1995). That tool was designed to improve the match between the communication skills required for successful employment in those settings and the abilities of the deaf worker. Although the assessments originally used by South Carolina and Alabama evolved over time, a presentation at the 2012 ADARA Breakout conference detailing each respective instrument and procedure inspired the goal of merging the two assessments into one tool that would be utilized in both states and made available to other programs (Crump & Williams, 2012). The assessment tool and procedure described here is the result of that collaboration.

As with any assessment for competence to stand trial, the linguistic assessor must be familiar with the skills required to participate in the court process effectively. These include the following:

- Whether the defendant understands what defenses are available;
- Whether the defendant can distinguish various pleas and understand the consequences of each plea;
- Whether the defendant has an awareness of their legal rights;
- Whether the defendant understands the range of possible verdicts and the consequences of conviction;
- Whether the defendant is able to recall and relate facts pertaining to their actions and whereabouts at certain times;
- Whether the defendant is able to maintain a consistent defense;
- Whether the defendant is able to listen to the testimony of witnesses and inform their lawyer of any distortions or misstatements;
- Whether the defendant has the ability to make simple decisions in response to well-explained alternatives.

The foregoing list is adapted from the work of Eric Eckes (2007) on linguistic incompetence in deaf individuals and is currently one of the few articles in the legal field on this topic. As is obvious from this list, all of these competencies require a minimal capacity to express and receive communication. However, rarely has a formal communication assessment been a part of the determination of competency. In my experience, sign language interpreters often do an informal communication assessment at the beginning of any assignment. In the not too distant past, interpreters were advised to spend a few minutes with the client in the waiting room before a session (Suggs, 2019). This, in theory, allowed the interpreter an opportunity to learn how the deaf person communicated. This informal assessment was often the extent to which a language assessment was conducted and yielded an impression as to whether the person was difficult or easy to understand. This analysis was often shared with the examiner and typically included comments such as "It's a tough one, they use ASL, but not well," "They have minimal language skills and are difficult to understand," or "They don't understand fingerspelling." These brief summary judgments were often overly simplistic, misleading, or outright wrong and gave little insight into the specific nature of the person's communication skills and deficits.

Neither did these brief assessments provide adequate guidance for the examiners to make a finding for the court on the question. In many situations, the interpreter's efforts may distort or interfere with that assessment. For example, an interpreter may provide too much information while interpreting a sentence or "clean up" the language used by the client to the point that the examiner thinks a client is competent when they are not. Similarly, an interpreter with insufficient linguistic competency may not be able to adequately express the message, leading the examiner to the finding of incompetency when the individual has the language competency but in ASL, not English.

An interpreter who chooses to interpret highly dysfluent language into coherent or even articulate spoken English may deprive the examiner of needed linguistic information regarding the accused individual's ability to comprehend the process. Yet an interpreter who glosses, providing a word-for-word transliteration, or simply states that the message does not make sense, without providing an analysis of why the message is incoherent, may bias their interpretation toward making the subject appear incompetent. In addition to violating Tenet 2.0 of the RID-NAD Code of Professional Conduct (Registry of Interpreters for the Deaf, 2005), such interpretive errors deny the defendant access to the court system and prevent the court from having an accurate report on which to base its decisions.

Having an objective communication assessment is one way to explore language abilities and deficits and eliminate ineffective communication approaches. It provides the examiner, and ultimately the court, guidance on an individual's ability to meet competence requirements.

Communication assessments are not psychological assessments, but they can certainly contribute to a fuller picture of the cognitive abilities of the client. Language and communication skills are strongly related to the "fund of information" that a person has about issues such as physical and mental health, interpersonal relationships, sexuality, society and the law, and how to work with an attorney (Esteban-Guitart & Moll, 2014). A person who is very language deprived is also likely to be information deprived (Hall et al., 2017). This means they need not only an interpreter to be competent in a court proceeding but also a staff who are prepared to help them learn the language, communication, and specific content areas.

The ability to communicate effectively is a major element in determining whether a person accused of a crime is competent to participate in their own defense. In the Appendix, a communication assessment report is included that was used as part of a forensic assessment of Serena to support the conclusion that she was not competent to work with her attorney in her defense.

The assessment report should be written for practitioners involved in the legal system, which is made up primarily of people who have limited background or experience working with individuals who are deaf. To ensure comprehension by attorneys and judges, the report must avoid jargon that is familiar only to those who work in the field of interpreting or deafness.

THE STRUCTURE OF THE COMMUNICATION ASSESSMENT

The communication assessment used in Alabama and South Carolina is designed to assess an individual's relative strengths and weaknesses across a continuum of communication modalities. It is also designed to identify an individual's most effective communication strategies. The assessment is structured in such a way as to permit those with severe language deficits to demonstrate skills. The definition of competence does not necessarily reflect a high degree of fluency or skill. The assessment was developed originally for use with individuals with significant communication dysfluencies and uses stimulus materials designed for easy comprehension. It does not allow for meaningful comparisons between individuals, nor does it compare one individual with a group norm. Attempts to interpret scores in these ways represent invalid applications of this instrument. Given the significant heterogeneity of the communication skills and experience of the population, the collection of background information is invaluable in understanding how an individual communicates. The assessment looks at the whole person and their communication environment. It looks at the individual's language and communication history, their communication strengths and weaknesses, and the degree of fit between these abilities and weaknesses as well as the communication demands of the environments they navigate. Data is collected in these domains:

- cause and nature of their hearing loss;
- family history;
- social background;
- psychiatric history;
- medical history;
- educational background;
- familiarity with, and use of, interpreters and adaptive equipment;
- visual or motor disabilities that impact language; and
- other medical issues such as dementia, stroke, cerebral palsy, or traumatic brain injury.

The language and communication capabilities examined include speech recognition and production, reading comprehension, writing, expressive and receptive fingerspelling, expressive and receptive manual communication skills, and familiarity with assistive communication devices. In addition, the evaluation attempts to describe and understand the specific kinds of sign language dysfluencies that are present.

Family communication background for each family member includes their age and gender, hearing status (hearing, hard of hearing, deaf), and method and quality of communication with the client (ASL; contact languages, such as Pidgin Signed English or manually coded English systems; cued speech; speech and lipreading; written notes; home signs; gestures; or other communication strategies). Some family members may use more than one system and will have different levels of fluency in different communication modalities. All applicable modes of communication used by each family member with the client should be indicated. This information should be obtained for each member of the client's household now and during childhood.

Of course, a person's formal school experiences will have a dramatic impact on the development of their language skills. As much as possible, either from a client report or record review, attempts are made to identify the complete trajectory of the individual's school experience. Considerations include the setting in which education occurred (e.g., mainstream, residential, self-contained classroom.) as well as the fluency of their language models. This information is essential in trying to determine potential language deprivation, as opposed to dysfluency caused by some other process. An individual educated for 12 years within a residential school for deaf people in a regular curriculum who has no coherent ASL presents significantly different concerns than someone with a similar lack of ASL fluency who attended mainstreamed classrooms without an interpreter for the same period.

During the interview portion of the communication assessment, the assessor should determine the person's familiarity with and ability to use a variety of assistive listening devices (e.g., videophones, hearing aids, signaling devices, assistive animals). In addition during the interview, various questions designed to assess the individual's experience and skill working with standard and deaf interpreters are asked. It is not unusual to find basic knowledge gaps, such as assuming the interpreter is the person generating the message or having no idea how to obtain an interpreter when they need one. During the administration of the assessment, the assessor(s) will be shifted between communication methods. These transitions between methods (as between speech recognition and speech, or writing and fingerspelling) should be explained to the client. If the client has questions or concerns, these can be discussed during the transitions. Signing clients may express a lack of enthusiasm for the speech-oriented components of the assessment, and oral deaf clients may express reluctance to shift from the speech-oriented subtest to the subtest assessing signing skills. The purpose of the assessment may need to be explained several times, and repeated efforts made to encourage the client to continue with a focused effort on all components of the assessment.

If the client's comprehension permits, the assessor may describe the process of the assessment and inform the client that all areas of communication will be included and specifically mention that speech, speech recognition/lipreading, reading, writing, fingerspelling, and signs will all be used. It is expected that individuals will have relative areas of strengths and weaknesses and that some areas of the assessment will be easier and relatively enjoyable, whereas other areas may involve some struggle for the client. Nevertheless, the assessor will make every effort to assist the client as much as possible to complete each component. The sole exception is the assistive communication section, which should be used only if the client uses a device or aid. The assessors note any differences between expressive or receptive communication abilities within specific modalities. For example, it is not uncommon to find that a person receives information better in one sign modality than another. There are some people who consistently demonstrate that they depend on ASL to receive information but whose language output is closer to Signed English. This is one of many reasons the individual is not asked directly for their communication preference, although it is often volunteered during the interview. Individuals will often answer what they think the "right" answer should be or what they have been told by others, whether that be teachers, interpreters, or family members.

Throughout the interview, the assessor should be looking for examples of dysfluency that are tabulated on a separate section. For instance, we regularly look for these common kinds of language weaknesses: If the client demonstrates the characteristic during the interview, it is noted on the assessment form. Additional dysfluencies not identified may be added, at the assessor's discretion, such as signs from a foreign sign language system being used with no recognition that they are not ASL or using signs that were created by an unqualified interpreter.

The scores from each of the areas (speech and speech recognition, reading and writing, fingerspelling, and expressive and receptive ASL) are then tallied, and a written report is produced. This report describes the results of the assessment, the demographic and historical data collected, and perhaps most importantly, recommendations for how information is best provided to the client.

The assessment will often include written material from the court setting, including documents the client has already seen, in an effort to determine whether the client has had effective access to those documents. Like any evaluation, assessing linguistic competence does not occur in a vacuum but is a reflection of the abilities required for the specific task at hand. As reflected in the list of competencies, a finding of competence must reflect the ability to perform these tasks in the course of the trial or proceeding, not merely to understand after several hours of explanation.

In addition to making a recommendation about competence to participate in the court process, a competency evaluation can also include an opinion as to the likelihood of an individual becoming competent in the future. As several cases have demonstrated, that process can take many years, if at all, but there is little legal guidance on how to retain someone who is neither mentally ill nor developmentally disabled (Eckes, 2007).

QUALIFICATIONS OF ASSESSORS

It took several decades for the awareness of ASL as a language to become widely accepted, and this can still be an ongoing issue. It also took decades for the field of interpreting to adopt formal standards, training, and a credentialing process. We need to adopt the same high standard for the new field of communication assessments with deaf persons. Being deaf or having fluency in a sign language is not a sufficient qualification to complete this type of assessment. A distinct knowledge base and skill set are required to do this work, and even if there are not many people yet who can do it, an untrained, unqualified person is likely to do more damage than not having an assessment.

We have, unfortunately, seen situations where assessments are completed with individuals who lack sufficient training and/or oversight. In these cases, the appearance of a valid communication assessment may give legitimacy to conclusions that are not supported by the actual evidence.

Like any assessment, the communication skills assessment requires that the assessor(s) be trained and qualified to administer the instrument. This is a test of the client's communication skills across the entire continuum of communication methods. Administration by an assessor who possesses less than native-level skills in the areas tested will not only represent an unethical use of this test and do a great injustice to the client but will also result in an invalid assessment.

In order to administer this instrument responsibly, the assessment team should consist of a native sign language user who is deaf and a sign-fluent hearing person. A sign-fluent person is defined as one who possesses demonstrated fluency in ASL by attaining a Superior Plus on the Sign Language Proficiency Interview, a certification from the National Registry of Interpreters for the Deaf, a certification from the National Association of the Deaf at level 4 or higher, a level 4.5 or higher on the Educational Interpreter Proficiency Assessment, a master or advanced level from the Texas Board for Evaluation of Interpreters, or an equivalent (Board for Evaluation of Interpreters, 2018; Center for Assessment of Sign Language Interpreters, 2016; Rarus, 1999; Schick, 2017). This includes the ability to fingerspell fluidly and proficiently at a rate of about three letters per second or slightly slower than ordinary conversation (Jerde et al., 2003). Receptive fingerspelling skills must also be excellent. In addition, the assessor who is hearing (or at least one member of the assessor team) must be able to hear and understand speech at the level of a quiet conversation or have access to this information through alternative strategies. This also includes being able to speak clearly and fluently, without a strong accent or speech impairment, or being able to utilize alternative strategies, such as using an interpreter. Since this communication assessment intentionally tries to describe competence, or lack thereof, across a broad spectrum of communication modalities, one of the assessors needs to be able to accurately describe the speech being used by the subject. It is for this reason that teams of assessors are recommended. Depending on the communication competencies of the subject, the assessors should also be proficient in manually coded English systems and visual-gestural communication. They must also be familiar with the assistive communication device or aid used by the client, if applicable. Each person should assess within their primary language strengths but also be willing to consult with the other members of the team when making determinations regarding language competencies.

The assessor(s) should have a minimum of eight (8) hours of training in the assessment, which includes an overview of the instrument, an overview of types and patterns of dysfluency, and samples of collected information and written assessments. After completing the training, new assessors should have a review by a qualified assessor of five assessments that include videotaped samples of their assessments, the raw data collected, and the final report. Ongoing training is recommended, on an annual basis, consisting of at least 8 hours, which may include additional training in assessment tools or in language use and dysfluency.

Assessments should be done by at least two individuals working collaboratively whenever possible. The team should include at least one native signer who is deaf, particularly when an individual's language is considered to be significantly dysfluent.

As with any new process, caution is important. When individuals who are unqualified to do the work, or individuals who work without having checks and balances in their system, provide assessments, their misuse can result in significant harm to the individuals being assessed and the judicial process. The concern about unqualified persons performing these assessments is based on too many experiences in dealing with the consequences of their actions. In psychology, there is something called the Dunning–Kruger effect (Kruger & Dunning, 1999), whereby people believe their abilities are much higher than they really are. When this happens, people can fail to recognize their own biases and limitations, at great cost to the people they serve. If this is true for people, in general, it is certainly true in the developing realm of assessing linguistic competence where standards and formal training and credentialing processes are rare. As the list of qualifications for communication assessors should make clear, this is highly demanding and specialized work, and an assumption of humility about one's own abilities is good clinical practice. Any review of a communication assessment must include a review of the process and the assessor who produced the report.

CONCLUSION

The use of a comprehensive communication assessment can provide the team doing an assessment with much of the information needed to make a finding to the court, both on the immediate question of competence but also on the likelihood of gaining competence in the future. Assessing competence to stand trial is often a complex task, but justice demands that thorough and accurate evaluations of linguistic ability become an essential component of such assessments when linguistic competence is in question. As noted, this is a new and developing area of practice. Additional research is needed to identify and validate additional assessment tools as well as expand the pool of trained assessors who have the competence to address this complex issue. Such tools will need to recognize the linguistic heterogeneity of individuals who are deaf as well as to be expanded to better work with individuals who are deaf/blind and have an intellectual disability. Laws need to be amended to provide specific direction to attorneys and jurists as to the specific definition of linguistic incompetence and, indeed, to recognize that linguistic incompetence even exists.

REFERENCES

American Psychiatric Association. (2013). *Diagnostic and statistical manual of mental disorders* (5th ed., DSM-5).

Andreasen, N. (1986). Scale for the assessment of thought, language and communication. *Schizophrenia Bulletin, 12*(3), 473–482. https://doi.org/10.1093/schbul/12.3.473

Board for Evaluation of Interpreters. (2018). *Board for evaluation of interpreters certification program*. https://hhs.texas.gov/doing-business-hhs/provider-portals/assistive-services-providers/board-evaluation-interpreters-certification-program

Center for Assessment of Sign Language Interpreters. (2016). *National Interpreter Certification (NIC) exam*. http://www.casli.org/national-interpreter-certification-exam-nic/

Crump, C. (2005). *Communication assessment for individuals who are deaf or hard of hearing*. [Unpublished document]. Alabama Department of Mental Health.

Crump, C., & Hamerdinger, S. H. (2017). Understanding etiology of hearing loss as a contributor to language dysfluency and its impact on assessment and treatment of people who are deaf in mental health settings. *Community Mental Health Journal, 53*(8), 922–928.

Crump, C., & Williams, R. C. (2012, July 1). *Communication assessments* [Paper presentation]. ADARA Breakout XI, Atlanta, GA, United States.

Eckes, E. (2007). The incompetency of courts and legislatures: Addressing linguistically deprived deaf defendants. *University of Cincinnati Law Review, 75*(4), 1649–1682.

Esteban-Guitart, M., & Moll, L. C. (2014). Funds of Identity: A new concept based on the Funds of Knowledge approach. *Culture & Psychology, 20*(1), 31–48. https://doi.org/10.1177/1354067X13515934

Gallaudet Research Institute. (2011). *Regional and national summary report of data from the 2009–10 Annual Survey of Deaf and Hard of Hearing Children and Youth*. https://research.gallaudet.edu/Demographics/2010_National_Summary.pdf

Glickman, N. (2005). Language disfluency and diagnosis in the deaf inpatient population. *JADARA, 38*(3), art. 3.

Glickman, N. (2009). *Cognitive-behavioral therapy for deaf and hearing persons with language and learning challenges*. Routledge.

Hall, W., Levin, L., Anderson, M., Hall, W. C., Levin, L. L., & Anderson, M. L. (2017). Language deprivation syndrome: A possible neurodevelopmental disorder with sociocultural origins. *Social Psychiatry & Psychiatric Epidemiology, 52*(6), 761–776. https://doi.org/10.1007/s00127-017-1351-7

Jerde, T. E., Soechtling, J. F., & Flanders, M. (2003). Coarticulation in fluent fingerspelling. *Journal of Neuroscience, 23*(6), 2383–2393. https://doi.org/10.1523/JNEUROSCI.23-06-02383.2003

Kruger, J., & Dunning, D. (1999). Unskilled and unaware of it: How difficulties in recognizing one's own incompetence lead to inflated self-assessment. *Journal of Personality and Social Psychology, 77*, 1121–1134. https://doi.org/10.1037/0022-3514.77.6.1121

Kuhl, P. K. (2000). A new view of language acquisition. *Proceedings of the National Academy of Sciences of the United States of America, 97*(22), 11850–11857. https://doi.org/10.1073/pnas.97.22.11850

Long, G., & Alvares, R. (1995). The development of a communication assessment paradigm for use with traditionally underserved deaf adults. *Journal of the American Deafness and Rehabilitation Association, 29*(1), 1–16.

Marschark, M., & Clark, M. D. (1998). *Psychological perspectives on deafness* (Vol. 2). Erlbaum.

Mathers, C. (2009). *The deaf interpreter in court: An accommodation that is more than reasonable.* National Consortium of Interpreter Education Centers, Legal Work Group. http://www.nciec.org/projects/docs/The_Deaf_Interpreter_in_Court62409.pdf

Miller, K. (2004). Linguistic diversity in a deaf prison population: Implications for due process. *Journal of Deaf Studies and Deaf Education, 9*(1). https://doi.org/10.1093/deafed/enh007

Miller, K., & Vernon, M. (2002). Assessing linguistic diversity in deaf criminal suspects. *Sign Language Studies, 2*(4), 380–390. https://doi.org/10.1353/sls.2002.0021

Morgan, G., Herman, R., & Woll, B. (2007). Language impairments in sign language: Breakthroughs and puzzles. *International Journal of Language & Communication Disorders, 42*(1), 97–105. https://doi.org/10.1080/13682820600783178

Mossman, D., Noffsinger, S. G., Ash, P., Frierson, R. L., Gerbasi, J., Hackett, M., & Zonana, H. V. (2007). AAPL practice guideline for the forensic psychiatric evaluation of competence to stand trial. *Journal of the American Academy of Psychiatry and the Law, 35*(4), 3–72.

Norbury, C. F., Gooch, D., Wray, C., Baird, G., Charman, T., Simonoff, E., Vamvakas, G., & Pickles, A. (2016). The impact of nonverbal ability on prevalence and clinical presentation of language disorder: Evidence from a population study. *Journal of Child Psychology & Psychiatry, 57*(11), 1247–1257. https://doi.org10.1111/jcpp.12573

Poizner, H., Klima, E. S., & Belllugi, U. (1987). *What the hands reveal about the brain*. MIT Press.

Pollard, R. Q. (1998). *Mental health interpreting: A mentored curriculum* [Videotape and user's guide]. University of Rochester School of Medicine.

Pollard, R. Q. (2013). *Mental health and Deaf individuals: On-line training for clinicians.* https://dmh.mo.gov/deaf-services/training

Provisions Applicable to Both Mentally Ill Persons and Persons With Intellectual Disability, 410, Pub. L. No. 44, 23 Stat. (2012).

Rainer, J. D., Altschuler, K. Z., & Kallmann, F. J. (Eds.). (1963). *Family and mental health problems in a deaf population.* Columbia University, Department of Medical Genetics.

Rarus, N. B. (1999). *A brief introduction to the National Association of the Deaf Interpreter Assessment and Certification Program (NIC).* http://www.jsu.edu/dept/dss/resource-vr/cer-nad.html

Registry of Interpreters for the Deaf. (2005). *NAD-RID code of professional conduct*. https://www.rid.org/ethics/code-of-professional-conduct/

Rost, G. C., & McGregor, K. K. (2012). Miranda rights comprehension in young adults with specific language impairment. *American Journal of Speech-Language Pathology/American Speech-Language-Hearing Association, 21*(2), 101–108. https://doi.org/10.1044/1058-0360(2011/10-0094)

Schick, B. (2017). *Educational interpreter performance test.* https://www.classroominterpreting.org/eipa/performance/index.asp

State v. Burnett, WL 32797 (Ohio App. 2 Dist 2005).

Suggs, T. (2019). *Managing the waiting room.* St. Catherine CATIE Center. https://healthcareinterpreting.org/managing-the-waiting-room/

Thacker, A. (1994). Formal communication disorder: Sign language in deaf people with schizophrenia. *British Journal of Psychiatry, 165,* 818–823. https://doi.org/10.1192/bjp.165.6.818

Thacker, A. (1998). *The manifestation of schizophrenic formal communication disorder in sign language* [Unpublished doctoral dissertation]. St. George Hospital Medical School.

Tomblin, J. B. (2010). The EpiSLI database: A publicly available database on speech and language. *Language, Speech & Hearing Services in Schools, 41*(1), 108–117. https://doi.org/10.1044/0161-1461(2009/08-0057

Trumbetta, S. L., Bonvillian, J. D., Siedecki, J. T., & Haskins, B. G. (2001). Language-related symptoms in persons with schizophrenia and how Deaf persons may manifest these symptoms. *Sign Language Studies, 1*(3), 228–253. https://doi.org/10.1353/sls.2001.0012

U.S. v. Jones, U.S. Dist. LEXIS 9257 (E.D. Tenn. 2006).

Vernon, M., & Miller, K. (2005). Obstacles faced by deaf people in the criminal justice system. *American Annals of the Deaf, 150*(3), 283–291. https://doi.org/10.1353/aad.2005.0036

Williams, R., & Critchfield, A. B. (2003). *Communication skills assessment* [Unpublished manuscript]. South Carolina Department of Mental Health.

Williams, R. C., & Crump, C. (2018). Communication skills assessment for individuals who are deaf in mental health settings. In N. Glickman & W. Hall. (Eds.), *Language deprivation and Deaf mental health* (pp. 136–158). Routledge.

World Health Organization. (1992). *ICD-10 classification of mental and behavioural disorders: Clinical descriptions and diagnostic guidelines.*

APPENDIX

Referral Information

Ms. Smith was referred for the Communication Skills Assessment by her attorney, Michelle Jones of the county public defender's office. During an earlier interview with Ms. Jones, the sign language interpreter had raised a concern about her American Sign Language (ASL) competence and ability to understand the language needed in a legal situation.

Background Information

Ms. Smith is a 35-year-old White deaf female with no motor disabilities or vision impairment. She reports no difficulty in seeing or understanding the examiner. Background information was obtained from Ms. Smith, and, as will be detailed in the report, she has severe language dysfluency, so some of the collected information is unclear or potentially inaccurate. This is particularly true when trying to get her educational history.

Ms. Smith has a severe congenital sensorineural hearing loss. She reports that she became deaf at 6 years of age, although she is not sure of the reason. She is unable to provide any information about the etiology of her hearing loss. She is the only deaf person in her family. No one in her family knows ASL, and they communicate with her by speech, which she reports she does not understand. She is the second eldest of four children, although her older brother is deceased. Her parents divorced when she was 12, and she remained with her father, who has since passed away.

Ms. Smith attended a school until age 12 but had no access to the instruction. She cannot identify anything she learned during her time in school except enjoying playing with the other students. She left school when her parents divorced and her father did not have the funds to pay for continued schooling. In 1995, she immigrated to the United States from her birthplace in a foreign country with her new husband and moved to two other locations before moving to her current residence. She lives with her husband, Johnnie, who is also deaf. Her father-in-law lives in the house next door. Her only language instruction has been provided by her husband, who apparently uses an idiosyncratic mixture of her native country's sign language and ASL.

Ms. Smith has a basic understanding of the role of an interpreter and is aware that she used one in the past. She does not know how to arrange for an interpreter, stating that her husband has that information. She knows she needs an interpreter for her interactions with her attorney or the court but does not seem to know that it is reasonable to ask for an interpreter for medical appointments or other situations. She does not wear a hearing aid or use an amplified telephone. She states she had a hearing aid for a short time when she was a child but that she is unable to keep the aid. She is unaware of signaling devices and does not have any. She does not know about videophones, but her husband has a cellular phone with text capacity. She would like to be able to have a phone but states she does not know how to read or write, which is consistent with this evaluation. She does not have captioning on her television.

Testing Administration

Ms. Smith is interviewed at the county detention center in a small town. The initial interview and testing instructions are conducted in ASL and gestures. The interview is conducted by a qualified mental health interpreter and a peer support specialist and native user of ASL. Ms. Smith appears to understand the instructions, although multiple repetitions are sometimes necessary. She is unsure of her answers, often stating that she does not know a signed language and that she is unable to complete sections that require speech or writing. She is very attentive to the examiner's responses and scoring and is visibly concerned when unable to complete a task. Once Ms. Smith understands the instructions, she is cooperative. Overall, her performance is thought to be a good representation of her communication abilities.

Testing Results

This client's profile is consistent with her reports of a complete lack of formal language instruction. She was not exposed to accessible language until age 29, significantly past the optimal language window of 3 years old. She has had limited opportunity to develop her language, whether in English or ASL. She lacks fluency in any area of communication. She has difficulties across the communication spectrum. For everyday communication and during the test administration, the client has performed best in ASL with considerable gestures and sign-mime. She has no usable skills in the oral or written communication domains. She does not know fingerspelling because she has no knowledge of the English needed to understand fingerspelling.

Her ASL reflects her limited contact with the Deaf community and ineffective education. She has difficulty with vocabulary and with many of the abstract grammatical structures of ASL. When sentence structure or nonmanual markers dictate sentence meaning, she is unable to comprehend the sentence, focusing on the few signs she recognizes, rather than understanding the whole sentence.

Similarly, her expressive ASL is lacking in ASL grammar or structure. For example, there is no evidence of eyebrow movement to indicate topic or the use of incorporated numbers in her sentences. She has some nonstandard signs, some signs from her native sign language, and at least one that is completely incomprehensible. When understanding ASL, she has difficulty with sentences that use the rhetorical question format or require spatial visualization. She can answer questions about identity and concrete events but cannot understand any question that requires reference to an abstraction. For example, she cannot answer a question such as "what would make you happy?" or "what do you wish for?"

Her signed communication is fraught with dysfluencies, including a lack of vocabulary, incorrect or absent grammar, major gaps in fund of knowledge, and a lack of spatial structure or nonmanual markers.

SCORING GRID

The scoring grid provides a quick visual representation of the assessment results. Although this individual does not have full fluency in any communication modality, her relative strengths are in expressive and receptive ASL. But, as can be seen, even in those areas, she is experiencing significant challenges (see Figure 1).

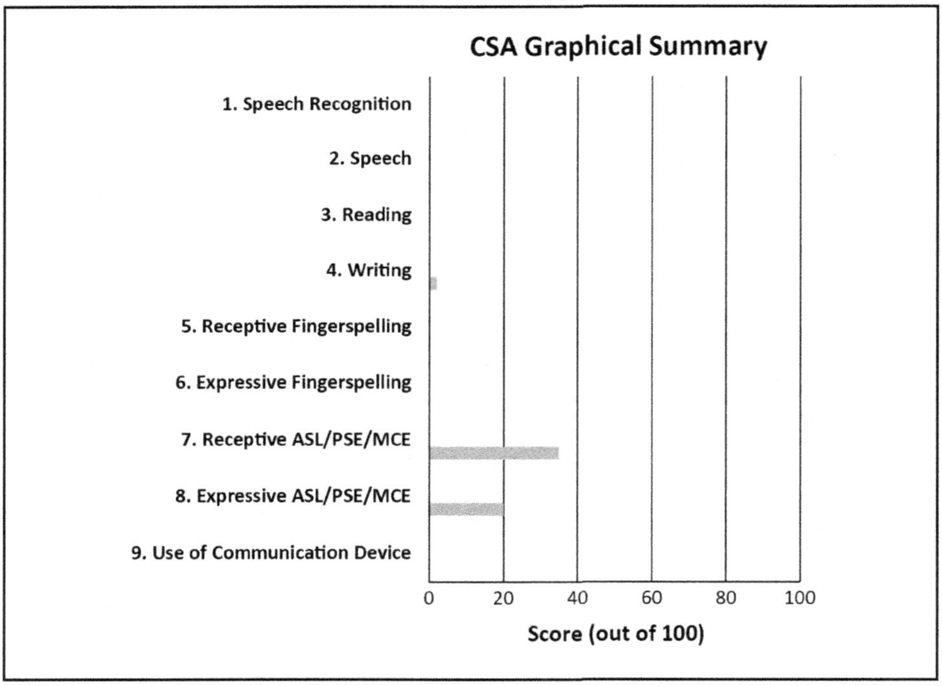

FIGURE 1. The scoring grid provides a visual representation of the assessment results.

Note. ASL = American Sign Language; MCE = Manually Coded English; PSE = Pidgin Signed English.

CONCLUSIONS

Ms. Smith's communication strength is in the manual communication arena, and this should be used as her primary mode of communication. However, in no communication arena were her communication skills sufficient to understand abstract or complicated information. Her oral and written skills are insufficient for any communication, although someone who knows her very well may be able to identify familiar words from her lip movements. Ms. Smith is aware of her communication limitations and perceives this as the result of intellectual deficiency, although her communication pattern is more consistent with language deprivation. She is likely to nod or respond as she thinks is appropriate without comprehending the interaction.

She is aware of some of the technological devices available such as captioning or text phones. However, her ability to use these devices is impaired by her lack of competence in English.

Ms. Smith would need significant and extensive instruction to improve her knowledge of ASL or to gain a basic understanding of English. It is unlikely that she would ever gain full fluency in any language, but she could improve her language skills. This could include an expansion of vocabulary and an improved ability to identify time sense and perspective (i.e., did the event she is reporting happen in the past or at present, and was she an observer or a participant). The types of errors she has made during the interview are fairly consistent and more likely reflect a lack of education and language exposure than a neurological or learning disorder.

As to the specific questions that resulted in Ms. Smith's referral, Ms. Smith's limited communication skills and inability to handle abstract information prevent her from comprehending or expressing the information needed to understand legal proceedings, including her ability to assist her attorney in her defense, understand her legal rights, or make choices about available options. She is able, with an experienced deaf/hearing interpreter team using a combination of visual–gestural communication and ASL, to communicate about concrete events and provide information about the events that led to her arrest. However, she lacks sufficient language fluency to understand witnesses in a courtroom during a proceeding, refute testimony, or assist her attorney when cross-examining witnesses. She lacks knowledge about the roles of individuals in a courtroom and does not know what a judge does or that there are other attorneys than Ms. Jones.

Outside of legal settings, information provided to Ms. Smith should include examples, demonstration, and visual representation, rather than depending on language to convey needed information. She should also have access to interpreters who are familiar with visual–gestural communication, ideally in deaf/hearing teams.

3

Research Methods With Deaf People in the Justice System

Raychelle L. Harris and Donna M. Mertens

The focus of this chapter is on the conducting of research related to linguistic and cultural issues associated with being deaf in the context of the justice system. These issues generally arise at the first point of contact with a law enforcement official and continue through the sequence of events between arrest, trial, incarceration, and probation (Mertens, 2000; Vernon & Miller, 2005). People doing research with deaf people within the justice system will find this chapter beneficial in designing their research methods. This chapter is also relevant for researchers focusing on deaf people who are victims of crimes. Although the processing of physical evidence is not different, depending on the accused person's hearing status, a multitude of linguistic and cultural issues arise when the person who is in contact with the justice system is deaf. Those issues are relevant when considering doing research with deaf people and their experiences with the justice system.

The Committee on Identifying the Needs of the Forensic Science Community (CIDNFSC, 2009) described the forensic research community as including crime scene investigators, crime laboratory staff, coroners, medical examiners, forensic pathologists, physicians and their assistants, law enforcement personnel, and court officials. The focus of the committee's work was on forensic evidence that is processed in crime laboratories, such as controlled substances, firearms, fingerprints, DNA, and other forms of technologically based evidence. This is also the focus of major textbooks on forensic research (James & Nordby, 2014). Although textbooks that address psychology and forensics do include reference to special populations, these are limited to youthful offenders and people with intellectual disabilities (Bartol & Bartol, 2015; Rosenfeld & Penrod, 2011). What is missing from this body of scholarly work is attention to issues related to deaf people who come into contact with the justice system and the particular issues that arise in ensuring that their rights are protected.

Despite the absence of a voice for Deaf communities in the forensic science research community, the concerns about the quality of material that surface in the CIDNFSC report (2009) do have relevance for members of Deaf communities. These concerns arise because information and testimony based on faulty forensic science contribute to wrongful convictions of innocent people. "Wrongful convictions have . . . demonstrated the potential danger of giving undue weight to evidence and testimony derived from imperfect testing and analysis. Moreover, imprecise or exaggerated expert testimony has sometimes contributed to the admission of erroneous or misleading evidence" (CIDNFSC, 2009, p. 4).

Research With Deaf People

Ethical concerns in research are pervasive throughout the research community and can be found in many statements. One such source is exemplified by the U.S. government's policies for the ethical conduct of research based on principles defined in the Belmont Report (National Commission for the Protection of Human Subjects of Biomedical and Behavioral Research, 1979) and overseen by the Office of Human Research Protections (www.hhs.gov/ohrp). The principles that govern research with human participants in the United States are defined as follows: Respect refers to treating people as autonomous agents and providing protection for those with diminished autonomy (Kitchener & Kitchener, 2009). Beneficence includes securing the participants' well-being by doing them no harm, maximizing possible benefits, and minimizing possible harms. Justice focuses not on the individual relationship between the researcher and the participants but on the distribution of goods and services in the research setting. This means that no group should be overburdened by excessive participation in research. This principle was viewed as important, especially for people who have diminished autonomy, such as prisoners (National Commission for the Protection of Human Subjects of Biomedical and Behavioral Research, 1979). In 1978, the U.S. Department of Health and Human Services added specific protections to prisoners who were subjects in research studies. These basic principles and protections are the bedrock of ethics in research. Nevertheless, multiple studies have identified contexts in which the rights of deaf people in contact with the justice system were not protected. Hence, a need exists to explore approaches to research that are framed by recognition of the specific needs of deaf people.

One challenge for researchers in deaf-related fields is the small size of the deaf population (Mitchell, 2006). This problem is magnified even further because most departments of corrections do not maintain a database of deaf prisoners (Ridgeway, 2009). In order to find and track Deaf community members, researchers would have to rely on assistance from Deaf community members throughout the United States. For example, according to Helping Educate to Advance the Rights of the Deaf's (HEARD) fact sheet, the Louisiana Department of Corrections announced that they have over 2,000 deaf prisoners;

however, as of 2018, HEARD was only able to find two deaf prisoners in Louisiana (HEARD Fact Sheet, 2018).

The difficulty in the identification of deaf prisoners is one manifestation of the challenges faced in conducting research with this population. Other factors that are explored in this chapter focus more directly on the status of the Deaf community as a cultural and linguistic minority group. To this end, we discuss the transformative paradigm as a framework for research that is explicitly designed to identify and develop solutions for members of marginalized communities. The transformative paradigm is a philosophical framework for research that emphasizes social justice and human rights (Mertens, 2009, 2020; Mertens & Wilson, 2019). This paradigm provides the structure for the discussion of an approach to research and addresses the cultural and linguistic issues associated with deaf persons who are in contact with the justice system. The ethical principles of the transformative paradigm are commensurate with those identified as sign language communities' terms of reference (SLCTR; Harris et al., 2009). These terms of reference (TOR) principles of ethics guide researchers in sign language communities (SLCs) that are specific to the conduct of culturally responsive research with deaf persons.

TRANSFORMATIVE PARADIGM: PHILOSOPHICAL ASSUMPTIONS

The transformative paradigm is based on the concept of paradigm in social science research as it was explained by Guba and Lincoln (2005) and modified by Mertens (2020). According to Guba and Lincoln (2005), a paradigm is made up of four basic sets of philosophical assumptions: axiological (the nature of ethics), ontological (the nature of knowledge), epistemological (the nature of knowledge and the relationships between the researcher and participants), and methodological (the nature of systematic inquiry). The philosophical assumptions for the transformative paradigm reflect the goal of research as supporting positive social transformation. When referring to deaf people in the justice system, this means positive transformation in terms of respect for their rights in all aspects of this system.

The transformative lens allows the researcher to explicitly seek to uncover systemic discrimination and oppression by working in partnership with the full array of stakeholders who are part of the criminal justice system. The goal is to challenge an oppressive status quo and support changes that further social justice. Thus, the transformative paradigm is used to inform the conduct of research that is rooted in a human rights agenda and that encompasses issues related to power and critical structural analysis.

Transformative Axiological Assumption

As stated previously, axiology asks the question: What is the nature of ethics or ethical behavior? The principles of respect, beneficence, and justice as described in the Belmont Report provide a beginning point to understand the nature of ethics in research. Ethical principles have been developed in the field of forensic science as well, but they are not inclusive of issues related to the culture and language in the Deaf communities (CIDNFSC, 2009).

The transformative axiological assumption challenges traditional interpretations of regulatory and professional ethics because they are not responsive to:

> ethical issues that arise in cultural contexts with differential power structures. . . . For example, within the context of a specific application in research with Deaf people, respect is defined in terms of the cultural norms of interaction within the Sign Language community and throughout the hearing and D/deaf worlds. Beneficence is defined in terms of the promotion of human rights and increased social justice. (Harris et al., 2009, pp. 108–109)

Within the parameters of the transformative axiological assumption, validity becomes an ethical issue in that research needs to be designed to make supported claims based on the findings. To establish such validity in the criminal justice context with deaf people requires that researchers collect valid data based on an understanding of the complexity of the community members by developing an accurate understanding of their context and by developing respectful relationships.

Culturally Appropriate Ethical Research Guidelines

Researchers in sign language communities (SLC) have explored the development of culturally appropriate guidelines that have relevance for researchers working in this community in the criminal justice system (Harris et al., 2009). They struggled with defining what the guidelines should include to enable respectful relationships and responsiveness to cultural issues and how partnerships with nondeaf researchers could be developed. The concept of cultural competency is relevant in the sense that it represents a critical disposition of the researcher to accurately portray the realities of members of a marginalized community. Cultural competence in research has been defined as:

> A systematic, responsive mode of inquiry that is actively cognizant, understanding, and appreciative of the cultural context in which the research takes place; it . . . employs culturally and contextually appropriate methodology, and uses community-generated, interpretive means to arrive at the results and further use of the findings. (Thompson-Robinson et al., 2004, p. 13)

Sign Language Communities' Terms of Reference (SLCTR)

Deaf people within SLC include the full range of diversity found in the general population with the added layers of complexity related to levels and type of auditory and speaking capabilities, including their use of auditory technologies such as hearing aids and cochlear implants (Harris et al., 2009). That definition also includes deaf people who may not have had access to sign languages early in life but instead may rely on their residual hearing, reading lips, making and reading gestures and facial expressions while communicating with other people. People who become deaf later in life are also included because, fundamentally, all deaf people experience barriers to communication, regardless of whether they are fluent in sign language or have some hearing or speaking abilities, particularly in our hearing-dominant and hearing-reliant society. TOR provides guidance for researchers in this context and ethical guidance for research conducted by, for, and with people who are deaf and part of the SLC. The SLCTR was originally conceptualized as guidelines for any research conducted with deaf individuals (Harris et al., 2009). Here, we modify and expand on these TOR to place them in the specific context of deaf people in the criminal justice system.

Ethical principles for researchers who conduct research in the SLC will be expanded on in the next section to reflect the needs of deaf people who do not use sign language and for hard of hearing people.

Principle 1: The Authority for the Construction of Sign Language Meanings and Knowledge Rests With the SLC Members

To do research with members of the Deaf community, a researcher not familiar with sign language or the Deaf community must work with deaf researcher(s) before proceeding any further. This approach is aligned with research methods protocol proposed by other marginalized, indigenous groups; for instance, research involving the Māori must be done "by Māori, for Māori, with Māori" (Cram et al., 2006, p. 176). That quote, Harris et al. (2009) argue, does not necessarily exclude hearing researchers, nor does it rule out the collaborative model; in fact, the last part of the phrase, "with Māori," emphasizes the joint role of both non-Māori and Māori researchers, "while keeping in mind the primacy of the latter and their essential roles in research projects" (p. 116). A historical analysis of research done on deaf and SLC members will show overwhelming evidence of published hearing researchers with very little actual collaboration with deaf stakeholders. The principle here emphasizes that the authority regarding deaf and SLCs belongs to deaf people and members of the SLC themselves (Harris et al., 2009).

The lack of knowledge about the Deaf community and about sign language is highlighted by deaf psychologists McCullough and Duchesneau (2006) in their interaction with a hearing forensic psychologist who did not know much about sign language or Deaf culture. The authors discussed whether specialized training (e.g., forensic psychology) supersedes cultural and linguistic knowledge of the community. McCullough and Duchesneau (2006) proposed that "the deaf professional should be in the front, with the hearing professional being available as a consultant, sharing specialized knowledge and allowing the deaf professional to grow and become an expert in the same area" (p. 1). Academic and employment opportunities for deaf researchers in a specialized area, such as forensic psychology, are limited, and hence the importance of the collaborative model with hearing people who have specialized training and, ideally, with deaf people leading the process.

Principle 2: Investigators Should Acknowledge That SLC Members Have the Right to Have Those Things That They Value to Be Fully Considered in All Interactions

Members of marginalized communities value direct communication, especially with people they trust, and often trust comes hand in hand with similar cultural and linguistic upbringing (Holcomb, 2013; Leigh et al., 2022). Simply put, these individuals are more likely to share with people similar to them. When researching deaf people in the justice system, they are most likely to represent a very diverse array of intersectionality, including but not limited to being deaf, a person of color, a member of an Indigenous community, transgender, disabled, blind, living in poverty, having limited education, and more. For example, to collect rich data from a specific population, such as deaf females of color, the contact person collecting the data would, ideally, also be a deaf female of color so as to build a genuine connection. In order to do this, a researcher who is not a member of the marginalized community would need to build a research team from the population being studied. Reaching out to, collaborating with, and learning from organizations such as the National Black Deaf Advocates, Council de Manos, and the National Association of the Deaf are some techniques that can be used when seeking members of a research team. Other methods include making the participants in the research project valued members of the research team. Like members of other marginalized groups, SLC members value this type of connection with their own people, and this should be fully considered in any type of research involving deaf people (McCullough, 2007).

Principle 3: Investigators Should Take Into Account the Worldviews of the SLC in All Negotiations or Dealings That Impact Those Members

Brunson (2008) used a qualitative approach in interviewing 12 deaf people about their experiences negotiating access with legal authorities. The questions were open-ended and done in a conversational style. The interviews were conducted in the participants' primary language, American Sign Language (ASL), at their homes. He used a grounded theory approach, where themes came from the analysis of statements from participants themselves, rather than prior to data collection. Brunson (2008) shared a disclaimer about the translation process from ASL to English, explaining that there is "no verbatim translation" for both languages and therefore that the translation was the researcher's own vernacular (p. 79). In his description of the participants, Brunson ensured that each of them was given a pseudonym and avoided any identifying information by using general terms (e.g., a college degree; lives in the Southwest), which is important when working with the Deaf community. Unlike the case with hearing participants, in the Deaf communities, it is easier to determine an individual's identity by revealing demographic information. With that as an example, Brunson (2008) clearly demonstrated an understanding of the worldviews of the SLC and incorporated them into his research methods.

Principle 4: Investigators Should Recognize the Diverse Experiences, Understandings, and Way of Life (in Sign Language Societies) That Reflect Contemporary Sign Language Cultures in the Application of SLC TOR

Researchers interested in exploring deaf individuals within the justice system need to recognize that members of this group and SLCs are very diverse with a similar, unifying experience—being deaf. Some may know ASL, some might know other signed languages, and some may not know any sign language at all. The auditory range and speaking levels of individuals within the Deaf community vary: some are completely deaf but can speak; some have partial hearing but do not speak; some have most of their hearing and cannot lipread and rely on their devices (hearing aid or cochlear implants) to understand spoken language or different combinations of those (Leigh et al., 2022). There may be additional layers of intersectionality (Crenshaw, 1993), such as gender, ethnicity, race, class, sexual orientation, disability, age, nationality, religion, and geography, and when those are included, the heterogeneity of the Deaf community becomes even more prominent. There are national organizations led by deaf women, Black deaf people, Hispanic/Latinx deaf people, LGBT deaf people, deaf Asians, Indigenous deaf people, DeafBlind people, to name a few (Leigh et al., 2022). All these groups represent diverse experiences, understandings, and ways of life for deaf people.

As an example, two of the most prolific researchers and publishers of the deaf prisoner population, Dr. Katrina Miller and Dr. McCay Vernon, both have strong connections with the Deaf community. Dr. Miller has a deaf sister (Suggs, 2002), and Dr. Vernon married a deaf woman (Vernon, 2013). Both are hearing, fluent signers, who graduated from colleges serving large deaf populations—Miller from Lamar University and Vernon from Gallaudet University—and are seen as members of the SLC. They demonstrate the ability to work effectively with deaf prisoners, as researchers with this type of understanding and approach, thus yielding richer opportunities to collect and access data.

Principle 5: Investigators Should Ensure That the Views and Perceptions of the Critical Reference Group (the Sign Language Group You Work With) Are Reflected in Every Process of Validating and Evaluating the Extent to Which SLC's TOR Have Been Taken Into Account

In Vernon and Rich (1997), the focus of their research was on deaf pedophiliac prisoners. Their research methods included both quantitative and qualitative approaches, with more emphasis on the latter. They employed purposeful sampling, working with extreme and/or deviant cases; however, they also employed the convenience sampling approach by identifying all deaf people with pedophilia cases that Vernon consulted on as a psychologist over a span of 45 years. A case study approach was utilized with each of the 22 cases of pedophilia, including in-depth interviews focusing on basic demographics, education, communication, history of sexual abuse (received and given), IQ, and psychiatric diagnosis. Vernon and Rich (1997) were able to build extensive and careful descriptions of the history and education of each prisoner in order to "represent a reasonable cross-section" of the deaf prisoner (p. 301). Their findings included a high prevalence of brain damage, and the majority had low educational levels. Most had a history of being sexually abused as children and had prior criminal records. The views and perceptions of the convicted deaf pedophiles in Vernon and Rich's study were interwoven in a narrative to help readers better understand what led to their crimes.

Principle 6: Investigators Should Negotiate Within and Between Sign Language Groups With the Aim of Establishing Appropriate Processes and Determining the Criteria for Meeting Cultural Imperatives, Social Needs, and Priorities

Miller, Vernon, and Capella (2005) studied the deaf population at a large prison in Texas. Part of their research methodology included individualized dialogue in sign language with each prisoner about informed consent because "of the high rate of functional illiteracy. . . . Concepts such as voluntary participation and right to withdraw without penalty could be explained using the language most readily understood by potential participants" (pp. 418–419). The authors adapted each informed consent dialogue using ASL, contact language, and Mexican Sign Language (known as *Lengua de señas mexicana*, or LSM) and included the use of gestures to work with inmates who have atypical language skills. This approach ensured respect and the development of trust, by using the language preferred by the inmate rather than the language typically used by the researchers.

Transformative Ontological Assumption

These ethical principles lead to an understanding of reality (the transformative ontological assumption) that reveals the possible different versions of reality as they are experienced by deaf people and others in the criminal justice system (Mertens, 2020). Examples of different versions of reality in this context are easy to come by. For example, in Texas, two young deaf people squeezed through a gate as a shortcut to get from their apartment complex to a convenience store; that is their version of reality (Lea, 2012). Once in the store, a police officer interpreted their behavior as suspicious and verbally indicated that he wanted them to come out of the store. The two deaf people's version of reality is that they did not know what the police officer was saying. The officer's version is that they did not respond to his order and were therefore handcuffed and treated roughly. The transformative ontological assumption holds that versions of reality emerge from different social positionalities, including hearing status, and that acceptance of one version of reality over another can have dire consequences for the less powerful. Researchers have an ethical responsibility to design their studies in ways that allow for the emergence of these different versions of reality, critical analysis of the sources of the versions of reality, and careful inferential analysis of the consequences of accepting one version of reality over another.

In *Nathan v. Municipality of Anchorage* (1998), Nathan, a deaf adult, was pulled over for a traffic violation. The officers proceeded to converse in writing and gestures. Nathan responded by nodding his head, which was interpreted by the officers to mean he understood, whereas in his case (and many others), "nodding may connote effort, rather than understanding" (Geer, 2003, p. 139). Nathan signed off on paperwork even though he did not understand the forms because he wanted "to please or placate the officer" (p. 138). The judge declared that Nathan "most likely understood, at least to the extent that he needed to understand" (p. 139). Geer (2003) argued that this line of faulty reasoning by this judge is less prevalent in the area of health care, where the absence of clear and effective communication can result in life or death. This leads to the next point, where researchers often give their participants informed consent forms with language that is typically obscure (Crasborn, 2010).

Deaf people who experience the legal system, anywhere from arrest, trial, incarceration, and probation, may be more inclined to sign off on forms and participate in research projects without fully understanding the implications (Singleton et al., 2014). The power imbalance between the researcher and the participants, especially prisoners, must be explicitly addressed. It is the researchers' obligation to ensure that deaf prisoners fully understand the research goals and their rights as participants (Singleton et al., 2014). This includes explaining that the informed consent paperwork indicating that the data collected are fully confidential may not be true if the researcher is taken to court because researchers' data is "not protected by law the way a lawyer's or physician's records are" (Mertens, 2020, p. 353). The reality of the fluctuating nature of confidentiality needs to be explicitly shared with research participants, including deaf prisoners. The problems with informed consent provide one example of the complexities associated with effective communication with members of the Deaf communities. Lack of appropriate interpretation in this situation is associated with misunderstandings that can lead to injustice.

The transformative ontological assumption also raises issues about diversity within the Deaf communities among those who are in contact with the criminal justice system. In Mertens's (2000, 2020) and Balch and Mertens's (1999) research on accessibility with deaf persons in the courts within the United States, the following types of individuals were identified on the basis of their hearing status and communication preferences:

- Highly educated ASL users
- Deaf ASL users with limited education and reading skills

- Deaf adults who had limited ASL skills and used gestures and pantomime primarily
- DeafBlind adults who used interpreters at close range or tactile interpreting
- Hard of hearing adults who used assistive listening devices (cochlear implants, hearing aids)
- Deaf adults who used LSM
- Deaf adults who relied on oral communication and print English

For each of these types of individuals, different support was necessary for effective communication, and different aspects of the court system were revealed from their experiences. Additional diversity was present within these groups in terms of gender, race/ethnicity, and status with the courts (e.g., juror, victim, witness).

Vernon and Miller (2005; Miller & Vernon, 2002) provided a comprehensive discussion of the challenges encountered by deaf people who are most at risk in the court systems for having their rights violated. These are people who were not given full access to language at home and school from birth, often reading at a fourth-grade level or below, having poor communication skills, and lacking a basic understanding and awareness of their legal rights. When they enter the legal system, it is the responsibility of the court to provide appropriate accommodations in the language most understood by the participant. Because of the diversity of communication needs within the Deaf community, particular attention needs to be given to the appropriateness of the interpretation choices that are made. In the case of deaf defendants who may struggle with comprehending and participating in legal proceedings involving dense concepts and legal jargon, they need to go through "adjudicative competence testing" (Miller & Vernon, 2001, p. 226). This test examines the defendant's state of mind at the time of trial, including the level of linguistic and cognitive functioning. Some deaf defendants may be assessed as linguistically and/or cognitively incompetent and thus unable to have a fair trial as a result of this test (Miller & Vernon, 2001).

The research strategies that Mertens (2000, 2020) and Balch and Mertens (1999) used were rooted in the importance of identifying the heterogeneity in the Deaf communities through the use of an advisory board that was reflective of the diverse positions in the court system, different hearing statuses, and modes of communication. The advisory board included two deaf judges (one used a cochlear implant and the other was an oral deaf judge), both of whom used laptop computers on their benches to read the court reporter's record during proceedings. Judicial educators were part of the advisory board because they control access to the dissemination of educative information for judges and other court personnel. Three attorneys were on the board; two were ASL signers and culturally deaf, whereas one was hearing but worked with a large number of deaf clients. Law enforcement was represented by a person with deaf parents who served as a liaison between the police department and the Deaf community. In addition, court interpreters were included.

The advisory board served to alert the researchers to the various dimensions of diversity that were present in the populations with whom they worked, as well as to the supportive strategies needed for effective communication. They ensured that the focus groups were homogeneous on the basis of the type of communication strategies that were used so that appropriate support could be provided. The focus groups were used as a needs assessment device to determine the experiences of deaf people in contact with the criminal justice system. This information was used to design and implement training for deaf people and court personnel to improve access to the court system.

The ontological assumption that diverse versions of reality exist and are the function of different positionalities led to the use of different communication supports for each focus group. For example, two comoderators were used in the ASL highly educated group; one was an experienced hearing moderator and the other a deaf moderator with less experience. In addition, two ASL court-certified interpreters were used, and two court reporters processed the spoken word into print that was visible on two large television sets in the focus group room. An individual who was deaf but used only minimal sign along with gestures and pantomime was included in another group with ASL users. The communication support was similar to the first group; however, an additional interpreter was added who was deaf and who acted out as much as possible what was being signed by the ASL interpreters. In the hard of hearing group that used assistive listening devices, an audio loop was provided. In the LSM group, LSM interpreters teamed with ASL interpreters to facilitate communication. In the oral deaf group, an oral interpreter was used to enunciate the words that were being spoken to support enhanced lipreading. These research strategies adhere to the TOR described earlier and allowed for the creation of research findings that accurately reflected diverse realities in the Deaf communities.

Transformative Epistemological Assumption

The transformative epistemological assumption leads researchers to consider how they can establish relationships that are respectful and supportive with deaf people in the justice system (Mertens, 2020). The transformative epistemological assumption reflects the need for an awareness of the various positions of power in the research context and to design research strategies that allow for the experiences of the full spectrum of stakeholders to be accurately expressed and documented.

Officers are trained to look at not only the language but also the gestures, body language, posture, and facial expressions made by potential suspects (Hoopes, 2003). Researchers also collect data on nonverbal language from their participants as a part of the data collection and analysis process. When researching a linguistic community that uses the face and body for grammatical signals and markers, researchers not familiar with SLCs may misunderstand facial grammar. These misinterpretations of facial grammar as facial expression used by nonsigners demonstrate why it is so important to work with deaf researchers who are experts in the language and culture of the SLC. The epistemological knowledge regarding language, especially for signed languages, is very complex and nuanced, to the point where much of the information can easily get lost in translation for a professional not familiar with the language used by the community (Hoopes, 2003; Mathers, 2007).

Transformative Methodological Assumption

The transformative methodological assumption emanates from the prior assumptions that have been discussed in terms of ethics, ontology, and epistemology. There is no single method that is associated with the transformative paradigm; rather, there is a need to devise methods that are culturally responsive and that support the attainment of accurate data that can be used for the purposes of social change.

Research Methods in Sign Language Studies: A Practical Guide (Orfanidou et al., 2015) has 19 chapters that discuss a variety of methods for collecting data within SLCs; they emphasize WITH deaf people (all caps in original). Within that edited book is a chapter by Singleton, Martin, and Morgan (2015), in which they argue that there are certain research methods that are more deaf-friendly (and result in more ethically sound research). These methods include the use of community-engaged research and action research that bring to the fore the importance of deaf-led research agendas.

Some have argued that with relatively small communities (as compared with larger populations), the research results cannot be applied (or generalized) (Ruddin, 2006). Counterarguments by researchers state qualitative methodological techniques can be implemented with small populations and can capture in-depth, genuine knowledge generated from the research process (Mertens, 2009; Ruddin, 2006; Stake, 2005). Examples of methods that can be used with small populations such as the Deaf communities in the legal system include focus group approaches, single-subject designs, case studies, participatory action research, ethnographic studies, and phenomenological studies, to name a few (Mertens, 2009).

In her study of Texas inmates in 2004, Miller used multiple techniques to strengthen her data collection process. One approach was Kannapell's (1989) bilingualism categories to assess inmates' knowledge of ASL and English. She included other people in assessing the inmates' language use, such as a hearing signer with 10 years of experience providing social services in the Deaf community and a certified sign language interpreter who had parents and worked full-time with the Texas deaf inmate population for more than 17 years. Although IQ tests were administered, there was no mention of whether the inmates' preferred language had been used. Miller (2004) used a hearing psychologist competent in sign language to assess the inmates through a series of in-depth interviews. Although using hearing people to assess the sign language skills of deaf inmates may be questionable, Miller's methods in using hearing people very familiar with the Deaf community and competent in sign language is certainly a step in the right direction. Eventually, the inclusion of more deaf researchers on the research team should become the standard.

Miller (2004) also argued for the inclusion of deaf interpreters working with hearing sign language interpreters, translating English-based signing into ASL. Deaf interpreters serve as valuable, equal members of the interpreting team, specializing in linguistic and cultural facilitation. Instead of the typical "spoken language interpreting model," deaf people in the legal system are best served by a "deaf-hearing interpreting team" (Mathers, 2009, pp. 5–6). Such a team consists of one hearing court interpreter and one deaf court interpreter who work together to ensure that the translation between languages is close to equivalent (Mathers, 2009). While the use of deaf interpreters is now a more accepted concept than it was back in 2004, Miller must be applauded for her forward thinking, particularly when deaf interpreters were, and in many cases are, not considered for most interpreting jobs. Brick and Beldon (2014) argued that any legal interpreting assignment that does not include a deaf interpreter violates the Registry of the Interpreters for the Deaf (RID) Code of Professional Conduct (CPC). In other words, all hearing interpreters certified by RID must have a deaf interpreter assigned to all of their jobs in order to ensure clear communication between all parties involved. In one example, a deaf individual used the sign for "crackers"; a hearing interpreter would have interpreted that as a food item, but it is more likely a deaf interpreter would immediately know that the witness was not talking about a food cracker but about crack cocaine (Brick & Beldon, 2014). In that situation, with a deaf-hearing interpreting model, the translation process is often more accurate than with a spoken language interpreting model. While this example may be interpreted as extreme, unfortunately, this happens more often than many of us realize (Mathers, 2009).

Mathers, a nationally renowned attorney and expert hearing interpreter, remarked, "My best interpretation, however, will never equal the value, skills, and contributions of a deaf interpreter" (p. 1). The trend of using deaf interpreters is continuing, as indicated in a recent landmark decision by the Administrative Office of the Courts in California that states that deaf interpreters must be:

> provided in all civil and criminal actions in which the service is needed for effective communication and in which the deaf individual is a party or witness in a case. These include traffic or other infractions, small claims court proceedings, juvenile court proceedings, family court proceedings, hearings to determine mental competency, and court-ordered or court-provided alternative dispute resolution, including mediation and arbitration. (Recommended Guidelines, 2010, p. 3)

The National Consortium on Interpreter Education Center states that "[i]t is best practice to collaborate with deaf interpreter specialists in law enforcement settings because they are able to enhance the accuracy, meaning, and effectiveness of the interpretation" (Stewart et al., 2009, p. 37). Taking this into account, hearing researchers should take note of the current protocol of including deaf interpreters in every step of deaf people's interaction with the criminal justice system, that is, on their research team and in all interactions with deaf people. The number of court-certified deaf interpreters is disproportionally low. For example, in Texas, a search of the Board of Evaluation of Interpreters public database (https://bei.hhsc.state.tx.us/PublicInterpreterSearch/) indicates there are four deaf court interpreters for the entire state of Texas. Of those four, several have a full-time job or commitment, rendering them unavailable for most legal settings, leaving only one or two deaf court interpreters available, with one nearing retirement age. Only one of those four is a person of color, a Latinx person. There are no Black deaf court interpreters in the state of Texas. Compounding this issue is the perception of conflict—deaf court interpreters cannot interpret for the same client in multiple legal settings, for instance, during the arrest and the booking process, then again in court, because what they saw, interpreted, or experienced during the booking process may influence their interpretation in court. Furthermore, the close-knit nature of the Deaf community often prevents deaf interpreters from interpreting for the majority of their clients owing to the level of their acquaintance prior to the job. Often, courts are forced to consider flying in deaf court-certified interpreters from out of state to alleviate this issue. With that, the limited number of deaf court-certified interpreters also impacts the ability of hearing researchers to work with deaf court-certified interpreters to support their research.

Barrow (2008) studied deaf crime victims within a theoretical framework that acknowledged the power inequities between potential criminals and victims, especially when the victims are deaf. Barrow used the National Crime Victimization Survey, in which she modified the vocabulary and syntax to accommodate the linguistic needs of the deaf victims. She included field testing of the instrument and review by various subcultures of the Deaf community prior to implementation. The field tests revealed that complete online surveys were not comfortable for the participants; they preferred to meet the researcher prior to completing the survey in order to ascertain whether they wanted to share their information with her. Barrow solicited and received permission to go into classrooms to introduce herself and her research before the participants agreed to be part of the study. Here is how Barrow (2008) describes her research approach:

> From the outset, this researcher recognized the importance of actively involving the Deaf community in the research effort, of remaining flexible to making necessary changes through the process as guided and instructed by the participants, and of remaining loyal to the primary goal of effectuating positive social change to benefit vulnerable victims of crime. (p. 75)

This statement illustrates many of the principles of transformative research, aspects of which Barrow included in her study. Rather than relying on a printed survey alone, she engaged with members of the Deaf community to ensure that the survey itself was culturally and linguistically appropriate for the intended respondents. Barrow provided flyers that listed counseling services that were available for anyone who felt anxious after completing the survey. She was accompanied by an interpreter who was a child of deaf adults (Coda) at each administration of the survey. Barrow reported her findings and recommendations in a book that is electronically available; however, she does not discuss whether she met with members of the Deaf community to interpret the findings or to facilitate their use.

The National Association of the Deaf Law Center "advocates the use of plain English notices about policies and services that comply with the law" (Geer, 2003, p. 86). Consumer protection advocates as well as other legislation and institutions such as the Model Life and Health Insurance Policy Language Simplification Act, and the Securities and Exchange Commission are pushing for greater use of plain language, avoiding archaic and obscure language choices that only serve to confuse people (Geer, 2003). This approach should be taken by researchers working with marginalized communities who often do not have the same level of access to English. This should also be considered for communities that are multilingual and/or speak other languages, such as the Deaf community. Research methods with deaf people and the justice system need to take into account the use of plain, accessible English as well as the deaf person's preferred language and communication modality, be it ASL, LSM, Protactile, Black ASL, or other dialects and language variations.

RECOMMENDATIONS FOR RESEARCH WITH DEAF PEOPLE IN THE CRIMINAL JUSTICE SYSTEM

Several essential points in researching deaf inmates emerged from the scholarly literature. The following is a compilation of our recommendations for research with deaf people in the criminal justice system:

1. **Study the Transformative Research Paradigm and related social justice material.** Crenshaw's 1993 work on intersectionality is pioneering and very relevant in understanding the foundation of social justice-infused research. Mertens's *Transformative Research and Evaluation* (2009) and *Research and Evaluation in Education and Psychology* (2020) include examples of research within the Deaf communities, a rarity for most research textbooks. Harris and Williams (2015) published an ASL videobook that aligns with the chapters of the latter book, thus making it accessible to those who may want to learn about research paradigms and methods in ASL that are aligned with the transformative, social justice paradigm. Mertens (2018), Shannon-Baker (2014), Habashi and Worley (2009), and other scholars who explicitly address issues of social justice expand the idea of the transformative paradigm in

their exploration of approaches to mixed methods research with members of marginalized communities.

2. **Create research teams.** Instead of a sole researcher directing the research, cultivate research teams with equal input and power. Teams also need to include deaf and hearing researchers representing different intersectionalities, with the aim of bringing different perspectives to the research process, keeping the process as authentic and representative of the experiences of deaf prisoners as possible. It would also be beneficial to invite deaf prisoners to be a part of the research team and/or research process.
3. **Include Deaf experts and professionals at every step of the research process.** Include Deaf professionals from several disciplines, such as linguists, psychology, interpretation, and research and evaluation. Also, keep in mind the inclusion of deaf people of color, such as African Americans, Latinx, Pacific Islanders, Asians, and Native Americans. Try to also include DeafBlind people and those with additional disabilities. Attempt to include deaf individuals who are lesbian, gay, bisexual, transgender, queer, asexual, intersex, etc. A deaf gay male prisoner who is African American will more likely connect better with a deaf gay male African American interviewer/researcher.
4. **Incorporate either mixed methods or qualitative approaches to research.** The collection of both quantitative and qualitative data can provide the mechanism for clearly and accurately portraying the experiences of deaf prisoners and lead to changes in policies that can create conditions to enhance justice (Mertens, 2018). Deaf prisoners need their stories to be told. Connections and trust are built when relationships are cultivated between the researchers and the community being researched. The data collected are much more authentic and richer. The combination of quantitative and qualitative data in a mixed-methods study can provide a better picture of the complexity of the issues and portray the extensiveness of the problems.
5. **Closely match the language used by the community being researched.** With a diverse research team (see number 2) of multiple experts, ensure that the team has a deaf expert to assess the language used by the participant by using the Language Rating Scale (Glickman, 2009) and Kannapell's bilingualism categories to assess deaf prisoners' knowledge of ASL and English. Once the sign language (and level) is identified, pair the prisoner with a deaf researcher fluent in the language to discuss the informed consent paperwork and subsequent interviews. For written (or spoken) English, identify the level and use plain English (Geer, 2003) at every step of the research process, including informed consent paperwork and subsequent publications and presentations.
6. **Closely match the culture used by the prisoners in the study.** As mentioned in number 5, we should try closely matching the intersectionality of the participants with their culturally competent interviewers (Thompson-Robinson et al., 2004). A prisoner may be hard of hearing, ASL fluent, a cochlear implant user, female-to-male transgender, and Latino. Efforts to find a transgender deaf person of color to work with the prisoner will more likely result in a much richer and more genuine data collection.

7. **Give back to the deaf prison population.** Share research results with the participants, perhaps in a presentation or through individualized narratives. If a profit is made from the results, give a percentage back to the deaf prison population. Keep in touch with the participants by sending them updates and news briefs. Immediately cutting off all ties when research ends is not an effective approach, especially in paving the way for future research by others. Developing and building genuine trust with marginalized communities requires a lifetime commitment.

Research regarding the deaf prison population is essential in opening people's eyes to what really happens to deaf prisoners from the very beginning, the first contact with a law enforcement official, and through the sequence of events between arrest, trial, incarceration, and probation. Having this information presented and published is paramount in bringing more attention and change to the current criminal justice system. We understand that taking into consideration the foregoing recommendations is critical in collecting data; however, it is understandable that time and financial constraints may hinder some aspects of including all of the recommendations in the research process. Ultimately, it is up to the researcher(s) to determine the capability of incorporating the recommendations in their research project.

REFERENCES

Balch, G., & Mertens, D. M. (1999). Focus group design and group dynamics: Lessons from deaf and hard of hearing participants. *American Journal of Evaluation, 20*(2), 265–277. https://doi.org/10.1177/109821409902000208

Barrow, L. (2008). *Criminal victimization of the deaf.* LFB Scholarly Publishing.

Bartol, C. R., & Bartol, A. M. (2015). *Introduction to forensic psychology.* Sage.

Brick, K., & Beldon, J. (2014). Interpreting without a deaf interpreter is an RID CPC violation. *Street Leverage.* http://www.streetleverage.com/2014/09/interpreting-without-a-deaf-interpreter-is-an-rid-cpc-violation/

Brunson, J. (2008). Your case will now be heard: Sign language interpreters as problematic accommodations in legal interactions. *Journal of Deaf Studies and Deaf Education, 13*(1), 77–91. https://doi.org/10.1093/deafed/enm032

Committee on Identifying the Needs of the Forensic Science Community. (2009). *Strengthening forensic science in the United States: A path forward.* The National Academies Press.

Cram, F., Ormond, A., & Carter, L. (2006). Researching our relations: Reflections on ethics and marginalisation. *AlterNative: An International Journal of Indigenous Peoples, 2*(1), 174–193. https://doi.org/10.1177/117718010600200108

Crasborn, O. (2010). What does "informed consent" mean in the internet age? Publishing sign language corpora as open content. *Sign Language Studies, 10*(2), 276–290. https://doi.org/10.1353/sls.0.0044

Crenshaw, K. (1993). Mapping the margins: Intersectionality, identity politics, and violence against women of color. *Stanford Law Review, 43*, 1241–1299. https://doi.org/10.2307/1229039
Geer, S. (2003). When "equal" means "unequal"—and other legal conundrums for the Deaf community. In C. Lucas (Ed.), *Language and the law in deaf communities* (pp. 82–167). Gallaudet University Press.
Glickman, N. (2009). *Cognitive-behavioral therapy for deaf and hearing persons with language and learning challenges.* Routledge.
Guba, E. & Lincoln, Y. (2005). Paradigmatic controversies, contradictions and emerging confluences. In N. Denzin & Y. S. Lincoln (Eds.), *Handbook of qualitative research* (3rd ed., pp. 191–216). Sage.
Habashi, J., & Worley, J. (2009). Child geopolitical agency. *Journal of Mixed Methods Research, 3*(1), 42–64. https://doi.org/10.1177/1558689808326120
Harris, R., Holmes, H. M., & Mertens, D. M. (2009). Research ethics in sign language communities. *Sign Language Studies, 9*(2), 104–131. https://doi.org/10.1353/sls.0.0011
Harris, R., & Williams, F. (2015). *Research and evaluation in education and psychology [ASL version].* ASLChoice. http://aslchoice.com/reep/
HEARD Fact Sheet. (2018). *#Deafinprison campaign fact sheet.* https://behearddc.org/wp-content/uploads/2018/11/DeafInPrison-Fact-Sheet-.pdf
Holcomb, T. (2013). *Introduction to American Deaf culture.* Oxford University Press.
Hoopes, R. (2003). Trampling Miranda: Interrogating deaf suspects. In C. Lucas (Ed.), *Language and the law in Deaf communities* (pp. 21–59). Gallaudet University Press.
James, S. H., & Nordby, J. J. (2014). *Forensic science.* Taylor & Francis.
Kannapell, B. (1989). An examination of deaf college students' attitude towards ASL and English. In C. Lucas (Ed.), *The sociolinguistics of the Deaf community* (pp. 191–210). Academic Press.
Kitchener, K. S., & Kitchener, R. F. (2009). Social science research ethics: Historical and philosophical issues. In D. M. Mertens & P. Ginsberg (Eds.), *Handbook of social research ethics* (pp. 5–22). Sage.
Lea, L. (2012, September 5). Caught on cam: Deaf couple gets arrested for no reason. *NBCLatino.* http://nbclatino.com/2012/09/05/caught-on-cam-deaf-couple-gets-arrested/
Leigh, I., Andrews, J., Harris, R., & González Ávila, T. (2022). *Deaf culture: Exploring Deaf communities in the United States* (2nd ed.). Plural Publishing.
Mathers, C. (2007). *Sign language interpreters in court: Understanding best practices.* AuthorHouse.
Mathers, C. (2009). Deaf interpreters in court: An accommodation that is more than reasonable. *National Consortium of Interpreter Education Centers Legal Interpreting Workgroup* (#H160A&B). http://www.interpretereducation.org/wp-content/uploads/2011/06/Deaf-Interpreter-in-Court_NCIEC2009.pdf
McCullough, C. (2007, September 23). Hearing researchers: Why do they study deaf people? *ASC on the Couch.* https://www.youtube.com/watch?v=3RiqeJZnDso&list=PLC8634F3F27BD09CD&index=4
McCullough, C. A., & Duchesneau, S. M. (2006, August 28). Walking on eggshells: Deaf and hearing in consultation. *ASL on the Couch.* https://deafcounseling.com/walking-on-eggshells-deaf-and-hearing-in-consultation/

Mertens, D. M. (2000). Deaf and hard of hearing people in court: Using an emancipatory perspective to determine their needs. In C. Truman, D. M. Mertens, & B. Humphries (Eds.), *Research and inequality* (pp. 111–125). Taylor & Francis.

Mertens, D. M. (2009). *Transformative research and evaluation.* Guilford Press.

Mertens, D. M. (2018). *Mixed methods design in evaluation.* Sage.

Mertens, D. M. (2020). *Research methods in education and psychology: Integrating diversity with quantitative, qualitative, and mixed methods* (5th ed.). Sage.

Mertens, D. M., & Wilson, A. T. (2019). *Program evaluation theory and practice* (2nd ed.). Guilford.

Miller, K. (2004). Linguistic diversity in a deaf prison population: Implications for due process. *Journal of Deaf Studies and Deaf Education, 9*(1), 112–119. https://doi.org/10.1093/deafed/enh007

Miller, K., & Vernon, M. (2001). Linguistic diversity in deaf defendants and due process rights. *Journal of Deaf Studies and Deaf Education, 6*(3), 226–234. https://doi.org/10.1093/deafed/6.3.226

Miller, K., & Vernon, M. (2002). Assessing linguistic diversity in deaf criminal suspects. *Sign Language Studies, 2*(4), 380–390. https://doi.org/10.1353/sls.2002.0021

Miller, K., Vernon, M., & Capella, M. (2005). Violent offenders in a deaf prison population. *Journal of Deaf Studies and Deaf Education, 10*(4), 417–425.

Mitchell, R. (2006). How many deaf people are there in the United States? Estimates from the survey of income and program participation. *Journal of Deaf Studies and Deaf Education, 11*(1), 112–119. https://doi.org/10.1093/deafed/enj004

Nathan v. the Municipality of Anchorage, Court of Appeals of Alaska (March 27, 1998). https://caselaw.findlaw.com/ak-court-of-appeals/1189568.html

National Commission for the Protection of Human Subjects of Biomedical and Behavioral Research. (1979). *The Belmont report.* U.S. Department of Health and Human Services.

Orfanidou, E., Woll, B., & Morgan, G. (2015). *Research methods in sign language studies: A practical guide.* Wiley Blackwell.

Recommended Guidelines for the Use of Deaf Intermediary Interpreters. (2010). *Judicial Council of California: Administrative office of the courts.* http://www.courts.ca.gov/documents/CIP_GID.pdf

Ridgeway, J. (2009, September 15). *The secret world of deaf prisoners.* https://thecrimereport.org/2009/09/29/the-secret-world-of-deaf-prisoners/

Rosenfeld, B., & Penrod, S. D. (2011). *Research methods in forensic psychology.* Wiley & Sons.

Ruddin, L. P. (2006). You can generalize stupid! Social scientists, Bent Fylvbjerg, and case study methodology. *Qualitative Inquiry, 9*(4), 643–668. https://doi.org/10.1177/1077800406288622

Shannon-Baker, P. (2014). Making paradigms meaningful in mixed methods research. *Journal of Mixed Methods Research, 10*(4), 319–334. https://doi.org/10.1177/1558689815575861

Singleton, J., Jones, G., & Hanumantha, S. (2014). Toward ethical research practice with deaf participants. *Journal of Empirical Research on Human Research Ethics, 9*(3), 59–66. https://doi.org/10.1177/1556264614540589

Singleton, J., Martin, A. J., & Morgan, G. (2015). Ethics, deaf-friendly research, and good practice when studying sign languages. In E. Orfanidou, B. Woll, & G. Morgan (Eds.), *Research methods in sign language studies: A practical guide* (pp. 5–20). Wiley Blackwell.

Stake, R. E. (2005). Qualitative case studies. In Y. S. Lincoln & N. K. Denzin (Eds.), *The Sage handbook of qualitative research* (3rd ed., pp. 443–466). Sage.

Stewart, K., Witter-Merithew, A., & Cobb, M. (2009). *Best practices: American Sign Language and English interpretation within legal settings.* National Consortium of Interpreter Education Centers. http://www.interpretereducation.org/wp-content/uploads/2011/06/LegalBestPractices_NCIEC2009.pdf

Suggs, T. (2002). Texas deaf inmates researched, results to become book. *Silent News.* http://www.trudysuggs.com/texas-deaf-inmates-researched-results-to-become-book

Thompson-Robinson, M., Hopson, R., & SenGupta, S. (2004). *In search of cultural competence in evaluation toward principle and practice [Special issue]. New Directions for Evaluation.* Wiley Periodicals.

Vernon, M. (2013). *McCay Vernon notice.* https://www.legacy.com/obituaries/washingtonpost/obituary.aspx?page=lifestory&pid=166674070

Vernon, M., & Miller, K. (2005). Obstacles faced by deaf people in the criminal justice system. *American Annals of the Deaf, 150*(3), 283–291. https://doi.org/10.1353/aad.2005.0036

Vernon, M., & Rich, S. (1997). Pedophilia and deafness. *American Annals of the Deaf, 142*(4), 300–311. https://doi.org/10.1353/aad.2012.0258

Part II

Theory, Practice, and Specialized Services

4

School-to-Prison Nexus: Deaf Youth and the Juvenile Justice System

Gabriel I. Lomas

Consider the case study of Caleb, a profoundly deaf teen, currently incarcerated at the county juvenile justice center, who has a history of familial rejection, school bullying, hanging out with delinquent hearing boys, and making bad decisions—all of which snowballed into dismal consequences for him.

Caleb's Story

From age 2, Caleb was raised by his grandfather, who struggled to balance his job demands and personal life and felt his grandson's needs were burdensome. Caleb's mother was addicted to drugs, and his father was in prison for manufacturing and selling drugs. Because his grandfather was unhappy about these circumstances, Caleb's home life with his grandfather was harsh, rigid, and cold. Caleb reported feeling abandoned and unloved by his family. In his neighborhood school, he had about 15 deaf peers, but he was generally introverted and worked hard to keep the teacher's attention off himself. Although typically quiet, Caleb was often caught bullying and provoking peers into misbehavior. His classmates regularly complained about his causing trouble, using foul language, and threatening to harm them, especially when out of view of the teachers. When he was 12 years old, he dropped a pill on the floor in class in view of a teacher and was sent to the office. The principal investigated and determined that the pill was his attention deficit hyperactivity disorder medication, which was only to be dispensed by the school nurse. Owing to a zero-tolerance drug policy, the school resource officer arrested him and took him to juvenile detention. His grandfather begrudgingly paid a $500 fine, and Caleb was ordered to do 100 hours of community service. After a 5-day suspension, Caleb returned to school with no changes in his educational program *and no new support services such as counseling in place. Two years later, he met with trouble again during a walk from his home to a convenience store, where he went to buy a snack. He ran into hearing peers who encouraged him to help them break into a nearby warehouse. The boys provided the gullible Caleb with the tools for him to commit the crime. Caught in the warehouse, the police arrived and took him into custody. This time, the judge ordered him to stay incarcerated for 6 months and then attend a special school for offenders. The hearing peers who enabled him to commit the crime all got off with no charges or probated sentences, whereas Caleb received a harsh jail sentence. Caleb did not have a sign language interpreter at any point during his incarceration, nor did he have access to a signing mental health professional, signing teachers, or deaf peers. Thus, rehabilitation services offered to hearing offenders were inaccessible to Caleb. When Caleb was released, he had no sign language interpreter at the alternative school for juvenile offenders. While in jail, he felt alone and depressed and learned to survive by imitating the behaviors of other inmates. When he returned home, Caleb was not rehabilitated but had learned new survival skills that are acceptable only within prison walls.*

How did Caleb fall through the cracks? Caleb's story is not a solitary one. In fact, today's deaf youth face seemingly insurmountable challenges as they attempt to navigate the systems in which they live. Current federal law, state law, and social policy all favor deinstitutionalization for students with disabilities, yet the result is typically a reduction of much-needed services for those who, like Caleb, need it the most.

Deaf youth are increasingly living at home with their families and are diffused in their communities. In the past, they were concentrated in larger numbers at schools for the deaf, but today they are increasingly represented in small numbers in their neighborhood schools and justice programs, both of which are often ill-equipped to serve them. Deaf youth are often faced with systems that are designed for hearing individuals. Although likely unintended, these systems end up funneling deaf children and youth into our criminal justice system. The term "school-to-prison pipeline" (the pipeline) or "school-to-prison nexus" is commonly used to reference the failures of school systems to support and educate children with challenging behaviors, pushing them into the juvenile and adult prison populations. Commentators on the nexus have drawn attention to the linkages among education, police power, and incarceration (Schept et al., 2015). This chapter addresses the contributing systems and explores both problems and solutions to disrupt the school-to-prison nexus for deaf youth (Lomas et al., 2017). Throughout this chapter, readers will see the terms "nexus" and "pipeline" used frequently. The nexus refers to the combination of multiple systems that pushes deaf youth toward a negative outcome and away from positive, rehabilitative resources. The pipeline refers to the rapid advancement toward prison. It is the nexus of multiple systems working against deaf youth that pushes them through a pipeline toward incarceration.

HISTORICAL PERSPECTIVE

In the early days of deaf education, youth with problem behaviors were often kept on residential campuses despite behavioral challenges. This practice is still common at some schools for the deaf. Although remaining on campus may be beneficial in terms of receiving accessible services, it can also have serious consequences that entail safety concerns for faculty, staff, and other students. If apprehended off campus by the authorities, deaf students were sometimes turned over to the school to be disciplined by the school administration, depending on the severity of the infraction. O'Rourke et al. (2013) point to what they characterize as "hearing guilt" as a factor in handling deaf lawbreakers. They contend that, in some situations, hearing people feel that offensive behavior by the deaf person should be tolerated, either because of their historical oppression by hearing people or because they feel a paternalistic pity for them for being deaf.

There are also historical accounts of deaf people with difficult behaviors who were wrongly incarcerated in state hospitals and other facilities for the criminally insane (Vernon, 2008). Vernon and Raifman (1997) point out that many of those placements were improper because of misdiagnosis by evaluators who were unfamiliar with deaf people and test administration in American Sign Language (ASL). Historical commentators agree that the high prevalence of behavior problems and language and cultural differences and the preponderance of clinicians unfamiliar with deaf people combine to create a higher likelihood that they are misdiagnosed with psychotic disorders (Glickman, 2009; Vernon & Greenberg, 1999). In extreme cases, deaf juvenile delinquents, including sex offenders, have remained on campus in classes with victims, a practice that is abhorrent to victims, survivors, and advocates. In most states, it is well established that juvenile sex offenders may not attend a school that is attended by the victim or a sibling of the victim. Separation of offenders and victims helps to promote a safe learning environment, show respect for the victim(s), and ensure the safety of all students and staff.

Whereas historical accounts from the field of deaf education point to schools for the deaf as the source of Deaf culture, language, and social experiences for deaf people (Miller et al., 2005; Moores, 2001), today more deaf youth are enrolled in public schools than schools for the deaf (Gallaudet Research Institute, 2013). Currently, deaf children and youth are more likely to be served by teachers and support staff who do not know ASL and use an interpreter. When deaf children in public schools need help, it is likely the individual they turn to for support will have no ability to communicate directly with them and will have little understanding of the experiences faced by deaf adolescents (Lomas et al., 2017).

POPULATION

Incarcerated Deaf People

The American carceral system is a closed one, with limited data released to the public. The organization Prison Policy Initiative (Sawyer & Wagner, 2020) estimates that there are currently 2.3 million prisoners in state and federal prisons. Although the exact numbers are not available for deaf persons, scholarly resources indicate there is an overrepresentation of deaf and hard of hearing inmates in state and county facilities, and 35% to 40% of the total population are estimated to have some degree of hearing loss (Jensema, 1990; Miller, 2001). Information about the juvenile justice system is even more limited, with a heavier emphasis on privacy for children.

Incarcerated Deaf Youth

Recently, attention has been drawn to the disproportionate numbers of youth with disabilities in the juvenile justice system. The U.S. Department of Education (2000) reported that a conservative estimate of the prevalence of youth with disabilities in the system is about 32%. Considering that the prevalence rate of disabilities among students in the United States is at about 9%, the disparity should be cause for alarm. Clearly, young people with disabilities are overrepresented in the juvenile justice system, and deaf youth are not immune to the effects of the nexus thrusting them into the school-to-prison pipeline.

A resource from Helping Educate to Advance Rights of the Deaf (HEARD), a nonprofit organization that advocates for deaf people in prison, estimates that tens of thousands of deaf people are in prisons across our nation. However, locating them has been difficult, as prison officials sometimes keep no records on the hearing status of inmates. Those who do keep such records sometimes work to prohibit access to this information. For an in-depth explanation of legal advocacy, readers are referred to Chapter 11 in this book.

Identifying the number of deaf youth in the juvenile justice system is equally challenging. One source reports that the entire juvenile justice system serves about two million youth annually (Stahl, 2006). If 30% to 60% of youth offenders have disabilities (U.S. Department of Education, 2017), it is estimated that between 600,000 and 1,200,000 youth with disabilities are in the system. If 1.5% is used as a conservative estimate of the number of youth with hearing loss, then there are between 9,000 and 18,000 youth who are deaf in the system each year. Sawyer and Wagner (2020) estimate confined youth at 52,000 nationally. Studies examining hearing loss and language deprivation among prison inmates range from a low of 30% (Melnick, 1970) in the United States to a high of 83% among the Indigenous inmates of New Zealand (Department of Corrections, 2013). Using those numbers, the estimate of deaf youth in American prisons ranges from 15,600 to 43,160.

Unfortunately, there is a paucity of data on deaf youth in the juvenile justice system, and no significant change aimed at improving fairness and equity in the justice system can occur in the absence of meaningful data. There are three sources of data on deaf juvenile offenders, which will be discussed. One set is from Miller, who studied deaf prisoners in her doctoral research (2001; Twersky Glasner & Miller, 2010); another is from Jernigan, who studied the risk factors and aggressive behaviors of deaf males (Jernigan, 2010); and a final set is unpublished combined clinical work from Drs. Jean Andrews and Gabriel Lomas. Ideally, all three data sets would offer objective and subjective information using the same instruments. Unfortunately, that is not the case with these data sets. Still, examination of these data has some value and may be the first step in advocacy for this population.

SCHOOL-TO-PRISON NEXUS FACTORS

As Caleb's story brings to light, several factors contribute to the high incidence of deaf youth in the juvenile justice system, some of which are addressed in what follows. These are related to cognition, adverse childhood experiences (ACEs), language and learning challenges, etiologies causing disabilities, deficits in social cognition and funds of information, education problems, low literacy levels, and financial factors related to who pays for treatment, assuming culturally appropriate services are available. It is important to note that a single factor is only rarely the sole contributor to the pipeline. Instead, it is more likely that two or more factors combine to form a "perfect storm" or a nexus that leads deaf youth to the prison pipeline.

Cognitive Factors

Based on the author's years of clinical experience with deaf individuals including juveniles, cognition is a significant factor that impacts the school-to-prison nexus for deaf youth. Although 30% to 50% of deaf school-age children have learning challenges (Guardino, 2008; Guardino & Cannon, 2015), few fall into the category of intellectually disabled (an IQ below 70). Until the *Diagnostic and Statistical Manual of Mental Disorders* (DSM-5), psychological evaluators were trained to assess cognition and adaptive behavior when determining cognitive functioning. Under DSM-IV, if one or both areas were determined to be above 70, the individual could not be labeled intellectually disabled. However, the DSM-5 has provisions that allow for a functional assessment of cognitive functioning. This gives examiners more flexibility in diagnoses. For example, there have been cases in which a deaf person has an IQ of 72 and adaptive behavior of 70 but the individual is unable to perform critical functions required to be independent. Historically, an individual with this profile would not be diagnosed as intellectually disabled. Today, we are able to examine the deaf individual through a functional lens and assign the appropriate diagnosis. This diagnosis is often critical in that it allows individuals access to essential services such as housing support, health insurance, and other social services.

Early Childhood Experiences

For any child, early affective bonds with parents are critical. As a baby becomes a toddler, language is acquired and communication skills are developed, all of which serve to deepen the parent–child bond. When these affective bonds do not develop, then the child is at risk for cognitive, language, and affective disorders that can be internalized into depression and malfunctioning or externalized into antisocial behaviors (Leigh & Andrews, 2017).

In a groundbreaking study on the health effects of ACEs, researchers from the Kaiser Permanente Health System, in collaboration with the Centers for Disease Control and Prevention, surveyed over 17,000 Kaiser patients on their ACEs and compared the findings with patient health outcomes (Felitti et al., 1998). The researchers queried seven ACE areas, including psychological, physical, or sexual abuse; violence against the mother; and living with household members who were substance abusers, mentally ill or suicidal, or ever imprisoned. When compared with measures of adult risk behavior, disease, and health status, the study revealed some disturbing results. In particular, a greater number of ACEs meant increased health risks for alcoholism, drug abuse, depression, heart disease, bone fractures, and other health problems in later life. The ACE study was revolutionary in that it tied health outcomes and leading causes of death for adults to early childhood experiences, an area of concern for many commentators in the field of deaf education.

Language and Learning Challenges

Language and learning challenges can be a major contributor to poor achievement and attachment between the child and caregiver, both of which are risk factors that may lead to unemployment, psychological problems, communication problems, and other risk factors in adulthood (Andrews, Leigh, & Weiner, 2004; Glickman, 2012; LaVigne & Vernon, 2003). Research reviewed by Andrews and colleagues (2004; Leigh & Andrews, 2017) has focused primarily on the importance of ASL in the development of children who are deaf. It is argued that a complete language system—either spoken language or ASL—is critical to the overall development of deaf children (Mayberry, 2002). When caregivers and teachers are all fluent users of ASL, deaf children are able to communicate effectively, and reading achievement is generally improved. In most cases, children fluent in ASL or who have full access to spoken language have better potential for healthy psychological adjustment when they reach adulthood. Of course, children fluent in

ASL often have deaf parents or hearing parents who are fluent in ASL and work toward building healthy attachments in early childhood. When deaf children are raised in an environment that limits access to communication, the likelihood of problems is heightened during adolescence and adulthood (Mayberry, 2002).

The presence of language and learning challenges adds to potential risk factors for deaf youth caught in the juvenile justice system. As first identified in 1969 by Vernon, and still a robust statistic found today (Guardino & Cannon, 2015), 30% to 50% of all deaf children have compounding disabilities that are educationally significant. Thus, the presence of disabilities is another risk factor for the pipeline and for poor outcomes as an adult. With few exceptions, public schools usually lack personnel to conduct proper diagnostic services. Public schools have often done a poor job of diagnosing disabilities and developing educational programming for these students (Guardino & Cannon, 2015). Schools for the deaf typically have programming designed to address this population. For example, schools for the deaf often have curricula for deaf people with intellectual disabilities, behavioral disorders, or gifted education. Deaf students who have cognitive delays are likely to have functional instruction, including employment skills, delivered by signing teachers at a school for the deaf. However, public schools often push these students into one program shared by all deaf students, whether they have additional disabilities or not. Teachers often struggle to meet the needs of this population, and deaf students with language and learning challenges frequently flounder in public schools. When behavior becomes a problem, public schools have few accessible resources available to them, and often turn to discipline to manage behavior. Often, this situation is the first step into the pipeline. Similar to Caleb in the earlier case example, deaf students with behavioral problems rarely receive appropriate support services to correct problem behaviors. Sadly, appropriate interventions for deaf youth with these challenges are available in very few communities.

In years past, this population took on a variety of labels, including "low functioning deaf" and "multihandicapped deaf." However, to reframe how we work with this population in psychotherapeutic settings, Glickman (2009) coined the term "language and learning challenged" deaf people. Glickman also pioneered innovative approaches to treatment, including the use of picture communication, role-play, and other approaches, to move away from talk therapy as a treatment mode and toward authentic, meaningful, action-oriented therapy. His work has been transformative in the field of psychotherapeutic treatment with deaf people and is arguably the preferred mode of treatment today among specialists in the field. Although Glickman's publications are widely available, his work is used primarily by clinicians who specialize in psychotherapy with deaf people. The result is that most deaf youth in need of counseling are working with hearing clinicians using interpreters or signing clinicians who lack the knowledge and skill needed to make an impact with these students. When the clinicians fail to facilitate progress, youth are often labeled "resistant" or "difficult" and are moved to a higher level of care—often a hospital or treatment center that is more restrictive linguistically. This situation serves to advance the youth forward in the pipeline, moving deaf youth away from their natural environments and toward more restrictive settings (Lomas et al., 2017).

Social Cognition

Other related conditions worth noting include components of social cognition that relate to problems with impulse control, problems with the environment, and communication difficulties (Leigh & Andrews, 2017). Researchers in developmental psychology agree that infants and children use behavior to communicate when they are very young and unable to use words to communicate their wants and needs. Once language emerges and affect vocabulary is used regularly, most young children begin to learn to self-regulate their behavior. They learn what developmental psychologists call social cognition, one component of which is "theory of mind" or understanding the feelings and intentions of others. A second component of social cognition is called "executive functioning" or understanding how to make plans, follow through on goals, and control their impulses for later gratification, which are important tools for learning (Hermans et al., 2015; Morgan, 2015). For example, when a child does not get what they want, they may impulsively begin to scream, cry, or use behaviors to demonstrate to their caregiver that they need attention. Typically, the caregiver will respond by saying something like "I see you are upset, but you are not allowed to have cake until you have eaten dinner." In that exchange, the child learns a great deal of information that fosters self-regulation. The child learns that the word "upset" is the label for the feeling they are experiencing and that the cake will be available to them if gratification is delayed. They also learn that their caregiver can simultaneously set limits and empathize with their feelings. However, this scenario changes drastically when a child is deaf. Deaf children raised in environments that are not rich in language experience difficulty learning how to "read others," learning self-regulation skills, and controlling their impulses. Often, they demonstrate significant deficits in their ability to use affect vocabulary, resulting in poor impulse control and increased behavior problems at school and in other settings, a risk factor and nexus point. The deprivation of language goes hand in hand with the deprivation of affect, poor psychological attachment, and delayed academic development.

Fund of Information

All of the aforementioned conditions and factors interact with each other to form what researchers call a poor "fund of information" (Lomas et al., 2017). Fund of information refers to the entire body of information that is available to an individual. Hearing people are inundated with information on a daily basis. Much of the information received is never sought out. For example, noises made by the squealing of brakes on a train or automobile are undesirable sounds but allow hearing people to integrate the noise as cognitive information for future use. When squealing is heard while driving a car, the driver will be triggered to consider servicing their brakes because the sound, originally undesirable, is a signal that the brakes are deteriorating. For hearing people, information can be so overwhelming that it triggers efforts to "unplug" and intentionally tune out environmental sources. Deaf children do not grow up with the same experiences in this regard, making their fund of information much smaller. Let us consider the traditional family dinner as an example. A hearing family sitting around the table may have discussion about the daily events. The discussion will contain rich information sources that go beyond mere data. Of course, children are often spoken to directly and have interactions with siblings. They may have a television on in the background, which provides another source of information. The parents may have a side conversation about budgeting for an upcoming event. Although the children may not engage in the financial discussion, they are listening and learning how their parents solve problems, manage money, manage stress, and much more. Family values are embedded in these types of discussions (saving money, planning, budgeting, not stealing, delaying gratification, and working for income). During this discussion, a mobile phone may ring or a tablet may vibrate as messages are received. A timer may ring to signal that the food in the oven is ready to eat. At every turn, senses are being stimulated with information that we store and use for decision making in the future. The deaf child with a hearing family will receive only information that is directly communicated to him or her. They will not benefit from the spoken side conversation about finances or from hearing the television story about a significant event that recently occurred in the community. Although a measurement of one's fund of information is impossible, deaf children and youth raised in environments that lack access to language are making decisions with much less information than their hearing peers. This has serious consequences when the stakes are high (Lomas et al., 2017). For example, the case of Andy (a pseudonym) is real, but information has been changed to maintain confidentiality.

Andy's Story

Andy, a Latin American deaf youth, moved with his parents and two younger sisters to the United States from Guatemala when he was 12 years old. His family settled in southern California, and his father found a good job with an oil company. His family moved because of the poor education Andy received in Guatemala, and they wanted a better life for him. Andy communicated using both Guatemalan signs and home signs. He was generally well adjusted emotionally and behaviorally. In school, he got along well with others, worked hard, and never got into trouble. At age 18, he graduated from high school and stayed at home with his parents. Although he should have sought out a transitional living and vocational training program, he and his parents lacked the knowledge needed to access those services. Culturally, it was important for children to stay home and help the family until they were married or working. Not only was Andy bored and lonely at home, his sex drive was strong, and he was seeking companionship from a gay peer. He turned to the internet to find a relationship and met several young people, including a 14-year-old teen who lived nearby and was interested in him. After exchanging some pictures electronically, the two met for their first date. When friends of the 14-year-old learned of the meeting, they called the police, who intervened immediately. The police found Andy undressed and preparing to have intercourse. They also found revealing photos of the 14-year-old on Andy's computer, along with other sexually explicit material. Andy was quickly arrested and charged with several crimes. Although Andy was not intellectually disabled and was a fairly fluent user of ASL, he did not fully understand the gravity of the situation until it was too late. Furthermore, Andy had no sense of how to defend himself with the authorities. When interrogated, he waived his right to legal counsel (although he did not understand what that meant) and fully confessed that he was seeking an intimate relationship with the minor. In court, Andy was faced with a young prosecutor who was seeking to build his résumé and had no mercy on Andy, who was represented by a public defender. Andy was found guilty and sentenced to 10 years in prison and lifetime registry as a sex offender.

A number of things went wrong in Andy's case. If Andy had been educated on how to develop and maintain intimate relationships appropriately, it is likely he would never have gotten into a romantic partnership with an underaged minor. Development of appropriate dating skills and boundaries is part of the curriculum at most schools for the deaf but is deemphasized or completely excluded in public school curricula. To make matters worse, Andy had no idea how to handle his interactions with the police after he was apprehended. When he was in jail, awaiting his trial, he was under the false impression that it was illegal to be gay. Unfortunately, Andy was faced with an overzealous prosecutor and a jury who did not fully grasp how the lack of information influenced his decision making. Furthermore, the options presented to Andy's attorney were all punitive and did not include rehabilitation. A treatment facility that is designed for deaf offenders would be the best of all the punitive options, if such a facility existed. Instead, he went to prison, where the climate for deaf inmates is described as horrific (Vernon, 2009). Any new behaviors Andy learns in prison may help him survive behind bars but will not serve him well once he is ready to be released.

Schools and Education

There is inadequate space in this chapter to address the evolution of the educational experiences of deaf children in the United States. Still, a brief review is offered as deaf education is a nexus point that contributes to the pipeline. The first school for the deaf in the United States was established in Hartford, CT, in 1817 by Thomas Hopkins Gallaudet. His model of a centralized, full-service, residential school proved successful, and other states began to establish schools for the deaf in subsequent years. Prior to Gallaudet's model, deaf children and youth were excluded from public schooling because they were viewed as "unable to benefit" from formal education. From 1817 to 1975, schools for the deaf experienced many struggles but generally enjoyed a period of peak enrollment (Gannon et al., 1981). In 1975, Public Law 94–142 established special education and ushered in a period of mainstreaming and inclusive education. The movement was led by parents of students with other disabilities, frustrated that their children were not educated in local public schools. Despite significant opposition by deaf alumni, public policy favored deinstitutionalization and the inclusion of students with disabilities in their neighborhood schools (Moores, 2001). Although this policy has been helpful for many students with disabilities, it has had consequences for deaf students. Two consequences, in particular, were limiting or eliminating deaf peer groups and limiting the number of service providers (teachers and other school staff) who could communicate directly with students in ASL. Deaf students at residential schools were seen by signing clinicians (counselors, psychologists, and social workers) when they experienced emotional and behavioral problems. However, deaf students in most public schools are served by staff who do not know sign language and misunderstand the impact of hearing loss and secondary disabilities on behavior. Although most clinicians in public schools are highly qualified, they are often ill-prepared to handle the challenges of deaf students with more significant emotional and behavioral problems (Lomas et al., 2017). If behavioral interventions are provided, they are often poorly constructed or ineffective for a deaf student. The practice of educating deaf youth with emotional and behavioral problems in our public schools is also a contributor to the pipeline. For example, most public schools have social–emotional programming to help students build empathy, reduce bullying, and improve overall student behavior. These programs are often delivered by staff or teachers, in large classrooms, not in small groups, and rarely by mental health professionals. Deaf students are sometimes left out of the delivery of social–emotional learning programs in public schools. If they are included, they may experience an interpreter instead of direct communication with a signing mental health professional using role-play and other strategies to ensure understanding (Lomas et al., 2017). Thus, their access to critical social–emotional programming is limited.

Literacy Levels

Another nexus point that contributes to the pipeline is the average reading level of deaf high school graduates, which has historically been about the 4th grade level (Traxler, 2000). Deaf youth who are recent immigrants, have psychosis, or who have language and learning challenges are likely to read English at an even lower level and may struggle with both receptive and expressive sign language. Thus, entanglements with those in authority (school leaders, law enforcement) are likely to be fraught with misunderstanding. If no interpreter is present, authorities often revert to writing to explain the infraction to the youth and are unaware that in many situations, writing is ineffective. If an interpreter is present, there is still no guarantee that the youth will understand the infraction and the consequences, especially if the deaf youth has language or learning challenges (LaVigne & Vernon, 2003). As a coping strategy, many deaf youths learn to nod and affirm, as if they understand (often referred to as the *deaf nod*) when they do not understand what is being said to them. Although it appears that communication is effective, the reality is that the nod has served to affirm misunderstanding, which leaves them more vulnerable to further injustices (LaVigne & Vernon, 2003).

Financial Reimbursement

A nexus point that contributes to the pipeline is that many facilities within the continuum of care are for-profit businesses, and this leads to problems related to financial reimbursement. The cost of treatment for deaf youth is typically much higher than for hearing youth at facilities that do not specialize in deaf services. A service provider who complies with the Americans With Disabilities Act (ADA) will be faced with costs that go beyond the typical price of treatment for hearing youth. At a minimum, the facility must employ an interpreter for several hours each day of treatment. Seeing their profit margins dwindle, administrators may actively work toward avoiding treatment of deaf youth or speed up the treatment, returning them to their communities before they have met the treatment goals. Thus, the quality of psychiatric care for deaf youth suffers, advancing their movement in the pipeline.

TREATMENT OPTIONS

Although treatment options vary, some common options are discussed in what follows. These include keeping the child in their home with their biological parents combined with school counseling; with a foster family, in a residential treatment center (RTC); in a group home; or in an adoptive family. The case study of Max illustrates each of these treatment options available to hearing youth and will illustrate the multitude of services traversed by one individual, most of which are inaccessible to deaf youth.

Max's Story

Max is a 14-year-old hearing youth who grew up in poverty. His father was murdered in a drug transaction, and his mother has struggled to stay sober. He has had poor school attendance and has not done well in a program for students with behavioral disorders. He has consistently refused to do any work in school and has been oppositional with teachers. He has been in and out of foster care since age 7. During his first trip to foster care, he was required to see a child therapist in her office. The two bonded, and Max showed clear signs of improvement in therapy and in his foster placement. However, his mother completed her services and, after 6 months in state custody, Max was returned to her care. Once protective services closed her case, Max's mother discontinued his counseling, and she eventually returned to drug use. Max's behavior has continued to decline, and he has had some serious rage outbursts. After threatening to kill peers last month, he was placed in a psychiatric hospital for a few days. Once he appeared to be stabilized and discontinued his overt threats of harm to others, he was moved into an RTC. His mother has reported that she cannot control him and has her own problems, so she desires to permanently relinquish custody to the state. The plan is for Max to move from his RTC into a group home for troubled boys. If Max does well in the group home, his caseworker told him, he may be placed in the foster care system—living with a family and attending daily therapy sessions at a local psychiatric hospital. If that setting shows improvement, he will stay in foster care while on the adoption list and will continue to see an outpatient therapist weekly until he is adopted or ages out of the system. Max sees this option as hopeful because he really wants to stay out of trouble and would like to find a family who will truly love and accept him.

Although the behavioral health system can be a challenge to navigate, there are resources available to youth in communities across our country. These agencies and institutions are staffed by people who are trained, usually licensed, and who work to help youth manage their emotions and improve behaviors. Their goal is to keep youth out of the pipeline and to move them toward hope and self-management. Although these institutions are far from perfect, they provide much-needed services for students who have emotional and behavioral demands that go beyond the purview of schools.

These mental health services, ranging from counseling at home or in an office to inpatient in a hospital, are seen collectively as a continuum of care. The continuum of mental health care in communities across our nation is designed for hearing individuals like Max in the prior case example. With few exceptions, institutions across the United States are ill-equipped to address the needs of deaf individuals within the care continuum. In a reference to services in the child welfare system, Lomas and Johnson (2012) reported that shelters and treatment programs for deaf children can be isolating and confusing and can exacerbate trauma that deaf children experience in systems that are supposed to be supportive. Figure 1 illustrates a continuum of common psychiatric services for children and youth, from the least restrictive, at the bottom of the pyramid, to the most restrictive, at the top. At the widest part of the pyramid, the largest number of people is served, and this narrows all the way up to the top of the pyramid, where the fewest are served.

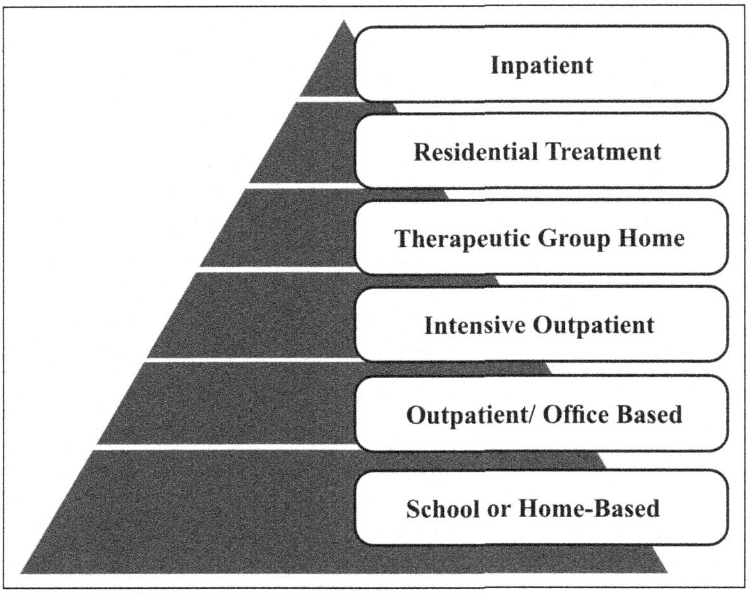

FIGURE 1. Continuum of common psychiatric services for children and youth.

Although not all children and youth do well in treatment, the continuum of psychiatric services is available in all urban areas across our nation. Furthermore, many suburban and rural areas have adequate access to the continuum of care. However, most of these systems are not designed to serve deaf children. In some urban areas, treatment programs accessible to deaf people are in operation. However, it is rare to find the entire continuum of psychiatric care, accessible in sign language and delivered by signing clinicians, available to deaf children and youth. Furthermore, it is also uncommon to find signing individuals in organizations that provide related services, such as signing caseworkers and foster parents, adding to the barriers to treatment. Because resources are unavailable or poorly delivered, deaf children and youth are placed at greater risk for unsuccessful outcomes. In communities that offer some accessible psychiatric care, there may be bureaucracy that impedes access to these services. For example, in some communities the county mental health agency handling a case is required to use an approved contractor. If the signing clinician is not on the approved list, caseworkers may be required to use a nonsigning clinician with an interpreter instead of an accessible provider. By limiting access to accessible treatment, these conditions serve to reinforce another nexus point toward the pipeline for deaf students (Lomas et al., 2017; Lomas & Johnson, 2012). All of these nexus points collide to form the school-to-prison pipeline (see Figure 2).

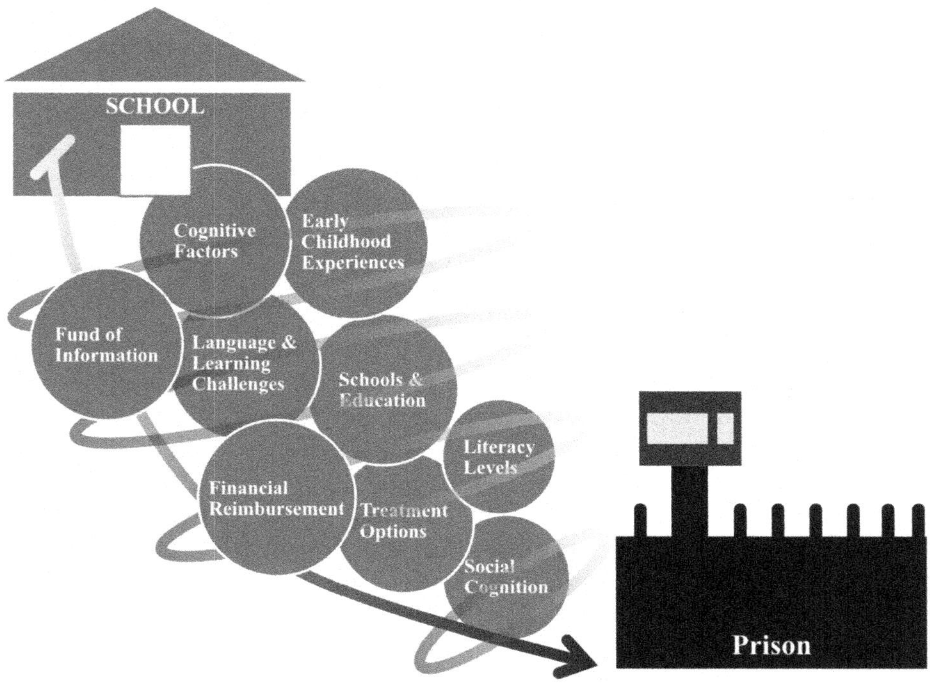

FIGURE 2. Nexus points in the school-to-prison pipeline.

DEAF YOUTH NAVIGATING THE JAIL/PRISON SYSTEM

Arrest and Booking

While arrest and incarceration can be traumatic for any individual, it is particularly upsetting for deaf juveniles. Deaf people are often victims of police brutality because they do not respond to verbal commands from the officer. The American Civil Liberties Union, in collaboration with HEARD, reported cases in which innocent deaf people have been beaten, shocked with a Taser, or shot because they did not respond to officers. Once arrested, hands are customarily cuffed behind the back, eliminating the ability to communicate using gestures, signs, or written language. Rarely are interpreters used at this stage of the process, a violation of the ADA (Vernon, 2009). Deaf youth are often extremely confused at this point because they may be expecting the arresting officer to allow them to explain themselves. The experience of being arrested and booked into detention facilities is demeaning and fraught with misunderstandings. Arrest is usually followed by an interrogation, which is frequently done without an interpreter. It is not unusual for an interrogation to last several hours, leading to exhaustion. In a compelling article on false confessions, Kassin (2012) asserted that false confessions are

> facilitated not only by dispositional characteristics of weak and vulnerable suspects (i.e., youth, intellectual impairment, mental illness, and personality traits that foster compliance and suggestibility) and situational aspects of custody and interrogation (i.e., lengthy sessions, threats, promises, presentations of false evidence, and minimization of themes that imply leniency, but by the phenomenology of innocence). (pp. 433–434)

While Kassin was referencing vulnerable people, in general, his descriptions of vulnerability are terms frequently used to describe deaf children and adults. Furthermore, Kassin described innocence as a

> mental state that leads innocent people to waive their Miranda rights to silence and to counsel; to behave in ways that are open and forthcoming in their interactions with police; to offer up alibis freely, without regard for the fact that police may view minor inaccuracies with suspicion. (p. 433)

Additionally, in studying mock juries, Kassin and Newmann (1997) revealed that confessions have a greater impact on verdicts than do other powerful forms of evidence. The conditions of arrest and interrogation, with ADA violations and intense questioning of a vulnerable population, advance deaf youth through the pipeline (Vernon & Andrews, 2012).

The Court Experience

The process of going to court for a trial is also fraught with problems. With their poor fund of information, deaf children and youth commonly do not understand the criminal justice system. Furthermore, many municipal and family courts do not provide interpreters unless there is advocacy by the family of the deaf defendant or plaintiff. Court interpreting requires a minimum of two interpreters, one to work at the table with the deaf person and their attorney and the other to work at the bench, interpreting the same content that is being recorded. Recently, the use of Certified Deaf Interpreters (CDIs) is becoming standard practice. CDIs are deaf adults with native ASL fluency who are certified and qualified to interpret to deaf people with a wide variety of communication modalities (Bienvenu, 2015). The use of a CDI is added assurance that the message will be understood by the deaf individual in court. Often, lawyers and judges are unclear about who is responsible for requesting an interpreter, resulting in no interpreter for the deaf person in court. The deaf person often ends up confused, allowing their lawyer to determine a course of action for them. Thus, they may accept plea deals that are undesirable, plead guilty when they are innocent, or take another course of action that was not understood by the deaf person (LaVigne & Vernon, 2003). Although there is an illusion of justice, many deaf youth and adult offenders are frequently locked up, whereas hearing people with the same charges would have been set free.

NEED FOR FUTURE RESEARCH

Although efforts have recently been made to disrupt the school-to-prison pipeline in some communities, more research is needed to do so with deaf children and youth. A good place to begin is collecting better data in existing programs. Schools are required to report the numbers of students with disabilities and the types of accommodations implemented for each student. However, youth correctional schools, jails, and prisons are not under the same obligation. Numbers of deaf children and youth who are educated or otherwise housed outside of traditional schools should be reported to the government, and those demographics should be available to the general public.

Furthermore, each factor that contributes to the school-to-prison pipeline for deaf youth should be the focus of research. For example, foster care programs for youth in need of care are available in all states, but few states have programs that identify foster parents who use sign language. Studies that address the outcomes of deaf youth in foster care with signing and nonsigning foster care should be conducted, and public policy should be established on the basis of best interest of youth in the foster care system. Each link in the system plays a role in making deaf youth either more resilient or more likely to advance in the school-to-prison pipeline. Areas of study should include the legal system, the child welfare system, the foster care system, the law enforcement system, and the school system. Those who work in these systems should identify ways to reinvent their nexus points and disrupt the pipeline.

SUMMARY

Nine nexus points have been identified as contributors to the school-to-prison pipeline for deaf children and youth. Some of these nexus points are rooted in the child and family and include poor language development, as well as poor fund of information, both of which lead to misunderstandings when interacting with law enforcement and the justice system. Additionally, there are variables that are rooted in our social system, including education, law enforcement, child welfare, and juvenile justice. Currently, deaf children and youth are overrepresented in the justice system. Researchers and practitioners working in these systems must be mindful of the contributors to the school-to-prison nexus and work to identify resources that lead to improved outcomes. The cases of Caleb and Andy must one day become the exception, rather than the rule, for deaf youth.

REFERENCES

Andrews, J., Leigh, I., & Weiner, M. (2004). *Deaf people: Evolving perspectives in psychology, education and sociology*. Allyn & Bacon.

Bienvenu, MJ. (2015). Bilingualism: Are sign language interpreters bilinguals? *Street Leverage Live*. https://www.youtube.com/watch?v=QfT3BvfCsVo&t=11s&frags=pl%2Cwn

Department of Corrections. (2013). *Trends in the offender population 2013* [Report]. http://corrections.govt.nz

Felitti, V. J., Anda, R. F., Nordenberg, D., Williamson, D. F., Spitz, A. M., Edwards, V., Koss, M. P., & Marks, J. S. (1998). Relationship of childhood abuse and household dysfunction to many of the leading causes of death in adults. *American Journal of Preventive Medicine, 14*(4), 245–258. https://doi.org/10.1016/S0749-3797(98)00017-8

Gallaudet Research Institute. (2013). *Regional and national summary report of data from the 2011–2012 Annual Survey of Deaf and Hard of Hearing Children and Youth*. Gallaudet Research Institute, Gallaudet University.

Gannon, J. R., Butler, J., & Gilbert, L. (1981). *Deaf heritage: A narrative history of deaf America*. National Association of the Deaf.

Glickman, N. (2009). *Cognitive-behavioral therapy for deaf and hearing persons with language and learning challenges*. Routledge.

Glickman, N. (2012). *Deaf mental health care*. Routledge.

Guardino, C. (2008). Identification and placement for deaf students with multiple disabilities: Choosing the path less followed. *American Annals of the Deaf, 153*(1), 55–64. https://doi.org/10.1353/aad.0.0004

Guardino, C., & Cannon, J. E. (2015). Theory, research, and practice for students who are deaf and hard of hearing with disabilities: Addressing the challenges from birth to postsecondary education. *American Annals of the Deaf, 160*(4), 347–355.

Hermans, D., Vuggs, C., Berkel-Van Hoof, M., & Knoors, H. (2015). Deaf children's executive functions: From research to practice. In H. Knoors & M. Marschark (Eds.), *Educating deaf learners: Creating a global evidence base* (pp. 231–260). Oxford University Press.

Jensema, C. K. (1990). Hearing loss in a jail population. *Journal of the American Deafness and Rehabilitation Association, 24*, 49–58.

Jernigan, J. (2010). *Risk factors and aggressive behaviors of deaf males: A longitudinal study* [Unpublished manuscript]. Lamar University, Beaumont, TX.

Kassin, S. M. (2012). Why confessions trump innocence. *American Psychologist, 67*(6), 431–445. https://doi.org/10.1037/a0028212

Kassin, S. M., & Newmann, K. (1997). On the power of confession evidence: An experimental test of the "fundamental difference" hypothesis. *Law and Human Behavior, 21*, 469–484. https://doi.org/10.1023/A:1024871622490

LaVigne, M., & Vernon, M. (2003). An interpreter is not enough: Deafness, language, and due process. *Wisconsin Law Journal, 5*, 843-935.

Leigh, I., & Andrews, J. (2017). *Deaf people in society: Evolving perspectives in psychology, education and sociology*. Routledge.

Lomas, G., Andrews, J., & Shaw, P. (2017). Deaf and hard of hearing. In J. Kauffman, D. Hallahan, & P. C. Pullen (Eds.), *Handbook of special education* (2nd ed., chap. 23). Routledge.

Lomas, G. I., & Johnson, H. A. (2012). Overlooked and unheard: Abuse of children who are deaf or hard of hearing and their experience with CPS and foster care. *The Family Journal, 20*(4), 376–383. https://doi.org/10.1177/1066480712452708

Mayberry, R. (2002). Cognitive development in deaf children: The interface of language and perception in neuropsychology. In S. J. Segalowitz & I. Rapin (Eds.), *Handbook of neuropsychology* (2nd ed., Vol. 8, Part 3, pp. 71–107). Elsevier Science.

Melnick, W. (1970). Hearing impairment in an adult penal institution. *Journal of Speech Hearing and Disorders, 35*, 173–181.

Miller, K. R. (2001). *Forensic issues of deaf offenders* [Unpublished doctoral dissertation]. Lamar University.

Miller, K., Vernon, M., & Capella, M. E. (2005). Violent offenders in a deaf prison population. *Journal of Deaf Studies and Deaf Education, 10*(4), 417–425. https://doi.org/10.1093/deafed/eni039

Moores, D. (2001). *Educating the deaf: Psychology, principles, and practices* (5th ed.). Cengage Press.

Morgan, G. (2015). Social-cognition for learning as a deaf student. In H. Knoors & M. Marschark (Eds.), *Educating deaf learners: Creating a global evidence base* (pp. 261–282). Oxford University Press.

O'Rourke, S., Glickman, N. S., & Austen, S. (2013). Deaf people in the criminal justice system: Is a culturally affirmative response possible or desirable? In N. S. Glickman (Ed.), *Deaf mental health care* (pp. 323–358). Routledge.

Sawyer. W., & Wagner, P. (2020). *Mass incarceration: The whole pie 2020*. Prison Policy Initiative. https://www.prisonpolicy.org/reports/pie2020.html

Schept, J., Wall, T., & Brisman, A. (2015). Building, staffing, and insulting an architecture of criminological complicity in the school-to-prison pipeline. *Social Justice, 41*(4), 96–112.

Stahl, A. L. (2006). *Delinquency cases in juvenile court, 2002*. U.S. Department of Justice, Office of Juvenile Justice and Delinquency Prevention.

Traxler, C. B. (2000). The Stanford Achievement Test, 9th edition: National norming and performance standards for deaf and hard-of-hearing students. *Journal of Deaf Studies and Deaf Education, 5*(4), 337–348. https://psycnet.apa.org/doi/10.1093/deafed/5.4.337

Twersky Glasner, A., & Miller, K. R. (2010). Communication isolation as reported by a group of deaf Texas inmates. *Western Criminology Review, 11*(2), 1–8.

U.S. Department of Education. (2000). *Twenty-second annual report to Congress on the implementation of the Individuals With Disabilities Education Act*.

U.S. Department of Education. (2017). *Supporting youth with disabilities in juvenile corrections*. https://sites.ed.gov/osers/2017/05/supporting-youth-with-disabilities-in-juvenile-corrections/

Vernon, M. (1969). *Multiply handicapped deaf children: Medical, educational and psychological considerations*. Council of Exceptional Children.

Vernon, M. (2008). Mental health services for people who are deaf. *American Annals of the Deaf, 152*(4), 374–381. https://doi.org/10.1353/aad.2008.0005

Vernon, M. (2009). The horror of being deaf and in prison. *American Annals of the Deaf, 155*(3), 311–321. https://doi.org/10.1353/aad.2010.0018

Vernon, M., & Andrews, J. (2012). Individuals with disabilities and the issue of false confessions. *The Champion, 36*(6), 34–42.

Vernon, M., & Greenberg, S. F. (1999). Violence in deaf and hard of hearing people: A review of literature. *Aggression and Violent Behavior, 4*(3), 259–272. https://doi.org/10.1016/S1359-1789(97)00058-X

Vernon, M., & Raifman, I. J. (1997). Recognizing and handling problems of incompetent deaf defendants charged with serious offenses. *International Journal of Law and Psychiatry, 20*, 373–487. https://doi.org/10.1016/S0160-2527(97)00010-1

5

Substance Use Disorders Among Deaf Offenders

Debra Guthmann and Marcia Kolvitz

Criminal justice experts recognize that many individuals who are incarcerated have substance abuse issues that may be compounded by co-occurring mental illness and that many may begin to use substances to cope with mental illness or physical pain (Kim et al., 2015). Among sentenced prisoners under the jurisdiction of state correctional authorities in December 2016, about 15%, or 190,100 prisoners, had been convicted of a drug offense as their most serious crime (Bronson & Carson, 2019). When individuals are incarcerated, there may be an opportunity to connect hard-to-reach and underserved people to treatment while in a fairly stable setting. However, substance abuse and addiction treatment is not widely available for incarcerated individuals, and very little has been reported about treatment for those who are deaf (Guthmann & Blozis, 2001). The National Center on Addiction and Substance Abuse (CASA) at Columbia University (2010) estimates that only 11% of incarcerated individuals in need of substance abuse treatment receive it in jail or prison. An Urban Institute report in 2015 found that more than half of all inmates in jails and state prisons have a mental illness of some kind. The report also found that only one-in-three state prisoners and one-in-six jail inmates who suffer from mental health conditions report having received mental health treatment since they were incarcerated. Although it provides a comprehensive summary of practice across the United States, this report does not address specific populations of inmates, such as those who are deaf. Little research has been done on the prevalence of deaf individuals who have been convicted or incarcerated and who experience substance abuse and/or mental health conditions (Vernon & Miller, 2005). If a deaf individual is able to receive treatment while incarcerated, they are not always provided with interpreters or other communication access, even though prisons are federally funded and required by law to do so.

The presence of co-occurring disabilities has been studied over the past few decades, but very limited information is available, especially related to deaf offenders who have substance abuse issues. Throughout this chapter, the experiences of two deaf men—**Alan** and **Robert**—are included to give the reader some insights into the life experiences of deaf offenders with substance abuse issues. These men started drinking alcohol and using other drugs as teenagers, committed crimes, and experienced significant consequences in their lives due to substance abuse and related interactions with the judicial system.

PREVALENCE OF SUBSTANCE USE AND CRIMINAL ACTIVITY

Substance misuse and addiction have reached epidemic proportions among inmates in the United States (James & Glaze, 2006). According to Bronson and Carson (2019), the Bureau of Justice Statistics estimates that there are currently 1.5 million prisoners in state and federal prisons. Almost two-thirds (64.5%) of the inmate population in the United States meet medical criteria for an alcohol or other drug use disorder and are seven times more likely than individuals in the general population to have a substance use disorder (National Center on Addiction and Substance Abuse at Columbia University, 2010). Within the general population, there is a high correlation between the use of substances (alcohol and drugs) and violent crime. In fact, as many as 60% of all people arrested for most kinds of crimes test positive for drugs (Fazel et al., 2006; Karberg & James, 2005). Between 1996 and 2006, the number of adults incarcerated rose by 33% to 2.3 million inmates, and the number of inmates who were substance involved jumped by 43% to 1.9 million inmates (National Center on Addiction and Substance Abuse at Columbia University, 2010).

A small research study by Vernon et al. (1999) found that limited data were available on drug and alcohol use by deaf offenders when their crimes were committed. Only four deaf violent offenders' medical records indicated that they had been intoxicated while committing their crime. According to the study, which included 64 subjects, 62.5% reported a history of alcohol and/or marijuana use, whereas 35.9% reported the use of other substances such as heroin, cocaine, inhalants, barbiturates, and hallucinogens. In a previous study of 29 deaf murderers, half were found to have been intoxicated at the time of the murder (Vernon et al., 1999). Although studies conducted about the nonoffender deaf population report a lower incidence of self-reported substance abuse, these responses may have been influenced by factors such as incorrect diagnoses by service providers and deaf individuals' lack of access to treatment services (Leigh & Pollard, 2004).

While back home in a rural community, **Alan** met a group of hearing people who drank and used drugs. To earn money, members of this gang stole furniture and sold it. Initially, they gave Alan drugs and alcohol for free, but eventually Alan became involved in selling stolen furniture in exchange for free meth. He started using meth intravenously and would stay high for long periods of time. Although he was not involved with making meth, he sold it for a short period of time.

Alan really wanted to change his lifestyle because he realized he was living a lie. At night, he would sleep with different groups of people—one group was sober and another group was using—and he would try to hide each part of his life from the other. He was very fearful of the gang members but tried to act as tough as possible. There were several occasions during which he could have been killed.

Alan's family knew he was hanging around with a bad group of people; they were afraid and they really didn't want him home. He would sometimes hide at his grandparent's home, clean up, get some sleep, and then hit the streets again. Alan was not at all stable. One night, he decided he needed to find his safe place and went to his grandmother's home. Within five minutes, he hurt his grandmother with a knife. He woke up in jail, remembering nothing about the previous evening.

Substance Use Disorders Among the General Deaf Population

Although little research has been done on prevalence rates, best practices related to prevention, assessment, or treatment, there is a great deal of speculation that the prevalence of substance use disorders (SUDs) among deaf individuals exceeds that of hearing individuals (Berman et al., 2010; Boros, 1979; Boros, 1980; Guthmann & Blozis, 2001; Guthmann & Graham, 2004; Guthmann et al., 2012; Guthmann & Sandberg, 1998, 2003; Kushalnagar et al., 2019; Lipton & Goldstein, 1997; McKee et al., 2018; Moore & McAweeney, 2006; Titus & Guthmann, 2010; Wilson et al., 2015). Substance abuse among deaf individuals is *at least* as prevalent as it is among hearing individuals, usually to the extent of 8% to 10% of the general population (Guthmann, 2007; Guthmann & Graham, 2004; Guthmann et al., 2012; Guthmann & Sandberg, 2003; Moore & McAweeney, 2006). Berman and colleagues surveyed over 800 deaf high school students and found lifetime use rates for alcohol and other substances to be as high as or higher than those for hearing youth (Berman et al., 2010; Guthmann, 2011).

This is supported by research conducted by Kushalnagar and colleagues. (2019), which showed a higher likelihood for increased alcohol consumption among younger male deaf adults, especially among those living in communities with a higher density of deaf individuals. In an analysis of 2013 to 2014 National

Health and Nutrition Examination Survey (NHANES) data that included 133 deaf adults, it was reported that deaf participants engaged in much heavier use of alcohol and regular use of cannabis than hearing participants (Anderson et al., 2018). In 2018, a study was done by Dr. Michael McKee et al. (2018), using the National Survey on Drug Use and Health data. The survey asked participants to identify whether they are deaf or have serious difficulty hearing. The results of the study from 2015 and 2016 of the National Survey on Drug Use and Health data were combined to compare SUDs among adults with and without self-reported hearing loss. Analyses indicated that adults with hearing loss ages 18 to 49 are more likely to meet the criteria for a SUD than their hearing peers. Those younger individuals with hearing loss appear more likely to develop a SUD (McKee et al., 2018).

Family and friends, often in a sincere but misdirected effort to help, rescue these individuals from the consequences of their behavior, robbing them of the opportunity to see how their alcohol or other drug use negatively impacts their lives (Guthmann, 2011). Failing to hold an individual accountable only serves to keep that person from seeking help. It is not uncommon for deaf individuals who are stopped by the police to be let off or merely cautioned for a number of reasons. Some officers may feel sorry for the deaf individual, whereas others do not want to deal with the communication barriers or the process of obtaining a sign language interpreter. This kind of enabling does not help the individual realize they have an issue and experience the natural consequences of their behavior.

Other factors that put some individuals at a higher risk for substance use are biological processes, personality traits, mental health disorders, family neglect and abuse, poor attachment to school and the community, and growing up in marginalized and deprived communities (Leyton & Stewart, 2014). Within the Deaf community, there are very few accessible community-based treatment programs, a low number of referrals to treatment at any given time, minimal alternatives for accessible self-help support groups, and a general lack of information about SUDs by deaf and hearing service providers (Guthmann & Blozis, 2001; Guthmann & Graham, 2004; Guthmann et al., 2012). Frequently, because of numerous communication and cultural barriers, deaf individuals lack access in their local communities to substance use and mental health services (Guthmann & Graham, 2004; Guthmann et al., 2012; Guthmann & Moore, 2007; Pollard & Barnett, 2009).

There is a need for drug and alcohol prevention to be provided to deaf individuals while in K–12 education to keep them better informed about the dangers of drugs and alcohol and prompt them to learn about the cycle of addiction. The primary objective of drug prevention is to help young people as well as people in general to avoid or delay the use of drugs and/or alcohol. If they have already started to use them, then the goal is for them to avoid developing disorders such as dependency. Very few prevention materials have been developed for working specifically with deaf individuals. When working with deaf individuals, interactive techniques that are highly visual are often preferred because they can be more conducive to behavioral and attitudinal changes than are lectures. The use of small group discussions and activities, role-play, hands-on projects, videos, and stories portraying real-life situations as well as other techniques that facilitate self-reflection and active involvement are also part of interventions that deliver desired prevention outcomes (Guthmann & Sternfeld, 2013).

Risk Factors

Individuals who start to drink before the age of 15 are four times more likely to also report meeting the criteria for alcohol dependence at some point in their lives (Substance Abuse and Mental Health Services Administration, 2015). Currently, there is no research that documents the average age that deaf individuals start to use alcohol and/or drugs. However, one of the first inpatient specialized treatment programs serving this population, the Minnesota Substance Use Disorder Program for Deaf and Hard of Hearing Individuals, has made some attempts to collect demographic information on their clients (Guthmann & Blozis, 2001; Guthmann & Graham, 2004; Guthmann & Sandberg, 1998). Since its inception in 1989, the program has served more than 1,600 deaf adolescents and adults and has collected information related to age, gender, ethnicity, drug of choice, funding sources, geographic location, and age of first use. During intake, when clients are asked about their first use of alcohol, many individuals indicate they started drinking around the age of 10. Unfortunately, many schools attended by deaf students may not offer formal prevention programs at all; but if they do, they frequently do not start until middle or high school (Guthmann, 1999, 2007). There continue to be questions as to whether it is more effective to focus prevention efforts on the nonusers who may benefit the most from primary prevention or whether prevention efforts that also reach higher risk youth or youth who are already experimenting make an impact. Primary prevention is designed to enhance protective factors of all students in order to keep problems from emerging. Secondary prevention interventions are designed to reverse the harm from exposure to known risk factors for a selected group of students. Tertiary prevention interventions are designed to reduce instead of reverse harm among a select group of students who are most at risk (Marsiglia et al., 2013).

A number of factors can put deaf individuals at higher risk for drug and alcohol use. Deaf youth may have a desire to fit in with hearing peers and face greater peer pressure, which could mean associating with those who use drugs (Dick, 1996; Titus et al., 2008). As previously mentioned, there is a lack of drug and alcohol prevention materials that are accessible and available for use by deaf individuals (Guthmann, 1999; Guthmann, 2007; Titus & Guthmann, 2010). Family and social issues may also increase substance abuse risk among deaf individuals. Additionally, communication challenges in families with a deaf individual may exist because 90% of parents of deaf children are hearing (Mitchell, 2006; Mitchell & Karchmer, 2004; Moores, 2001; Schein, 1974).

Deaf individuals who are unable to communicate with their peers often experience isolation in mainstreamed settings (Angelides & Aravi, 2007; Guthmann & Graham, 2004). Because of the lack of available support services, this isolation can extend beyond the educational environment into the community. After completing treatment, additional sober living options are needed but are very limited. For example, a deaf individual who was in treatment for 1 month learned about a sober living house for deaf people where he might be able to go after treatment. He was accepted into the program, but owing to space and funding issues, he was not able to move in immediately after completing treatment. In some situations, individuals may have to stay in shelters until space is available. Without some kind of immediate support available, the risk of relapse is high. Self-help and peer support are important elements of recovery but are largely missing for many deaf individuals. In most communities, hearing people have the option to attend an Alcoholics Anonymous (AA), Cocaine Anonymous (CA), or Narcotics Anonymous (NA) meeting any day of the week. Because most communities may only have few (if any) accessible meetings available, deaf individuals do not have the option to select the type of 12-step meeting they may attend. Whereas hearing people have a multitude of choices in aftercare resources, deaf people lack these resources. Deaf individuals who have been in the Minnesota treatment program have continually expressed their wishes for an accessible sober house and access to 12-step meetings.

COMMUNICATION ACCESS FOR INDIVIDUALS WHO ARE DEAF

Deaf people are afforded protection from discrimination under U.S. civil rights laws. The Americans With Disabilities Act (ADA) of 1990 and the Rehabilitation Act of 1973 clearly and comprehensively prohibit discrimination based on disability. Section 504 of the Rehabilitation Act of 1973 applies to federal executive agencies, including the Federal Bureau of Prisons and any program receiving federal funding in addition to both state and local prisons and jails. For a detailed discussion of these laws, see Chapter 9 in this volume.

While at the state hospital, **Alan** participated in substance abuse treatment. He was given lectures related to drugs and alcohol and attended 12-step meetings with interpreters. It didn't bother Alan to be the only deaf person there; he had grown up as the only deaf member of his family and was used to communicating through writing. After his discharge, he attended 12-step meetings as required. However, when his case was closed and meetings were no longer mandated, he stopped attending them. He thought that the sad and depressing stories that others shared were not helpful to him. If he attended meetings with other deaf people, he felt very stressed because he felt responsible for them and thought he should be helping them. Alan now gets his support from his family and his church. Over the years, he helped sponsor other deaf people, and will talk with people and go to sober events in his community.

Although laws have been enacted in the United States to protect individuals with disabilities in prison, a great deal of case law demonstrates that the intent of these laws has not been achieved. The services and accommodations prisons provided for deaf inmates—so that they can function at least as well as nondeaf inmates—do not seem to provide enough support to ensure their equal accessibility. Although the Rehabilitation Act and the ADA are intended to protect disabled individuals from discrimination and require deaf inmates to have equal access within correctional facilities, the laws are not implemented as they should be throughout our criminal justice system. Deaf inmates face greater risks of miscommunications that can lead to wrongful convictions, isolation, and emotional, physical, and sexual abuse by fellow inmates (Twersky Glasner & Miller, 2010; Vernon & Miller, 2001). Reform of the criminal justice system is needed to ensure that the laws are enforced and that due process is provided to deaf people.

Some deaf individuals in the criminal justice system grew up in homes where family members spoke English and did not know or use American Sign Language (ASL). Lack of language input during a child's earliest years and the underdevelopment of a formal language system can result in an adult without fluency or competence in any language, including ASL (Bavelier et al., 2003; De Houwer, 2009; Mayberry, 2010; Sacks, 1989). If you think about it, a lot of what goes on around us is picked up through incidental learning (Brackenbury et al., 2006). "Incidental" is defined in the dictionary as "occurring as a minor accompaniment" or "occurring by chance in connection with something else." Therefore, according to the *Merriam Webster Dictionary* (n.d.), incidental learning occurs merely by chance or without intention or calculation. Note that deaf individuals do not have the opportunity to be exposed to conversations going on around them. These individuals miss out on the discussions going on at home related to family issues or expectations. For example, there may be a discussion about a family member or friend who got into some kind of trouble and the ramifications of what might happen if those same actions were repeated. Therefore, discussions occurring in the home, at family gatherings, or during other times are not accessed by the deaf individual.

Alan, the only deaf member of his family, recalled going to different local public schools in his home area. Mostly, he remembered that there was no language or communication in his preschool years, but he went to school to play. Eventually, his grandparents found out about the state school for the deaf, and Alan started school there when he was about 4 or 5 years old. He lived on campus and would come home only about once each month. He enjoyed hanging out with his uncles when they watched car racing. He indicated that some of his aunts and uncles learned some sign language, but he otherwise communicated with family members through writing.

We can distinguish incidental learning from deliberate or intentional learning. The latter takes place when we conduct an activity with the specific aim of learning something. Think about all the information that is obtained through incidental learning, that is, our parents discussing the news or having the TV or radio on so hearing family members can listen to what is happening. We "overhear" discussions in a number of different settings, and all this information helps us to be aware of what is going on around us. This incidental learning also happens by overhearing conversations at school, work, or in other settings. Often, on overhearing such information, family members may go home and ask their parents or siblings questions about it. Therefore, for deaf individuals to acquire this same information, it needs to be shared through direct conversation or instruction. For individuals from nonsigning families, family discussions and incidental learning about the dangers of drug use may be limited.

In school, there is often a great deal of focus on developing reading and writing skills as well as on meeting all the state standards required of students in K–12 programs. Sometimes, because of this academic pressure, other information not considered pertinent to graduation may not be available. States require that health education be taught in high school, and there is some information related to drug education in this material. However, deaf youth may not receive direct drug and alcohol prevention information or learn about the dangers and effects when using alcohol and/or other drugs (Guthmann & Graham, 2004; Guthmann & Sandberg, 1998). One study of deaf young adults who did not have access to prevention materials during adolescence recommended that such materials would be helpful to adolescents with hearing loss, especially if they were available in sign language (Mason & Schiller, 2006).

Telecommunication Access

Throughout the criminal justice system, deaf people are often at a disadvantage owing to the lack of accessible communication and the inability to get due process equal to that available to hearing individuals. Because deaf inmates are at special risk for mistreatment and/or abuse by guards, other correctional employees, as well as other inmates, it is critical that safe, appropriate, and accessible facilities and programming are provided to ensure safety during incarceration and facilitate successful reentry upon release.

Many prisons do not provide the same communication options to deaf inmates as they do to hearing individuals. Because of lawsuits that have been filed on behalf of deaf inmates, more states are installing videophones (VPs) in prisons allowing inmates to communicate with their families and friends. When the technology is available, deaf inmates must go through a registration process before access is given to use the video relay service (VRS) or a VP.

Although teletype (TTY) devices are outdated, inappropriate, and ineffective for many deaf inmates, some prisons are still using them, even with deaf persons who have low English literacy. Some deaf inmates have indicated a preference for videophones because they use ASL; however, videophones may not be readily available. One inmate serving time for drug-related crimes indicated a preference for using the TTY because lines for the videophones were often much longer (J. Smith, personal communication, May 30, 2020).

In his early 20s, he was drinking heavily every day. After being arrested for getting into a fight, **Robert** spent several weeks in jail. He went to court twice, but no interpreter was provided. It wasn't until his third appearance that an interpreter was present, and he was able to get out on probation. During another time when Robert was in jail for 3 weeks, he had to ask hearing people to make calls for him, as there were no TTYs or video phones.

Alan was the only deaf person in the county jail in his small community. One of the female guards had a son who was deaf, so she tried to communicate with him, which eased some of the isolation. In retrospect, Alan didn't think his sign language communication back then was very clear in ASL, but the guard made things better when he was in jail. She also got Alan a TTY so he could communicate with other people. He still has that same TTY.

As an anecdotal example of the impact a videophone can have on a deaf inmate, consider the case of an individual who is serving a life sentence for committing first degree murder while high on heroin. In the more than 30 years that he has been in prison, his elderly mother and sister would visit him weekly and communicate with him by writing back and forth. There were frequently misunderstandings because the inmate struggled with reading and writing. After learning that this inmate had never used a videophone before, another deaf inmate helped him to learn how to use a videophone and get his family registered so they could talk with him through VRS. The first time he used VRS, the interpreter was able to translate every word he signed to his mother and sister. They all cried because they finally understood each other for the first time in 30 years. Now this inmate can regularly communicate with his mother and sister (B. Johnson, personal communication, January 15, 2017).

DEAF INMATES WITH SUBSTANCE USE DISORDERS

A number of issues impact incarcerated individuals who are deaf and also have substance abuse and mental health issues. For example, there is a lack of prevention, assessment, and treatment options within the Deaf community (Guthmann, 2011; Guthmann & Graham, 2004). Prisons should use appropriately trained health care professionals to screen, assess, and treat substance-involved inmates using comprehensive, evidence-based approaches tailored to the needs of deaf individuals. In prison settings, access may be reduced even further because interpreters are not always provided for deaf inmates who are participating in various kinds of programming. There is also a lack of appropriately trained professionals to treat substance-involved offenders using evidence-based approaches tailored to meet the needs of deaf offenders. Treatment support for individuals who are deaf and in prison should cover the full continuum of care, including prevention, job skill development, life skills training, substance abuse, and mental health assessment and treatment as well as access to self-help groups such as 12-step meetings. We know that deaf inmates who have been incarcerated for violations of the law that occurred while they were under the influence of drugs and/or alcohol may need SUD treatment. Although treatment programs in the prison system may be available to hearing inmates, individuals who are deaf may not have the same opportunities for access. Many deaf inmates cannot access specialized services such as drug/sex offender programs in prisons because the prisons may not provide interpreters. Even with interpreters, the deaf individual may not be able to follow the conversations in group discussions. The inmates are unable to write in their journals or read the materials given to them because they are usually written at a high reading level.

Inmates are usually up for parole once a year and, in preparation, put together a packet of information justifying why they think they are ready to be released and what support they will have when they get out of prison. For an individual who has issues with substance abuse, having a treatment program they will attend or demonstrating their efforts while in prison to address addiction issues is viewed positively by the parole board. Prisons sometimes have secular or faith-based treatment programs that allow inmates to work on their dependency issues. Anecdotally, we know of at least one deaf inmate who was accepted into a faith-based treatment program but was denied an interpreter. During the 2-year program, the inmate tried to lipread providers and peers and worked hard to teach other inmates sign language so as to get more out of the program.

As part of the parole package, indicating the willingness to go to a treatment program upon release may be an important part of the plan presented to the board. Because most states do not have specialized linguistically accessible treatment programs for deaf people and, in most cases, the parole board will not permit an inmate being released from prison to leave the state, it is challenging to find appropriate programs. This can mean extending the time the deaf person may be incarcerated because the support plan for when they are released may not be considered viable. Lewis (2018) described the situation of Jonah Wooden, a deaf plaintiff who was supposed to attend substance abuse classes as a condition of probation but could not understand the classes because he had no interpreter. He asked for an interpreter but was told he would have to pay for one himself. Although unable to afford the cost of an interpreter, he continued attending the classes, but later, out of frustration, decided to stop. He was arrested for violating the terms of his probation and sentenced to 2 years in prison.

There are deaf inmates housed in prisons located at short distances from designated substance abuse felony treatment facilities. Inmates may be authorized to participate in a felony treatment program by the Board of Pardons and

Parole as a modification of their parole. Some deaf individuals may qualify for these programs but are not guaranteed the provision of interpreters if they are accepted and do attend. As of this writing, there are some lawsuits underway that are addressing these issues.

In another situation, the parole board wanted to know whether a deaf individual had completed any self-help programs during his incarceration because this is seen as an indication that the individual may have been rehabilitated and is able to return home (Michaels, 2018). This deaf individual had attended groups at the substance abuse treatment facility (SATF) within the prison system, but because no interpreter was provided, he had problems understanding and benefited little from the meetings. Yet he continued to attend the meetings on a regular basis. However, the parole board denied his request for release even though he had attended all the meetings consistently. This inmate was reprimanded for not participating in more programs and was told that he would have to wait 5 years before applying for another hearing! Prisons should provide communication access, including qualified interpreters for deaf inmates, to help them participate in education and self-help classes, and communicate with guards. Unfortunately, this access is not provided consistently in many of the prison settings.

What Deaf Inmates Experience

Although many teenagers and youth might have limited knowledge about the legal system, the foregoing factors certainly contribute to the lack of understanding that many deaf people may have about it. If a deaf person is stopped by the police, it can be overwhelming and frightening for many reasons, including the lack of communication access. It can be frightening for a deaf individual who is handcuffed, arrested, taken into police custody, convicted, and incarcerated. Deaf inmates may not understand the arrest and questioning process for a number of reasons, including dysfluency and limited fluency in English, ASL, or both languages (Vernon, 2009). Additionally, there may be a lack of qualified sign language interpreters, including the limited use of certified deaf interpreters (CDIs; see Chapter 7). A number of deaf individuals who have participated in the Minnesota Substance Use Disorder Program for Deaf and Hard of Hearing Individuals have reported being stopped by a police officer while under the influence of alcohol and/or drugs and being let off because they are deaf. Some deaf offenders are let off for escalating infractions until, finally, they commit more serious offenses and are imprisoned.

There has been very little information written about deaf individuals who are incarcerated and even less documentation about the reasons why the imprisonment occurred. Various reports indicate that many deaf prisoners may face some kind of abuse in prison. Rape is common within prison walls and often goes unreported and even unpunished when reported to guards (Vernon, 2010). A deaf prisoner is unlikely to be able to communicate effectively with other inmates and is less likely to have a friend or group to protect him if a conflict arises. Because deaf prisoners often cannot hear other inmates approaching, they may not be aware of possible attacks that may occur. Deaf inmates may also face abuse or taunting by coprisoners or guards because deaf individuals tend to rely on them to gain vital information about the prison (Vernon, 2010).

When **Robert** was walking by himself to the chow hall, one of the correctional officers found out that he was deaf after shouting at him several times and getting no response. The officer then walked toward Robert from behind, grabbed his coat hood, and pulled it with full force until he fell and hit the ground. Disoriented and confused about what had just happened, Robert turned his head and saw that it was the correctional officer that many deaf inmates didn't like because of his attitude toward them. Robert immediately informed him that he was deaf. Still sitting on the floor, he lipread the officer's comment: "I know you are deaf, and you are dumb to ignore my calls!" Robert indicated that he has seen situations worse than what happened to him, and it would be easy to feel sorry for oneself while in that situation.

COMMUNICATION BARRIERS IN THE LEGAL SYSTEM

Within the criminal justice system, deaf individuals may encounter barriers, beginning with their first encounter within the legal system. This includes situations in which individuals may be stopped by police or arrested if suspected of being under the influence. There are many examples of deaf individuals being arrested and taken to jail without being able to explain the situation to the police or being informed of the charges against them (American Civil Liberties Union, National Prison Project, 2012; National Association of the Deaf, 2000). When interpreters or other communication access is not provided, miscommunication can happen, which may result in a host of consequences, including confusion, frustration, and the possibility of a wrongful conviction (Vernon, 2009, 2010; Vernon & Miller, 2005).

Deaf individuals may end up in jails and prisons where the lack of communication access makes their daily life very difficult and makes it challenging to get the support that is available to hearing individuals who are in prison. Although prisoners may be required to participate in a program as part of a sentence, deaf defendants are unable to access prison services such as religious services, educational classes, and AA meetings (Jeffers et al., 2016; Vernon, 2010). Without an interpreter or other support service, a deaf inmate cannot participate in these programs and may be released much later than they would have been if an interpreter or other assistance was provided. Deaf inmates should be provided with interpreters for all disciplinary hearings, medical and counseling appointments, job training, and rehabilitative and educational classes (National Association of the Deaf, 2000).

Robert described the mixed feelings he had about how he and the other deaf prisoners were being treated. Feeling disrespected, he also realized that he felt helpless to do anything about it because he was powerless. He continued feeling sorry for himself and also lying to himself that things would be much better for him when he was released. Even worse, he lied to his own family and said he was doing much better in prison. The truth was that he sat, watched TV, gazed into space, and slept a lot. For a long time, he pretended that he was ok, without addressing his addiction.

Making Changes in the Legal System

There are numerous examples of deaf individuals who have been incarcerated and denied communication access. The lack of effective communication in a prison system can result in other very serious outcomes. In *Corrections Today*, a publication of the American Corrections Association, Talila A. Lewis (2015) stated that there was "a marked increase in the number of lawsuits brought against law enforcement agencies, departments of correction, private prison companies and reentry service providers on behalf of deaf individuals" (p. 44). These lawsuits are signs of the ongoing violation of rights, which are unacceptable and also end up costing taxpayers a great deal of money.

In a noteworthy case, Joseph Heard, a man who was deaf and mentally ill, spent 22 months in a Washington, DC, jail after a judge dismissed the charges against him and ordered his immediate release. The jail failed to provide telecommunications access and interpreters for the duration of his unlawful 2-year confinement. Owing to his isolation, he was unable to communicate effectively to anyone that he was being illegally held. During this unlawful detention, the contracted medical health care provider performed medical testing on Heard and gave him potentially dangerous, antipsychotic medications without communicating with him or obtaining his informed consent. In 2005, Helping Educate to Advance the Rights of the Deaf (HEARD) won a $1.5 million settlement for these and other egregious rights violations (Lewis, 2015).

For over 10 years, Talila A. Lewis, a cofounder and volunteer director of HEARD, has been working with incarcerated and formerly incarcerated people who are deaf and wrongly imprisoned. HEARD initiated a deaf prisoner phone campaign to create awareness about the lack of videophones in many of the prisons. They pointed out that several prisoners who face abuse in prison have no means of contacting family members or friends, let alone sexual or physical abuse hotlines (HEARD, 2014). Talila Lewis submitted five comments to the Federal Communications Commission in 2013 that included letters from several inmates requesting access to videophones within the facilities that held them. One letter from a deaf inmate detailed a problem he faced with the TTY because the calls required longer durations than were permitted, while other inmates reported they could use the phone only at very limited times throughout the day or week. Another letter from an inmate representing a group of deaf inmates at a facility reported that the TTY did not work and that the inmates were unable to dial the rape hotline to report the abuse faced by deaf prisoners at that facility (HEARD, 2014).

ACCESS TO TREATMENT WHILE INCARCERATED

While incarcerated, few inmates receive evidence-based services, including access to pharmacological treatments, and well-trained staff are in limited supply. Of the 1.5 million prison and jail inmates who met clinical diagnostic criteria for a SUD in 2006, only 11.2% had received any type of professional treatment since admission. Only 16.6% of facilities offer treatment in specialized settings that can produce better outcomes for offenders as measured by drug use and arrests post release (National Center on Addiction and Substance Abuse at Columbia University, 2010). Simply offering treatment, even in specialized settings, does not mean that the treatment is available to all who need it or is of adequate quality.

After a number of years of being sober, **Robert** got involved with drugs and ended up back in prison serving a lengthy term. He was admitted into a faith-based dorm program in the prison, which involves taking classes that focus on developing moral principles to become a better citizen, as well as cognitive intervention classes that help inmates better understand the importance of making responsible choices. With over 100 participants, the program offers a variety of classes, has big brothers, includes many spiritual activities, and uses DVDs to help participants find more meaning in their lives and deepen their relationship with God. Most of the classes are taught by exemplary inmates who had graduated from the program. Three participants are deaf but no interpreters were provided.

Robert felt he learned a lot through this program, and he is motivated to enter a substance abuse treatment program but has been turned down multiple times. The judge has not been willing to permit him to leave the state for a treatment program, and none exist in his state.

Some correctional facilities house their deaf inmates together in the same area of the prison. Research has shown that a deaf individual can feel very isolated and that this can be a major cause of psychological breakdowns and psychosis for prisoners (Reutter, 2008, 2009; Weinstein, 2009). Another rationale for a separate unit for deaf inmates is that they are often denied programs in prison that hearing inmates have the ability to access.

The best example is the Unit for the Deaf in Huntsville, Texas, where there are around 100 inmates who are deaf (Miller, 2001). The inmates that most likely would want to be in that unit would be those who use ASL and are culturally Deaf. Because they are extremely vulnerable in the general population setting, a separate facility is important for these individuals (Vernon, 2009). In prison, deaf individuals are more at risk for encountering sexual assaults, physical violence, intimidation, and exploitation with other inmates. Some deaf inmates would like to participate in a substance abuse program while in prison. However, according to Miller (2001), even though such programs are often provided to hearing inmates, many deaf inmates are denied access to them (e.g., drug rehabilitation), owing to the cost of sign language interpreters. Often, there is a lack of interpreting services for medical attention or educational, addiction, and faith-based programs and services (Vernon, 2010). The inability to benefit from educational programs to improve their lives in and out of prison, such as joining an addiction class, is a violation of the ADA legislation. Those deaf individuals who are accepted into faith-based or other programs are expected to participate without having access to any sign language interpreters. Although failure to provide accommodations such as interpreters may be a violation of the ADA, the practice is common in prisons (Vernon, 2009). If deaf inmates are grouped together, one interpreter can provide a number of inmates with communication access at the same time, which is more cost-effective. For example, when a separate unit was established in Texas, one interpreter was able to serve numerous functions, unlike before, when many interpreters were required at a greater expense (Miller, 2001). Although cost-effective, the provision of an interpreter for this larger group of people may not be equitable because it may require the entire group to agree on the same activity. However, having a part-time or full-time interpreter on-site means that if an inmate needs to see a doctor or has other appointments, it is more likely that the resource will be available to them. Correctional facilities need to investigate the issue related to the lack of interpreting services and make them available to deaf prisoners.

Although there are approximately 60 deaf inmates in the same prison, they are not all in the same wing. Many of them were also students from the same school for the deaf that **Robert** attended. Knowing that it takes a lot of energy to fight for access and strive for improvement, he described feelings of helplessness and powerlessness. Still, he indicated that his dream was to have a blog that could help other deaf inmates who are also addicts. He hopes to write a book one day that will share his experiences about being a deaf addict in prison.

Providing Treatment Programs

For many individuals who need alcohol and drug treatment, contact with the criminal justice system is their first opportunity to get treatment and be diagnosed with a substance abuse problem. Providing effective treatment and aftercare to offenders with SUDs may help improve health and reduce crime and its costs to society. According to the Center for Substance Abuse Treatment Improvement Protocol (2005), there is evidence that substance abuse treatment reduces crime. Without treatment, the odds are that substance-involved offenders will end up back in prison. Providing treatment and training to inmates and using treatment-based alternatives to incarceration through drug courts or prosecutors both saves taxpayer dollars and reduces crime. With so few hearing inmates getting access to treatment while incarcerated, we can assume that it is very challenging for deaf individuals in prison to access treatment services. Criminal justice costs are extremely high, and in 2005, according to the CASA report (2010), federal, state, and local governments spent $74 billion on incarceration, court proceedings, probation, and parole for substance-involved adult and juvenile offenders and less than 1% of that amount—$632 million—on prevention and treatment. In addition, the report found that only 11% of all inmates with addiction received any treatment during their incarceration. Without treatment, the odds are that substance-involved offenders will end up back in prison. Providing treatment and training to inmates and using treatment-based alternatives to incarceration through drug courts or prosecutors both saves taxpayer dollars and reduces crime.

In 2013, the SATF in California, which is a state-run correctional center, was not providing interpreters even though a judge ordered them to provide qualified interpreters for any inmate who enrolled in an educational or vocational class and needed sign language (Michaels, 2018). However, it was then reported that when deaf inmates tried to enroll in programs, they would often not be accepted, and this was thought to be because of the need for additional support, that is, sign language interpreters. California faces unique challenges; because of its size and because the SATF is in a remote part of California, finding qualified interpreters presents additional challenges. The California Department of Corrections and Rehabilitation did hire additional full-time interpreters for the SATF after the 2013 order and is now using staff interpreters, contract interpreters, and video remote interpretation to provide inmates with reasonable access to programs. According to an article published in Mother Jones by Samantha Michaels, on June 7, 2018, the warden at SATF also directed his staff to draft a new policy memo for sign language interpreters and to implement training.

According to Michaels (2018), lawsuits have been filed by deaf individuals to improve access to prison programs. Michaels indicated that in 2016, a deaf man in Washington, DC, was awarded $70,000 after he was jailed for 2 months without an interpreter and that several states, including Maryland, Kentucky, and South Carolina, have also reached settlements to improve access to interpreter services in prisons.

Although deaf individuals may suffer a violation of their rights during incarceration, such situations also occur during court appearances or when a person is on probation or parole. For example, Jeremy, an 18-year-old deaf 12th-grade student at a residential school for deaf people, was arrested for a drug-related offense and taken to jail. The student had some limitations and would be considered a vulnerable individual. Several days after the incident, when staff assumed the family had picked up the student and taken him home, it was discovered that he was still being held in a jail facility that has a reputation of housing seriously violent offenders. It took significant effort, but the school staff was finally able to reach someone in authority at the prison. The school staff shared safety concerns for this individual and advocated for his rights to have access to communication. The prison authority understood the situation and put the deaf individual in a separate part of the prison that was known to be less violent. When it was time for the student to go to court, the trial had to be postponed because the court was unsuccessful in obtaining a certified sign language interpreter. The deaf student had to return to jail for another week to allow the court to schedule an interpreter. The fact that this individual had to stay in jail longer than he should have because the court had not been able to find a sign language interpreter was inexcusable.

When deaf individuals leave prison, many struggle to access interpreters for parole meetings and mandated services, especially if they live in rural areas. One deaf parolee in California allegedly did not have access to an interpreter for four out of five parole-mandated mental health appointments (Michaels, 2018). He was soon rearrested and, although there may have been many reasons for his reoffending, the lack of access to interpreter services is a likely contributor to his recidivism. With the wide use of video remote interpreting, services can be provided to most deaf people, including those who live in rural areas.

Prisons should use appropriately trained health care professionals to screen, assess, and treat substance-involved offenders using evidence-based approaches tailored to the needs of offenders. The National Institute on Drug Abuse (NIDA) published a research-based guide outlining 13 principles of drug abuse treatment for criminal justice populations (NIDA, 2014). The guide describes treatment principles and research findings of relevance to the criminal justice community and treatment providers working with drug-abusing offenders. In 2010, CASA published a report on substance abuse and the U.S. prison population that included similar findings. Some of the items included in the original NIDA report were as follows:

- treatment should target factors that are associated with criminal behavior;
- criminal justice supervision should incorporate treatment planning for drug-abusing offenders, and treatment providers should be aware of correctional supervision requirements;
- offenders with co-occurring drug abuse and mental health problems often require an integrated treatment approach;
- medications are an important part of treatment for many drug-abusing offenders; and
- treatment planning for drug-abusing offenders who are living in or reentering the community should include strategies to prevent and treat serious, chronic medical conditions, such as HIV/AIDS, hepatitis B and C, and tuberculosis.

According to the 2010 CASA report, offenders who receive evidence-based treatment and recovery services have the best outcomes, including reduced relapse and recidivism rates.

Providing addiction treatment to offenders benefits the correctional system as well (National Center on Addiction and Substance Abuse at Columbia University, 2010). In correctional facilities where substance abuse treatment occurs, staff reported a less stressful job environment, a higher level of job satisfaction, lower rates of staff sick leave, less inmate-on-inmate and inmate-on-staff assault, and less disruptive behavior among inmates. Violent behavior is more than twice as likely to occur among inmates in the general population compared with those in treatment programs. Drug abuse treatment can be incorporated into criminal justice settings in a variety of ways. These include having treatment as a condition of probation, drug courts that involve judicial monitoring and sanctions with treatment, treatment in prison followed by community-based treatment after release, and treatment under parole or probation supervision. Drug abuse treatment can benefit from the cross-agency coordination and collaboration of criminal justice professionals, substance abuse treatment providers, and other social service agencies.

Substance abuse treatment requires two-way communication of information, including treatment expectations, personal information, and emotional expression. In a criminal justice setting, the levels of distrust and possibilities for misunderstanding are magnified. Although all correctional staff members are seen, to some extent, as representatives of the dominant culture, the potential for misunderstanding can increase when inmates and staff providing treatment support are from different ethnic or cultural backgrounds. These misunderstandings can jeopardize the client's chances of success in treatment. The most common misunderstandings in counseling originate in culture, socioeconomic class, and language (Taxman et al., 2007).

Robert indicated that he had two great sponsors who knew ASL. Although he could communicate with those sponsors, things did not work out the way he had hoped. He had the wrong idea about how sponsors were supposed to work with him. For instance, he expected them to solve his substance abuse struggle instantly so he could move on and begin pursuing his goals. Now in recovery, Robert realizes what his responsibilities are and believes he owes those sponsors a huge apology.

It is important to note that currently there are no evidence-based programs specifically designed to serve deaf individuals, whether incarcerated or not. This means that if an evidence-based treatment program designed for hearing persons is to be provided in the prison system, there must be full access to communication. The prison system must also provide appropriate care for co-occurring physical and mental health problems as well as offer and encourage participation in literacy, education, job training, and parenting programs. The prison system also needs to improve its release planning for inmates with SUDs to ensure the transition to reentry services. There is a huge need for the expansion of the use of treatment-based alternatives to prison, including drug courts, diversion programs, and the possibility of postrelease supervision.

Deaf individuals are at a severe disadvantage in receiving and realizing long-term benefits from treatment for drug and/or alcohol issues because many programs are not culturally appropriate or fully accessible. Ideally, individuals who successfully complete an alcohol and/or drug treatment program should be able to return to the community that they lived in prior to entering the treatment program. However, that environment must include a sober living option, family/friend support, professionals trained to work with clients on aftercare issues, and accessible 12-step/AA meetings. This kind of support is unavailable for the majority of deaf individuals because currently only four residential treatment programs in the United States are fully accessible with staff who are fluent in ASL (Guthmann, 2011; Guthmann & Blozis, 2001; Guthmann & Koster, 2003; Titus & Guthmann, 2010).

There are AA meetings in the prison where **Robert** is incarcerated; however, they do not have ASL interpreters for these meetings. Instead, Robert takes classes through the faith-based program that helps him overcome life-controlling problems. Still, there are no interpreters available for these classes either. He relies on lipreading and writing back and forth for program access. He indicated that he works the program primarily through the readings.

He wants to participate in a treatment program, and he has been discussing with his attorney the possibility of asking the judge to resupervise his sentence. There is a nearby treatment program that has ASL interpreters for deaf inmates. He believes it is time for him to get proper help and proper services for his substance abuse issues.

Over the past few years, Robert has also applied for parole. Although it has not yet been granted, he recognizes that he will need support when he is released. He has already identified a halfway house with 12-step meetings that he learned about through the pastors involved with the deaf Bible study class.

DEAF INMATES WITH DISABILITIES

Hidden disabilities, such as mental illness, learning disabilities, and/or attention deficit disorder, impact a number of deaf individuals. The disabilities these and other individuals may experience have been linked to increased rates of substance abuse (Weiss, 2013). Because recent data suggest that as many as 40% of deaf children experience co-occurring diagnoses (Gallaudet Research Institute, 2013), it must be noted that the inmate population likely includes deaf individuals who have additional disabilities. Given the prevalence of disabilities in incarcerated populations, especially among offenders with SUDs, treatment providers should be able to screen for coexisting disabilities and make accommodations for offenders who have them. Information on treatment for clients with coexisting disabilities can be found in *TIP 29, Substance Use Disorder Treatment for People With Physical and Cognitive Disabilities* (Moore, 1998).

Co-Occurring Disorders

The number of people with mental health diagnoses or issues who encounter the criminal justice system is high. A U.S. Department of Justice study showed that approximately 45% of people in federal prison, 56% of people in state prison, and 64% of people in jail displayed symptoms or had a history of a mental health disorder; among female inmates in state prisons, the rate was nearly three out of four (James & Glaze, 2006). In comparison, according to the National Institute of Mental Health, approximately one of four adults in the general U.S. population is diagnosed with a mental health disorder in a given year (Skeem & Louden, 2006).

As with substance abuse, there is little data on a national basis regarding the rate of mental health issues within the incarcerated deaf population. However, based on older research done in Texas, we know that approximately 32.8% of their deaf violent offender population was diagnosed with a psychiatric condition and that over half of them reported symptoms of depression or a depression-related illness (Miller & Vernon, 2003). Self-reported substance abuse appeared to be somewhat lower in the deaf violent offender population than is estimated for the general inmate population in Texas. However, the incidence of diagnosed mental disorders among deaf violent offenders was double what was self-reported for inmate populations in other states (Vernon & Miller, 2001). A joint report completed in 2014 by the Treatment Advocacy Center and National Sheriff's Association disclosed that ten times more mentally ill people are in prisons than in state psychiatric hospitals. The report was based in part on a survey completed in 2012 that focused on the treatment of persons with mental illness in prisons and jails and indicated that approximately 356,268 inmates with severe mental illness were in prisons and jails, whereas about 35,000 severely ill patients were in state psychiatric hospitals (Treatment Advocacy Center, 2014). In 2005, more than half of all prison and jail inmates had a mental health problem, including 705,600 inmates in state prisons, 78,800 in federal prisons, and 479,900 in local jails. These estimates represented 56% of state prisoners, 45% of federal prisoners, and 64% of jail inmates (James & Glaze, 2006).

While **Alan** was in jail, he tried hanging himself by climbing up on a table and using a bedsheet. The guards caught him and he was moved to a cell where the guards could monitor him. The police caught him when he was trying to hang himself again with a bedsheet, and he was put into solitary. The jail supervisor knew Alan's family, and he asked Alan to please not try that again. Knowing that people cared what happened to him had a positive impact on Alan.

After being in jail for several months, Alan was evaluated for mental health issues and was sent to a state hospital for treatment. Unfortunately, he did not understand what the psychologist told the court and did not grasp that he would be staying at the hospital for a long time. The unit to which he was assigned was very strict, and there were no other deaf people there.

Alan was very angry while in the hospital, and he was confused about why he was there and how long he would have to stay. Most of the time, two skilled interpreters were provided. Alan learned that he was diagnosed as mentally ill and dangerous (MID). Through group sessions, he started to learn more about himself. Eventually, he was more honest about his recovery, and the staff explained more about his illness. He found out that he was schizophrenic. He had always seen things that weren't there, but he thought it would stop when he stopped using meth. The hallucinations continued, however, and he continued to see ghosts/spirits that he thought were watching him.

When Alan was young, school staff thought he had attention deficit hyperactivity disorder. Actually, his mental health issues began around the third grade and were full blown by the time he was 27 years old. Using meth made him feel more paranoid, and he didn't know if the ghosts/spirits were real or fake. He was in the state hospital for 4 years. During this time, his medication was changed several times. Alan was stable for the first time when he was taking medication. After 3 years in a secure unit, he was given more independence so the staff could observe his progress. During his last year there, he was transferred to a less secure part of the hospital and able to sign himself out for short periods of time and go to town.

When he was discharged, he moved into a group home to learn independent living skills such as preparing meals, doing laundry, and handling other responsibilities. He has had a variety of jobs over the years, but currently works part-time as a certified peer support provider (CPSP). In this role, he works with other deaf individuals who have mental health issues.

Conducting appropriate assessments and providing accurate diagnoses are important keys to understanding mental health issues among deaf individuals. Misdiagnosing nonfluent (but otherwise healthy) deaf individuals as psychotic is not a new phenomenon. But what may be equally common are deaf individuals who are psychotic but whose illness is overlooked by clinicians who attribute symptoms to poor interpretation, deafness, or minimal language skills (Pollard, 2005). The ability to determine specific kinds of mental illness can be compounded when a deaf individual has limited language ability and/or when they are under the influence of drugs and/or alcohol. Standards of care for mental health services provided to deaf persons have been established (Myers, 1995). However, there continue to be problems with misdiagnosis, denial of appropriate services, lack of resources, lack of appropriate medical care (assessment and treatment), and significant language and communication barriers (Titus et al., 2008).

In order to serve the multitude of offenders with mental health and SUDs, a number of diversionary and corrections-based programs have been developed for offenders with co-occurring disorders. These programs, generally referred to as mental health courts, currently exist in a handful of counties across the United States (Lattimore et al., 2003). As we have discussed, mental illness and co-occurring disorders of drug or alcohol abuse are directly linked to repeat criminal offenders. Being mentally ill in the criminal justice system can be associated with greater substance use, longer sentences, higher rates of physical violence, and increased homelessness.

A great deal of stigma is associated with mental disorders, even within the culture of prisons and jails. At the same time, in correctional institutions, substance abuse does not carry the same degree of stigma as it does in the outside community. In some prison settings, procedures such as public medication lines expose the inmate with a mental disorder to public ridicule, adding to the stigma and reinforcing the inmate's reluctance to admit to his or her disorder. Offenders may be willing and able to talk about their criminal activity or substance abuse but reluctant to discuss their mental disorder. Consequently, actual rates of mental disorders in this population are likely to be higher than self-reported rates (Thompson, 2004).

One of **Alan's** goals was to have the "D" removed from his MID diagnosis. This lengthy process included about a dozen expectations, such as following orders given to him after his provisional release from the state hospital, meeting with his psychologist, attending recovery meetings, taking his medication, and having no contact with some of his family. He participated in a psychological assessment—initially thought to take approximately an hour—that lasted 3 hours with one interpreter. This turned out to be a very open and honest meeting in which Alan was clearly able to state why it was appropriate to have the "D" removed and why he felt he was not a threat to society. He indicated that he was in a positive place in his life with a job and was sober and actively involved in a program of recovery. He had positive relationships with his girlfriend and young daughter, as well as other friends. Within a week of this assessment, Alan was notified that the "D" had been removed from his diagnosis.

In addition to diversion programs such as mental health courts, there has been an increase in corrections-based co-occurring programs during recent years. However, few state systems have procedures in place for identifying and tracking prison inmates with co-occurring disorders. Moreover, little research has yet been done on the effectiveness of these programs. Preliminary outcome data from one study comparing a modified therapeutic community (MTC) program for prison inmates with co-occurring disorders with treatment as usual with a mental health group showed the MTC group to have fewer new arrests, less use of illicit drugs, and better compliance with treatment regimens (Sacks et al., 2012).

Several features distinguish programs that treat inmates with co-occurring disorders from other criminal justice substance abuse treatment programs (Sunrise House, 2019). For example, an integrated treatment approach is used whenever possible. Mental health treatment staff, substance abuse treatment staff, and criminal justice staff often share in decision making. In some jurisdictions, both correctional officers and community supervision officers have been successfully involved in treatment team meetings, treatment groups, and other therapeutic activities. A wide range of treatment approaches is implemented, according to the client's stage of treatment. Both disorders are treated as "primary." Integrated treatment involves simultaneous consideration of both disorders and attention to the interactive nature of these disorders. Comprehensive treatment services are flexible and individualized. Treatment is provided in "phases" or "stages," using a highly structured psychoeducational treatment approach. Treatment should be adapted to address different levels of symptom severity, functioning, and commitment to treatment (Finkelstein et al., 2004).

The focus of treatment is long-term and emphasizes continuity of treatment in aftercare and postrelease settings. The offender needs to be monitored carefully during transition periods when stress levels are high and there is an increased risk for recurrence of mental health symptoms, substance abuse relapse, and recidivism. Staff should be trained and experienced in treating both mental disorders and substance abuse. A blend of staff experience is needed, including those trained in working with symptoms of mental health disorders and those who have worked in specialized substance abuse treatment settings.

Robert knows that he can't change his past, but he can work to make things right with himself and others. Anger issues led to losing his temper and control of himself, resulting in domestic violence episodes during which he physically abused his wife. Although he wanted to control his temper, he didn't know how to do it or where to get help. Angry at the world and addicted to crack, Robert relapsed after his son was born. He was arrested and sent to jail.

Now able to look at his behavior through a more honest lens, Robert realizes that deaf addicts need to get the right resources and have better services. These form the foundation for his goals when he is released from prison. Deaf addicts and inmates need a community support recovery. Twenty-four-hour hotlines that provide counseling and referrals as well as up-to-date listings of treatment programs are critical services. He hopes to write a book about his experiences to help other deaf inmates and addicts.

Cognitive Disabilities

Evidence suggests that people with cognitive disabilities are disproportionately involved in the criminal justice system (Cockram, 2005). Nearly one-third of inmates in state prisons and one-quarter of those in federal prisons report having a physical or cognitive disability. These data, derived from self-reports, may underrepresent some conditions, including learning disabilities, of which inmates themselves may not be aware. Ten percent of state and 5% of federal prison inmates report having a learning disability, and these inmates are less likely to have a hearing loss; however, this can be accounted for by the age and gender differences from the general population (Maruschak & Beck, 2001). People with cognitive disabilities are at a significant disadvantage in engaging with the criminal justice system. For example, offenders with these kinds of challenges are disproportionately more likely to be arrested and coerced into a confession for a crime they did not commit. They may not understand their Miranda rights and are eager to please, do not understand the value of remaining silent, could be susceptible to leading questions, do not understand nonverbal cues, and want to appear competent (Cockram, 2005). They are also easily led into criminal activity by others. In their desire to feel that they belong to a group, some individuals may even view arrest and incarceration as a positive achievement.

INTERACTIONS WITH LAW ENFORCEMENT PERSONNEL

Law enforcement officers are typically the first responders to incidents ranging from suicide attempts to complaints about people potentially endangering themselves. They also encounter individuals in mental health crisis while on patrol. Despite this kind of interaction between law enforcement and individuals experiencing mental health issues, in most states training requirements to address these situations are minimal. In one state, out of 664 hours of basic training, academy recruits are required to receive only 6 hours of instructional time, which covers mental health and all disabilities. Even after graduating from the academy, most officers are not required by law to receive much, if any, additional or refresher training in these areas.

In addition to a lack of training provided to first responders, insufficient training is provided to officers in communicating with deaf individuals if encountered while on duty. Training is needed for first responders, law enforcement officers, and prison staff so they are equipped with the knowledge, skills, and attitude to perform their duties with respect to everyone they encounter, including those who are deaf. The American Civil Liberties Union, Academy Award-winning actress Marlee Matlin, and HEARD collaborated to create a video in ASL to ensure deaf people know their rights when interacting with law enforcement. The video outlines some communication challenges that may arise as officers respond to calls for service involving deaf people and warns of possible communication obstacles as officers interact with deaf individuals who use ASL as their primary mode of communication. Advocacy training should be provided in school so children will grow into adults with a better understanding of the criminal justice system. The video is available at https://aclu.org/video/marlee-matlin-deaf-and-police-interaction (American Civil Liberties Union, n.d.).

POSTINCARCERATION PLANNING AND SERVICES

When inmates approach the end of their sentences or are eligible for parole, plans need to be made to support the transition back to the community. A variety of resources may be utilized, depending on the individual's plans. In addition, a parole package, including questions and supporting documentation, is presented to the parole board. Some of these questions may include:

- Does the parolee have a trade or skill to assist in getting employment?
- What classes and personal improvement activities has the parolee participated in while incarcerated?
- How will family members be participating or available to assist in the parolee's release plan?
- What other activities and organizations does the parolee plan on attending or participating in?
- What are the parolee's future goals?

To assist an individual who is incarcerated for drug and/or alcohol-related offenses, examples of what might be included in a parole package are available online at https://forum.jpay.com/forum/prison-resources/prison-legal-help/4343-the-components-of-my-parole-package and https://prisonchat.wordpress.com/tag/parole-package/.

Robert has access to a service called JPay (www.jpay.com) to communicate with others outside the prison. Friends or family members can type letters online and send them to the prison via JPay, and prison authorities print them for inmates to read. Any responses from the inmate are either handwritten or typed on a typewriter, if one is available.

As part of a treatment program and in anticipation of being released, deaf inmates may become familiar with other community resources that may be of help to them. For example, vocational rehabilitation is a federal-state program that helps people who have physical or mental health diagnoses get or keep a job. Although many state agencies resist specialized caseloads, a strong argument can be made for ensuring that communication access is a critical issue and services are enhanced when provided by counselors with an understanding of the unique employment needs of individuals who are deaf (Watson et al., 2008).

In a follow-up study of 100 clients who had completed a specialized inpatient treatment program for deaf individuals, one of the factors that contributed to their sobriety was being employed (Guthmann & Blozis, 2001). The inpatient treatment program had vocational rehabilitation counselors provide lectures and information to clients while in treatment and follow up with them on discharge. This same connection should be considered with individuals who are incarcerated. It is important to connect the deaf individual with vocational rehabilitation because finding employment may help the individual maintain recovery and reduce future criminal behavior. Chronic joblessness or underemployment limits the ability to give up the drug crime lifestyle, to support a family, and to successfully transition from the treatment program to the community.

As part of the preparation for employment, some deaf individuals may seek additional education or training. Those without high school diplomas may seek high school equivalency and/or adult basic education (ABE) programs. A high school equivalency program may assist the individual in preparing to take the General Educational Development (GED) test. ABE programs frequently address reading and math skills and English foundations. This coursework may support college and career readiness skills that lead to employment or the transition to postsecondary education. In addition, it may help parents to obtain the educational skills necessary to participate more fully in their children's education. Because there are very few ABE or GED programs nationwide that offer instruction in ASL, access services as described previously in this chapter should be part of the student's participation in these programs.

Once an individual has been released, the Centers for Independent Living (CILs) may provide services such as peer counseling, information and referral, and training in areas such as independent living skills, consumer education, and self-advocacy. For deaf individuals, having direct communication with CIL staff supports the peer-based approach that CILs use in assisting people in achieving their goals. In addition, specialized services may include interpreter referral, telephone access, resource sharing, and training on assistive technology.

RECOMMENDATIONS

Effective treatment and aftercare should be provided to deaf offenders with SUDs. The provision of these support services would not only help to improve the overall health of the offenders but may reduce crime and its costs to society. We recognize that it is not a simple process but that the criminal justice system can take the appropriate and necessary steps to build and implement programming that can be effective. The following recommendations can thus serve as a base from which to achieve better outcomes.

Qualified sign language interpreters should be provided for deaf individuals who are in substance use and/or mental health programs while incarcerated. Whenever possible, CDIs should be teamed with qualified ASL interpreters to ensure the communication needs of the deaf individual are met (see Chapter 7).

Prisons should use appropriately trained health care professionals to screen, assess, and treat substance-involved offenders using comprehensive, evidence-based approaches tailored to the needs of offenders.

Communication assessments should be developed and utilized for all inmates, ensuring that the assessment tools are periodically reevaluated so that accommodations or modifications create equal access for each individual (see Chapter 2).

Training should be provided for prison personnel to ensure that deaf individuals who are incarcerated have equal access to the programming and services that are available to the general inmate population. As an example, any recovery-related supports that are offered to hearing inmates should also be available to deaf individuals. Training that is provided should address the agency's legal obligations as well as cultural diversity and communication and language challenges that are faced by many deaf individuals.

Members of the Deaf community should be utilized when creating training for officers and administrators who work in prison settings.

When possible, deaf inmates should be housed together, taking care not to violate federal disability rights law requirements forbidding discrimination, segregation, or isolation (Vernon & Miller, 2005).

No-cost videophones should be installed, and requests for proposals for inmate calling services should include an updated section on deaf and disability access such that contractors' services always include products compatible with videophones, video remote interpreting, telephones with amplification capabilities, captioned telephones, and the like (see Chapter 9).

Sign language interpreters or other sources of appropriate access should be utilized for the provision of self-help groups such as 12-step meetings for deaf individuals.

Deaf individuals should have the opportunity to participate in accessible treatment options while incarcerated. Before release, deaf inmates should also be connected with local community agencies such as vocational rehabilitation and CILs because finding employment is crucial to maintaining recovery and reducing future criminal behavior (Guthmann & Blozis, 2001).

There is a need for additional accessible and culturally appropriate treatment programming to address substance use among deaf individuals prior to and following incarceration.

Certification needs to be developed for interpreters working in substance abuse and mental health settings, particularly because many deaf who are incarcerated also have a high prevalence of co-occurring disorders. Sign language interpreters or other sources of appropriate access should be utilized for the provision of self-help groups such as 12-step meetings for deaf individuals.

CONCLUSION

There is an enormous gap in state and federal prisons between available addiction treatment, inmate participation, and the need for such services. As discussed in this chapter, the lack of treatment options for hearing inmates is a huge concern and an even greater problem for the Deaf community. Without appropriate access and service provision, deaf individuals will continue to be incarcerated with ongoing recidivism and no opportunity to become contributing members of their community. There is a need to provide a continuum of services to deaf individuals, starting with prevention, assessment, treatment, and aftercare. Without accessible assessment and screening tools, we are unable to accurately identify deaf persons who may be at risk for behavioral disorders (Guthmann et al., 2012). It is also important to use appropriately trained professionals to assess and treat substance-involved offenders using evidence-based approaches tailored to the needs of the offenders. There is a need to address the lack of evidence-based programs for this population as well as shortages of accessible substance abuse and mental health programs nationally. Treatment support for deaf individuals in the prison system must include sign language interpreters and the use of videophones and cover the full continuum of care, including prevention, job skill development, life skills training, substance abuse, and mental health assessment and treatment.

REFERENCES

American Civil Liberties Union, Multimedia. (n.d.). *Marlee Matlin on police and deaf interaction* (video). https://aclu.org/video/marlee-matlin-deaf-and-police-interaction

American Civil Liberties Union, National Prison Project. (2012). *Know your rights: Legal rights of disabled prisoners.* https://www.aclu.org/files/assets/know_your_rights_—_disability_november_2012.pdf

Americans With Disabilities Act of 1990, Pub. L. No. 101–336, 104 Stat. 328 (1990).

Anderson, M. L., Chang, B. H., & Kini, N. (2018). Alcohol and drug use among deaf and hard-of-hearing individuals: A secondary analysis of NHANES 2013–2014. *Substance Abuse, 39*(3), 390–397. https://doi.org/10.1080/08897077.2018.1442383

Angelides, P., & Aravi, C. (2007). A comparative perspective on the experiences of deaf and hard of hearing individuals as students at mainstream and special schools. *American Annals of the Deaf, 151*(5), 476–487. https://doi.org/10.1353/aad.2007.0001

Bavelier, D., Newport, E. L., & Supalla, T. (2003, January 1). Children need natural languages, signed or spoken. *The Dana Foundation.* http://www.dana.org/Cerebrum/Default.aspx?id=39306

Berman, B., Streja, L., & Guthmann, D. (2010). Alcohol and other substance use among deaf and hard of hearing youth. *Journal of Drug Education, 40*(2), 99–124. https://doi.org/10.2190/DE.40.2.a

Boros, A. (1979). The role of action research in services for the deaf alcoholics. *Journal of Rehabilitation of the Deaf, 12*(4), 1–5.

Boros, A. (1980). Alcoholism intervention for the deaf. *Alcohol Health & Research World, 8*(2), 26–30.

Brackenbury, T., Ryan, T., & Messenheimer, T. (2006, January). Incidental word learning in a hearing child of deaf adults. *Journal of Deaf Studies and Deaf Education, 11*(1), 76–93. https://doi.org/10.1093/deafed/enj018

Bronson, J., & Carson, E. (2019, April). *Prisoners in 2017. Bureau of Justice Statistics: NCJ 252156*. U.S. Department of Justice. http://www.bjs.gov/content/pub/pdf/p17.pdf

Center for Substance Abuse Treatment. (2005). *Substance abuse treatment for adults in the criminal justice system* (Treatment Improvement Protocol [TIP] Series 44). U.S. Department of Health and Human Services, Center for Substance Abuse Treatment.

Cockram, J. (2005). People with an intellectual disability in the prisons. *Psychiatry Psychology and Law, 12*(1), 163–173. https://doi.org/10.1375/pplt.2005.12.1.163

De Houwer, A. (2009). *An introduction to bilingual development*. Multilingual Matters.

Dick, J. E. (1996). *Signing for a high: A study of drug and alcohol abuse by deaf and hard-of-hearing adolescents* [Doctoral dissertation, The State University of New Jersey, Brunswick]. ProQuest Dissertations and Theses Global.

Fazel, S., Bains, P., & Doll, H. (2006). Substance abuse and dependence in prisoners: A systematic review. *Addiction, 101*, 181–191. https://doi.org/10.1111/j.1360-0443.2006.01316.x

Finkelstein, N., Vandemark, N., Fallot, R., Brown, V., Cadiz, S., & Heckman, J. (2004). *Enhancing substance abuse recovery through integrated trauma treatment*. The National Trauma Center Consortium. https://www.samhsa.gov/sites/default/files/wcdvs-article.pdf

Gallaudet Research Institute. (2013). *Regional and national summary report of data from the 2011–12 Annual Survey of Deaf and Hard of Hearing Children and Youth*. https://www.gallaudet.edu/office-of-international-affairs/demographics/

Guthmann, D. (1999). Is there a substance abuse problem among deaf and hard of hearing individuals? In *Unrealized visions: What's next for the deaf and hard of hearing community?* (pp. 33–36). National Association of the Deaf.

Guthmann, D. (2007). Accessing alcohol and drug abuse service for people who are deaf or hard of hearing. *California Association of Addiction Recovery Resources: Disability Access Project, 3*(1), 1–7.

Guthmann, D. (2011). What to consider when deaf individuals have substance abuse issues. *Paradigm Magazine, 16*(1), 20–22.

Guthmann, D., & Blozis, S. A. (2001). Unique issues faced by deaf individuals entering substance abuse treatment and following discharge. *American Annals of the Deaf, 146*(3), 294–304. https://doi.org/10.1353/aad.2012.0085

Guthmann, D., & Graham, V. (2004). Substance abuse: A hidden problem within the D/deaf and hard of hearing communities. *Journal of Teaching in the Addictions, 3*(1), 49–64. https://doi.org/10.1300/J188v03n01_04

Guthmann, D., & Koster, T. (2003). Steps towards recovery: Substance abuse treatment for deaf and hard of hearing people. *NADmag, 2*(5), 28–29.

Guthmann, D., Lazowski, L. E., Moore, D., Heinemann, A. W., & Embree, J. (2012). Validation of the Substance Abuse Screener in American Sign Language (SAS-ASL). *Rehabilitation Psychology, 57*(2), 140–148. https://doi.org/10.1037/a0028605

Guthmann, D., & Moore, D. (2007). The Substance Abuse in Vocational Rehabilitation-Screener in American Sign Language (SAVR-S-ASL) for persons who are deaf. *JADARA, 41*(1), 8–16.

Guthmann, D., & Sandberg, K. (1998). Assessing substance abuse problems in deaf and hard-of-hearing individuals. *American Annals of the Deaf, 143*(1), 14–21. https://doi.org/10.1353/aad.2012.0080

Guthmann, D., & Sandberg, K. (2003). Culturally affirmative substance abuse treatment for deaf persons: Approaches, materials and administrative considerations. In N. Glickman & S. Gulati (Eds.), *Mental health care of deaf people: A culturally affirmative perspective*. Erlbaum.

Guthmann, D., & Sternfeld, C. (2013). Substance abuse treatment and recovery: Adaptations to best practices when working with culturally deaf persons. In N. Glickman (Ed.), *Deaf mental health care* (pp. 234–267). Taylor & Francis.

Helping Educate to Advance the Rights of the Deaf. (2014). *Deaf in prison fact sheet.* http://www.behearddc.org/images/pdf/deafinprison%20fact%20sheet%20.pdf

James, D. J., & Glaze, L. E. (2006). *Mental health problems of prison and jail inmates* (NCJ 213600). U.S. Department of Justice, Bureau of Justice Statistics. https://bjs.gov/content/pub/pdf/mhppji.pdf

Jeffers, J., Ellis, E., & Paul, P. (2016). *Disability and criminal justice reform: Keys to success.* RespectAbility. https://www.respectability.org/2016/06/disability-and-criminal-justice-reform-keys-to-success/

jpay Forum. (n.d.). *The components of my parole package*. https://forum.jpay.com/forum/prison-resources/prison-legal-help/4343-the-components-of-my-parole-package

Karberg, J. C., & James, D. J. (2005). *Substance dependence, abuse, and treatment of jail inmates, 2002*. Bureau of Justice Statistics, U.S. Dept. of Justice. http://www.bjs.gov/index.cfm?ty=pbdetail&iid=1128

Kim, K., Becker-Cohen, M., & Serakos, M. (2015, April 7). *The processing and treatment of mentally ill persons in the criminal justice system: A scan of practice and background analysis* (Urban Institute Research Report). https://www.urban.org/research/publication/processing-and-treatment-mentally-ill-persons-criminal-justice-system

Kushalnagar, P., Hoglind, T., Simons, A. N., & Guthmann, D. (2019). Prevalence of alcohol use: A national survey of deaf adults in the United States. *JADARA, 52*(2), 24–33.

Lattimore, P., Broner, N., Sherman, R., Shafer, M., & Frisman, L. (2003). A comparison of prebooking and postbooking diversion programs for mentally ill substance-using individuals with justice involvement. *Journal of Contemporary Criminal Justice, 19*(1), 30–64. https://doi.org/10.1177/1043986202239741

Leigh, I. W., & Pollard, R. Q. (2004). Mental health and deaf adults. In M. Marschark & P. Spencer (Eds.), *Oxford handbook of deaf studies, language, and education* (pp. 203–215). Oxford University Press.

Lewis, T. (2015). Deaf inmates: Communication strategies and legal considerations. *Corrections Today, 77*(3), 44–49.

Lewis, T. A. (2018, June 20). In Georgia, imprisoned deaf and disabled people don't stand a chance. *Speak Freely, a blog of American Civil Liberties Union*. https://www.aclu.org/blog/disability-rights/disability-rights-and-criminal-justice/georgia-imprisoned-deaf-and-disabled

Leyton, M., & Stewart, S. (Eds.). (2014). *Substance abuse in Canada: Childhood and adolescent pathways to substance use disorders.* Canadian Centre on Substance Abuse.

Lipton, D. S., & Goldstein, M. F. (1997). Measuring substance abuse among the deaf. *Journal of Drug Issues, 27*(4), 733–754. https://doi.org/10.1177/002204269702700404

Marsiglia, F. F., Becerra, D., & Booth, J. M. (2013). Alcohol and drug problems: Prevention. In C. Franklin (Ed.), *Encyclopedia of social work*. Oxford University Press. http://socialwork.oxfordre.com

Maruschak, L., & Beck, A. (2001). *Medical problems of inmates, 1997* (Bureau of Justice Statistics Special Report NJC 181644). U.S. Department of Justice.

Mason, T. C., & Schiller, J. (2006, January). *College drinking among deaf and hard of hearing students: Problems and prevention.* [Poster presentation]. Society for Social Work and Research meeting, San Antonio, Texas.

Mayberry, R. I. (2010). Early language acquisition and adult language ability: What sign language reveals about the critical period for language. In M. Marschark & P. E. Spencer (Eds.), *The Oxford handbook of deaf studies, language, and education* (Vol. 2, pp. 281–291). Oxford University Press.

McKee, M. M., Meade, M. A.., Zazove, P., Stewart, H. J., Jannausch, M. L., & Ilgen, M. A. (2018). The relationship between hearing loss and substance use disorders among adults in the U.S. *American Journal of Preventive Medicine, 56*(4), 586–590. https://doi.org/10.1016/j.amepre.2018.10.026

Merriam-Webster. (n.d.). Incidental. *Merriam-Webster Dictionary.* http://www.merriam-webster.com/dictionary/incidental

Michaels, S. (2018, June 7). Without interpreters, California's deaf prisoners are getting stuck behind bars. *Mother Jones.* https://www.motherjones.com/crime-justice/2018/06/without-interpreters-californias-deaf-prisoners-are-getting-stuck-behind-bars/

Miller, K. R. (2001). *Forensic issues of deaf offenders* [Unpublished doctoral dissertation]. Lamar University, Beaumont.

Miller, K., & Vernon, M. (2003). Deaf sex offenders in a prison population. *Journal of Deaf Studies and Deaf Education, 8*(3), 357–362. https://doi.org/10.1093/deafed/eng011

Mitchell, R. E. (2006). How many deaf people are there in the United States? Estimates from the Survey of Income and Program Participation. *Journal of Deaf Studies and Deaf Education, 11*, 112–119. https://doi.org/10.1093/deafed/enj004

Mitchell, R., & Karchmer, M. (2004). Chasing the mythical ten percent: Parental hearing status of deaf and hard of hearing students in the United States. *Sign Language Studies, 4*(2), 138–163. https://doi.org/10.1353/sls.2004.0005

Moore, D. (1998). *Substance use disorder treatment for people with physical and cognitive disabilities* (Treatment Improvement Protocol [TIP] Series 29). U.S. Department of Health and Human Services, Center for Substance Abuse Treatment.

Moore, D., & McAweeney, M. (2006). Demographic characteristics and rates of progress of deaf and hard of hearing persons receiving substance abuse treatment. *American Annals of the Deaf, 151*(5), 508–512. https://doi.org/10.1353/aad.2007.0005

Moores, D. F. (2001). *Educating the deaf: Psychology, principles, and practices.* Houghton Mifflin.

Myers, R. R. (Ed.). (1995). *Standards of care for the delivery of mental health services to hard of hearing people.* National Association of the Deaf.

National Association of the Deaf. (2000). *Rights of deaf and hard of hearing inmates.* https://www.nad.org/resources/justice/police-and-law-enforcement/

National Center on Addiction and Substance Abuse at Columbia University. (2010). *Substance use and America's prison population behind bars, a report by CASA Columbia.* https://thehill.com/sites/default/files/behind%20bars%20ii%20report%20final%202-24-10_0.pdf

National Institute on Drug Abuse. (2014, April 18). *Principles of drug abuse treatment for criminal justice populations: A research-based guide* (NIH Publication No. 11–5316). https://www.drugabuse.gov/publications/principles-drug-abuse-treatment-criminal-justice-populations/principles

Pollard, R. (2005). *Psychological testing studies: Psychosis symptom rating scale. Deaf Health Task Force.* University of Rochester School of Medicine.

Pollard, R., & Barnett, S. (2009). Health-related vocabulary knowledge among deaf adults. *Rehabilitation Psychology, 54*(2), 182–185. https://doi.org/10.1037/a0015771

Rehabilitation Act of 1973, Pub. L. No. 93–112, 87 Stat. 394 (1973).

Reutter, D. M. (2008, September 15). Massachusetts mental health treatment policies prove deadly for public, prisoners. *Prison Legal News.* https://www.prisonlegalnews.org/news/2008/sep/15/massachusetts-mental-health-treatment-policies-prove-deadly-for-public-prisoners/

Reutter, D. M. (2009, January 9). A prisoner's view: The mentally HI in prison. *Prison Legal News.* https://www.prisonlegalnews.org/news/publications/david-reutter-mental-health-article-2009/

Sacks, O. (1989). *Seeing voices: A journey into the world of the deaf.* University of California Press.

Sacks, S., Chaple, M., Sacks, J. Y., McKendrick, K., & Cleland, C. M. (2012). Randomized trial of a reentry modified therapeutic community for offenders with co-occurring disorders. Criminal outcomes. *Journal of Substance Abuse Treatment, 42,* 247–259. https://doi.org/10.1016/j.jsat.2011.07.011

Schein, J. (1974). *The deaf population of the United States.* National Association of the Deaf.

Section 504 of the Rehabilitation Act of 1973, Pub. L. No. 93–112, 87 Stat. 394 (Sept. 26, 1973), codified at 29 U.S.C. § 701.

Skeem, J. L., & Louden, J. E. (2006). Toward evidence-based practice for probationers and parolees mandated to mental health treatment. *Psychiatric Services, 57*(3), 333–342. https://doi.org/10.1176/appi.ps.57.3.333

Substance Abuse and Mental Health Services Administration. (2015). *Risk and protective factors and initiation of substance use: Results from the 2014 National Survey on Drug Use and Health* (NSDUH Data Review).

Sunrise House. (2019, November 4). *How to treat addiction with co-occurring disorders.* https://sunrisehouse.com/treat-co-occurring-disorders/

Taxman, F., Young, D., Wiersema, B., Rhodes, A., & Mitchell, S. (2007). The National Criminal Justice Treatment Practices survey: Multilevel survey methods and procedures. *Journal of Substance Abuse Treatment, 32*(3), 225–238. https://doi.org/10.1016/j.jsat.2007.01.002

Thompson, A. C. (2004). *Navigating the hidden obstacles to ex-offender reentry,* 45 B.C.L. Rev. 255. http://lawdigitalcommons.bc.edu/bclr/vo145/iss2/1

Titus, J. C., & Guthmann, D. (2010). Addressing the black hole in substance abuse treatment for deaf and hard of hearing individuals: Technology to the rescue. *Journal of the American Deafness and Rehabilitation Association, 43*(2), 92–100.

Titus, J. C., Schiller, J. A., & Guthmann, D. (2008). Characteristics of youths with hearing loss admitted to substance abuse treatment. *Journal of Deaf Studies and Deaf Education, 13*(3), 336–350. https://doi.org/10.1093/deafed/enm068

Treatment Advocacy Center. (2014, April 8). *The treatment of persons with mental illness in prisons and jails: A state survey.* Author. http://www.treatmentadvocacycenter.org/storage/documents/treatment-behind-bars/treatment-behind-bars.pdf

Twersky Glasner, A., & Miller, K. (2010). Communication isolation as reported by a group of deaf Texas inmates. *Western Criminology Review, 11*(2), 1–8. https://www.westerncriminology.org/documents/WCR/v11n2/TwerskyGlasner.pdf

Vernon, M. (2009). ADA routinely violated by prisons in the case of deaf prisoners. *Prison Legal News, 20*(7), 14–15.

Vernon, M. (2010). The horror of being deaf and in prison. *American Annals of the Deaf, 155*(3), 311–321. https://doi.org/10.1353/aad.2010.0018

Vernon, M., & Miller, K. R. (2001). Linguistic incompetence to stand trial: A unique condition in some deaf defendants. *Journal of Interpretation, Millennial Edition,* 99–120.

Vernon, M., & Miller, K. (2005). Obstacles faced by deaf people in the criminal justice system. *American Annals of the Deaf, 150*(3), 283–291. https://doi.org/10.1353/aad.2005.0036

Vernon, M., Steinberg, A. G., & Montoya, L. A. (1999). Deaf murderers: Clinical and forensic issues. *Behavioral Sciences and the Law, 17,* 495–516. https://doi.org/10.1002/(SICI)1099-0798(199910/12)17:4<495::AID-BSL361>3.0.CO;2-6

Watson, D., Jennings, T., Tomlinson, P., Boone, S., & Anderson, G. (2008). *Model state plan for rehabilitation of persons who are deaf, deaf-blind, hard of hearing, or late deafened.* University of Arkansas Rehabilitation Research & Training Center for Persons Who Are Deaf or Hard of Hearing. http://www.rehabnetwork.org/wp-content/uploads/2008-Model-State-Plan-for-Deaf-DB-HoH-or-Late-Deafened.pdf

Weinstein, C. (2009, October 15). Perpetrators and enablers of torture in the U.S. *Prison Legal News,* p. 10. https://www.prisonlegalnews.org/news/2009/oct/15/perpetrators-and-enablers-of-torture-in-the-us/

Weiss, T. (2013). *Addiction and substance abuse among persons with disabilities.* Disabled World.com (Revised/Updated 2017–11–24). https://www.disabled-world.com/medical/pharmaceutical/addiction/serious.php

Wilson, J., Guthmann, D., Embree, J., & Fraker, S. (2015). Comparing outcomes from an online substance abuse treatment program and residential treatment programs for consumers who are deaf: A pilot study. *JADARA, 49*(3), 172–184. http://repository.wcsu.edu/jadara/vo149/iss3/3

6

Deaf People Within the Justice System: Insights From the United Kingdom

Susan O'Rourke, Sally Austen, and Elizabeth Wakeland

In this chapter, we consider the research carried out concerning offending by deaf people in the United Kingdom—whether there are certain patterns of offending that are more likely within the Deaf community or indeed less likely. Research on pathways to offending within this population is lacking, but drawing on what we know from other areas and considering this in the context of the developmental experiences of deaf people may shed some light on how and why a deaf person may choose to commit a crime. Similarly, the research on desistance does not address deaf people; we will consider the available related research on how deaf people who have offended may subsequently choose not to offend.

The criminal justice system faces particular challenges when dealing with deaf offenders, from arrest through the court process to providing fair and equal treatment in the prison system. We will explore some of these experiences, documenting how the system appears to oscillate from making no allowances for the deaf person and not accommodating their needs at all to being overly lenient and colluding with the view that they are deaf and therefore "cannot help it."

PREVALENCE OF OFFENDING IN DEAF COMMUNITIES

There are no agreed-upon figures of the incidence of offending among people who are deaf. One difficulty of gathering such information is that there are no formal monitoring practices of individuals who come into contact with the criminal justice system concerning their hearing status. An attempt at gathering such information was undertaken by Gahir and colleagues (2011) in a survey sent to all 139 prisons and young offender institutions in England and

Wales. They found an overrepresentation of deaf people in the prison system, in the ratio of 1 deaf prisoner to every 566 hearing prisoners, compared with one deaf person to every 1,500 hearing people in the general population. An overrepresentation was also found within mental health hospitals, where the prevalence was 12 times higher than the expected figure, given the size of the deaf population (Mitchell & Braham, 2011). This overrepresentation may be attributable to deaf prisoners having less access to the means to exit prison, for example, difficulties accessing education, work, and offending behavior courses (McCulloch, 2012). This lack of opportunity could have a profound impact on their ability to demonstrate change while in prison. It may even prevent release in some cases (e.g., those with a tariff or indeterminate sentence). Similar findings were reported by Haualand (2015) in a Norwegian sample of deaf prisoners.

RISK FACTORS AND PROTECTIVE FACTORS

Emerson (1995) defined challenging behavior as "culturally abnormal behavior(s) of such an intensity, frequency or duration that the physical safety of the person or others is likely to be placed in serious jeopardy, or behavior which is likely to seriously limit use of, or result in the person being denied access to ordinary community facilities" (p. 44).

Not dissimilarly, the definition of "offend" is to violate a rule or law. When discussed in terms of "challenging behavior," it is generally agreed that there is a higher prevalence within the deaf population (Austen & Jeffery, 2007) and that this may be reflected in the overrepresentation of deaf people in the prison population and within secure mental health services.

In the context of offending, risk factors are those conditions or variables associated with a higher likelihood of delinquency and/or justice system contact; protective factors are those conditions that lessen this likelihood. The question pertinent to this chapter is whether deaf and hearing people are likely to similarly experience risk factors and protective factors and whether there are additional risks of offending in the developmental pathway of deaf people.

The impact of culture on the prevalence of offending is potentially twofold. First, a minority culture could regard certain behaviors as acceptable and therefore flout the national laws. For example, within some cultures resolving disagreement through violence is considered preferable to involving the police. Second, people within certain minority cultures may share common demographic or developmental factors that influence their risk or protective factors.

Deaf culture does not appear to be connected in any way with beliefs that run counter to the national laws of their lands. However, demographic and developmental differences may have some effect on a deaf person's behavior and, therefore, their chances of offending (Figure 1).

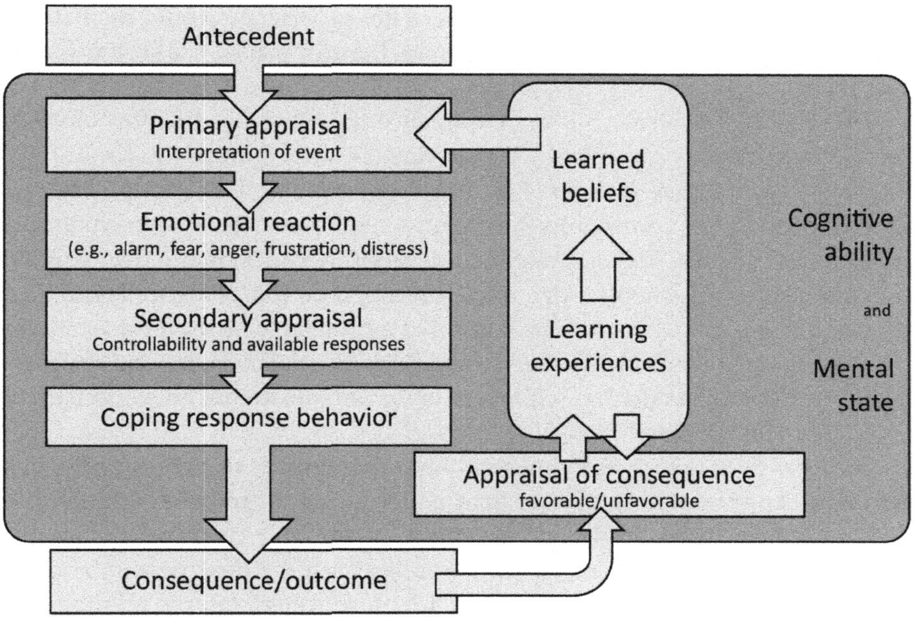

FIGURE 1. Appraisal Model of Behavior. Adapted from Lazarus and Folkman (1984) by Paijmans (2007).

The well-established psychological explanation of behavior by Lazarus and Folkman (1984) was expanded by Paijmans (2007) to include the variability of an individual's cognitive ability and mental state, and, as such, some of the commonly experienced facets of deafness could be represented.

The original model describes how a person's choice of behavior varies depending on their primary and secondary appraisal of a situation. The primary appraisal results in an emotional reaction, such as fear or anger; the secondary appraisal relies on cognitive controllability responses such as inhibition, empathy, self-talk, and reasoning. This process is identical for all people, whether deaf or hearing.

For example, if while I am chopping vegetables, a man jumps in through my window brandishing what appears to be a blood-soaked ax, my primary appraisal is to fear for my life and defend myself by stabbing him with my knife first. However, my secondary appraisal is that it is Halloween and that I have invited some very excitable friends to my house for a costume party, so this character is likely to be harmless. I need to inhibit my stabbing decision and manage my sky-high adrenaline in a more peaceful way.

Lazarus and Folkman (1984) described how our coping responses evolve from our previous experiences. The consequences of our previous coping strategies and how we appraise them create our learned experiences and learned beliefs that then affect the way we react to the next event. The consequences and learned experiences that fuel our behavior are the essences of our development. It is in considering this model that we can see that deaf and hearing people have different developmental experiences. These life experiences could increase the deaf person's risk of coming into contact with the criminal justice system (Miller et al., 2005).

The majority of deaf children experience significantly different developmental environments compared with hearing children (Hindley & Kroll, 1998). Some are very positive and serve as a protective factor. For example, being a member of the Deaf community has many developmental benefits, including language and identity development. Until recent decades, many deaf children attended residential schools, often for an extended period, compared with hearing peers. This experience may have acted as a protective factor for deaf adolescents, reducing the opportunities to engage in antisocial behavior and drug use. With a decrease in residential schools in favor of mainstream education, this is less likely to be the case.

For deaf people in a predominantly hearing world, social support is less prevalent. Approximately 96% of deaf children are born to hearing families (Mitchell & Karchmer, 2004), and most will be the only deaf family member. Many families do not share a fluent language with the deaf person, and this communication barrier may also lead to complicated family relationships (Humphries et al., 2019), attachment-related difficulties (Weisal & Kamara, 2005), and social isolation (Peterson, 2020). This lack of ability to communicate effectively has an impact on the parent's capacity to deliver sufficient and adequate boundaries and punishment (Knutson et al., 2004), as does a traumatic reaction of a hearing parent on the diagnosis of a deaf child (Kentish, 2007). This can have a substantial impact on that child's acquisition or understanding of appropriate or inappropriate behaviors and thus increase their vulnerability to abuse, victimization, and perpetration (Black & Glickman, 2006; Schenkel et al., 2014).

The Lazarus model shows the importance of consequences in shaping future behavior. Unfortunately, guidance and feedback from others can be significantly substandard for deaf people compared with hearing people. Appropriate use of behavioral reinforcement (reward and punishment) to shape behavior differs greatly depending on whether a child (or adult) is deaf or hearing (Kentish, 2007). For example, deaf people (whether a small child who has thrown sand at a peer or adults facing trial for a violent offense) may be less likely than hearing people to be given negative consequences for bad behavior (from hearing caregivers). This may be because the "bad behavior" is considered an inevitable feature of their deafness; because of misplaced sympathy for the "poor" deaf person; or because of fear, ignorance, and communication difficulties on the part of the hearing person/system who may have little experience of interacting with deaf people (Wakeland et al., 2019). It is unfortunate that a problem initially belonging to the hearing person has negative consequences for the deaf person. In terms of consequences and outcomes, the existence of good boundary settings is the difference between the protective and risk factors for all children. It is crucial to note that research shows that deaf children of deaf parents (where there is more likely to be a shared language and a less traumatic reaction to the diagnosis of deafness) are more likely to receive appropriate behavioral boundaries (Kentish, 2007). Deaf children born into deaf families are also less likely to experience difficulties associated with self-esteem, communication, and behavioral concerns (Crowe, 2005). This highlights how important it is that any study or intervention clearly needs to be on the psychosocial and linguistic experience of the person, rather than their audiological status.

A 27-year-old woman in forensic services (mental health services designed for individuals with a forensic history or severe challenging behavior) due to problematic behavior and self-harm reflects on her childhood:

> If I wanted something, I would get it because my family were frightened of what I would do if they said "no." On the rare occasion my mum did say "no," I would scream and bang my head until she changed her mind.

This behavioral response could also be present in a hearing child; however, in the absence of fluent communication in most hearing families with a deaf child, there is a greater risk of such responses, which begin as a result of frustration at being unable to communicate and are maintained by being positively reinforced.

An older deaf man described being let off numerous very significant offenses before going to prison and forensic services in conditions of high security:

> One time, coming out of a match with friends, we joined in a big fight, really kicking people hard and stamping on them. I really enjoyed that. The police came straight away. They wanted to arrest me, and since they had cameras, I was sure they had got me this time, but they only moved me on. Later that night me and some friends started a fight at a disco, pushing past the bouncer . . . started kicking everything in. The police said . . . "Oh, it's you again is it?" and sent me home. I didn't go home. I stayed in town and continued to drink.

Paijmans (2007) specified in his adaptation of the Lazarus and Folkman model that in order to consider the experience of any person (although in this instance he was referring to deaf clients), we must consider how potentially differing cognitive abilities and mental states may influence the entire process of appraisal and behaviors.

Cognitive ability is affected by static intelligence, educational experience, and life experience. For example, if I see a teacher trying to caress a primary school child, my appraisal of that situation will be affected by my intelligence (including whether I have a metaunderstanding of other people's interactions); my education (do I know that there are laws against an adult having sexual relations with a child); and my own experience (if, as a child, I was sexually abused by an adult I may see this as acceptable or inevitable).

Educational provision for deaf people is exceptionally variable. Many deaf people will struggle with a lack of access to appropriately resourced and supported education (Stinson & Antia, 1999), resulting in gaps in learning and literacy (Mayberry, 2002), which in turn has negative effects on work and finance. However, when it comes to risk and protective factors relating to offending, the authors of this chapter are more concerned about language fluency, which has significant effects on some of the more subtle and abstract aspects of cognitive functioning.

Unfortunately, preventable cognitive deficits are common in deaf people who experience language deprivation and language delays; these tend to be deaf children of hearing parents. Children who do not have a consistently stimulating and challenging language environment, with adults who can role model both sides of complex conversations (including such features as abstract thought, emotional awareness, and negotiation), are at risk of delayed or incomplete theory of mind (the ability to think that others think differently from us, have different information, and have an appropriate sympathetic response) and poor executive functioning (the ability to combine different skills such as working memory, inhibition, and attention to enable us to plan and regulate our behavior). These experiences may also impact the deaf person's moral reasoning and consequential thinking, putting them at risk of engaging in criminal behavior (Young et al., 2000).

In the general prison population, between 50% and 60% of prisoners have been found to have subtle or not so subtle cognitive deficits, and these are considered to contribute to difficulties in self-regulatory behavior (Farrer & Hedges, 2011; Shiroma et al., 2010). In hearing people, the cause of the cognitive deficit is often associated with acquired brain injury (Farrer & Hedges, 2011). While there is no research on the prevalence of acquired deficits in a deaf prison population, what is known is that some deaf people will have experienced neurological risks associated with their cause of deafness. Incidental brain damage may occur because of meningitis, premature birth, rubella, and cytomegalovirus (CMV). These neurological risk factors increase the prevalence of autistic spectrum disorder and attention deficit hyperactivity disorder as well as nonspecific difficulties with self-regulation. Both congenital damage to the brain and paucity of language development reduce the person's ability to use frontal lobe-generated "self-talk" as a regulatory strategy: a personal feedback system to observe, reflect, and guide oneself, and the initiation of a second appraisal to temper their first appraisal (Paijmans, 2007).

Mental state and mental health also affect how experiences will be appraised and future behaviors shaped. Although deafness is not directly connected with mental health issues, and the research can often be criticized on methodological grounds, it has been suggested that deaf people do have a higher rate of mental health conditions than hearing people (Department of Health, 2005; Fellinger et al., 2012). There is no definitive opinion as to whether mental health conditions increase the risk of offending. However, we know that the appraisal of experience is affected by mental state and mental health. For example, if I notice someone looking at me and laughing, I am more likely to assume this is a personal affront (and possibly react violently) if I am depressed, anxious, or experiencing persecutory delusions.

The Paijmans (2007) extension of the Lazarus–Folkman model is particularly welcome in the understanding of offending in different demographic and cultural groups because it has no room for prejudice or assumption. Each person's appraisal is unique to them, affected by their own unique experience of consequences and outcome, cognitive state, and mental state. Where experiences share similarities, we can hypothesize about similarities between groups.

SEXUAL OFFENDING

Our use of the Paijmans (2007) model to consider sexual offending specifically does not differ from consideration of other types of offense. However, the issue of sexual offending deserves additional analysis because it is reported that there is a greater proportion of sex offenders within the population of deaf offenders than within the population of hearing offenders (Miller & Vernon, 2003). It may be that deaf people are less likely to offend in other ways and that therefore the proportion of sexual offending is greater. It may also be that deaf people are less likely to be prosecuted for lesser crimes for a variety of reasons but would be prosecuted for offenses that are considered serious (such as sex offenses), thus representing a greater proportion of offenders in prison or in forensic mental health services, which is where most of the research is conducted in both the United Kingdom and the United States (Iqbal et al., 2004; Miller & Vernon, 2003).

Lack of knowledge about the law, age of consent, and nature of consent can play a part in some sexual offenses, whereas poor social and emotional understanding, lack of empathy, and delayed theory of mind, as described previously, may prevent inhibition of sexual or aggressive drives. The inability to negotiate relationships or communicate one's emotional and sexual needs or a lack of social skills may all contribute to some deaf people falling foul of the law in sexual matters. Although this applies equally to hearing people and certainly does not apply to most deaf people, we would argue that the experiences of some deaf people are relevant to the development of such behavior.

Deaf children present a particular case of vulnerability to being victims of sexual abuse (Mertens, 1996; Wakeland et al., 2018). Deaf children, often far away from their parents in a residential school where their communication needs may not well be met, certainly lacking sexual knowledge, make up a pool of potential victims. They are even less likely to disclose than their hearing peers because communication with parents and teachers is often problematic (Paul & Cawson, 2002). The incidence of offending against deaf children is not known. Still, a literature review identified deaf children as being at a higher risk for all types of abuse than their hearing peers (Wakeland et al., 2018), with an estimate of around 50% being reported by Sullivan et al. (1987) in a U.S. school-based deaf sample and 35% in the general Norwegian deaf population (Kvam, 2004).

This is compared with the hearing population, estimated in the United Kingdom by the Office for National Statistics (2020) at around 7.5% for 2019 and 5% by the National Society for the Prevention of Cruelty to Children (NSPCC, 2019) although some studies have suggested that it is considerably higher. Underreporting is likely to have affected the results in both hearing and deaf samples, and several high-profile abuse cases in deaf schools in the United Kingdom have since been reported.

Although we do not wish to suggest that those who have been abused as children will inevitably go on to become abusers themselves, the experience of sexual abuse constitutes a risk factor for developing distorted views of relationships and sex, which for some people can be a contributory factor.

A 30-year-old man reflects on his sexual offense that took place when he was 19:

> I have learnt a lot since then; at the time, I had no idea how to talk to girls, and I thought because the woman smiled at me, it meant she fancied me. When I grabbed her, I had no idea she would be frightened; when I look back, I can't believe I did that.

Overprotection, or protection of deaf people in a broader sense, is relevant to offending and has a positive and negative effect. Anecdotal evidence suggests that parents frequently shelter deaf children more than their hearing peers, and this can protect against the influences that can lead to crime. On the other hand, overprotection can lead to a naivete that makes the individual more vulnerable to such influences later in life.

Anecdotal evidence indicates that there appears to be a view, going hand in hand with overprotection, that deaf people cannot help themselves. This sympathy stance is behind a myriad of problems ranging from deaf children not being disciplined by parents to the courts being overly lenient on deaf offenders. Failing to learn the consequences of minor misdemeanors can be a powerful means of developing a sense of entitlement associated with the individual's deafness and leading to further more serious offenses. These factors can apply equally to sexually inappropriate behavior and sexual offending as to other types of offending.

PUNISHMENT OR REHABILITATION?

The discussion about prison being either for punishment or rehabilitation is somewhat ironic where deaf clients are concerned. Lack of accessibility for deaf people throughout their journey from arrest to court is a punishing experience, whether the client is innocent or guilty. And those who end up in prison or secure services are rarely offered services that could be considered rehabilitative. Their experience of isolation, lack of access to communication, and vulnerability may mirror their risk factors on the path to their offending.

The journey of a deaf person from arrest through the criminal justice system presents particular challenges at each stage, as illustrated by the experience of deaf people in the United Kingdom.

Arrest

Despite the requirements of legislation relating to equality and discrimination and police guidelines in the United Kingdom (Police and Criminal Evidence Act, 1984) and the United States (Americans With Disabilities Act, 1990) illustrating best practices when working with deaf people and those with disabilities, there is no absolute requirement for police officers to know anything at all about deaf people. Research in the United Kingdom indicates that the level of awareness among police officers is low, and when asked to consider this, the officers identify a need for training (Wakeland et al., 2019). At the point of arrest, communication is paramount. Yet the police officer may find themselves unable to communicate with the person they are arresting and, unless it is a planned arrest, unable to obtain the services of an interpreter (Wakeland et al., 2019). Relying on gesture, writing, lipreading, all of which are unreliable, and assuming there is some understanding based on context, they proceed as best they can. This situation is highlighted within the U.S. Department of Justice (2006a) guide for law enforcement officers on communicating with deaf people—it discusses methods such as lipreading, writing, and gesture as adequate ways of communicating with deaf people at the time of arrest or interview. Positively, it also includes a list of practical suggestions, such as minimizing background noise, not covering the mouth while talking, and the use of visual aids. If a deaf person nods, this is often deemed sufficient to indicate a level of understanding. Even if the deaf person understands the reason for arrest, the police caution in the United Kingdom or the Miranda warning in the United States presents particular problems, and without the benefit of a qualified sign language interpreter (SLI), it is unlikely to be understood.

Once at the police station, interviews should be conducted with an SLI and need to be video recorded to capture the original evidence. Audio recording only captures the voice of the interpreter and not the signs of the individual being interviewed. The consequence of this is that possible errors in interpretation are lost and cannot be challenged later in court. In the United Kingdom, this type of guidance and information can be found within the Police and Criminal Evidence Act guidelines (1984) but is not well known among all police officers. The U.S. Department of Justice (2006b) guide does not include video recording interviews.

Court

Despite clear equality acts and some developments in access to justice for deaf people in court, some cases go ahead without qualified SLIs, deaf interpreters/relays, or specialist deaf experts. Deaf experts could be deaf people such as intermediaries or include hearing or deaf experts in deafness, such as psychologists or psychiatrists. The language and concepts used in court are extremely sophisticated, and legal professionals who have never worked with deaf people need expert advice to understand the deaf people's disadvantaged position in this situation. In the United Kingdom, considerable work has been undertaken to protect vulnerable people in court, including the development of tool kits to give introductory information on a range of topics, such as questioning people with autism spectrum disorder or mental health conditions. There is also a tool kit on deafness (see www.theadvocatesgateway.org/toolkits). Although still rarely done, it is feasible to have all the court documents translated into British Sign Language (BSL) and recorded.

For the deaf person who has difficulties with abstract language or a poor fund of background information to draw upon, a significant proportion of the most common aspects of court functioning prove impossible to navigate. In the United Kingdom, the introduction of deaf intermediaries as part of the permissible special measures to protect vulnerable populations has helped dramatically, not only in improving access to proceedings but also in raising the court's awareness of the difficulties deaf people face in that environment. The intermediary can work with the deaf person from arrest through to court (although they are often not appointed until the defendant appears in court). The intermediaries identify difficulties in understanding resulting from lack of prior knowledge and explain legal matters to the person while educating the court about matters relating to deafness and communication. Where there is a question of a possible intellectual disability or mental health needs, the intermediary is often the person who alerts the court to this so that an expert psychological assessment can be carried out.

How the court deals with the evidence of deaf people adds another layer of vulnerability to the deaf person; in only audio recording the voice of the SLI, the original signed evidence is lost, and the interpretation cannot be effectively challenged. The reluctance of courts to video record evidence is often based on cost and practicality but also belies a misunderstanding of the difficulties of interpretation and the risks inherent in the process (O'Rourke & Wade, 2016). A landmark case in the United Kingdom, with both victims and defendants who were deaf, saw the evidence that video recording of all the participants allowed any disputes over meaning to be clarified and was hailed as a "big step forward" (Raynor, 2014, p. 1) for disability rights. Far from the anticipated lengthening of the trial, the number of disputes over interpreting appeared to be reduced because all parties worked together in the interests of clarity (Raynor, 2014). If deaf people are to have real access and equitable treatment in court proceedings, we would argue that evidence should be routinely video recorded so that interpretations can be challenged if necessary.

If the deaf defendant is convicted, disposal* within the criminal justice system or within mental health services provides limited options because few facilities can meet their needs. Arguably, a deaf person with a mental health condition is at an advantage, with at least some opportunities for accessible treatment within secure mental health facilities. By contrast, the prison service

* The term "disposal" is used within the U.K. court system to describe those actions after conviction.

does not have a strategic approach to dealing with deaf prisoners, who generally remain isolated from each other and within the prison environment.

Prison and Secure Hospital

The authors of this chapter provide expert witness reports in the United Kingdom to cases involving deaf defendants. They are regularly asked to comment on the plight of deaf prisoners, allowing the legal team to raise the issues of isolation and lack of access to prison rehabilitation as a reason for avoiding or reducing a custodial sentence. True parity (particularly for the victim) would be for prisons to provide accessible service and the judge to give the same sentence regardless of whether the complainant or the defendant is deaf or hearing.

A significant negative effect of deaf clients sometimes not being prosecuted for less serious crimes is a continuation of the lack of learning from mistakes, which prevents development and reflection on the consequences of one's actions. In addition to the fact that they do not then accumulate a formal criminal record, it may be that they are considered to have mental health issues. Although they may have concurrent mental health issues, equivalent hearing clients would more likely remain within the criminal justice system. By labeling the criminal behavior as a symptom of a mental health issue, this shifts the responsibility from the client to the mental health professional and perpetuates the belief that this behavior is out of the patient's control. Within clinical mental health services, individuals are commonly found to have a history of arson or severe violence and yet have never been charged with any offenses and do not have the expectation of any consequences for their continued violent behavior.

When deaf people are sentenced to prison or secure hospitals, these facilities often fail to provide any specialist support, resulting in their being socially isolated, vulnerable, and unable to make use of the rehabilitative aspects of the prison sentence (McCulloch, 2012). This results in many deaf prisoners experiencing the difficulties of imprisonment more severely than their hearing peers (Kelly, 2018). This inequitable service appears to be accepted as the norm. Simple interventions such as ensuring hearing aids have adequate batteries and maintenance can be blocked by health and safety concerns (as hearing aid batteries can be used in suicide attempts), by lack of resources, or by staff ignorance. Obvious inequities result from a lack of signing staff and peers, but lipreading is also restricted through environmental barriers such as small windows into cells and poor lighting. Deaf people report being kept separate from other deaf prisoners, presumably because officers are concerned about what may be signed to each other, being punished for "not listening" and thus missing information, and not being able to access basic services such as healthcare (O'Rourke & Reed, 2007).

> A deaf offender described how, after 20 years of no sign language in prison, he received visits from a deaf mental health worker. He said that his own sign language had been very limited, and he didn't even know the sign for sorry. Working with the deaf member of staff he described increasing

his vocabulary and with it his understanding. He said he began for the first time to understand how his victims might have felt (Austen & Jeffery, 2007, p. 8).

Within the United Kingdom, efforts have been made to improve the situation for deaf people in prison. Several specialist mental health teams or individual therapists have been contracted to work in prisons, not only offering individual interventions but also trying to support prison staff and providing ad hoc deaf awareness and consultancy. However, such developments have been initiated by enthusiastic individuals and do not reflect a much needed strategic approach, with the necessary investment.

DESISTANCE

Desistance, the process by which offenders make the change from criminal to law-abiding prosocial behavior, is complex and involves both subjective/agency factors and social/environmental factors, with the interaction between the two being poorly understood (LeBel et al., 2008). Many young offenders "grow out of" their offending behavior before too much damage is done. This implies a process of maturation, which may be more difficult for some deaf offenders given developmental experiences, lack of access to information, and lack of opportunities.

Once patterns of offending are established, professional services exist to try to manage risk and reduce recidivism. Although the efficacy of offender interventions is modest, in terms of internal change, it is of concern that deaf people in a prison setting have little or no access to therapeutic programs designed to reduce offending. Prison staff have few skills to engage and assist the development of prosocial attitudes in a deaf offender and, as a result, may rely solely on observation of "good behavior" rather than an assessment of attitudes toward offending.

In terms of environmental factors, these generally reflect the offender's engagement with society and investment in an alternative way of behaving. This might be attributable to relationships with partners, children, or employment. Arguably, deaf people start this process from a position of being doubly disenfranchised, that is, being both offenders and deaf. Anecdotal evidence suggests that for the deaf person, more generally, feeling isolated and "left out" of hearing culture is likely to be the norm, with very practical implications, such as even more difficulties in achieving and sustaining employment. Factors that encourage desistance need to address the place of deaf people in the broader society.

CONCLUSIONS

In any deaf research, the heterogeneity of the deaf population makes subcategorization crucial yet, for statistical reasons, extremely difficult. Multiple variables, some within the individual's control and some not, influence the biopsychosocial development of a person, such as having deaf or hearing parents, parental languages, one's language literacy level, educational opportunity, parents' previous experience of deafness, how the deaf baby's diagnosis was explained to the parents, and physical or sensory illness or disability.

Despite these variables, it would be fair to say that there are likely to be sufficient differences between the experiences of deaf offenders compared with hearing offenders, and we are prompted to revisit our understanding of risk factors and protective factors in deaf people.

Deaf culture does not advocate any behaviors that are outside of the law. A majority of deaf people are psychologically healthy and live satisfying and productive lives (Fellinger et al., 2012; Lane et al., 1996). The same range of crimes are committed by deaf people as by hearing people. Causes, however, may be rooted in different developmental experiences, particularly for the linguistically and culturally isolated deaf children of hearing parents, where there is an increased risk of language and educational delay. Unsurprisingly, preventative interventions at an individual and societal level, which address exclusion and deficits in language development and education, are likely to have a beneficial impact on the development of prosocial attitudes and affect the reduction of crimes committed by deaf people. Such interventions would include working with parents and schools to promote social understanding and an understanding of the law and a more general development of resilience and skills of self-management. Beginning this education early would create preventative strategies, rather than the current reactive model of working.

Once deaf people are in the criminal justice system, they appear to be at risk of staying there longer or leaving without having addressed their offending behavior. Strategic changes in how deaf people are treated in prisons, with the development of specialist deaf prison services akin to those in mental health, would address this and promote desistance in deaf offenders. This would also require staff training and education, which has repeatedly been identified in previous research (McCulloch, 2012; Wakeland et al., 2019). Further research would be supported if governments kept a record of defendants' and prisoners' hearing status and language skills alongside that of their age, gender, and criminal history. This knowledge would allow for a more detailed analysis of crimes committed by deaf people and the deaf person's experience within the criminal justice system.

REFERENCES

Americans With Disabilities Act. Pub. L. No. 101–336, 104 Stat. 328 (1990).

Austen, S., & Jeffery, D. (2007). *Deafness and challenging behavior.* Wiley.

Black, P. A., & Glickman, N. S. (2006). Demographics, psychiatric diagnoses, and other characteristics of North American Deaf and hard-of-hearing inpatients. *Journal of Deaf Studies and Deaf Education, 11,* 303–321. https://doi.org/10.1093/deafed/enj042

Crowe, T. (2005). Self-esteem scores among deaf college students: An examination of gender and parents hearing status and signing ability. *Journal of Deaf Studies and Deaf Education, 8*(2), 199–206. https://doi.org/10.1093/deafed/eng003

Department of Health. (2005). *Mental health and deafness: Towards equity and access*. HMSO.

Emerson, E. (1995). *Challenging behaviour: Analysis and intervention in people with severe intellectual disabilities*. Cambridge University Press.

Farrer, T. J., & Hedges, D. W. (2011). Prevalence of traumatic brain injury in incarcerated groups compared to the general population: A meta-analysis. *Progress in Neuro-Psychopharmacology & Biological Psychiatry, 35*, 390–394. https://doi.org/10.1016/j.pnpbp.2011.01.007

Fellinger, J., Holzinger, D., & Pollard, R. (2012). Mental health of deaf people. *The Lancet, 379*, 1037–1044. https://doi.org/10.1016/S0140-6736(11)61143-4

Gahir, M., O'Rourke, S., Monteiro, B., & Reed, R. (2011). The unmet needs of deaf prisoners: A survey of prisons in England and Wales. *International Journal on Mental Health and Deafness, 1*, 58–63.

Haualand, H. (2015). Punished and isolated: Disabled prisoners in Norway. *Scandinavian Journal of Disability Research, 17*, 74–87. https://doi.org/10.1080/15017419.2014.945956

Hindley, P., & Kroll, L. (1998). Theoretical and epidemiological aspects of attention deficit and overactivity in deaf children. *Journal of Deaf Studies and Deaf Education, 3*, 64–72. https://doi.org/10.1093/oxfordjournals.deafed.a014341

Humphries, T., Kushalnagar, P., Mathar, G., Napoli, D. J., Rathmann, C., & Smith, S. (2019). Support for parents of deaf children: Common questions and informed, evidence-based answers. *International Journal of Pediatric Otorhinolaryngology, 118*, 134–142. https://doi.org/10.1016/j.ijporl.2018.12.036

Iqbal, S., Dolan, M., & Monteiro, B. (2004). Characteristics of deaf sexual offenders referred to a specialist mental health unit in the UK. *Journal of Forensic Psychiatry and Psychology, 15*(3), 494–510. https://doi.org/10.1080/14789940410001703291

Kelly, L. (2018). Sounding out d/Deafness: The experiences of d/Deaf prisoners. *Journal of Criminal Psychology, 8*(1), 20–32. https://doi.org/10.1108/JCP-03-2017-0015

Kentish, R. (2007). Challenging behaviour in the young deaf child. In S. Austen & D. Jeffery (Eds.), *Deafness and challenging behavior* (pp. 75–88). Wiley.

Knutson, J., Johnson, C., & Sullivan, P. (2004). Disciplinary choices of mothers of deaf children and mothers of normally hearing children. *Child Abuse & Neglect, 28*, 925–937. https://doi.org/10.1016/j.chiabu.2004.04.005

Kvam, M. (2004). Sexual abuse of deaf children. A retrospective analysis of the prevalence and characteristics of childhood sexual abuse among deaf adults in Norway. *Child Abuse and Neglect, 28*, 241–251. https://doi.org/10.1016/j.chiabu.2003.09.017

Lane, H., Hoffmeister, R., & Bahan, B. (1996). *A journey into the Deaf world*. DawnSignPress.

Lazarus, R., & Folkman, S. (1984). *Stress, appraisal and coping*. Springer.

LeBel, T., Burnett, R., Maruna, S., & Bushway, S. D. (2008). The chicken and egg of subjective and social factors in desistance from crime. *European Journal of Criminology, 5*(2), 131–159. https://doi.org/10.1177/1477370807087640

Mayberry, R. (2002). Cognitive development in deaf children: The interface of language and perception in neuropsychology. In S. J. Segalowitz & I. Rapin (Eds.), *Handbook of neuropsychology* (2nd ed., Vol. 8, Part 2, pp. 71–107). Elsevier.

McCulloch, D. (2012). Not hearing us: An exploration of the experience of deaf prisoners in English and Welsh prisons. *The Howard League of Penal Reform*. https://howardleague.org/wp-content/uploads/2016/03/Not_hearing_us.pdf

Mertens, D. (1996). Breaking the silence about sexual abuse of deaf youth. *American Annals of the Deaf, 141*, 352–358. https://doi.org/10.1353/aad.2012.0257

Miller, K., & Vernon, M. (2003). Deaf sex offenders in a prison population. *Journal of Deaf Studies and Deaf Education, 8*(3), 357–362. https://doi.org/10.1093/deafed/eng011

Miller, K., Vernon, M., & Capella, M. (2005). Violent offenders in a deaf prison population. *Journal of Deaf Studies and Deaf Education, 10*, 417–425. https://doi.org/10.1093/deafed/eni039

Mitchell, R., & Karchmer, M. (2004). Chasing the mythical ten percent: Parental hearing status of deaf and hard of hearing students in the United States. *Sign Language Studies, 4*, 138–163. https://doi.org/10.1353/sls.2004.0005

Mitchell, T., & Braham, L. (2011). The psychological treatment needs of deaf mental health patients in high-secure settings: A review of the literature. *International Journal of Forensic Mental Health, 10*, 92–106. https://doi.org/10.1080/14999013.2011.577135

National Society for the Prevention of Cruelty to Children. (2019). *Statistics briefing: Child sexual abuse*. https://learning.nspcc.org.uk/media/1710/statistics-briefing-child-sexual-abuse.pdf

Office for National Statistics. (2020). *Child sexual abuse in England and Wales: Year ending March 2019*. https://www.ons.gov.uk/peoplepopulationandcommunity/crimeandjustice/articles/childsexualabuseinenglandandwales/yearendingmarch2019

O'Rourke, S., & Reed, R. (2007). Deaf people and the criminal justice system. In S. Austen & D. Jeffery (Eds.), *Deafness and challenging behaviour* (pp. 257–274). Wiley.

O'Rourke, S., & Wade, C. (2016). Making special measures special. Reasonable adjustments for deaf witnesses and defendants. In P. Cooper & L. Hunting (Eds.), *Addressing vulnerability in justice systems*. Wiley, Simmonds, & Hill.

Paijmans, R. (2007). Neuropsychological, behaviour and linguistic factors in challenging behaviour in deaf people. In S. Austen & D. Jeffery (Eds.), *Deafness and challenging behaviour* (pp. 89–100). Wiley.

Paul, A., & Cawson, P. (2002). Safeguarding disabled children in residential settings: What we know and what we don't know. *Child Abuse Review, 11*, 262–281. https://doi.org/10.1002/car.755

Peterson, C. (2020). Theory of mind and conversation in deaf and hearing children. In M. Marschark & H. Knoors (Eds.), *The Oxford handbook of deaf studies in learning and cognition* (pp. 213–231). Oxford University Press.

Police and Criminal Evidence Act. (1984). https://www.gov.uk/guidance/police-and-criminal-evidence-act-1984-pace-codes-of-practice

Raynor, J. (2014). Sign language trial "big step forward." *Law Society Gazette*. https://www.lawgazette.co.uk/practice/sign-language-trial-big-step-forward/5041926.article

Schenkel, L. S., Rothman-Marshall, G., Schlehofer, D. A., Towne, T. L., Burnash, D. L., & Priddy, B. M. (2014). Child maltreatment and trauma exposure among deaf and hard of hearing young adults. *Child Abuse & Neglect, 38*, 1581–1589. https://doi.org/10.1016/j.chiabu.2014.04.010

Shiroma, E. J., Ferguson, P. L., & Pickelsimeree, E. E. (2010). Prevalence of traumatic brain injury in an offender population: a meta-analysis. *Journal of Correctional Healthcare, 16*, 147–159. https://doi.org/10.1177/1078345809356538

Stinson, M., & Antia, S. (1999). Considerations in educating deaf and hard of hearing students in inclusive settings. *Journal of Deaf Studies and Deaf Education, 4*, 163–175. https://doi.org/10.1093/deafed/4.3.163

Sullivan, P., Vernon, M., & Scanlan, J. (1987). Sexual abuse of deaf youth. *American Annals of the Deaf*, 256–262. https://doi.org/10.1353/aad.2012.0614

U.S. Department of Justice. (2006a). *Americans With Disabilities Act information for law enforcement*. https://www.ada.gov/policeinfo.htm

U.S. Department of Justice. (2006b). *Communicating with people who are deaf or hard of hearing: ADA guide for law enforcement officers*. U.S. Department of Justice, Disability Rights Section.

Wakeland, E., Austen, S., & Rose, J. (2018). What is the prevalence of abuse in the deaf/hard of hearing population? *Journal of Forensic Psychiatry & Psychology, 29*(3), 434–454. https://doi.org/10.1080/14789949.2017.1416659

Wakeland, E., Rose, J., & Austen, S. (2019). Professionals' experiences of deaf offenders with mental health difficulties. *American Annals of the Deaf, 164*(1), 137–157. https://doi.org/10.1353/aad.2019.0012

Weisal, A., & Kamara, A. (2005). Attachment and individuation of deaf/hard-of-hearing and hearing young adults. *Journal of Deaf Studies and Deaf Education, 10*(1), 51–62. https://doi.org/10.1093/deafed/eni003

Young, A., Monteiro, B., & Ridgeway, S. (2000). Deaf people with mental health needs in the criminal justice system: A review of the UK literature. *Journal of Forensic Psychiatry, 11*, 556–570. https://doi.org/10.1080/09585180010004810

7

Discourse, Sign Language Interpreters, and the Criminal Justice System: Implications for Communicating With Deaf People

Theresa B. Smith

Someone once asked me what the difference is between being bilingual and being an interpreter. After some thought, my answer was that being bilingual is equivalent to managing one's personal finances, while being an interpreter is equivalent to being an accountant. Bilinguals are assumed to be able to communicate effectively in either of two languages about their own thoughts, and on topics and in situations with which they themselves are familiar. Although this is broadly true, in practice, it is more complicated. Some concepts are much easier to express in one of the languages than in the other. Something may be funny in one language but not in the other, and some things may be assumed by speakers of one language but not by speakers of the other. For example, a linguist once asked a Navajo how to translate the phrase "The horse kicked the man" into Navajo. The man obligingly did so but added that a Navajo would never say such a thing because a man "must allow the horse to kick him" (Gary Witherspoon, personal communication). Thus, language is more than vocabulary and grammar. Each language is a unique system employing a set of social rules, historical references, shared values, and "received wisdom" expressed through a unique discourse to "make sense." (See Condon & Yousef, 1975.)

It is easy, therefore, to overlook the complexity of what it means to interpret. Indeed, it has taken many decades, even centuries, for philosophers and researchers to come to our current understanding of what constitutes a language.[1] As already noted, meaning is not in the words, grammar, or even the language alone. To reach a common understanding, speakers must share a minimum of common history, cultural knowledge, values, and practices, as described, for example, by Condon and Yousef (1975), Clyne (1994), and Ortner (2006).[2]

American Sign Language (ASL) interpreters themselves recognize some of the challenges of interpreting, especially in more formal settings where the register[3] or style itself carries one part of the meaning (Joos, 1967; Tannen, 1989). One hears among interpreters that they are not comfortable interpreting in legal situations; they mention as reasons the linguistic challenge, specifically all the terminology or legal terms of art[4] and the great responsibility of the task given potentially serious outcomes. In addition, legal discourse[5] and differences in background between the parties (in this case, users of ASL and those of English) make a mutual interpretation of the interaction challenging.

Perhaps the most important factor that makes effective communication difficult is the *adversarial* nature of most encounters between deaf people as citizens and members of the criminal justice system.[6] Although other professional situations may also include the use of specialized terminology and also carry great responsibility (e.g., serious medical situations), these situations are *cooperative* in nature. In cooperative interactions, both parties have the same goal in mind (e.g., a patient's health); there is therefore an underlying trust between all parties (e.g., between patient, nurse, and physician) who work cooperatively to achieve both mutual understanding and their mutual goal (the health of the patient). In adversarial interactions, however, the goal is not shared. There is tension rather than trust; indeed, there is often an underlying suspicion between the parties (e.g., a police officer and suspect, prosecutor and defendant), and meaning may be contested. (See, for example, Hoopes, 2003 and Shuy, 2003.)

Indeed, where one is "coming from" in terms of personal background, imagined identity, internalized beliefs, values, and ideas about other people, as well as education and professional position, all influence how we metaphorically see or frame a situation before any verbal exchange takes place. This framing of one another and of the interaction is critical to how each participant *interprets* what is done and said and what is meant (Tannen, 1993).

Finally, providing effective communication in the criminal justice system is made more complex by the sociopolitical position of deaf people and the various languages, language varieties,[7] and codes they use,[8] compounded by the small numbers of qualified interpreters.[9]

Case Analyses

I now turn to the case of Frank[10] to point out some of the issues that together cause miscommunication and their implications.

Frank's Story

Frank's teenage stepson was pulled over for speeding one dark summer evening on a country road. The boy could not find the car's registration papers asked for by the officer and was understandably nervous. In the presence of the officer, he telephoned his mother for help, who in turn asked the deaf[10] *stepfather, Frank,*

> *to go take care of it. Frank got into his pickup truck (this was a semirural area) and drove to the spot the boy had described. Frank, who is Caucasian, was in his 40s, had shoulder-length bushy hair and a beard. He pulled up at the scene, parked just ahead of the other cars, got out of his pickup truck, and began walking back toward his stepson and the officer to help. The officer, however, walked toward Frank, pointing back toward the truck, and ordered him to get back in his truck. Despite the dark, and headlights in his eyes, and the fact that he could neither hear nor lipread the instructions of the officer, Frank correctly interpreted the officer's approach and gestures to mean he should return to his truck, which he did, climbing back into the driver's seat, and reattached his seat belt to wait.*
>
> *The officer followed him and, with the truck window rolled down, began questioning him. Both the officer and Frank were irritated, the officer at having this unexpected intrusion and Frank at having to leave home, where he was relaxing.*
>
> *When the officer came to the driver's window and began talking, Frank reached up quickly to pull back his hair to show his hearing aid (indicating he could not hear or understand the officer); the officer interpreted this move as aggressive. He punched Frank, then grabbed him by his jacket and attempted to pull him out of the truck. Once free of the seat belt, Frank was dragged from the truck and arrested.*

The officer was not expecting gestures as communication and perceived Frank's raising of his hand (even though it was directed at himself) as a threat, to which the officer responded physically.

In the subsequent trial, the scene and interactions were described, first by the officer, and then by Frank. The concluding question the defense attorney had of Frank was whether he had indeed "resisted arrest." Herein lies the linguistic problem. There is a gloss for *resist* in ASL; it does not, however, have the legal denotation of fleeing, hiding from, or threatening an officer. A gloss in this sense is a superficial/approximate rendition of a word or phrase in another language.[11] Indeed, the ASL sign RESIST has a more mental or attitudinal meaning of "resisting an idea" and is semantically related to the sign for *protect* or *defend*. There is no exact equivalent of the legal phrase "resisted arrest" in ASL.[12]

The court interpreter, however, given the pressure of simultaneous interpreting[13] and the existence of the gloss "resist," used this ASL sign while interpreting the question "did you resist arrest?" The defendant, Frank, having previously denied any aggression, or uncooperativeness, nevertheless replied yes (i.e., he resisted the idea that he would be arrested), adding that the officer had no reason (to arrest him).

Frank was convicted. In a posttrial interview, the defense attorney asked one of the jurors why she thought he was guilty, and she replied, somewhat defensively, "He admitted it. He said he resisted arrest."

I report Frank's case to make the following points:

- Expectations of each of the participants influence their interpretation of actions, specifically both Frank and the police officer.
- Simultaneous interpreting, although a common practice, adds pressure and increases errors (Russell, 2002).
- To properly defend a client, an attorney must understand potential issues of translation and have a strategy to accommodate them.

ASL and English are distinct languages in which there are rarely word-for-word equivalences.[14] In Frank's arrest, the issue was in framing (and associated expectations). In Frank's trial, the issue was semantic (i.e., the meaning of "resist").

The misunderstanding began when Frank first arrived on the scene. Frank framed his actions as "helping out," whereas the officer framed Frank's arrival as "interference." They each interpreted Frank's footing (role, status) differently as well. Frank saw himself as a stepfather coming to help, whereas the officer saw him as a possible intruder coming to disrupt.

DISCOURSE AND PRAGMATICS: FRAME, FOOTING, AND PERSPECTIVE

Most of us have a pretty clear idea about what is meant by the words "terminology," "vocabulary," and "grammar" but are less familiar with what is meant by "discourse," "pragmatics," or "semiotics." The simplest definition of "discourse" is language above the level of the sentence: a "chunk" of language: a conversation, a chapter, a sermon, etc. Discourse analysis includes its organization and style, possible bias, and so on; signs and symbols such as a truck, long hair, and a beard in this case constitute meaning the study of which is "semiotics." "Pragmatics" is defined as meaning within context, including presupposition[15] and implicature.

Together, semiotics, pragmatics, and discourse set the frame. The frame identifies the situation, tells us what we are doing here (e.g., investigation, interrogation, deposition). The frame includes the footing (i.e., identifies the role[s] and status of the participants within the frame). Together, frame and footing inform who may speak, to whom, when, on what topic, and so on. The frame of a trial is the same for all the participants, but the authority and footing varies. To participate effectively, each participant in the situation (including the interpreter) must share an understanding of both frame and footing.

Finally, each participant within a given frame will have a specific perspective informed by previous life experiences and routine strategies.[16] Charles, in the next case, misread both the *frame* and his *footing*.

Charles's Story

Charles was an African American deaf man of approximately 35 years of age. He had been raised in a poor family and been poorly educated.[17] *He was unemployed, living in shared housing with several others, all of whom, like Charles, were early school dropouts and deaf.*

One late night, Charles stumbled down the street on his way home after leaving a bar. As he walked through the neighborhood, he felt the urge and stopped to relieve himself in someone's yard. As he did so, he was mugged, and his wallet was stolen. He did not report the theft, but the police later found the wallet with Charles's ID in the belongings of the thief when they arrested him. Because of this, the police then contacted Charles and brought him down to the police station to interview as a victim-witness, a role unfamiliar to Charles.

An interpreter was called, and the police questioned him about what had happened. The interview was not successful. Charles was later called to testify in court, and a different interpreter was called, one with a specialist certificate to interpret for legal matters. As the prosecutor talked with Charles, the interpreter noticed how nervous and upset Charles seemed, inconsistent with his being asked to be a witness against his mugger. The interpreter asked Charles if he knew what he was doing there (the frame) and what the prosecutor wanted. He understood that the topic was "that night" but thought he had been interrogated by the police[18] *(rather than being interviewed) and was himself in trouble for trespassing, was possibly even going to jail for relieving himself in someone's yard; that is, he thought that he was there as a perpetrator, not as a victim. Because he misinterpreted his role, he also, therefore, misinterpreted the frame of the questioning and what it would be appropriate to say.*

Once the second interpreter was able to explain that he was there to help the police as a witness, he became much more relaxed and able to help. From this perspective, he felt more comfortable interacting and indeed even asking questions to better understand the process.

Charles's life experiences and therefore his mental maps were very different from those of the officers, the prosecutor (all White, male, educated professionals), and the first interpreter. In his experience, interactions with police officers were framed as trouble. He was unaccustomed to having people in authority benevolently ask his perceptions.

This case implicates the *role* of the interpreter. The first interpreter stayed at the level of transmitting what was said. This interpreter did not go beyond what was explicitly stated, and thus the confusion expressed by Charles and the prosecuting attorney was left unclarified. I will return to the role of an interpreter in a later section, but first, I turn to discourse style.

DISCOURSE: ORGANIZATION AND STYLE

Different languages organize chunks of language in different ways (Bennet, 1985; Christie et al., 1999; Condon & Yousef, 1975; Gumperz, 1982; Gumperz et al., 1987). Even when someone uses English vocabulary and grammar well, it may be difficult to follow the thread or recognize the point they are trying to make. For example, one linguaculture may begin with the most important element and then add details that are less and less significant.[19] Others use a more narrative style, setting the scene (time, place, introducing characters) before moving to a conclusion (Gumperz, 1982; Tannen, 1989).[20] Some discourse styles emphasize quantitative descriptions or data as explanations or evidence, whereas others emphasize more contextualized, qualitative descriptions and data as explanation or evidence. Discourse style can be contrasted as direct versus indirect, reserved versus animated, intimate versus formal, and so on[21] (Gumperz, 1982; Wierzbicka, 2003).[22]

In addition to culture, the organization and style of an individual speaker's discourse will be influenced by additional factors, including the person's race, gender, profession, and footing (power and authority) in the situation (Fairclough, 1989, 1992; Matoesian, 2001; Stubbs, 1983; Tannen, 1994). Here, the importance of "style" is that a listener who is unfamiliar with a style may perceive it to be unclear or hard to follow; they may impute a lack of credibility to the speaker (Lawrence, 1994; Lewis, 2000).[23] They may perceive a different organizational style as intentional obfuscation; meanwhile, the speaker may impute a lack of intelligence to the listener who fails to get the point. One strategy that interpreters use is to insert discourse markers such as "Let me first give you some background . . ." or "So, my point is . . ." to help the listener identify those elements that were only implied in the original by the discourse style/organization (Tannen, 1994).

Allowing the interpreter to work *consecutively*, with time to adjust for different culturally appropriate *styles*, will allow the interpreter time to make the interpretation more intelligible as well as less prone to error.

DISCOURSES

Discourses taken together form a collection of themes, perspectives, evaluations, or assumptions that repeat and interweave to construct a reality.

The Social Construction of People Who Are "Disabled"

Discourses on the topic of "disability," although distinct, cannot be entirely separated from discourses of deaf people, all of which reflect themes of inability, impairment, the need for rehabilitation, and dependence on others as well as distaste.[24]

Meanings of the Word "Deaf"

1. From the medical perspective, the word "deaf" or "hearing impaired" references a lack or deficiency in the ability to hear.
2. Metaphorically, "deaf" means a certain kind of stubborn refusal to listen, or attend, a cavalier dismissal of what could be heard.[25]
3. Within a legal context, it identifies a category of "disability" used, for example, by the Social Security Administration to determine qualifications for benefits[26] as well as within a public policy context to determine rights to accommodations[27] or accommodation in public education systems.[28]
4. From a sociolinguistic perspective, the category "deaf"—often capitalized—identifies a group of people who are both deaf in the audiological sense and who use a variety of ASL as their primary language.[29]
5. The term "Deaf community" refers to a network of people using a variety of ASL, not all of whom are audiologically deaf.

The term is then polysemous (i.e., has different meanings—and implications—in different contexts). The various meanings are not mutually exclusive or discrete but rather implicate one another.

Everyday discourses about "deaf" refer to a loss[30] or a disability[31] that imputes an incapacity—even of intelligence (as in deaf and dumb).[32] Indeed, nowhere else in this book is it assumed that the deaf person in question is an attorney or judge within the criminal justice system (see Kolb, 2016). This is parallel to discussions of other disabled people. (See Basas, 2018, for a commentary on stigmatizing and liberating models of disabilities.)

Deaf people are often essentialized as "a deaf" or a walking set of nonfunctioning ears. Indeed, there is an ASL sign that identifies this. It can be translated as "framed-as-an-ear [invisible as a whole person]." That is to say, "deafness" (the fact that the person is deaf) seems to obliterate awareness of any other factor or characteristic of who the person is. In the cases outlined here, the reader will notice that the individuals encountering the criminal justice system share very little other than that they are all deaf (and male).

Deaf people are not uncommonly suspected of faking it, a version of "refusing to hear" referred to previously. I have heard a version of the following more than once: "They can hear me when they want to,"[33] which is not a denial of any hearing loss but imputes an exaggeration of it for devious reasons. (See the cases of George and Christopher further on).

Discourses of Sign Language

Some laypeople assume that any form of signing used in America is ASL. Conversely, others assume that signing is universal, used by deaf people around the world. Still, others think it is a code for English or a semilanguage that requires fingerspelling[34] (borrowing from English) to convey abstract ideas.[35] Indeed, the concept of "language" in the largely monolingual United States is limited. New ASL students often ask, "What is the sign for . . . ?" and must be schooled to frame their question in a way that does not assume a word-for-word equivalent, even when the denotation is the same (e.g., referencing a feline: English: "cat" and ASL: CAT the connotations and the use are not the same). There is, for example, no sense of "catting around" or being "catty" in the ASL sign for the animal;[36] ASL and English also differ in which lexical items can be either a noun or a verb. For example, using morphological inflection, the sign for AIRPLANE becomes FLY (in-an-airplane), or CHAIR becomes SIT-DOWN; whereas a single sign is the equivalent of the English phrase "sit-side-by-side-facing-forward."

Modality: a signed language is not a code for a spoken language.[37] It is important to distinguish between the visual-gestural modality, medium, or channel[38] of communication versus the language that is being used. As natural languages, English, French, and Farsi are spoken. ASL, *Langue des signes française*, or *Zaban Eshareh Iran* are natural languages that are signed.

A natural language is a human language that has evolved organically, over time, as people interact within a group or community.[39] Gestures constitute "paralanguage" behaviors that supplement or augment speech (Kendon, 2004, p. 156) or kinesic codes (Kendon, 2004, p. 284).[40] Morse code (a set of electronic-auditory signals representing letters of the alphabet) is an example of an invented code used to spell out words.[41]

ASL is not simply "on the hands"[42] but rather a visual-gestural language that includes facial gestures, head tilts, and body shifts. Nonsigners may perceive signing (waving hands and facial expressions) as indicating anger. On a visit to Guadalajara, I asked a tour guide if he knew where the local deaf people gather,[43] and he said he knew a local church commonly attended by deaf people. He said he had seen them waving their arms in the courtyard after mass. At first, he thought they were fighting, but after passing by a few times, he realized they were deaf and signing. This perception of signing as fighting or angry communication has implications for the perception of deaf witnesses or defendants by naive nonsigners, particularly jurors and judges. Indeed all of this implicates what the naive person thinks the interpreter is doing.

These negative constructions of (1) deaf people as impaired or limited (intellectually) on the one hand or stubborn and suspect on the other, together with (2) misconceptions of sign language as a code for English on the one hand or a crude but universal system of concrete gestures on the other, have been shown to be widespread, including even trained, professional educators of deaf children (Pennucci et al., 2007). For this reason, it may be assumed to also influence professionals in the criminal justice system, including jurors, and implicate the perceived need for and use of interpreters.

Discourses of Suspects

A person suspected of a crime is, by definition, suspect, a person not to be trusted. All of these discourses are relevant to the case of George.

George's Story

George, a White, deaf, 34-year-old man, was arrested for burglary. The police found him to be regularly uncooperative, and records indicated that, in addition to being deaf, he had a long history of being in trouble with the law. Official descriptions of George's mental competence were somewhat mixed, and so he was referred for a psychiatric examination to determine his competence to stand trial.

Relying on past records of criminal history, an interview with the defendant's mother, observations by custody officers, and his own observations during his interview with George, the psychiatrist came to a provisional diagnosis that included a certain amount of malingering. [I will return to the psychiatrist's report later, after I have discussed the process.] For the diagnostic interview, a team of two sign language interpreters was used. Both interpreters were certified by the Registry of Interpreters for the Deaf (RID). Interpreter A has hearing within the normal range, whereas interpreter B is profoundly deaf. Interpreter A interpreted the questions of the psychiatrist into ASL, which interpreter B then converted to gestures. George's responses were then converted by interpreter B into standard ASL and thence into spoken English by interpreter A.

The interview was videotaped, a practice I strongly recommend. Significantly, George communicated using only basic gestures throughout the interview. Interpreter B relied heavily on world knowledge, knowledge about the case, and professional skill to infer the meaning(s) of George's gestures and body language. These he then translated into standard but simple ASL, which interpreter A then rendered into simple English sentences without comment or elaboration.

At times during the interview, George seemed not to understand a question. He then either simply failed to respond or responded inappropriately (i.e., in a way that had nothing to do with the question).

The psychiatrist observed in his report:[44]

Most of our questions to [George] were interpreted using American Sign Language. [*sic*] His responses to most of these questions were characterized by either refusals to answer or simple, primitive gestural signs rather than American Sign Language. At first, it appeared that perhaps [George] had little or no knowledge of American Sign Language; however, several times during both interviews, [George] was capable of engaging in basic communication utilizing American sign language [*sic*] *when it suited his need to do so* [emphasis added].

It is unclear how the psychiatrist determined that George was using ASL, having had no linguistic background with which to do so, and at no time during the interview did the interpreters indicate as much. Furthermore, he said

> Indeed, examiners were left with the impression that [George's] obvious refusals to answer and use of simple gestural communication vis-à-vis sign language were designed to give the examiner the impression that he was so low functioning that he was not accountable for his actions.

The psychiatrist concluded that

> [George] . . . functions at a higher cognitive level than he is willing to present upon forensic interview; in my opinion, [George] has the capacity to appreciate the nature of the legal proceedings against him and the capacity to rationally assist defense counsel if he so chooses. In my opinion, despite his many problems,[45] [George] is competent to stand trial. Moreover, based upon the available information, there was no reason to believe that [George] would have lacked either the capacity to perceive the nature and quality of his actions or the capacity to tell right from wrong . . . [George] appears to have learned that by presenting himself as a helpless, non-communicative, hearing impaired person, he can avoid criminal responsibility for his actions. If the information provided to me by the defendant's mother Ms. ___ is correct that the defendant is probably not mentally retarded as previously reported by Dr. ___.

Competence

First, it must be observed that cognitive impairment, like hearing levels, is not black and white. George clearly indicated from time to time, using body language, that he understood that certain behaviors were bad, but even very young children understand at a concrete level that their behavior is bad when they have been scolded; this does not, however, index a mature moral sense. In the subsequent trial, early school records were presented by the defense, which clearly stated that George was severely mentally retarded.[46]

A report by an expert who had reviewed the videotaped interview reported that she did not see any use of standard ASL and that given the approach used by the interpreters, it had been clear to them also that George was severely mentally retarded. The expert concluded that the questions George failed to respond to appropriately or at all were simply above his comprehension level rather than a refusal to answer, as the psychiatrist concluded, and that he was unable to respond appropriately because it had not made sense to him.

Here we see several things happening. The interpreters working with George did not appear to have communicated their process to the psychiatrist.

The translation of George's gestures into simple English sentences may have been misleading, especially if he was influenced by the discourses of sign language (myths) described previously. Second, George's mother's statement that George was indeed smart may have been taken literally rather than to indicate that he was not totally without ability. Another factor that might have influenced the psychiatrist in suspecting that George was exaggerating "his problems" was reports by officers who supervised George in jail that George seemed at times to respond to sounds. Finally, the position of the psychiatrist was to be suspicious, and he was. His lack of expertise led him to erroneous conclusions.

However, it was not only the officers and the psychiatrist but also the interpreting team who made assumptions. Perhaps to the interpreters, their process of going from English to ASL to gesture and back was obvious and did not need to be made explicit. Indeed, sign language interpreters commonly assume that what they are doing is transparent to others or does not warrant comment.[47] Alternatively, they may have overly interpreted the constraints of their role.

TWO-STEP INTERPRETING

The team of interpreters working with George was composed of one interpreter with "normal hearing" and another who was audiologically deaf. Converting the psychiatrist's questions was thus a two-step process: The first interpreter relayed the spoken English questions in ASL (changing both the modality and the language), and the second (deaf) interpreter then converted the question into gestures. When George responded, this two-step process was repeated in reverse. This process relies heavily on context and, as indicated, special skills. It is nevertheless imprecise and limited.[48]

Before discussing the use of interpreters who are themselves deaf, it is necessary to explore what is meant by "fluency" in a language.

LANGUAGE FLUENCY

Clearly mastering a first language is an important part of maturation neurologically, socially, and educationally. It affects our success in life, in society as a social being, in school, and in our careers. Yet, normal as learning language is, an analysis of what this means can be eye-opening. The development of fluency in using a language goes hand in hand with the ability to think well (e.g., organize, recall, analyze, synthesize) and how to operate as a social being within a specific linguaculture. Nippold (2007), for example, identifies the following topic areas of linguistic competence:[49]

> Having a literate lexicon; able to use derivational morphology; lexical storage and retrieval; inductive reasoning (analogies); deductive reasoning (syllogisms); understanding rhetorical devices such as metaphors and

similes; idioms and slang terms; proverbs and fables; ambiguity and sarcasm; use in various situations (e.g., social, academic) requiring expanded syntactic attainment;[50] conversation and narration; persuasion, negotiation, and explanation; and finally the special skills of reading and writing. (pp. vii–xii)

Bilingualism

Contrary to general belief, bilinguals are rarely equally fluent in their languages; some speak one language better than another, others use one of their languages [only] in specific situations, and others still can only read or write one of the languages. (Grosjean, 1982, p. vii)

Li Wei (2000) lists the categories of bilinguals, which include balanced, receptive, dominant, dormant, functional, incipient, minimal, and subordinate (pp. 6–7). The Foreign Services Administration uses proficiency tests designed by the American Council on the Teaching of Foreign Languages (ACTFL, 2012).[51] It is a functional evaluation of one's language proficiency, designed through the lens of application. As the diagram on their webpage indicates, gains in proficiency are exponential rather than linear. That is, it takes much more language skill to be able to carry on a conversation than to simply use the language for travel (book a hotel, find a restaurant, etc.) and more proficiency still to be able to perform one's work in the target language. ACTFL designates one's first language as L1, second language as L2, and so on.

. . . L2 learning after the primary language (L1) has been learned is called *successive bilingualism* . . . starting later may offer the advantages of a well-developed L1 system, including literacy skills and metalinguistic competence, which can support the process . . . [however, success] is also affected by the amount and consistency of exposure to the language, the type and quality of instruction offered, the learner's motivation and aptitude, and frequent opportunities to use the new language. (Nippold, 2007, p. 9)[52]

Others also emphasize the importance of immersion in a community of speakers.

The quality of the language environment is of paramount importance to success in learning a new language. If students are exposed to a list of words and their translations, together with a few simple readings in the new language, they will perhaps be able to attain some degree of reading skills in the language, but listening and speaking skills will remain fallow. As many high school and college students have learned to their chagrin,

> if one is exposed only to classroom drills and dialogs, one may acquire substantial mastery of classroom communication skills but still remain at a loss in other areas of social discourse. (Dulay et al., 1982, p. 13)

While students of Sweden in the United States can travel abroad to obtain such immersion, obtaining a parallel experience is more difficult for students of ASL because there is no parallel geographically bound community of ASL users.

Heritage Language Users

Some people come from families that use a language at home that differs from the one used in the wider community. There may be multiple combinations. Here are a few examples:

- All members of the family are bilingual and use Language A at home and Language B in the community.
- Only the children are developing fluency in the language of the community (Language A used at home by parents who are not fluent in Language B, the community language).
- Parents are multilingual and want their children to also acquire multiple languages (At home, the mother uses Language A, the father uses Language B, whereas in the wider community, all use Language C).[53]
- The situation in which a *marginalized* language is used only at home and with family friends rarely results in the children of these families becoming fluent: "Due to socio-political pressure from the majority language spoken in their community, their heritage language does not fully develop" (Montrul, 2016, frontispiece).

First, Native, and Primary Language

We might assume that, all things being equal, babies naturally acquire a *native language* from their parents, which they study later in school. This is the case for most people in the United States. Children of immigrant parents might learn one language at home, which is different from that spoken by the majority of people in the neighborhood and school (see the previous section on heritage language). Their first language is therefore not quite the same as a native language despite learning it first. An expatriate might be competent in their native language but living and working in another country using their second language (L2) as their primary language.[54] People who become deaf as adults, after having learned a spoken language and gained much world knowledge, will likely retain that language as both their first and their primary language, whether or not they later learn some form of signing.

Children born deaf or severely hard of hearing to nondeaf, nonsigning parents[55] represent a distinct instance of bilingualism; their early access to a natural signed language such as ASL depends greatly on several key factors, including family perspectives and resources; local school district's philosophy and resources; and the size, composition, and accessibility of the local community of ASL signers. Too often, a negative combination of these factors results in language delay or deprivation[56] (Humphries et al., 2017).[57] On the other hand, deaf children born to deaf or hearing parents who use ASL will likely develop linguistically and cognitively along a more typical trajectory. Deaf children in the United States will be taught English in school, and their level of achievement will again depend on many factors. Thus, the level of fluency in English or ASL of deaf people in the criminal justice system cannot be assumed.[58]

Bilingualism, Fluency, and Domain

Even native speakers are not fluent in the language used in all domains. As previously indicated, learning a profession requires learning the concepts, knowledge, and procedures specific to it (van Dijk, 2014) as well as the language (lexicon, syntax, and discourse style) to convey them.[59] Obvious examples from criminal law include *mens rea* and *voir dire*, whereas deceptively, seemingly clear terms such as *evidence* or *standing* carry special meanings within the context of a trial.[60] Learning such specialized discourse distances members of the profession from nonmembers. Bienvenu (2015) pointed out that sign language interpreters are called upon to interpret in many situations that would require proficiency in various domains[61] and suggests the impossibility of mastering them all.[62]

Power and Privilege: Language of a Marginalized Community

As mentioned earlier, in the sections on discourses of "deaf" and "sign language," there are many common negative or simplistic associations with each. Well-intentioned or not, educational philosophies that privilege codes for English and the teaching of speech over a natural signed language not only postpone or deny access to ASL (Baynton, 1996; Humphries et al., 2017; Lane, 1992) but often ironically (and harmfully) result in isolation (Oliva, 2004), as well as poor social and cognitive skills (Gulati 2014, 2019).[63] Any failure of these approaches may be projected onto the "disability" in the form of inappropriately low academic expectations (Pennucci et al., 2007). Deaf people themselves have long critiqued and resisted any attempt to suppress sign language and contested the perception of them as impaired.[64]

Shame

Marginalized people (including deaf people) often internalize a sense of shame (David, 2014; Davis, 1995), which leads to a strategy of pretending to understand[65] to avoid angering the person in authority or prolonging an uncomfortable situation. Discourses of deafness, misunderstanding of what it means to have a heritage language or to be bilingual, and the stigma of being deaf are all implicated in the case of Christopher.

Christopher's Story

Christopher was an exceptionally intelligent young man with a nonverbal or "performance" IQ score in the 99th percentile.[66] *His parents had always identified him as "hard of hearing" and pressured him to lipread and talk, while in reality he was profoundly deaf from birth.*[67] *While he was assigned to a school in which the modality of signing was used, he internalized his parents' stigmatized view of deafness and adopted the self-identification of hard of hearing. Because he was so exceptionally smart, he was often able to figure out what people in his family or in the community said, from a combination of experience, environmental cues, body language, facial expressions, and some lipreading. When he did not understand, he often used face-saving strategies of faking understanding, feigning disinterest, or making jokes. In this way, he reinforced the idea that he was not really that deaf.*

As a recent high school graduate, Christopher was at a loose end, not yet employed, and with no plans for college, he began using drugs. One day while he was, as he said, "fucked up on drugs," he got into an altercation with someone wanting to sell him a used car and became lethally violent. He was soon arrested and interrogated. During the interrogation, an officer who had been raised by deaf parents (who used ASL) was used to interpret. This officer had also internalized the shame of his parents' disability and their marginalized language and had never learned to sign well. Despite the officer's protestations, he was nevertheless ordered by his superior officer[68] to act as an interpreter during the interrogation and reluctantly agreed. As you might expect, it did not go well. The officer tried his best, and Christopher employed his lifelong strategies of going along to get along. As smart as he was, Christopher was still young, somewhat naive, and did not know his rights; he did not understand the officer's signing. He did, however, feel troubled about what he had done and felt a lot of guilt. In the interview, he incriminated himself.

Subsequently, however, it became evident that:

a. Christopher was profoundly deaf and not hard of hearing,
b. The officer had only a very basic command of sign language, and
c. Christopher had not understood his right to remain silent, to not incriminate himself, and so on.

All evidence gained from the interrogation was deemed inadmissible.

Ways of (Not) Understanding

There are many ways (levels) of misunderstanding from the lexical or word level, to the discourse (frame and footing), to the pragmatic, that is, the level of implications. As illustrated by the preceding cases, *not understanding* may be due to a term of art; it may mean not understanding the frame (e.g., an interrogation) or one's footing in that interaction (witness); it may mean having incorrect assumptions about what it means to grow up with parents using another language (a heritage language) as was the case of the supervisor ordering the officer to interpret and the implications: dismissal of evidence gathered. Indeed, when individuals have different values and priorities, they will have difficulty understanding one another even though the language itself is clear (Ridington, 1990; Verschueren, 1989).

COMMUNICATION SKILL AND INTERPRETERS

Beyond native-like fluency in two or more languages and their cultures, interpreters need at least average social skills (which go beyond manners and include communicative competence). Communicative competence, which is related to but distinct from linguistic fluency, involves the ability to:

- Mentally take the listeners' perspective and to predictively infer how they might understand what is to be said[69]
- Read the listeners' responses (retroactively infer how the listeners understood what was said)
- Adapt as necessary
- Command a wide variety of communication strategies (beyond language)

Communication skills, like language fluency, is measured along a continuum and is situated. In other words, if the interlocutors are peers who share similar experiences and a similar outlook on life, average communication skills will be all they need. If, on the other hand, the interlocutors differ significantly in background, worldview, and/or assumptions, then to be effective, the process will demand much more skill. To interpret accurately, the interpreter needs to be able to inhabit the speaker/signer's mind and that of the listener (i.e., how it is intended, and how it will be understood by the listener[s]) and to adjust accordingly.

The Process of Interpreting

Interpreting is a complex process (Cokely, 1992; Larson, 1998).

1. To explain or tell the meaning of: present in understandable terms
2. To conceive in the light of individual belief, judgment, or circumstance: construe

3. To represent by means of art: bring to realization by performance or direction (~s a role) ~vi: to act as an interpreter between speakers of different languages (Merriam-Webster, 2009)
4. To derive meaning within context (It is difficult to interpret these statistics without knowing how they were obtained; https://dictionary.cambridge.org/us/dictionary/english/difficult)

Interpreting effectively is more than knowing a language, as has been well established (see Clyne, 1994; van Dijk, 2014; Wierzbicka, 2003).[70] To state the obvious, interpreters are sought because two or more interlocutors are unable to understand one another without such an intermediary.[71] To ensure the interpretation is as accurate, impartial, and as effective as possible, it is necessary to use qualified interpreters and, in some situations, a team (discussed next).

The Role of the Interpreter

As outlined earlier, the process of interpreting is distinct from the practice of specific behaviors. It is to *convey meaning between interlocutors* and will be defined more narrowly or broadly, depending on (a) the situation and (b) the interlocutors.[72] There is often a tension between form, on the one hand, and function, on the other (Guenther, 1962).

Too often (in this author's opinion), it is defined too narrowly. As we saw in the case of Frank, staying too close to the original form can be counterproductive. On the other hand, some deaf people achieve a very high level of fluency in English (written or signed), in which case the role of the interpreter is appropriately narrow.

- Had the interpreter for Frank framed the question as "Did you attempt to strike the officer when he approached the truck?" it might have been more accurate.
- On the other hand, had Frank been a criminal attorney himself, glossing the term (resist arrest) would not have been an issue, as he would have been able to do the interpreting for himself.

In the case of Charles, the first interpreter again felt too constrained and did not interpret Charles's nonverbal communication, failing to frame and thereby failing to convey the *meaning* of the prosecutor's questions. The failure of the interpreters for George to make their process explicit to the psychiatrist negatively influenced his final assessment.[73]

The ability of interlocutors to assume part of the responsibility[74] for the communication will affect the interpreter's role; for example, the more informed and bilingual the deaf person, the less burden on the interpreter. This requires, however, that the interpreter be able to accurately read the interlocutors as well as the situation to correctly adjust their own role. When the interlocutors are less able to be "responsible" in Joos's sense, and the interaction is adversarial, then the challenge to the interpreter is much greater. Thus, the role of the interpreter, as in any profession, requires judgment in addition to knowledge, skill, and ethics.

The Preparation and Practice of Interpreters

Most professional interpreters begin by learning ASL in a postsecondary setting[75] (i.e., as adults). Such programs do their best to provide opportunities to use the language outside the classroom. Unfortunately, this is rarely sufficient to achieve fluency.[76] Classes in ASL are then followed with coursework in interpreting itself, including such topics as text analysis, the role of an interpreter, and ethics, or professional behavior. The attrition rate at each level is high, as reflected by the decreasing number of sections offered by year and the relatively few people successfully certified each year.[77]

Unlike people who use spoken language interpreters, deaf, hard of hearing, and deafblind people will use interpreters throughout their lives in many different settings (including college and university classrooms, theaters, churches, and corporations like Boeing or Google).[78]

Deaf professionals may use interpreters virtually every day for telephone calls, for meetings with colleagues or clients, as well as for professional conferences and training. ASL interpreters typically choose one setting in which to work primarily, supplemented by fewer hours in a secondary setting (e.g., interpreting regularly in a postsecondary school, supplemented by occasional appointments at medical clinics).[79]

DEAF INTERPRETERS

Some interpreters are themselves audiologically deaf. These deaf interpreters typically work in teams with at least one other interpreter who has English as an L1 and has average or better hearing acuity, and then relay what is said from English to ASL to gesture as in the case of George, or another signed language (e.g., Korean Sign Language).[80] Among the advantages to such a team is that—unlike the majority of interpreters who have learned ASL as adults and have not achieved native-like fluency—deaf interpreters have ASL as their primary (and typically first) language. Interpreters who are deaf also obtain certification (see next section), demonstrating that they are sufficiently bilingual and able to interpret, understand the role, and understand how to practice ethically.

INTERPRETER CERTIFICATION

ASL interpreters are currently certified by the Center for the Assessment of Sign Language Interpretation, the testing arm of the national organization RID. As might be clear from the foregoing description of interpreter training, not all interpreters are qualified to interpret within the criminal justice system, despite being certified. The generalist certification test establishes only a minimum criterion for fluency in ASL (Bienvenu, 2015; Graybill, 2015; Padden, 2015).[81]

INTERPRETING TEAMS

The problem of fluency can be mitigated by using a team of interpreters whose linguistic skills complement each other, that is, one who is English dominant (nondeaf) and one who is ASL dominant (deaf), both of whom are qualified interpreters.

For this reason, a small but growing segment of the interpreting profession is critically composed of people who are themselves deaf, who bring needed native skills/insight to the interpreting team, and who have studied to become interpreters. These are most often people born to deaf parents/families who then become translators and language mentors for their classmates and peers from an early age (Bienvenu, 2015), an experience that is critical to their ability to accommodate the communication needs of a variety of deaf, hard of hearing, and deafblind people.[82]

Deaf interpreters, as well as nondeaf interpreters, do not work in all domains. Examples include conference work (using formal or presentation-level language), medical or legal settings, or with deaf people who use a different signed language as their primary language (i.e., not ASL).[83] Some deaf interpreters work with deaf children who have limited world experience and schema or adults who have very limited language for a variety of reasons, including having a cognitive impairment.

A FINAL WORD

Availability of Interpreters

Interpreting as a profession is relatively new (Ball, 2013; Fant, 1990). Demand for qualified interpreters has grown exponentially in the past 50 years for a variety of reasons, including the passing of laws mandating communication access in education, public accommodations, and telecommunications (PL 94-142,[84] the Americans With Disabilities Act,[85] and the Telecommunications Act of 1996[86]), and continues to outstrip supply.

The interpreter demand is compounded by the need for a team of interpreters. Extended sessions such as during an interrogation, a trial, or programming while incarcerated will require a team to avoid errors due to fatigue. Providing native-like fluency in ASL most often requires the use of a team of interpreters having complementary skills. The list of currently certified interpreters on the RID website shows that there are seven states with no interpreters certified to do legal work and 14 states with no certified deaf interpreters (CDI); an additional 14 states have only one CDI in the state. Without funds to bring in qualified interpreters from a distance and without advance planning, this can create delays with unintended and negative consequences.

Clearly, the criminal justice system does not exist or operate in a vacuum. There are larger issues, some of which have been touched on in this chapter, that are outside both the control of the criminal justice system and beyond the scope of this chapter, that nonetheless influence both the communication itself and the interpretation of the said communication within the criminal justice system. These include, but are not limited to, the hierarchical and somewhat rigid nature of institutions, the lack of supply and availability of qualified interpreters, discourses of "deaf" and "sign language," and, finally, educational policies based on ideologies of normalcy (*sic*) that hinder rather than facilitate linguistic and communicative competence of children born deaf.

INTERPRETING IN THE CRIMINAL JUSTICE SYSTEM

Within the criminal justice system, a deaf person might be involved in a variety of ways: as a suspect, defendant, codefendant, inmate, or parolee. Alternatively, an interpreter might work for a deaf witness, juror, attorney, or judge.[87] How the deaf person is involved is important. Factors such as the following implicate the difficulty of the interpretation and potential effects of misunderstandings during the interaction:

- First encounter and/or other interactions with police officers
- Questioning by officers/detectives
- Miranda warnings or explanation of rights
- Interrogation
- Communication while in custody (with police officers)
- Meeting with defense counsel
- Arraignment
- Psychiatric or other examinations by experts
- Trial: presentation of testimony/evidence
- Judgment and sentencing
- Programming, religious services, and so forth while incarcerated
- Administrative hearings for infractions while incarcerated
- Probation hearing
- Mandated treatment (e.g., anger management)
- Polygraph test
- Meetings with a probation officer (sometimes called a community corrections officer or CCO)

Each of these interactions is qualitatively different. Accuracy is most crucial whenever the interaction is adversarial. Unfortunately, this is often during the early stages when (because of time pressure) it is most difficult to ensure an appropriate interpreting team. It is therefore critical that each jurisdiction have a system in place to procure the services of qualified teams of interpreters and to preserve the complete record (both video and audio) of these interactions which is then kept available for later review.

IT'S COMPLICATED

- Not everyone who is audiologically deaf is unable to hear at all: a deaf person may be able to hear sirens, shouts, certain dog barks, and so forth.[88]
- Not everyone who is deaf is "just deaf" because a person who is deaf may also, for example, have limited cognitive ability or visual acuity.
- Not everyone who is labeled *deaf* uses a sign language,[89] and not everyone who uses a sign language is deaf.[90]
- Not everyone who uses ASL is using the same standard variety of the language in all situations (Edwards, 2014; Hill, 2012; Kannapell, 1993; Lucas, 1996; Lucas et al., 2001; Lucas & Valli, 1989).
- Most certified ASL-English interpreters are not nativelike in both languages (Bienvenu, 2015; Padden, 2015) and not always able to understand/convey more than the surface meaning of what is said (Graybill, 2015).
- Not all certified ASL-English interpreters are qualified to interpret in all domains (Bienvenu, 2015).
- Some interpreters for the deaf are themselves audiologically deaf.
- Deaf people and their language are often stigmatized, resulting in shame (Davis, 1995), which in turn negatively affects communication.
- Communication is broader than just language.
- The demand for interpreters is greater than the supply of qualified professionals, and availability may be an issue.
- Whether or not the interactions are adversarial is a critical consideration.

RECOMMENDATIONS

Establish a System

First, it is important to establish a system—a set of policies and procedures, as well as a budget for hiring qualified teams of interpreters. I recommend using only ASL specialist referral businesses. As of this writing, there is a trend to contract with an organization that provides or refers interpreters in many languages because it is seen as more efficient. Unfortunately, these businesses are rarely equipped to locate or identify which sign language interpreter is qualified for which situation and which client.[91]

Given the current scarcity of qualified interpreters,[92] especially outside major metropolitan areas, I would recommend having a contract with a qualified, as well as reliable, ASL specialist referral business,[93] which can help locate and screen interpreters. It may be necessary at times to hire interpreters from outside the area, possibly even from another state. All of these considerations will impact the budget and is not something that can be thought through or arranged at the last minute.

Use Qualified Experts

Maintain an up-to-date roster of experts (psychiatrists, linguists) who are qualified to evaluate the cognitive state of deaf, hard of hearing, and deafblind people and the interpretations given. Experts such as Gulati (2014, 2019) emphasize the difficult challenge of diagnosing the underlying reasons for atypical language in deaf patients. These experts may themselves be deaf. ASL specialist interpreter referral businesses may help locate and identify such experts.

Consider Factors in the Situation: Role, Identity, Complexity, and Severity

The position and footing of the deaf person is a factor in arranging interpreters (juror, witness, defendant, or inmate). Does the deaf person need a team of specialists (e.g., a signed language other than ASL) or evaluation by a specialist (e.g., a psychological examination), for which the interpreting team may need additional skills/background. Some cases are more complex, such as one that involves more than one deaf person (e.g., domestic violence between a couple, each of whom is deaf). Finally, the more complex the situation and the more severe the charges and possible jeopardy, the more important it is to both use a team (or teams) of qualified interpreters and to preserve the record for any later challenges.

Use a Team of Interpreters

Use a team of interpreters with complementary skills, that is, a deaf interpreter with a nondeaf interpreter (Mathers, 2009). This will ensure native-like fluency in both languages (ASL and English).

Use specialists when needed. Use multiple teams for trials involving charges that may result in incarceration over a year or other severe consequences—*three teams*: one for the court and one team for each side (prosecution and defense). The prosecution/defense team can act as "table interpreters" during a trial and can monitor the accuracy of the court interpreter for the attorneys.

A Word About (the Perception of) Bias

Given that a sign language interpreter is involved in the criminal justice system only when a deaf person is involved, it is sometimes assumed by nondeaf people that there is a bias in favor of the deaf person. This perception may be falsely reinforced by more eye contact or touch between the interpreter and the deaf person than is typically used by English speakers (Mathers, 2007). A suspicion may even be raised by the use of a language not understood by others.[94] Deaf people, on the other hand, often perceive a bias on the part of the (nondeaf) interpreter in favor of the dominant society and its authority or simply self-interest as in the ASL idiom glossed as "smell money."[95] Having three mixed teams for serious cases will help minimize any bias, as well as its perception.

Prepare the Interpreters

As is clear by now, interpreting is a challenging process that is best done consecutively and with preparation. The more the interpreters understand the elements of the case, attorney strategies, and points to be contested and have time to analyze possible sticking points regarding the interpretation, the better and more accurate the interpretation will be (Cokely, 2013). Having a defense/prosecution team monitoring the signed interpretation can act as a check on possible errors.

Do Not Rush

Consecutive interpreting is more accurate than simultaneous (Russell, 2002) and avoids error resulting from fatigue (Brasel, 1976; Moser-Mercer et al., 1998) and cognitive load. Given that this is an unusual pace at which to listen, it is important that one can later review the record.

Preserve the Record

Preserving an accurate record, especially of the interrogation and informing of rights, is key. This will require a video record from more than one angle, as well as an audio record. It is important to record the signed interpretation as well as what is signed by the deaf person. Preserve any notes or written communication between police officers and the deaf person(s) as well.

CONCLUSION

Discourse is where language, culture, and the situation meet, merge, and create meaning. The listener's personal and collective experiences establish expectations and influence the "interpretation" of exchanges and encounters, that is, pragmatics. Communicating across linguacultures is even more prone to failings than otherwise. Precautionary measures include those in the foregoing recommendations.

NOTES

1. Less than 100 years ago, it was recognized that a signed language could have all the essential characteristics of a spoken language: phonology, syntax, etc., and the ability to express both abstract and complex ideas as well as systematic ways of creating new lexical items (Baynton, 1996; Klima & Bellugi, 1979; Stokoe et al., 1965).

2. These, in turn, are reflected in as well as partially formed by discourses or ways of talking about certain topics, as discussed under the section Discourses or Tropes.

3. "Register" includes a level of formality. The salience of the use of different forms of language according to situation was identified in the seminal work of Joos (1967).

4. "Terms of art" is a phrase used to describe terminology having special meaning within a particular profession. This meaning is often not clear to people who are not members of that profession (e.g., "chain of custody" is a term of art used in legal contexts to mean the documentation of "the movement and location of physical evidence from the time it is obtained until the time it is presented in court" (https://legal-dictionary.thefreedictionary.com/chain+of+custody). Indeed the phrase "term(s) of art" may itself be said to be a "term or art" used by lawyers.

5. This can generally be described as formulaic, precise, and attentive to detail; formal and authoritative in nature; and quite distinct from conversational register or style (Stygall, 1994).

6. For example, police interrogations, trials, and administrative hearings.

7. Sometimes called "dialects."

8. Although many deaf people do share a common linguistic and cultural heritage (Lane et al., 2011), not all deaf people can be assumed to share a common identity, linguistic variety, or level of fluency (Gutierrez, 1998).

9. The Americans With Disabilities Act (1990) requires the use of "qualified interpreters" (42 U.S.C. § 12141 *et seq*). A qualified interpreter is one "who is able to interpret effectively, accurately, and impartially both receptively and expressively, using any necessary specialized vocabulary" (28 C.F.R. § 35.104).

10. All names used in case examples are changed. Technically, Frank was severely hard of hearing, but his primary language is ASL.

11. One might gloss the English word "dish" as "plato" in Spanish, literally "plate." But in the sentence "[Chef] Julianna created a wonderful *dish* for my birthday," it is not accurately interpreted by the gloss "plato."

12. As with other languages, there are also ASL signs and references that have no clear equivalent in English (Cokely, 2001).

13. Interpreting into ASL what has just been said—with only a slight "lag" in time—while the speaker (in this case, the attorney) continues to talk, meaning that the interpreter is simultaneously mentally translating into ASL while listening to what is concurrently being said requires an in-depth discussion of the cognitive load this places on the interpreter that is beyond the scope of this chapter.

14. The difference may be one of semantic breadth (e.g., the sign RESIST discussed earlier). The difference may be one of connotation (e.g., one of the three signs for "cochlear implant," indicating neutrality, opposition, or a slightly medicalized perspective). The difference might be one of register or formality (e.g., the two signs for DEAF). It may be morphological: indicating aspect or mood (e.g., work, work-for-a-long-time-continuously, work-hard). The difference may be syntactic; for example, the basic English words "walk, milk, and water" can serve in English both as a verb and as a noun, but in ASL the verb form and the noun form ASL are expressed either by a different sign for the verb and the noun (e.g., "walk" becomes the equivalent of "walkway" or "path," and "milk" has different movements in ASL for the noun or a verb form; while the verb form of "water" uses a compound: water+action to distinguish watering by hose or by pouring

water as in using a watering can, etc. The difference might be rhetorical, for example, whether a word/sign can be used metaphorically or not (e.g., "read" as in to "read the room") or by a sociolinguistic variation for signs (e.g., the multiple ASL signs for "birthday") that have no equivalent in English versus the multiple words for "soda," "pop," or "soft drink," which have no equivalent in ASL.

15. Things tacitly assumed, preconceptions, or assumptions.

16. For example, is the person used to being in a position of authority, being given the benefit of the doubt, or looked down upon as a "loser"?

17. There is copious documentation of institutionalized and social racism affecting the employment of African American men and their reasons for fearing authorities such as the police or courts. For example, see Alexander (2012) and Anderson (2017).

18. The police and Black people (especially men) in the United States often have a contentious relationship (Morin & Stepler, 2016).

19. Much like a newspaper with headlines at the top followed by fewer and fewer significant facts.

20. Think "movie," in which the scene is set before the action begins.

21. These differences are best understood as being along a continuum rather than as absolute categories.

22. These are generalizations that need much more parsing by factors such as gender, age, and topic, all beyond the scope of this chapter. (See for example Smitherman, 1977; Tannen, 1994.)

23. Furthermore, in some groups experience may be a more credible attribute than years of formal study, whereas in other groups, advanced degrees give one more credibility.

24. See *The Ugly Laws* (Schweik, 2009).

25. See, for example, Hefler (2012): "The critics of the recent sale of Burlington County's hospital for the poor say the freeholders were *deaf to their cries* [emphasis added] and cavalier in handling the controversy" (https://www.inquirer.com/philly/blogs/burlington/Freeholders-Deaf-To-Cries-Of-Hospital-Sale-Critics.html).

26. Office for Civil Rights. (1978). Section 504 of the Rehabilitation Act of 1973.

27. The Americans With Disabilities Act (ADA, https://www.ada.gov) as well as Section 504 of the United States Health, Education, and Welfare's Rehabilitation Act of 1973 (https://www.dol.gov/agencies/oasam/civil-rights-center/statutes/section-504-rehabilitation-act-of-1973 and various state laws mandate such access/accommodation).

28. As outlined, for example, in the Individuals With Disabilities Education Act.

29. See Brueggemann (2008) and Bechter (2008) for discussions of d/Deaf distinctions as too absolute.

30. It is in challenge to this narrative (discourse) that Bauman and Murray edited a collection of "deaf gains" (2014).

31. Victoria Ann Lewis (2000) in "The Dramaturgy of Disability" reported how the disabled individual is a representation of moral failure, disability itself as punishment for sin, or, conversely, an innocent (Tiny Tim) and disability a blessing from the gods to "overcome" or to inspire others. She adds a further perspective of the disabled person as ill, a problem to be fixed, cured, and if not, a life to be ended or at least hidden away. See also Longmore (2003) and Longmore and Umansky (2001). These tropes operate largely below the surface of our consciousness.

32. Language policy in the United States strongly favors English (Adams, 1996; Ramsey, 1989; Schiffman, 1996), which is also applied to deaf children specifically (Burch, 2002; Gertz, 2008). A lack of ability to speak may then be seen to indicate a lack of ability or a stubbornness. Pennucci et al. (2007) found that teachers' expectations of deaf and hard of hearing children were consistently reported to be inappropriately low.

33. This is most likely caused by (a) an inconsistent response from the "deaf person" because of context, lighting, acoustics, and other elements of the environment outside the awareness of the speaker and (b) a feeling of frustration or annoyance at not being heard.

34. A form of "spelling out" words using a handshape for each letter.

35. Elaboration and possible reasons for some of these misconceptions about deaf people and about language are outside the scope of this chapter.

36. This is not to imply that ASL does not use words metaphorically; it clearly does but not reliably the same metaphors as those found in English.

37. ASL is not a code for English. There are, however, gestural codes for some English words and morphemes, invented by educators for the purposes of teaching. They are analogous to logograms, that is, not a natural language.

38. Sometimes called medium or channel. Here these terms are used interchangeably in reference to the means of expression or reception: auditory, visual, or tactual.

39. Of the many definitions of language, we have chosen these two: "a system of conventional spoken, manual, or written symbols by means of which human beings, as members of a social group and participants in its culture, express themselves. The functions of language include communication, the expression of identity, play, imaginative expression, and emotional release" (Robins & Crystal, 2019) and "a system of relatively arbitrary symbols and grammatical signals that change across time and that members of a community share and use for several purposes: to interact with each other, to communicate their ideas, emotions, intentions, and to transmit their culture from generation to generation" (Baker & Cokely, 1980, p. 15). This is in contrast to artificial or invented "languages" such as programming "language" or codes.

40. Kendon (2004) distinguishes between *primary* signed languages (e.g., ASL) and *alternative* sign languages found in some speaker–hearer communities (ibid). Indeed, it was a conflation of language with speech and gestures with paralanguage that obscured the recognition of natural signed languages (i.e., true language) in another channel.

41. "Fingerspelling" (a set of handshapes used to spell out words) was originally a manual code for letters and can still be used in that way, but some commonly fingerspelled words have become lexicalized (Battison, 1978). As a fingerspelled word becomes lexicalized, it gradually shifts in form (phonology) to become a sign itself, sometimes with the original meaning (e.g., the name JOHN) and at other times shifting even more to take on a distinct meaning.

42. See, for example, Neidle et al. (2000); Reilly, McIntire, and Bellugi (1990).

43. Large cities often have regular gathering places for deaf people who live there. Common locations include agencies serving deaf people, select taverns, all-night restaurants, food courts, or churches.

44. Excerpted from the psychiatrist's report to the court (defendant's name has been replaced and others deleted).

45. It is not clear which "problems" he is referring to here.

46. ___ State School for the Deaf stated that at the age of 5 George was still unable to dress himself and was eventually sent home for "failure to learn." This was before laws were enacted mandating "education for all" children.

47. Historically, using a team including an interpreter who is themself deaf has implied that the deaf interlocutor was somehow atypical. The practice is changing, and the role of nonhearing interpreters is expanding.

48. Communicating, for example, whether or not George *took* an object, and to some extent how he *felt* about it (scared or worried he would get in trouble), but not *higher level of* concepts of "theft" and "guilt." Abstract concepts of ownership, and "wrong" in the moral sense, even the ability to explain "rationale" or "motive" require both more intelligence and more language than George possessed.

49. These are listed as section headings in her text; each is then further parsed out. I have modified them slightly for clarity.

50. Intrasentential growth and intersentential growth.

51. https://www.actfl.org/publications/guidelines-and-manuals/actfl-proficiency-guidelines-2012

52. Citing work by Fred Genessee of McGill University.

53. A full discussion goes beyond the scope of this chapter. For a full discussion, see Montrul (2016).

54. How a given individual feels about their heritage language will often be influenced by the view of the dominant society. See, for example, Rodriguez (1982).

55. Although there is virtually no recognized set of accurate numbers, which may fluctuate over time, it is generally recognized by people serving deaf people that this is true of the majority.

56. See Guitierrez (1998), Gulati (2014, 2019), and Humphries et al. (2017).

57. A full description of language acquisition by deaf, hard of hearing and deafblind people is beyond the scope of this chapter. (See Humphries et al., 2017.)

58. Rarely, they may be a-lingual or too often semilingual.

59. Sholeen Nett, MD, assured me that despite having a bachelor's degree in Spanish followed by living and working in Guatemala for more than 2 years, then passing the American Council on the Teaching of Foreign Languages (ACTFL) "oral proficiency interview" at the level of average native speaker, she always used a professional interpreter while practicing (medicine) because "I don't know *medical* Spanish" (Sholeen Nett, personal communication).

60. Indeed, what properly counts as "evidence" for cultural anthropologists is different from what counts as "evidence" for sociolinguists.

61. Such as medical, legal, academic, religious, or ceremonial (weddings and funerals).

62. As the profession of interpreting has grown, it has become common since 2010 for interpreters (at least in urban areas) to focus their practice on one or a few domains (Hauser et al., 2008; Smith, 2014).

63. Sanjay Gulati lecture at Brown University (2014) https://www.youtube.com/watch?v=8yy_K6VtHJw.

64. (See, for example, Ballin, 1998; Burch, 2002; Gertz, 2008; Jacobs, 1980; Jankowski, 1997; Kolb, 2016; Ladd, 2003, 2008; Levesque, 1991; and Roots, 1999.) This is only a sampling.

65. There is indeed an ASL sign for "nodding without understanding" in order to be agreeable, to maintain the conversation, or to avoid angering the person with more authority.

66. An IQ of 140, measured on the Wechsler Adult Intelligence Scale (WAIS), which is composed of two parts, verbal and performance. The performance section of the WAIS uses a combination of block design, matrix reasoning, picture completion, object assembly, picture arrangement, digit-symbol coding, and symbol search measuring perceptual reasoning, inductive reasoning, working memory, and processing speed.

67. Unable to hear speech sounds.

68. He later said that a fellow officer from a Spanish-speaking family who had refused to act as interpreter had been fired for insubordination.

69. Psychologists refer to this as "theory of mind."

70. These are but a few examples of the substantial literature on differences in linguacultures that apply to interpreting.

71. For a fuller elaboration of the interpreter's role, see Wadensjö (2002).

72. As professionals, maintaining confidentiality, avoiding a conflict of interest, and exercising good judgment are always a part of the role. A breach of ethical behavior can result in the removal of certification through a grievance procedure. (See RID enforcement: https://rid.org/ethics/enforcement-procedures/)

73. Wherein he notes that "several times during both interviews [George] was capable of engaging in basic communication utilizing American sign language [*sic*] when it suited his need to do so."

74. Joos (1967, pp. 11–18).

75. Not all of the students in ASL classes intend to become interpreters.

76. The Deaf community is based on networks of personal connections rather than on geography, and so the students cannot simply travel to the "home country." A minority of students are from families where they learned ASL as a heritage language, and another minority of students do manage to make their way into this community network and so become more fluent.

77. The availability of qualified interpreters varies significantly by geographic region and by population for whom the interpreters work.

78. They work for faculty members as well as for students, for systems analysts as well as for factory workers, and for attorneys as well as for defendants.

79. Survey of certified interpreters in Washington state in 2005.

80. Exceptions include doing translation from a written text or working in a group of deaf signers, interpreting for a deafblind person using either modified ASL or Protactile.

81. The specialist certification for interpreting in legal situations (SC:L) is a much better indicator of qualifications to work within the criminal justice system. Unfortunately, for logistical reasons, the test for this specialist certification has been temporarily suspended as of this writing.

82. Interpreters who are deaf are also certified by the Center for the Assessment of Sign Language Interpretation (see previously) identified as certified deaf interpreter (CDI). Requirements to obtain the CDI were updated in 2014. Beldon (2014) explained the changes (https://www.youtube.com/watch?v=oU1Y8TvMpP0).

83. Including a variety of ASL such as Protactile (PT; Edwards, 2014).

84. Public Law 94-142, also known as the Education for All Handicapped Children Act (EAHCA) of 1975, is the landmark federal legislation pertaining to the education of children with disabilities.

85. Commonly referred to as the ADA, 42 U.S.C. § 12141 *et seq*.

86. Public Law 104-104, 110 Stat. 56 (1996).

87. Deaf attorneys and judges are professionals, able to manage their own communication, experienced, and knowledgeable in the use of interpreters with procedures in place.

88. The perception of sound may be distorted such that a person can hear but not understand speech. Hearing is measured by audiologists along two axes: decibels or loudness, and Hertz or pitch.

89. Senior citizens, for example, who have gradually become deaf with age, do not typically learn a sign language.

90. Family members or students of ASL in college, for example.

91. These businesses should demonstrate a record of the ability to fill requests appropriately, and not simply a statement of their ability, or an avowed willingness "to learn."

92. See, for example, an article on Citylimits.org titled "Shortage of Sign Language Interpreters in City Courts Creates delays" https://citylimits.org/2019/09/23/shortage-of-sign-language-interpreters-in-city-courts-creates-delays/

93. Agencies that are "one-stop shops" offering rosters of spoken language interpreters and certified ASL interpreters simply schedule interpreters; that is, they are not qualified to match teams of interpreters with individual deaf people whose primary language they do not know and are not equipped to evaluate.

94. This is not to say that there is never any bias on the part of an interpreter but rather to recommend the use of three teams for serious cases. The topic is complex and beyond the scope of this chapter (Metzger, 1999).

95. Or the folktale of the interpreter who betrays an innocent farmer and the Mafioso who hired her to keep the money for herself.

REFERENCES

Adams, D. W. (1996). *Education for extinction: American Indians and the boarding school experience, 1875–1928*. University of Kansas.

Alexander, M. (2012). *The new Jim Crow: Mass incarceration in the age of colorblindness*. The New Press.

American Council on the Teaching of Foreign Languages. (2012). *Proficiency guidelines 2012*. https://www.actfl.org/publications/guidelines-and-manuals/actfl-proficiency-guidelines-2012

Americans With Disabilities Act of 1990, Pub. L. No. 101–336, 104 Stat. 328 (1990).

Anderson, C. (2017). *White rage: The unspoken truth of our racial divide*. Bloomsbury.

Baker, C., & Cokely, D. (1980). *American Sign Language: A teacher's resource on grammar and culture*. TJ Publishers.

Ball, C. (2013). *Legacies and legends: History of interpreter education from 1800 to the 21st century*. Interpreting Consolidated.

Ballin, A. (1998). *The deaf-mute howls*. Gallaudet University Press.

Basas, C. G. (2018, February 12). *Short bus to social justice*. Ignite Education Lab. https://www.youtube.com/watch?v=KCZyyqgsQ_s&frags=pl%2Cwn

Battison, R. (1978). *Lexical borrowing in American Sign Language*. Linstok Press.

Bauman, H. D., & Murray, J. J. (Eds.). (2014). *Deaf gain: Raising the stakes for human diversity*. University of Minnesota Press.

Baynton, D. (1996). *Forbidden signs: American culture and the campaign against sign language.* The University of Chicago Press.

Bechter, F. (2008). The deaf convert culture and its lessons for deaf theory. In H-D. Bauman (Ed.), *Open your eyes: Deaf studies talking* (pp. 60–79). University of Minnesota Press.

Beldon, J. (2014). *Certified deaf interpreter (CDI) requirements.* https://www.youtube.com/watch?v=oU1Y8TvMpP0

Bennet, A. (1985). Contextualization conventions. In A. Bennet (Ed.), *Language and social identity studies in interactional sociolinguistics* (2nd ed., pp. 95–107). Cambridge University Press.

Bienvenu, M J. (2015). *Bilingualism: Are sign language interpreters bilinguals?* Available from Street Leverage Live. https://www.youtube.com/watch?v=QfT3BvfCsVo&t=11s&frags=pl%2Cwn

Brasel, B. B. (1976). The effects of fatigue on the competence of interpreters for the deaf. In H. J. Murphy (Ed.), *Selected readings in the integration of deaf students at CSUN. Number 1, center on deafness publication series* (pp. 19–23). California State University at Northridge. https://files.eric.ed.gov/fulltext/ED123812.pdf

Brueggemann, B. J. (2008). Think-between: A deaf studies commonplace book. In H-D. L. Bauman (Ed.), *Open your eyes: Deaf studies talking* (pp. 35–41). University of Minnesota Press.

Burch, S. (2002). *Signs of resistance: American deaf cultural history, 1900–1942.* New York University Press.

Christie, K., Wilkins, D. M., McDonald, B. H., & Neuroth-Gimbrone, C. (1999). Get to the point: Academic bilingualism and discourse in American Sign Language and written English. In E. A. Winston (Ed.), *Storytelling and conversation discourse in deaf communities* (pp. 162–177). Gallaudet University Press.

Clyne, M. (1994). *Inter-cultural communication at work: Cultural values in discourse.* Cambridge University Press.

Cokely, D. (1992). *Interpretation: A sociolinguistic model.* Linstok Press.

Cokely, D. (2001). Interpreting culturally rich realities: Research implications for successful interpretation. *Journal of Interpretation,* 1–46.

Cokely, D. (2013). *Sign language interpreters: The importance of the day before.* Street Leverage Live. https://live.streetleverage.com/tag/streetleverage-live/

Condon, J. C., & Yousef, F. S. (1975). *An introduction to intercultural communication.* Bobbs-Merrill.

David, E. J. R. (Ed.). (2014). *Internalized oppression: The psychology of marginalized groups.* Springer.

Davis, L. (1995). *Enforcing normalcy: Disability, deafness, and the body.* Verso.

Dulay, H. C., Burt, M. K., & Krashen, S. K. (1982). *Language two.* Oxford University Press.

Education For All Handicapped Children Act of 1975, P. Law No. 94-142, 89 Stat. 773 (1975).

Edwards, T. (2014). *Language emergence in the Seattle deafblind community* [Unpublished doctoral dissertation]. University of California, Berkeley.

Fairclough, N. (1989). *Language and power.* Longman.

Fairclough, N. (1992). *Discourse and social change.* Polity Press.

Fant, L. (1990). *Silver threads: A personal look at the first twenty-five years of the Registry of Interpreters for the Deaf.* Registry of Interpreters for the Deaf.

Gertz, G. (2008). Dysconscious audism: A theoretical proposition. In H-D. L. Bauman (Ed.), *Open your eyes: Deaf studies talking* (pp. 219–234). University of Minnesota Press.

Gibbons, J. (2003). *Forensic linguistics: An introduction to language in the justice system.* Blackwell Publishing.

Graybill, P. (2015). *Genuine confidence: Implicit and explicit meaning; implications for sign language interpreters.* Street Leverage Live. https://streetleverage.com/live_presentations/implicit-explicit-meaning-implications-for-sign-language-interpreters/

Grosjean, F. (1982). *Life with two languages: An introduction to bilingualism.* Harvard University Press.

Guenther, P. F. (1962). Faithful ugliness or faithless beauty: The translator's problem. *The German Quarterly, 35*(4), 504–510. https://doi.org/10.2307/401586

Gulati, S. (2014, April 1). *Language deprivation syndrome* [Lecture]. Brown University, Providence, RI. https://www.youtube.com/watch?v=8yy_K6VtHJw

Gulati, S. (2019). Language deprivation syndrome. In N. S. Glickman & W. C. Hall (Eds.), *Language deprivation and deaf mental health.* Routledge.

Gumperz, J. (Ed.). (1982). *Discourse strategies.* Cambridge University Press.

Gumperz, J. J., Aulakh G., & Kaltman, H. (1987). Thematic structure and progression in discourse. In J. J. Gumperz (Ed.), *Language and social identity* (pp. 22–56). Cambridge University Press.

Gutierrez, P. S. (1998). The relationship of educational policy to language and cognition in deaf children. In C. Lucas (Ed.), *Pinky extension and eye gaze: Language use in deaf communities* (pp. 103–134). Gallaudet University Press.

Hauser, P. C., Finch, K. L., & Hauser, A. B. (Eds.). (2008). *Deaf professionals and designated interpreters: A new paradigm.* Gallaudet University Press.

Hefler, J. (2012, March 16). Freeholders deaf to cries of hospital sales critics. *Philadelphia Inquirer.* https://www.inquirer.com/philly/blogs/burlington/Freeholders-Deaf-To-Cries-Of-Hospital-Sale-Critics.html

Hill, J. C. (2012). *Language attitudes in the American deaf community.* Gallaudet University Press.

Hoopes, R. (2003). Trampling Miranda: Interrogating deaf suspects. In C. Lucas (Ed.), *Language and the law in deaf communities* (pp. 21–50). Gallaudet University Press.

Humphries, T., Kushalnagar, P., Mathur, G., Napoli, D. J., Padden, C., Rathman, C., & Smith, S. (2017). Discourses of prejudice in the professions: The case of sign languages. *Journal of Medical Ethics, 43*(9), 648–652. https://doi.org/10.1136/medethics-2015-103242

Individuals With Disabilities Education Act, 20 U.S.C. § 1400 *et seq.* (2004).

Jacobs, L. M. (1980). *A deaf adult speaks out* (2nd ed.). Gallaudet College.

Jankowski, K. A. (1997). *Deaf empowerment: Emergence, struggle, and rhetoric.* Gallaudet Press.

Joos, M. (1967). *The five clocks: A linguistic excursion into the five styles of English usage.* Harcourt, Brace, & World.

Kannapell, B. (1993). *Language choice—identity choice: A sociolinguistics study of deaf college students.* Linstok Press.

Kendon, A. (2004). *Gesture: Visible action as utterance.* Cambridge University Press.

Klima, E., & Bellugi, U. (1979). *Signs of language.* Harvard University Press.

Kolb, R. (2016, September 28). The deaf body in public space. *The New York Times.* https://www.nytimes.com/2016/09/28/opinion/the-deaf-body-in-public-space.html

Ladd, P. (2003). *Understanding deaf culture: In search of deafhood.* Multilingual Matters.

Ladd, P. (2008). Colonialism and resistance: A brief history of deafhood. In H-D. L. Bauman (Ed.), *Open your eyes: Deaf studies talking* (pp. 42–59). University of Minnesota Press.

Lane, H. (1992). *The mask of benevolence: Disabling the deaf community.* Knopf.

Lane, H., Pillard, R. C., & Hedberg, U. (2011). *People of the eye: Deaf ethnicity and ancestry.* Oxford University Press.

Larson, M. L. (1998). *Meaning-based translation: A guide to cross-language equivalence* (2nd ed.). University Press of America.

Lawrence, S. (1994). Discourse: English to ASL expansion. In E. A. Winston (Ed.), *Mapping our course: A collaborative venture.* (pp. 205–215). CIT.

Levesque, J. (1991). Do we continue this tragedy? In L. Bragg (Ed.), *Deaf world: A historical reader and primary sourcebook* (pp. 205–206). New York University Press.

Lewis, V. A. (2000). The dramaturgy of disability. In S. Crutchfield & M. Epstein (Eds.), *Points of contact: Disability, art, and culture* (pp. 93–108). University of Michigan Press.

Longmore, P. K. (2003). *Why I burned my book and other essays on disability.* Temple University Press.

Longmore, P. K., & Umansky, L. (Eds.). (2001). *The new disability history: American perspectives.* New York University Press.

Lucas, C. (Ed.). (1996). *Multicultural aspects of sociolinguists in deaf communities.* Gallaudet University Press.

Lucas, C., Bayley, R., Valli, C., Rose, M., & Wolf, A. (2001). Sociolinguistic variation. In C. Lucas (Ed.), *The sociolinguistics of sign languages* (pp. 61–110). Cambridge University Press.

Lucas, C., & Valli, C. (1989). Language contact in the American deaf community. In C. Lucas (Ed.), *The sociolinguistics of the deaf community* (pp. 11–40). Academic Press.

Mathers, C. (2007). *Sign language interpreters in court: Understanding best practices.* Author House.

Mathers, C. (2009). *The deaf interpreter in court: An accommodation that is more than reasonable.* National Consortium of Interpreter Education Centers. http://www.interpretereducation.org/wp-content/uploads/2011/06/Deaf-Interpreter-in-Court_NCIEC2009.pdf

Matoesian, G. M. (2001). *Law and the language of identity: Discourse in the William Kennedy Smith rape trial.* Oxford University Press.

Merriam-Webster. (2009). *Merriam-Webster's collegiate dictionary* (11th ed.).

Metzger, M. (1999). *Sign language interpreting: Deconstructing the myth of neutrality.* Gallaudet University Press.

Montrul, S. (2016). *The acquisition of heritage languages.* Cambridge University Press.

Morin, R., & Stepler, R. (2016, September 29). *The racial confidence gap in police performance.* Pew Research Center. http://www.pewsocialtrends.org/2016/09/29/the-racial-confidence-gap-in-police-performance/

Moser-Mercer, B., Kunzli, A., & Korac, M. (1998, January). Prolonged turns in interpreting: Effects on quality, physiological and psychological stress (Pilot study). *Interpreting, 3*(1), 47–64. https://doi.org/10.1075/intp.3.1.03mos

Neidle, C., Kegl, J., MacLaughlin, D., Bahan, B., & Lee, R. G. (2000). *The syntax of American sign language: Functional categories and hierarchical structure.* The MIT Press.

Nippold, M. A. (2007). *Later language development: School-age children, adolescents, and young adults* (3rd ed.). PRO-ED.

Office for Civil Rights. (1978). *Section 504 of the Rehabilitation Act of 1973. Fact sheet: Handicapped persons rights under federal law.* Department of Health, Education, and Welfare.

Oliva, G. A. (2004). *Alone in the mainstream: A deaf woman remembers public school.* Gallaudet University.
Ortner, S. B. (2006). *Anthropology and social theory: Culture, power, and the acting subject.* Duke University Press.
Padden, C. (2015, May 13). *Do sign language interpreter accents compromise comprehension?* Street Leverage Live. https://streetleverage.com/live_presentations/do-sign-language-interpreter-accents-compromise-comprehension/
Pennucci, A., Smith, T. B., & Roth, R. I. (2007, June). *Educational services for deaf, hard of hearing, and deaf-blind children in Washington state: Stakeholder views.* Washington State Institute for Public Policy. http://www.wsipp.wa.gov/ReportFile/987/Wsipp_Educational-Services-for-Deaf-Hard-of-Hearing-and-Deaf-Blind-Children-in-Washington-State-Stakeholder-Views_Full-Report.pdf
Ramsey, C. (1989). Language planning in deaf education. In C. Lucas (Ed.), *The sociolinguistics of the deaf community* (pp. 123–146). Academic Press.
Reilly, J., McIntire, M., & Bellugi, U. (1990). The acquisition of conditionals in American Sign Language: Grammaticized facial expressions. *Applied Psycholinguistics, 11*(4), 369–392. https://doi.org/10.1017/S0142716400009632
Ridington, R. (1990). *Little bit know something: Stories in a language of anthropology.* University of Iowa Press.
Robins, R. H., & Crystal, D. (2019). Language. In *Encyclopedia britannica.* https://www.britannica.com/topic/language
Rodriguez, R. (1982). *Hunger of memory: The education of Richard Rodriguez.* Bantam.
Roots, J. (1999). *The politics of visual language: Deafness, language choice, and political socialization.* Carleton University Press.
Russell, D. L. (2002). *Interpreting in legal contexts: Consecutive and simultaneous interpretation.* Linstok Press.
Schiffman, H. F. (1996). *Linguistic culture and language policy.* Routledge.
Schweik, S. M. (2009). *The ugly laws: Disability in public.* New York University Press.
Shuy, R. W. (2003). The language problems of minorities in the legal setting. In C. Lucas (Ed.), *Language and the law in deaf communities* (pp. 1–20). Gallaudet University Press.
Smith, T. B. (2014). Going forward, is interpreting a viable career? [Abstract]. In D. I. J. Hunt & S. Hafer (Eds.), *Our roots: The essence of our future. 2014 Conference of Interpreter Trainers Proceedings* (p. 137). CIT.
Smitherman, G. (1977). *Talkin and testifyin: The language of Black America.* Wayne State University Press.
Stokoe, W. C., Casterline, D. C., & Croneberg, C. G. (1965). *A dictionary of American Sign Language on linguistic principles.* Linstok Press.
Stubbs, M. (1983). *Discourse analysis: The sociolinguistic analysis of natural language.* University of Chicago Press.
Stygall, G. (1994). *Trial language: Differential discourse processing and discursive formation.* John Benjamins.
Tannen, D. (Ed.). (1984). *Conversational style: Analyzing talk among friends.* Ablex.
Tannen, D. (1989). *Talking voices: Repetition, dialogue, and imagery in conversational discourse.* Cambridge University Press.
Tannen, D. (1993). What's in a frame? Surface evidence for underlying expectations. In D. Tannen (Ed.), *Framing in discourse* (pp. 14–54). Oxford University Press.

Tannen, D. (1994). *Gender and discourse*. Oxford University Press.
van Dijk, T. A. (2014). *Discourse and knowledge: A sociocognitive approach*. Cambridge University Press.
Verschueren, J. (1989). English as object and medium of (mis)understanding. In O. Garcia & R. Otheguy (Eds.), *English across cultures. Cultures across English.* (pp. 31–53). De Gruyter Mouton.
Wadensjö, C. (2002). The double role of the dialogue interpreter. In F. Pöchhacker & M. Schlesinger (Eds.), *The interpreting studies reader* (pp. 354–370). Routledge.
Wei, L. (2000). Dimensions of bilingualism. In L. Wei (Ed.), *The bilingualism reader* (pp. 3–25). Routledge.
Wierzbicka, A. (2003). *Cross-cultural pragmatics: The semantics of human interaction* (2nd ed.). De Gruyter Mouton.

Part III

Legal Aspects

8

Deafness, the Individuals With Disabilities Education Act, and the Juvenile Delinquency System

Daniel Shaw

Approximately 2 to 3 of every 1,000 children born in the United States have a congenital hearing loss in one or both ears (Gaffney et al., 2005). There is very little research regarding the correlation between deafness and mental health (Glickman, 2013). Many studies (see, for example, Ohre et al., 2011) suggest that a disproportionate number of deaf individuals are more likely to experience depression, anxiety, and substance abuse as compared with hearing people. This has been sought to be explained by various hypotheses, such as a lack of communication access with family members and the community at large and a lack of appropriate mental health services. Nonetheless, it is believed that mental health issues and substance abuse issues lead to incarceration (Lyons et al., 2001). This presents a problem for deaf youth.

An obvious problem for deaf youth in the United States is how we treat mental health and substance abuse. Generally, mental health and substance abuse are treated through some form of therapy involving one-to-one or group communication. For many deaf individuals, this is a challenging endeavor. The moment an interpreter is involved in the situation, what is meant to be an intimate conversation is lost by design. Furthermore, there are very few deaf trained mental health practitioners and even fewer who are fluent in American Sign Language (ASL). And we know that communication deprivation is directly linked to mental health (Hindley, 2005). In turn, mental health issues become a catalyst for incarceration (Atkins et al., 1999). The lack of appropriate mental health and substance abuse services for deaf individuals cannot be ignored and is directly related to the incarceration of deaf youth.

As advocates for deaf youth, it is critical that we understand what supports and services are available to help deaf youth deal with issues of depression, anxiety, and substance abuse. The purpose of this chapter is to focus on the correlation between deafness, the Individuals With Disabilities Education Act (IDEA), and the juvenile delinquency system.

BRIEF HISTORY OF SPECIAL EDUCATION AND THE INDIVIDUALS WITH DISABILITIES EDUCATION ACT

Prior to the mid-18th century, individuals with disabilities were not a recognized group of people as much as they were viewed as a social liability. Individuals were not identified by their unique types of needs but, rather, were all lumped together under the broad banner of *idiot* (Statutes [1907], 34:899; U.S. Public Health Service, Regulations, 30–31).

In the United States, it was not until the 19th and 20th centuries that educational institutions began to be developed for individuals with disabilities. Most of these programs were either private or residential, and this prevented the majority of youth with special needs from attending. In 1817, Thomas Gallaudet started the first school for deaf people (https://www.gallaudet.edu/about/history-and-traditions/thomas-hopkins-gallaudet). In the mid-1800s, Samuel Gridley founded what is known as the Perkins Institution—the first school for the blind (Hall, 2008). And in 1848, Samuel Gridley developed schools for "feebleminded" children (https://www.brown.edu/Administration/News_Bureau/Databases/Encyclopedia/search.php?serial=H0280). What began as a humanitarian movement in the 19th century to address injustices against youth with special needs also contributed to institutionalization and segregation of many individuals with disabilities because these settings were neither publicly funded nor integrated into public schools.

It was not until the 20th century that we began to see a clear path toward desegregation and inclusive practice for youth with special needs. In 1941, Elise Martens, a senior specialist in the United States Office of Education, issued a scathing report, titled "Education of Exceptional Children" (Martens, 1941). The report highlighted the numerous issues facing American public schools in the education of children with special needs.

But the greatest catalyst in educating children with special needs in public school came in a U.S. Supreme Court decision dealing with racial segregation in America's public schools. In 1954, the U.S. Supreme Court issued what is largely recognized as the most pivotal public education rights decision in *Brown v. Board of Education* ("*Brown*") (1954). In *Brown*, the Supreme Court recognized that segregation had no place in public education. *Brown* not only inspired the civil rights movement, which resulted in the Civil Rights Act of 1964, but also inspired individuals with disabilities, parents, teachers, and others to begin to advocate for the desegregation of children with special needs from public education (Yell & Rogers, 1998).

In 1965, U.S. President Lyndon B. Johnson signed the Elementary and Secondary Education Act, which included funding for public schools to provide services for children with special needs (P.L. 89–10; 79 Stat. 27). However, the impetus for significant change came with two cases in 1970 that highlighted the challenges faced by children with special needs in public schools.

In 1971, a federal court in *Pennsylvania Ass'n for Retarded Children v. Commonwealth* (*PARC*) dealt with the issue of excluding children with intellectual disabilities from public schools (*PARC*, 1971). In *PARC*, the court recognized the importance of a free and appropriate public education in the least restrictive environment when it was ordered:

> It is the Commonwealth's obligation to place each mentally retarded child in a free, public program of education and training appropriate to the child's capacity, within the context of a presumption that, among the alternative programs of education and training required by statute to be available, *placement in a regular public school class is preferable to placement in a special public school class and placement in a special public school class is preferable to placement in any other type of program of education and training.*

The *PARC* case recognized that parents and their children had a protected right to a free public education. The court noted the importance of ensuring the right to a continuum of placement options in which a placement in a regular public school environment is *preferable* to any other placement.

In 1972, a federal court in *Mills v. Board of Education of District of Columbia* ("*Mills*") dealt with the practice of suspending, expelling, and excluding children with special needs from public school (1972). In *Mills*, the court found that the District of Columbia had failed to provide a public education to children with special needs. More important, the court determined that children with special needs could not be excluded from public school absent due process of law.

Because of *PARC* and *Mills*, national attention focused on the treatment of children with special needs in public education. In 1972, Congress embarked on an investigation into the status of children with unique and special needs and found that millions of children with special needs were not receiving an appropriate education (U.S.C.C.A.N., 1975, p. 1433). On November 19, 1975, Public Law 94–142 was enacted with the clear purpose, rooted in years of civil rights litigation, of ensuring children with special needs were not forced into segregated environments absent a meaningful attempt to educate those children in America's public schools. Public Law 94–142 has been amended frequently over the years and is now known as IDEA.

In enacting the IDEA, Congress found that it was an essential element of our national policy to improve the educational outcomes for individuals with disabilities, which had been impeded by low expectations and insufficient focus on proven methodologies to teach disabled youth (20 U.S.C. § 1400(c)(1) & (4)). The IDEA ensures that students with disabilities—such as deaf students—have access to special education and related services through an individualized education plan (IEP).

BRIEF HISTORY OF THE JUVENILE DELINQUENCY SYSTEM

For just about 100 years, the United States has defined the adult criminal justice system and the juvenile delinquency systems differently. The juvenile delinquency system was founded on the presumption that children were worthy of rehabilitation and that society had an obligation to foster youth offenders to become productive members of society. The Juvenile Justice and Delinquency Prevention Act of 1974 codified the idea of diverting delinquent youth from the formal, punitive process of the adult justice system. Although each state has separate statutes providing the framework for juvenile criminal justice, the underlying philosophy that youth offenders can be rehabilitated is the same.

For example, the juvenile system in California is described, per relevant statutes, as noncriminal. California Welfare and Institutions Code section 203 provides that "[a]n order adjudging a minor to be a ward of the juvenile court *shall not be deemed a conviction of a crime* for any purpose, nor *shall a proceeding in the juvenile court be deemed a criminal proceeding*." Furthermore, in describing the purpose of the juvenile system, California Welfare and Institutions Code Section 202 states, "[m]inors under the jurisdiction of the juvenile court who are in need of protective services *shall receive care, treatment, and guidance consistent with their best interests and the best interests of the public*."

According to the U.S. Department of Education, there are approximately 54,000 youth residing in juvenile correction facilities on any given day. There is little credible research analyzing how many of those youth have disabilities. Estimates highlight that approximately 70% of youth encountering the juvenile delinquency system suffer from a mental health disorder (Shufelt & Cocozza, 2006).

It is overwhelmingly clear that the youth who encounter the juvenile justice system have multifaceted needs. The notion that the juvenile delinquency system alone can rehabilitate these youth is unsustainable. The goal of rehabilitation becomes even more daunting for deaf youth because they make up only a small percentage of incarcerated youth. The percentage of delinquent youth who are deaf is not specifically provided by the data. However, according to the National Center for Education Statistics, deaf students (including hard of hearing and Deafblind students) make up a little more than 1% of the total number of children served under the IDEA. Thus, it is easy to conclude that only a very small percentage of juvenile delinquents are deaf.

Most incarcerated disabled youth are not provided the basic educational services they are entitled to (Twomey, 2008). There are few juvenile detention facilities, if any, prepared to meet the needs of deaf youth. Incarcerated deaf youth are still entitled to their IDEA services. However, despite the IDEA, little has been done to ensure that incarcerated deaf youth get the services they are entitled to. There is a severe shortage of mental health professionals with the training and experience to assess deaf individuals (Luckner & Bowen, 2006). In 2015, according to the National Association of School Psychologists, fewer than 2% of practicing school psychologists were fluent in ASL, and, furthermore, there are very few mental health measures that are designed for deaf students (Fellinger et al., 2012). Ultimately, incarcerated deaf youth are rarely appropriately diagnosed and treated with effective mental health interventions using their mode of communication.

THE IDEA AND THE DELINQUENCY SYSTEM

Perhaps the greatest tool preventing deaf youth from being swallowed up by the youth delinquency system is the IDEA, which guarantees that every child with a disability who is between the ages of 3 and 21 will have access to a free and appropriate public education (FAPE) (20 U.S.C. § 1412(a)(1)(A)). The IDEA is premised on the understanding that it is an essential element of national policy to ensure youth with disabilities are afforded "equality of opportunity, full participation, independent living, and economic self-sufficiency" (20 U.S.C. § 1400(c)(1)). More important, this is a federal right that continues even if a deaf youth becomes involved in the juvenile delinquency process (20 U.S.C. § 1412(a)(1)). There is, however, one caveat. The IDEA does not protect incarcerated adults (between the ages of 18 and 21) if the individual was not identified as eligible for IDEA services prior to incarceration (20 U.S.C. § 1412(a)(1)(B)(ii)(I) & (II)).

It is critical to understand that when a deaf youth becomes involved in the juvenile delinquency system, they do not lose their right to a FAPE. A FAPE is defined as special education, and related services, that are available at no cost to the parent or guardian (20 U.S.C. § 1401(9)). "Special education" is instruction specially designed to meet the unique needs of a child with a disability (20 U.S.C. § 1401(39)). A student's unique needs are to be broadly construed to include the child's academic, social development, health, emotional and communicative needs, and physical and vocational needs (*Seattle Sch. Dist., No. 1*, 1996). Deaf youth, whether incarcerated or not, continue to have a right to special education designed to meet their unique communicative needs.

The IDEA ensures that deaf youth be provided "related services." "Related services" are supportive services that may be required to assist a child in benefiting from special education (20 U.S.C. § 1401(26)). The list is nonexhaustive and can include services such as speech therapy, audiology services, interpreting services, psychological services, counseling services, residential treatment, and social work services (20 U.S.C. § 1401(26)). The IDEA also requires the consideration of "special factors" when developing an IEP (34 C.F.R. 300.324(a)(2)(i)-(v)). Particularly important for deaf youth is that the IDEA requires a school district to provide the communication mode normally used by the individual (e.g., sign language or oral language) (34 C.F.R. 300.29(b)). Additionally, the education agency must provide opportunities for deaf students to engage in direct communication with peers and teachers utilizing their preferred mode of communication and to receive direct instruction in the student's preferred mode of communication (34 C.F.R. 300.324(a)(2)(iv)).

The U.S. Supreme Court has issued two important decisions interpreting the standards advanced by the IDEA. In 1982, the U.S. Supreme Court determined that a deaf youth named Amy Rowley did not require an ASL interpreter in class to receive a FAPE (*Board of Educ. of Hendrick Hudson Central School District, Westchester County v. Rowley*, 1982). The court held that the school district was merely required to create an IEP that provided "some educational benefit." In *Rowley*, the court noted that the student was integrated into a regular education classroom and making grade-level advancement.

In 2017, the U.S. Supreme Court revisited the "some educational benefit" standard in *Endrew F. ex rel. Joseph F. v. Douglas County School Dist. RE-1 (Endrew F.*, 2017*). Endrew F.* dealt with a youth who could not be integrated into a regular classroom. The court determined that given such facts, the IEP must be reasonably calculated to enable the student "to make progress appropriate in light of the child's circumstances." The court refused to set a "bright line rule" or to explain what progress could be expected. Nonetheless, it clearly set a higher standard for students who could not be integrated into a regular education classroom.

It is unclear how *Rowley* and *Endrew F.* will impact deaf youth in the future. What does appear clear, however, is that deaf youths who are educated in a regular classroom and making grade-level progress are held to a lower standard than deaf students who are educated outside a regular classroom and are not making grade-level progress. Nonetheless, the IDEA continues to serve as the most potent tool for addressing the needs of incarcerated deaf youth—as well as preventing incarceration in the first place.

It is believed that the majority of delinquent youth suffer from mental health issues. However, many juvenile delinquency facilities are not prepared to meet the needs of delinquent youth with mental health needs. Research indicates that effective mental health interventions should extend beyond the juvenile detention setting (Underwood & Washington, 2016). If juvenile delinquency systems are struggling to meet the needs of youth with mental health issues, imagine how they are doing meeting the unique needs of deaf youth, particularly when most juvenile courts have little understanding of the IDEA. Not one delinquency facility in the United States specializes in serving deaf youth. For these reasons, it is imperative that the IDEA rights of delinquent deaf youth are protected. The IDEA can serve as a shield in ensuring that deaf youth continue to receive the unique array of special education and related services they are entitled to in an effort to aid in the rehabilitation process prescribed by the Juvenile Justice and Delinquency Prevention Act of 1974.

Some states have recognized the importance of the IDEA in the juvenile delinquency system. For example, the California State Legislature recognized this when it enacted California Rule of Court 5.651. California Rule of Court 5.651 (CA 5.651) exists solely to protect the IDEA rights of wards and dependents of the juvenile court (Ca. St. Fam. Juv. Rule 5.651(a)(1)). This rule applies to all hearings before the juvenile court that can affect a youth's education (Ca. St. Fam. Juv. Rule 5.651(a)(2)). CA 5.651 incorporates the rights that flow from the IDEA, the Americans With Disabilities Act (ADA), and Section 504 of the Rehabilitation Act (Ca. St. Fam. Juv. Rule 5.651(a)(3)). Under CA 5.651, the court must take into account other statutory considerations (e.g., IDEA, ADA, and Section 504) regarding a youth's placement that promotes educational stability (Ca. St. Fam. Juv. Rule 5.651(b)(1)(E)). And the court must determine the youth's special education needs and develop a plan to meet them (Ca. St. Fam. Juv. Rule 5.651(b)(2)). These procedures mandate compliance with the IDEA as the juvenile court determines what to do with incarcerated special education students.

However, many states lack specific legislation to create interplay between the juvenile delinquency system and the IDEA. For deaf youth, such interplay is critical in meeting their unique needs and in preventing recidivism. But even in states like California, where CA 5.651 attempts to protect the rights of deaf delinquent youth, it is rarely implemented with fidelity. Many juvenile courts in California, much like most juvenile courts in the United States, treat IDEA rights as a check-the-box analysis, rarely spending the time needed to understand the unique needs of the youth. Such an approach is even more impactful on deaf youth.

It is imperative that those involved with incarcerated deaf youth familiarize themselves with these protections. Whether or not a state has enacted specific legislation aimed at protecting the IDEA rights of incarcerated youth, the rights that flow from the IDEA are federal rights and are guaranteed regardless of state law.

Although the Juvenile Justice and Delinquency Prevention Act of 1974 codified the idea of diverting youth from the formal punitive process of the adult justice system, federal law has yet to utilize the IDEA as part of the rehabilitative process to the extent possible. Sadly, this has significantly impacted the ability of deaf youth to meaningfully obtain an array of rehabilitative services while incarcerated and to prevent recidivism.

UNATTENDED CONSEQUENCES OF HIGHLY MOBILE DEAF YOUTH

The IDEA is a framework designed specifically to allow flexibility to state recipients in providing IDEA services. However, this flexibility also becomes a major hurdle for some of our most vulnerable youth—that is, deaf youth protected under the IDEA. There is no specificity in the IDEA as to how incarcerated deaf youth are treated under IDEA, which entity is responsible for the youth's right to a FAPE, and how those unique rights are protected provided the complexities of being in a state delinquency system. To be eligible to receive funding under the IDEA, a state or local education agency must ensure that they have enacted effective policy and procedures that offer a FAPE to all eligible children (20 U.S.C. § 1412). But how states develop those policies and procedures can directly affect how incarcerated disabled youth are treated.

There are unattended consequences for deaf youth because of the flexibility offered to states under the IDEA. Using California as an example highlights this issue when we analyze the state's residency laws. Many states have similar types of residency laws. In California, the general rule is that the responsible educational agency for the provision of IDEA services is based on the residency of the parent or legal guardian (California Education Code sections 48200, 48204, and 56028 [definition of parent]). However, the responsible educational agency can become quite fluid under California state law. When deaf youth are incarcerated in California, the responsible educational agency changes from the entity where the parent or guardian resides to the county office of education where the juvenile detention facility is located (California Education Code § 48645.2). Thus, in California, a deaf student arrested for criminal conduct and incarcerated becomes the legal responsibility of an entirely new entity.

This creates many issues. The new entity does not know the student and is now responsible for providing this individual with a FAPE. The new entity likely has little experience serving deaf youth. This serves to undermine the IEP planning process because the responsible decision makers do not know the student or his or her unique needs. A deaf youth could go from a school placement where they are educated alongside other deaf students with an ASL-fluent teacher to a setting with typical students and a teacher who cannot communicate directly with the student without the assistance of an interpreter. This can further isolate deaf youth at a time when they likely require additional supports and services.

Under California law, the county office of education where the juvenile detention facility is housed also becomes financially responsible for the student's IDEA services. This creates a financial burden on these entities when dealing with the complexities of meeting the needs of deaf youth. For example, a deaf youth might require (besides specialized academic instruction using their preferred form of communication) cognitive behavioral therapy or some other form of mental health intervention. It is much costlier to provide such services to deaf youth because they require a clinician fluent in their form of communication and experienced in serving that population.

The IDEA also requires the responsible educational entity to provide students with a continuum of placement options (34 C.F.R. § 300.115(a)). For deaf youth, this can include placement in a general education setting with appropriate supports to placement in a residential treatment center (34 C.F.R. § 300.115(b)(1)). Many deaf incarcerated youths require placement in residential treatment centers. In California, for students placed in a juvenile detention center, the law requires the county office of education to fund a deaf student's placement in a residential treatment center if such a placement is included in the student's IEP (Cal. Code Regs., tit. 2, § 60010, subd. (k)). However, these placements are far more costly than residential treatment centers for hearing students. This creates an incentive for the responsible educational entity to not offer such services to deaf youth. Thus, in California, a county office of education can wait until the student is placed in another setting by the juvenile court to avoid funding an expensive placement because once that student leaves their facility, they are no longer responsible for funding the student's education.

California law complicates this issue even further because when the juvenile court places a deaf youth in a licensed children's institution or foster home, the responsible educational entity is the entity where the institution or home is located (Ed. Code, § 48204, subds. (a)(1) & (6)). If a deaf youth is placed by the juvenile court out of his community, the educational planning process under the IDEA starts over with an entirely new team of educators. A state's fluid residency laws can create a pattern of highly mobile deaf youth treated as moving targets often not being anywhere long enough to get the services the IDEA guarantees. This can also create disputes among different entities as to which entity is financially responsible to fund an expensive placement for deaf youth and also results in substantial delay for deaf youth getting the supports and services they require. If a deaf student is highly mobile (i.e., subjected to multiple placements by the juvenile court), the responsible education agency knows the student is likely to be moved, alleviating their financial responsibility to fund an expensive placement.

THE PATH TO THE YOUTH DELINQUENCY SYSTEM

How deaf children end up in the juvenile delinquency system is complicated and varies from child to child. However, for those who work with these children there are anecdotal trends that share common themes. Here, we will use the case of Bobby to illustrate this complicated path toward incarceration. Bobby's actual name has not been used here to protect his identity. This case study is drawn from the author's personal experience.

Bobby was abandoned by his parents when he was 11 months old. His mother had substance abuse issues, and his father lacked the tool set to carry out his duties. Bobby was raised by his two elderly grandparents. He lost his hearing around age 4 because of meningitis. Although an attempt was made to provide Bobby with cochlear implants, it was short-lived. Bobby's cochlea had ossified because of the illness, making the cochlear implant wholly ineffective.

Bobby received no early intervention services until kindergarten. But even then, subsequent services were insufficient. Bobby resided in a rural community where there were very few deaf youths to communicate with. He spent the first 3 years of public education learning Signing Exact English. Signing Exact English is a type of sign system that attempts to encode spoken English. However, Signing Exact English is not taught in most public schools and has very limited use in the real world because it is rarely utilized by other deaf individuals. Teaching Bobby Signing Exact English made him unable to communicate effectively with other deaf students fluent in ASL.

Around the fourth grade, it was determined that Bobby needed to learn ASL and that the local educational system could not meet his needs. As a result, Bobby was sent to a residential school for deaf students. At age 8, Bobby was forced to leave the care of grandparents and spend 5 days a week far from his home. Because he never learned ASL, he struggled to communicate with other deaf students at his new school. Bobby was alone and not fitting into Deaf culture or the hearing world. Bobby—a boy abandoned by his parents—became depressed about having to be so far away from his grandparents with whom he had bonded. It was determined that Bobby's emotional well-being was deteriorating, so he returned to his rural community and continued to receive inappropriate services.

In junior high, Bobby began to develop serious mental health issues that often manifested in significant maladaptive behavioral outbursts. Bobby began to reject the deaf world and despised being a deaf youth. He longed to be part of the hearing world but found no acceptance because of the language barrier. Bobby had clear mental health issues yet was provided no services to address these budding needs. Moreover, there was no qualified mental health professional trained in assessing deaf students to properly diagnose his mental health issues.

By the end of junior high, Bobby rarely attended school. He began to abuse drugs and alcohol and would spend a lot of time living in homeless encampments. Although initially law enforcement did not take an interest in Bobby because of his deafness (law enforcement did not know what to do with a deaf youth), that too changed. As Bobby began to engage in more significant criminal conduct, he was eventually arrested and incarcerated.

What is clear is that Bobby's path to the youth delinquency system was all too familiar. His mental health issues were largely ignored. Not even once, until he was initially arrested, was Bobby ever evaluated by a deaf psychologist or any mental health professional fluent in ASL. Nor was he ever provided any appropriate mental health interventions. His mental health needs were minimized by a system of care ill-equipped to recognize the internal struggles he was dealing with on a daily basis.

THE PATH BEYOND THE YOUTH DELINQUENCY SYSTEM

Bobby was initially placed in the county juvenile hall in 2012. The local county office of education became responsible for his IDEA services. Approximately 30 days later, he was uprooted from the county that he resided in and placed, by the juvenile court, at a group home in another part of the state that served deaf youth. Bobby was enrolled in the local school district, which then became responsible for IDEA services. Bobby barely attended any school before he eloped to the streets, where he would exchange sexual favors for access to drugs and alcohol, exposing him to more trauma.

Only 5 months after being placed in a group home, Bobby was kicked out of the group home and placed in a youth shelter back in the rural community he came from. Bobby's IDEA services became the responsibility of the local school district where he had been placed. However, Bobby ran away and continued to live on the streets and use drugs. In late 2012, he was arrested for being drunk in public and returned to the juvenile hall in the town in which his grandparents resided (approximately 60 days after being placed within the school district where the youth shelter was located). Again, the educational entity responsible for Bobby's IDEA services changed because in his state the educational entity responsible for his IDEA services changed every time the juvenile court placed him in a different living setting. Bobby remained incarcerated in the juvenile hall for approximately 9 months until mid-2013. During that time, he received no mental health services through his IDEA-mandated educational program.

Bobby was shuttled between four educational entities responsible for his IDEA rights in less than a matter of a year. Each move involved a new group of educators responsible for ensuring that Bobby's IDEA rights were safeguarded. Each move further eroded his ability to access those rights and his right to appropriate intervention based on his unique needs as a deaf youth.

In 2013, Bobby was, for the first time, evaluated by an experienced deaf psychologist, who recommended his placement in a residential setting. Bobby was incarcerated in the juvenile hall, but his legal guardians requested the local education agency to provide him with placement in a residential treatment setting for deaf youth. However, the education agency, on the basis of an evaluation conducted by a school psychologist, claimed that Bobby did not require a residential placement as part of his IDEA services. The psychologist had, however, never evaluated deaf students (except one), was not fluent in ASL, and minimized Bobby's significant mental health needs. Furthermore, the school psychologist determined that Bobby had no mental health issues other than dysthymia (i.e., minor depression).

As a result, Bobby's guardians sought a due process hearing against the various educational entities involved in his case to compel them to provide a placement in a residential treatment center for deaf youth as part of his IDEA services. After a 7-day trial, the administrative law judge (ALJ) issued a 75-page decision finding that Bobby's IDEA rights had been severely violated. The ALJ ordered the educational entities to fund numerous evaluations by individuals trained in assessing deaf students and approximately 100 hours of compensatory educational services in various areas. Most important, the ALJ found that Bobby's mental health needs had been significantly misunderstood by the local school district and juvenile hall because the mental health professionals involved had no experience assessing or working with deaf students.

The ALJ ordered the educational entities to fund Bobby's placement in a residential treatment center designed to serve deaf students. If no such placement could be found, the educational entities were ordered to fund Bobby's placement in a residential treatment center with numerous educational, developmental, and behavior services specifically designed for deaf youth. The ALJ made her point clear: Bobby's case was caused by a common mistake made by educational professionals who were not experienced or trained in working with deaf individuals, resulting in the minimization of Bobby's individual and unique needs.

Bobby's case not only highlights some of the problems faced by deaf delinquent youth, but also illustrates how the IDEA can provide additional tools to prevent the incarceration of deaf youth. It cannot be understated that Bobby's unique needs as a deaf mentally ill youth went unmet for years. Had appropriate IDEA services been provided to him years before his incarceration, he would have never likely ended up in the delinquency system. Bobby would not have been a highly mobile deaf youth moving from one school setting to another simply because no one knew how to meet his unique needs. Had he been provided with educators and clinicians trained in serving deaf individuals, his significant mental health needs would not have gone unmet or unrecognized.

Multiple studies have shown how juvenile delinquency systems fail to meet the needs of most disabled youth in the system. However, deaf youth are even more vulnerable to such disparate treatment because they represent such a small proportion of juvenile delinquent youth. Very few placements in the entire United States specialize in working with deaf delinquent youth. It is critical that individuals involved in cases such as Bobby's are familiar with a deaf student's IDEA rights.

CONCLUSION

Bobby's story helps us understand the often-ignored path many deaf youth take to the delinquency system, the complexities of serving deaf youth, how the IDEA can aid in supporting deaf youth, and how the IDEA (or relevant state law) can undermine the need to address the unique issues of deaf youth once incarcerated. To better address these issues, it is imperative that deaf youth, parents, advocates, attorneys, educators, social workers, judges, and all those involved in raising our deaf youth familiarize themselves with the IDEA. Furthermore, it is imperative that we, as advocates for deaf youth, consider the following:

1. Identifying methods to foster healthy identities for deaf individuals, in part, by respecting their preferred mode of communication, especially during incarceration;
2. The need to focus on developing state laws aimed at protecting deaf youth to ensure that during incarceration their IDEA, Title II, and Section 504 rights are realized;
3. Ensuring that deaf youth have access to quality ASL instruction and interpreters as guaranteed by the IDEA;
4. Ensuring that deaf youth have access to trained school-based mental health professionals fluent in their mode of communication and trained in their unique needs;
5. Fostering the development of more standardized assessments and mental health measures for deaf youth that can be used by school districts;
6. Fostering the development of residential treatment centers that focus solely on deaf youth;
7. Providing more academic research on the correlation between mental health and deafness;

8. Providing more academic research on the effectiveness of traditional mental health interventions with deaf youth;
9. Ensuring that deaf youth are provided evidence-based interventions under the IDEA beginning at a very young age;
10. Continuing to educate juvenile courts about the unique needs of deaf youth.

One of the keys to prevention seems to be early intervention, with educators and clinicians trained in identifying deaf needs, as well as the availability of better assessment tools and deaf trained assessors. Although we have only a few—if any—appropriate residential treatment center placements for deaf youth, our focus should be on preventing our youth from even getting to that point.

REFERENCES

Atkins, D. L., Pumariega, A. J., Rogers, K., Montgomery, L., Nybro, C., Jeffers, G., & Sease, F. (1999). Mental health and incarcerated youth. I: Prevalence and nature of psychopathology. *Journal of Child and Family Studies, 8*, 193–204. https://doi.org/10.1023/A:1022040018365

Board of Education of Hendrick Hudson Central School Dist., Westchester County v. Rowley. (1982) 458 U.S. 176, 177 [102 S.Ct. 3034, 3036, 73 L.Ed.2d 690].

Brown v. Board of Education, 347 U.S. 483 (1954).

California Code of Regulations; Cal. Code Regs., tit. 2, § 60010, subd. (k).

California Ed. Code, § 48200.

California Ed. Code, § 48204, (a)(1), & (6).

California Ed. Code, § 48645.2.

California Ed. Code, § 56028.

California Rule of Court; Ca. St. Fam. Juv. Rule 5.651(a)(1).

California Rule of Court; Ca. St. Fam. Juv. Rule 5.651(a)(2).

California Rule of Court; Ca. St. Fam. Juv. Rule 5.651(a)(3).

California Rule of Court; Ca. St. Fam. Juv. Rule 5.651(b)(1)(E).

California Rule of Court; Ca. St. Fam. Juv. Rule 5.651(b)(2).

California Welf. & Inst. Code, § 202.

California Welf. & Inst. Code, § 203.

Elementary and Secondary Education Act of 1965. H. R. 2362, 89th Cong., 1st sess., P. Law 89-10 (1965).

Endrew, F. ex rel. Joseph F. v. Douglas County School Dist. RE-1 (2017) 137 S.Ct. 988, 991 [197 L.Ed.2d 335].

Fellinger, J., Holzinger, D., & Pollard, R. (2012). Mental health of deaf people. *Lancet, 379*(9820), 1037–1044. https://doi.org/10.1016/S0140-6736(11)61143-4

Gaffney, M., Eichwald, J., Grosse, M. A., & Mason, C. A. (2010, March 5). Identifying infants with hearing loss—United States, 1999–2007. *Centers for Disease Control Morbidity and Mortality Weekly, 59*(8), 220–223. https://www.cdc.gov/mmwr/preview/mmwrhtml/mm5908a2.htm

Glickman, N. (2013). *Deaf mental health care*. Routledge.

Hall, E. M. (2008). *Howe, Dr. Samuel Gridley*. Center on Philanthropy at Indiana University. http://learningtogive.org/papers/paper105.html

Hindley, P. (2005). Mental health problems in deaf children. *Current Pediatrics, 15*, 114–119. https://doi.org/10.1016/j.cupe.2004.12.008
Individuals With Disabilities Education Act of 2014; 20 U.S.C. § 1400.
Individuals With Disabilities Education Act of 2014; 20 U.S.C. § 1400(c)(1) & (4).
Individuals With Disabilities Education Act of 2014; 20 U.S.C. § 1401(9).
Individuals With Disabilities Education Act of 2014; 20 U.S.C. § 1401(26).
Individuals With Disabilities Education Act of 2014; 20 U.S.C. § 1401(39).
Individuals With Disabilities Education Act of 2014; 20 U.S.C. § 1401(26)(A).
Individuals With Disabilities Education Act of 2014; 20 U.S.C. § 1412.
Individuals With Disabilities Education Act of 2014; 20 U.S.C. § 1412(a)(1).
Individuals With Disabilities Education Act of 2014; 20 U.S.C. § 1412(a)(1)(A).
Individuals With Disabilities Education Act of 2014; 20 U.S.C. § 1412(a)(1)(B)(ii)(I) & (II).
Juvenile Justice and Dequincy Prevention Act of 1974; 42 U.S.C. § 5600.
Luckner, J., & Bowen, S. (2006). Assessment practices of professionals serving students who are deaf or hard of hearing: An initial investigation. *American Annals of the Deaf, 151*(4), 410–417. https://doi.org/10.1353/aad.2006.0046
Lyons, J., Baerger, D., Quigley, P., Erlich, J., & Griffen, E. (2001, June). Mental health service needs of juvenile offenders: A comparison of detention, incarceration, and treatment settings. *Journal of Children's Services, 4*(2), 69–85. https://doi.org/10.1207/S15326918CS0402_2
Martens, E. L. (1941). State supervisory programs for the education of exceptional children. *United States Office of Education Bulletin, 6* (Monograph No. 10).
Mills v. Board of Education of District of Columbia, 348 F. Supp. 866 (D. DC 1972).
Ohre, B., Tetzchner, S., & Falkum, E. (2011). Deaf adults and mental health: A review of recent research on the prevalence and distribution of psychiatric symptoms and disorders in the prelingually deaf adult population. *International Journal on Mental Health and Deafness, 1*(1), 3–22.
Pennsylvania Assn. for Retarded Children v. Commonwealth, 334 F. Supp. 1257 (E.D. Pa 1971).
Seattle Sch. Dist., No. 1 v. B.S., 82 F.3d 1493, 1500 (9th Cir. 1996) (Seattle), citing H.R. Rep. No. 410, 1983 U.S.C.C.A.N. 2088, 2106.
Shufelt, J. L., & Cocozza, J. J. (2006, June). *Youth with mental health disorders in the juvenile justice system: Results from a multi-state, multi-system prevalence study* (Research and Program Brief). National Center for Mental Health and Juvenile Justice.
Twomey, K. (2008). The right to education in juvenile detention under state constitutions. *Virginia Law Review, 94*(3), 765–811.
Underwood, L., & Washington, A. (2016). Mental illness and juvenile offenders. *International Journal of Environmental Research and Public Health, 13*(2), 228–242. https://doi.org/10.3390/ijerph13020228
United States Code of Federal Regulations; 34 C.F.R. § 300.115(a).
United States Code of Federal Regulations; 34 C.F.R. § 300.115(b)(1).
United States Code of Federal Regulations; 34 C.F.R. § 300.324(a)(2)(i)-(v).
United States Code of Federal Regulations; 34 C.F.R. § 300.324(a)(2)(iv).
United States Code of Federal Regulations; 34 C.F.R. 300.29(b).
United States Code Congressional and Administrative News 1975 (U.S.C.C.A.N. 1975).
Yell, M. L., & Rogers, E. L. (1998, July–August). The legal history of special education: What a long, strange trip it's been! *Remedial and Special Education, 19*(4), 219–228. https://doi.org/10.1177/074193259801900405

9

Nondiscrimination in the Criminal Justice System: An Examination of the Americans With Disabilities Act and Section 504 of the Rehabilitation Act

Barry C. Taylor and Rachel M. Weisberg

Discrimination within the U.S. criminal justice system is an issue of critical importance, regularly addressed on the news, in political campaigns, and within government and local communities. Although the public discussion is not always focused on issues about disability and deafness, recent statistics suggest that people with disabilities encounter the criminal justice system more frequently than their nondisabled counterparts, demonstrating one of the many reasons this topic is extremely important to the disability community, including deaf people (Bronson et al., 2015). It is essential for all stakeholders to understand the federal laws that protect the rights of deaf people within the criminal justice system: the Americans With Disabilities Act of 1990 (ADA), Section 504 of the Rehabilitation Act (Section 504), Section 255 of the Telecommunications Act of 1996, and the Hearing Aid Compatibility Act of 1988. These laws, as well as the U.S. Constitution, apply to different aspects of the criminal justice system, including law enforcement, correctional facilities, and criminal court proceedings.

This chapter addresses the federal laws that prohibit the criminal justice system from discriminating against deaf people. This chapter starts by providing an overview of the relevant statutory text and regulations and then provides an in-depth review of important case law and settlement agreements in the criminal justice context.

HOW THE ADA AND SECTION 504 PROTECT THE RIGHTS OF DEAF PEOPLE IN THE CRIMINAL JUSTICE SYSTEM

The ADA and Section 504 are federal civil rights laws that prohibit discrimination against people with disabilities in various aspects of life (ADA, 2016a; Rehabilitation Act, 2016a). Title II of the ADA applies to all programs, services, and activities of state and local governments (ADA, 2016b).[1] Section 504 applies only to entities that receive federal financial assistance (Rehabilitation Act, 2016).[2] Even if a state and local entity does not receive federal financial assistance, it still has nondiscrimination obligations under Title II of the ADA. As a practical matter, however, virtually all entities involved in the criminal justice system are state or local entities that receive federal funding, and, thus, the ADA, Section 504, and their respective regulations usually apply. Such entities include state and local law enforcement agencies, correctional facilities, and court judicial systems. The Rehabilitation Act has exclusive jurisdiction with respect to disability discrimination protection for facilities and programs in the criminal justice systems that are managed by the federal government, such as federal prisons.

Title II of the ADA and Section 504 are similar in many respects. They will be referred to interchangeably throughout this chapter unless there is a reason to note a difference. The ADA and Section 504 have both general and specific nondiscrimination requirements. Generally, state and local law enforcement agencies, correctional facilities, and court judicial systems must provide equal access to programs, services, and activities to people with disabilities (ADA, 2016c). Title II provides that that "no qualified individual with a disability shall, by reason of such disability, be excluded from participation in or be denied the benefits of the services, programs, or activities of a public entity, or *be subjected to discrimination by any such entity* [emphasis added]" (ADA, 2016d). Likewise, Section 504 provides that no "qualified individual with a disability shall, solely by reason of her or his disability, be excluded from the participation in, be denied the benefits of, or be subjected to discrimination under any program or activity receiving Federal financial assistance."

Like other government entities covered by the ADA, law enforcement agencies, correctional facilities, and court judicial systems must make reasonable modifications of policy (ADA, 2016e; Judicial Administration, 1991a),[3] provide legally required architectural and programmatic access (Judicial Administration, 1991a), and provide programs and services in the most integrated setting available (ADA, 2016f; Judicial Administration, 1991b).[4] Arguably most important for individuals who are deaf is the obligation that covered entities provide the auxiliary aids necessary to ensure effective communication (ADA, 2016g).[5] Exactly what the requirement to provide effective communication means in the criminal justice context is examined in detail within this chapter.

LEGAL BACKGROUND REGARDING EFFECTIVE COMMUNICATION

Statutory and Regulatory Text

When Congress passed the ADA in 1990, it recognized that people with disabilities "encounter various forms of discrimination," including "communication barriers" (ADA, 2016h). It then defined discrimination to include

> a failure to take such steps as may be necessary to ensure that no individual with a disability is excluded, denied services, segregated, or otherwise treated differently than other individuals because of the absence of auxiliary aids and services unless the entity can demonstrate that taking such steps would fundamentally alter the nature of the good, service, facility, privilege, advantage, or accommodation being offered or would result in an undue burden. (ADA, 2016i)

This statutory requirement has come to be known as the obligation to provide effective communication. For people with communication-related disabilities, including people who are deaf, the ADA's requirement to provide effective communication has proven to be a crucial way to achieve equal access.

The U.S. Department of Justice (DOJ), the federal agency charged with interpreting and enforcing Title II (*C.V. v. Dudek*, 2016) (and Title III, which covers public accommodations) of the ADA, has promulgated regulations that provide additional clarification on the meaning of the effective communications requirements. In 2010, the DOJ amended these regulations, which became effective on March 15, 2011.

The Title II regulations regarding effective communication contain two important requirements. First, they provide that "[a] public entity shall take appropriate steps to ensure that communications with applicants, participants, members of the public, and companions with disabilities are *as effective* [emphasis added] as communications with others" (ADA, 2016j; Judicial Administration, 2010b). Second, they specify that public entities must "furnish appropriate auxiliary aids and services where necessary to afford an individual with a disability an equal opportunity to participate in, and enjoy the benefits of, a service, program, or activity conducted by a public entity" (ADA, 2016k; Judicial Administration, 2010c).

What Are Auxiliary Aids and Services?

The ADA requires the provision of "auxiliary aids and services," and, thus, the logical next question is, what are auxiliary aids and services?

The ADA (2016l) defines this term by listing four categories:

- Qualified interpreters or other effective methods of making aurally delivered materials available to individuals with hearing impairments

- Qualified readers, taped texts, or other effective methods of making visually delivered materials available to individuals with visual impairments
- Acquisition or modification of equipment or devices
- Other similar services and actions

The ADA's regulations include additional examples of possible auxiliary aids and services to ensure communication access for people who are deaf. In addition to "qualified interpreters," the regulations include a host of other possibilities, including the following:

> notetakers; real-time computer-aided transcription services; written materials; exchange of written notes; telephone handset amplifiers; assistive listening devices; assistive listening systems; telephones compatible with hearing aids; closed caption decoders; open and closed captioning, including real-time captioning; voice, text, and video-based telecommunications products and systems, including text telephones (TTYs), videophones, and captioned telephones, or equally effective telecommunications devices; videotext displays; accessible electronic and information technology; or other effective methods of making aurally delivered information available to individuals who are deaf or hard of hearing. (ADA, 2016m; Judicial Administration, 2010)

Notably, and as discussed in more detail later, the regulations also specify that qualified interpreters may be provided "on-site or through video remote interpreting (VRI) services" (ADA, 2016m; Judicial Administration, 2010).

Finally, the regulations reinforce the ADA's text that auxiliary aids and services include the "[a]cquisition or modification of equipment or devices" and "[o]ther similar services and actions" (ADA, 2016m; Judicial Administration, 2010). However, the court cases concerning effective communication do not typically analyze whether something is an auxiliary aid or service. Perhaps this is because of the extensive list of examples in the regulations and the fact that the regulations specify that the list of examples is a nonexclusive list. Instead, a key issue in almost every case involving effective communication is whether a covered entity was required to provide a particular auxiliary aid or service.

Deciding Which Auxiliary Aid or Service to Provide and "Primary Consideration"

A central dispute in most litigation involving effective communication is whether a particular auxiliary aid or service should have been provided. This tends to be a recurring issue in effective communication litigation because the ADA's effective communication requirements do not specify which auxiliary aid should be provided in every instance. To answer this question, one must engage in a highly fact-specific inquiry. There is no one-size-fits-all solution when it comes to the provision of auxiliary aids and services under the ADA.

Instead, there must be an individualized assessment of the nature, length, complexity, context of the communication, and the person's typical method of communication (ADA, 2016n; Judicial Administration, 2010d).

Although it is important for any covered entity to consider the requests made by the deaf person, public entities are held to a higher standard under Title II of the ADA than places of public accommodation under Title III. Under Title II, public entities must give "primary consideration to the requests of individuals with disabilities" (ADA, 2016n; Judicial Administration, 2010d). As a result, public entities have an obligation to consult with and defer to the person with the disability when deciding which auxiliary aid or service to provide. One reason for this is that the person with the communication-related disability is the one most informed about her needs.

The "primary consideration" requirement has been applied in the case law as well. In *Chisolm v. McManimon* (2001), in response to an ADA lawsuit, a detention center asserted that it did not violate the ADA even though it failed to provide an American Sign Language (ASL) interpreter for a deaf inmate for certain complex communications because it employed alternative, but equally effective, auxiliary aids (*Chisolm v. McManimon*, 2001). The court rejected this argument, noting that the "most obvious problem" with this argument is that it conflicts with the "regulatory mandate that a public entity honor a disabled person's choice of auxiliary aid or service" (*Chisolm v. McManimon*, 2001).

Moreover, settlement agreements with public entities regularly require the inclusion of the "primary consideration" language. For example, in 2018, the United States entered into a settlement agreement with the Philadelphia Police Department (PPD), discussed in greater detail in Section III.A.3. Under the terms of this agreement, the PPD agreed that when it determines which auxiliary aid and service to provide for a person who is deaf, it will give "primary consideration" to the person's expressed preference for a particular auxiliary aid or service (*United States v. City of Philadelphia Police*, 2016).[6]

Video Remote Interpreting (VRI)

When the DOJ amended its ADA regulations in 2010, it included a technology called VRI as an example of an auxiliary aid or service. VRI technology connects an off-site interpreter through the use of a videoconferencing system to facilitate communication. Guidance from the DOJ explains that covered entities can choose either VRI or an on-site interpreter "in situations where either would be effective" (U.S. DOJ, 2014). As with many other technologies, VRI can be useful to serve people with disabilities in rural areas where interpreters may not be geographically available and in emergency situations where an interpreter is not available on-site.

However, the DOJ cautions that VRI is not appropriate in all circumstances because there are situations where it will not lead to effective communication. Specifically, VRI will not lead to effective communication where the person who is deaf cannot access the screen owing to his own vision loss or cannot properly position the screen, perhaps because of an injury.

Moreover, if VRI is used, DOJ regulations require that the VRI used meet the following four performance standards:

1. Real-time, full-motion video and audio over a dedicated high-speed, wide-bandwidth video connection or wireless connection that delivers high-quality video images that do not produce lags, choppy, blurry, or grainy images, or irregular pauses in communication
2. A sharply delineated image that is large enough to display the interpreter's face, arms, hands, and fingers, and the participating individual's face, arms, hands, and fingers, regardless of their body position
3. A clear, audible transmission of voices
4. Adequate training to users of the technology and other involved individuals so that they may quickly and efficiently set up and operate the VRI (ADA, 2016o; Judicial Administration, 2010e)

Many people in the Deaf community are concerned about the overreliance on VRI (NAD, 2018). VRI can be an inferior means of communication as compared with an on-site interpreter because VRI has less mobility and less access to visual and auditory cues in the environment. There are also concerns about technological problems when interpretation services are needed and lack of adequate staff training. Because of these limitations, the general consensus in the Deaf community is that VRI should be implemented as a last resort (NAD, 2018).

Although not specific to the criminal justice context, there have been cases challenging the use of VRI, especially when technical issues result in ineffective communication. See, e.g., *Silva v. Baptist Health South Florida* (2017) (reversing and remanding summary judgment where plaintiffs "routinely experienced problems with the VRI devices not working at all or failing to transmit a clear screen image" during visits to a hospital).

Within the criminal justice context, the DOJ has entered into settlement agreements on behalf of the United States, outlining the specific parameters required when a public entity opts to use VRI. A good example of this is the settlement agreement with the Arlington County sheriff in 2016 (*United States v. Elizabeth F. Arthur*, 2016).[7] That settlement agreement involved a person who was deaf and was incarcerated for 40 days. During that time, he repeatedly requested an ASL interpreter for his housing, medical, and classification assessments, as well as for his meeting with the ADA coordinator. Instead of providing a qualified ASL interpreter, however, the Arlington County sheriff used unqualified staff members to facilitate conversation. As part of the settlement agreement, the sheriff agreed that when they used VRI, they would adhere to the four DOJ regulatory requirements (ADA, 2016o; Judicial Administration, 2010e). In addition to these regulatory requirements, the agreement expressly restricts the sheriff from using VRI if the technology would be ineffective for other reasons—including a person's limited ability to move his head, hands, or arms; vision or cognitive issues; significant emotional distress or pain; and/or space limitations in the room. Finally, and importantly, the agreement also outlines a protocol whereby the sheriff must call an on-site interpreter if the VRI is not functioning properly and staff cannot get it to work within 30 minutes of the malfunction.

Owing to the issues that frequently arise in the context of VRI, more settlement agreements are requiring this type of protocol, including in settlement agreements outside of the criminal justice context. See, for example, the Settlement Agreement Between the United States of America and Mountain States Health Alliance Under the Americans With Disabilities Act (2016) (establishing protocol whereby staff must call an on-site interpreter if the VRI is not functioning properly and they cannot get it to work within 30 minutes of the malfunction); *Morales v. Saint Barnabas Medical Center* (2017) (requiring hospital staff to provide an on-site interpreter if the VRI is not operational and staff have tried for 45 minutes).

Extension to Companions

It is well settled that the ADA's effective communication obligations extend to companions with disabilities. Companions are defined as "a family member, friend, or associate of an individual" accessing the public entity, "who, along with such individual, is an appropriate person with whom the [public entity] should communicate" (ADA, 2016p; Judicial Administration, 2010e). Title II regulations provide that "[a] public entity shall take appropriate steps to ensure that communications with applicants, participants, members of the public, *and companions with disabilities* [emphasis added] are as effective as communications with others" (ADA, 2016p; Judicial Administration, 2010b).

ADA, SECTION 504, AND CRIMINAL JUSTICE FOR DEAF INDIVIDUALS

With this legal framework in mind, this chapter now delves into the ADA and Section 504 as applied to the criminal justice system.

Law Enforcement

Ensuring effective communication during police encounters and arrests has been an extremely important issue for people with disabilities. The majority of cases addressing effective communication during police encounters focus on whether police departments must provide ASL interpreters during arrests.

Exigent Circumstances: Case Law

When discussing the ADA and police encounters, a critical preliminary legal issue is whether the ADA also applies to the arrest process. It has been the long-standing position of the DOJ that the ADA applies to law enforcement personnel in nearly every facet of their work, including interrogating witnesses, booking and holding suspects, enforcing laws, operating 911 centers, and, notably, arrests. The DOJ reiterated this position in its Statement of Interest filed in June 2016 in *Robinson v. Farley* (2016), citing the broad scope of Title II and the ADA's legislative history (*Robinson v. Farley*, 2016). Despite the DOJ's consistent position, there is currently a circuit court split over the question of whether the ADA applies to arrests.

The Fifth Circuit's decision in *Hainze v. Richards* (2000) is important to review even though the case does not involve a deaf plaintiff. In this case, the Fifth Circuit held that the ADA "does not apply to an officer's on-the-street responses to reported disturbances or other similar incidents . . . prior to the officer's securing the scene and ensuring that there is no threat to human life" (*Hainze v. Richards*, 2000). In *Hainze*, a woman called 911 asking for assistance with transporting her nephew, Hainze, who was suicidal, to a hospital for mental health treatment. The woman advised that Hainze had a history of depression, was currently under the influence of alcohol and antidepressants, was carrying a knife, and was threatening either to commit suicide or "suicide by cop," a term used to describe a suicide method where an individual intentionally engages in threatening behavior for the purpose of eliciting a deadly response from a police officer (*Hainze v. Richards*). When the police arrived on the scene, they saw a shoeless Hainze talking to individuals in a pickup truck and holding a knife. The police officer drew his weapon and ordered Hainze to walk away from the truck. Hainze responded with profanities, began to walk toward the officer, and was ordered again to stop. Hainze did not stop, and when he was within 4 to 6 feet of the officer, the officer shot Hainze twice in rapid succession in his chest. Hainze survived.

The Fifth Circuit concluded that because law enforcement personnel face the "onerous task" of having to "instantaneously identify, assess, and react to potentially life-threatening situations," it would pose an "unnecessary risk to innocents" to require officers to comply with the ADA "in the presence of exigent circumstances . . . prior to securing the safety of themselves, other officers, and any nearby civilians" (*Hainze v. Richards*). It concluded that Congress could not have intended the ADA to be preserved at the expense of public safety, especially when there are other remedies available under the law, such as a Section 1983 or a state law claim. Thus, it held that these specific situations fall outside the scope of the ADA.

However, the majority of circuits have rejected this type of categorical exemption. Instead, most courts have held that Title II applies to arrests and that the existence of exigent circumstances and criminal activity simply factors into the analysis of whether the police officer's actions are reasonable. For instance, in *Loye v. County of Dakota* (2010), police officers responded to an environmental and public health emergency after two boys released two bottles of mercury while playing (*Loye v. County of Dakota*, 2010). Police officers knocked on doors to notify people who had been exposed and then set up a decontamination tent.

Among the people who were contaminated were the four plaintiffs, all of whom were deaf. Plaintiffs brought an ADA lawsuit asserting that they were not provided with ASL interpreters during the decontamination process, among other communications. The court found for the county, explaining that waiting for an interpreter was not reasonable given the "exigent circumstances of an emergency hazardous materials decontamination" (*Loye v. County of Dakota*).

See also *Seremeth v. Board of County Commissioners Frederick County* (2012) (finding first that "in light of *Yeskey's* expansive interpretation, the ADA applies to police interrogations" and then applying that reasoning to the facts in the case to hold that "the ADA applied once the deputies attempted to question and obtain information from Seremeth"); *Bircoll v. Miami-Dade County* (2007) (holding that "the question is not so much one of the applicability of the ADA because Title II prohibits discrimination by a public entity by reason of [a person's] disability. The exigent circumstances presented by criminal activity and the already onerous tasks of police on the scene go more to the reasonableness of the requested ADA modification than whether the ADA applies in the first instance"); and *Gohier v. Enright* (1999) (concluding that "a broad rule categorically excluding arrests from the scope of Title II . . . is not the law"). See also, *Waller ex rel. Estate of Hunt v. City of Danville* (2009) ("Just as the constraints of time figure in what is required of police under the Fourth Amendment, they bear on what is reasonable under the ADA."); *Tucker v. Tennessee* (addressing a Title II reasonable accommodation claim in which the plaintiffs asserted that police officers "discriminated against them in violation of the ADA by failing to provide a qualified sign language interpreter or other such reasonable accommodation(s) during the domestic disturbance call that resulted in their arrest").

Even so, under this analysis, courts have concluded that exigent circumstances allow a police officer to forego a request for accommodations or effective communication, such as the provision of a sign language interpreter. In *Bircoll v. Miami-Dade County* (2007), the plaintiff, a deaf man, asserted that the police department violated the ADA by failing to provide him with an oral interpreter[8] both during a field sobriety test and at the police station before he took an Intoxilyzer test (*Bircoll v. Miami-Dade County*, 2007). The court rejected both claims. With respect to the field sobriety test, the court held an oral interpreter's presence at a field sobriety test is not a reasonable modification of police procedures owing to the "exigent circumstances of a [driving under the influence] DUI stop on the side of a highway, the on-the-spot judgment required of police, and the serious public safety concerns in DUI criminal activity" (*Bircoll v. Miami-Dade County*, 2007). Additionally, waiting for an interpreter jeopardized the officer's ability to obtain an accurate measure of the driver's blood-alcohol level. The court also rejected the plaintiff's argument that the police should have accommodated him by skipping the field sobriety tests altogether and going directly to the station for the breathalyzer test. This proposal, explained the court, would force police to arrest all deaf DUI suspects, which is not reasonable. The court was also persuaded by the fact that the plaintiff admitted that he reads lips (though he understands only about 50% of what is said), that he had received both verbal and physical demonstrations of the field sobriety tests, and that he had admitted that he had understood.

The key is to determine whether there were truly exigent circumstances that required immediate communication. This legal principle is well-illustrated by the Eighth Circuit's decision, *Bahl v. County of Ramsey* (2012). In *Bahl*, a deaf arrestee who used ASL as his primary language sued the city, arguing that he received ineffective communication at various points of his arrest after a traffic stop. The Eighth Circuit declined to consider whether the traffic stop was a covered service but found that, assuming it was, the officer's decision to communicate through simple communications and gestures (rather than in writing, as requested by the plaintiff) was reasonable under the circumstances where the situation "quickly escalated" and was "no longer controlled." The Eighth Circuit said it would not second-guess judgments of police officers presented with exigent or unexpected circumstances.

However, with respect to the plaintiff's postarrest interview, the Eighth Circuit concluded there was a question of fact about whether the police officer started to engage in a postarrest interview and then stopped the interview so that the city did not have to provide an interpreter. The court explained that the postarrest interview would have given the defendant certain benefits, such as the right to ask questions and give his side of the story, which could have affected the prosecutor's decision to charge him with an offense. The court further reasoned that the city bears the burden of showing that providing an interpreter would have resulted in an undue financial burden. Thus, the court reversed the decision to grant summary judgment concerning the communication provided during the postarrest interview (*Bahl v. County of Ramsey*, 2012).

Courts have cautioned that law enforcement should not overextend the argument that exigent circumstances preclude effective communication. In *Taylor v. City of Mason* (2013), a deaf man called the police after having a physical altercation with a partially deaf woman at his home. The police came to the man's house and used the woman—who also alleged that the man had sexually assaulted her—as an interpreter while waiting for the qualified interpreter to arrive. The court explained that the situation was under control and that there was no imminent safety risk, so the police could have waited for the interpreter to arrive on the scene. It further explained that the woman was not an appropriate person to use as an interpreter, given the circumstances and the fact that he had not consented to her acting as one. Further, at the police station, the city provided the defendant with an interpreter who was not ASL certified and refused to replace the interpreter upon the man's request. For those reasons, the court denied the city's motion to dismiss, holding that the burden is on law enforcement to ensure that communications with a deaf individual are as effective as communications with hearing individuals when a law enforcement agency does not defer to the deaf individual's requests.

Exigent Circumstances: Settlement Agreements and Practical Guidance

Recent settlement agreements resulting from investigations brought by the DOJ offer guidance for law enforcement departments about when and how to provide specific auxiliary aids and services during and after exigent circumstances. For instance, the 2018 settlement agreement with the PPD creates a comprehensive process under which PPD will assess communication needs and provide auxiliary aids and services. This process is discussed at length in what follows. However, the agreement also makes the following provision:

> When there is an emergency involving an *imminent threat* to the *safety or welfare* of an individual (including law enforcement personnel or members of the public), and there is *insufficient time* to make available appropriate auxiliary aids and services, law enforcement personnel will use whatever auxiliary aids and services are *most effective* under the circumstances to communicate with persons who are deaf or hard of hearing, *consistent with an appropriate law enforcement response to the imminent threat*. [emphasis added] (*United States v. City of Philadelphia Police*, 2016)

This agreement suggests that under certain limited situations, it will not be reasonable to stop to secure specific auxiliary aids and services. However, even in those situations, officers should provide the most effective auxiliary aids and services they can under the circumstances. As soon as there is no longer an imminent threat, the agreement requires PPD to follow its procedures to assess and provide appropriate auxiliary aids and services to ensure effective communication.

This mirrors the requirements found in an earlier settlement agreement between the United States and the police department of Columbia, South Carolina, discussed in more detail later (*United States v. City of Columbia Police*, 2016). There, the agreement sets forth different requirements for communication during exigent circumstances and routine interactions. When there is an exigent circumstance and insufficient time exists to make appropriate auxiliary aids and services available, police are permitted to use what is available, consistent with an appropriate law enforcement response—such as exchanging written notes or using the services of a person who knows sign language but is not a qualified interpreter—for an interim period while the imminent threat is ongoing, even if the person who is deaf would prefer an appropriate auxiliary aid or service such as a qualified sign language interpreter. As soon as there is no longer an imminent threat, the police department agreed to follow its comprehensive procedures to provide appropriate auxiliary aids and services.

The Effectiveness of the Communication

Other cases about effective communication during police encounters turn on the question of whether an alternative auxiliary aid or service was effective in light of the individual's communication skills and the public entity's efforts.

For instance, in *Valanzuolo v. City of New Haven* (2013), a deaf individual was arrested by the New Haven police department for failing to appear in court. At no time during the plaintiff's arrest, 10-hour hospital stay in police custody, or transportation to booking and processing was the plaintiff provided with an ASL interpreter. The plaintiff alleged a deprivation of rights under the ADA for failure to provide an ASL interpreter. The court entered judgment in favor of the defendant and held that the City of New Haven had provided the plaintiff with effective communication through the use of pen and paper. Specifically, it cited the fact that during the initial arrest, the plaintiff had a pen and paper at his door with which he regularly used to communicate, had communicated using that method previously, had read the arrest warrant, and had communicated via a handwritten note with the police on three or four pages of the officer's pad and had done so in complete sentences with proper spelling.[9]

Similarly, in *Hoffman v. Marion County Texas* (2014), after only a cursory analysis, the Fifth Circuit held that the county had not violated the ADA by failing to provide a deaf arrestee with an interpreter because the plaintiff could effectively communicate with the officers, even initiating the conversation at times, so he was not "excluded as a result of not having an interpreter during the investigation or arrest."

On the other hand, in *Williams v. City of New York* (2015), the New York Police Department (NYPD) arrested and detained the plaintiff, who was deaf, without making any effort to communicate with her at all (*Williams v. City of New York*, 2015). The plaintiff and her husband attempted to secure police presence when evicting their tenants, given prior incidents between the parties. The police failed to respond, and after some minor disputes with the tenants transpired, the plaintiff's husband, who was also deaf, called the police through video relay service, asking for police assistance because he believed that the tenant's boyfriend had a firearm.

When the police arrived, the police hardly engaged with the owners. The owners requested an ASL interpreter, but one was not provided. Further, another tenant (who was being evicted but not part of the alleged physical altercation) knew ASL and offered to interpret, but the police declined this option as well. The police spoke with the tenant and the tenant's boyfriend, who reported that the owner had engaged in an assault but had failed to make an effort to adequately communicate with the owner. The plaintiff was arrested and held overnight and at no time was an ASL interpreter provided, nor did the police try to communicate with her in any other way to advise why she was under arrest or how long she would be in custody.

In her ADA lawsuit, the NYPD asserted that it had no responsibility under the ADA to provide any accommodation until after the individual had been arrested and booked, a position the court rejected and called "extraordinary" (*Williams v. City of New York*, 2015). The NYPD also asserted that it was unreasonable to provide an accommodation prior to arrest because they needed to secure the scene. The court rejected this argument because the facts suggested that no one was in imminent danger and permitted the case to move forward.

Following this decision, the parties settled the lawsuit, which also included constitutional claims under Section 1983, and state law tort claims of assault, battery, and false imprisonment, for $750,000 (*Williams v. City of New York*, 2015). This case demonstrates the importance of effective communication both during an arrest and while in police custody.

Settlement Agreements, Policies, and Practical Guidance

The DOJ has entered into settlement agreements on behalf of the United States with law enforcement departments across the country on the topic of communication access for deaf individuals.

Given the comprehensive nature of these agreements, they provide a helpful template for law enforcement departments looking to evaluate and revise their own policies, including policies on how to implement training, change signage, modify handcuffing policies, and a variety of other topics.

As noted previously, on August 2, 2018, the DOJ entered into a settlement agreement on behalf of the United States with the city of Philadelphia and the PPD (*United States v. City of Philadelphia Police*, 2016), which served to resolve the legal violations identified by investigations led by the DOJ, resulting in a letter of findings about PPD (U.S. Department of Justice, 2016). The DOJ's investigation was prompted by a complaint from a person who was deaf who asserted that PPD failed to provide him with effective communication during his arrest and detainment. When PPD arrested the complainant, officers handcuffed him with his hands behind his back, which prevented him from communicating with officers using ASL, his primary language. Officers then escorted the complainant to the PPD detective's office, where the detective asked an unqualified interpreter, a radio room staffer, to explain the detention process. The complainant could not understand what the radio room staff was signing, so he wrote a note requesting a qualified interpreter, which PPD never provided. PPD held him in the detention area overnight until he was arraigned the next morning via video. He could not understand the judge because the video had no captioning, and PPD failed to inform the court that he was deaf.

After being charged with simple assault, the complainant had to write a note to a staffer asking them to call his mom for him because there was no TTY or videophone. Later, PPD arrested him again for failing to appear at a hearing. The hearing had actually been rescheduled, and he had not failed to appear, but he was unable to communicate this because the arresting officer had handcuffed him. He was taken to a PPD precinct, where he was processed and detained. At the precinct, "PPD staff took [his] blood, administered a tuberculosis test and urine test, [and] strip-searched him," all without ever providing him with a qualified interpreter to explain what was happening (U.S. Department of Justice, 2016). During the course of its investigation, the DOJ identified four other deaf people with similar allegations against the PPD. It concluded that PPD had failed to provide appropriate auxiliary aids and services, had improperly relied on an accompanying adult to interpret, and had failed to take appropriate steps to train officers.

As part of the settlement agreement, PPD will ensure that appropriate auxiliary aids and services, including qualified interpreters, are made available, establish contracts with interpreting agencies, ensure that all personnel who have contact with individuals who are deaf understand how to assess the need for auxiliary aids and services, and notify the court that detainees are deaf with sufficient notice for auxiliary aids or services to be provided. In addition, PPD agreed that when officers handcuff individuals who are deaf and who use ASL to communicate, the officers will, safety permitting, handcuff the person with their hands in front of their body so they can still communicate by signing or writing.

To assist in its communication assessment process, PPD law enforcement personnel will use a communication card during routine interactions, which are defined as all interactions in which no imminent threat exists. The communication card uses pictograms to communicate basic information, as well as to inquire into the individual's preferred method of communication (*United States v. City of Philadelphia Police*, 2016). Then, for routine interactions, law enforcement personnel, in consultation with the individual, will assess what auxiliary aids and services are necessary using a communication assessment form (*United States v. City of Philadelphia Police*, 2016). The form asks what auxiliary aids and services the individual desires and includes a list of possibilities. It also makes clear that any auxiliary aids and services provided will be free of charge.

The agreement also specifies that when a qualified interpreter is required, one should be provided at the earliest reasonable time, which, in most cases, means within 1 hour of first identifying a need. To ensure this type of timely response, the agreement also requires PPD to maintain contracts with qualified interpreter agencies to ensure that services will be available on a priority basis (or hire qualified interpreters with availability 24 hours a day, 7 days a week).

Another settlement agreement of interest was entered into on May 3, 2016, between the United States and the police department of Columbia, South Carolina, mentioned earlier, which contains many of the same requirements (*United States v. City of Columbia Police*, 2016). This settlement agreement was reached after the DOJ investigated a complaint alleging that the complainant was not provided with an ASL interpreter for police questioning over a 3-month period, including at the time of his arrest.

In addition to revised policies and training requirements, some of the highlights of the settlement include Columbia Police Department's agreement to designate at least one employee as the ADA coordinator responsible for ADA compliance; provide appropriate auxiliary aids and services, including qualified sign language interpreters; create communication cards to aid in communication with persons who are deaf during routine interactions in the field; use pictograms to determine whether someone requires an interpreter in all nonexigent circumstances; and use a communication assessment form while taking a deaf individual into custody for processing (*United States v. City of Columbia Police*, 2016).

To ensure that these requirements are met, the police department has also agreed to form and maintain working relationships with one or more qualified oral/sign language interpreter agencies to ensure interpreter availability on a priority basis 24/7. The department also agreed to modify its handcuffing policy by handcuffing an individual in front of his body to enable sign language or writing. It also agreed to ensure a sufficient number of working TTYs and videophones at each station, but no fewer than one of each, and to provide signage to inform the community about their availability.

In other settlement agreements, police departments agreed to provide auxiliary aids and services, including sign language interpreters, to citizens who are deaf (U.S. Department of Justice, 2015a–d). To facilitate this communication, the departments created new policies, trained their employees about the policies, and, at times, entered into contracts with qualified sign language interpreting agencies.

An older settlement agreement with the Rochester Police Department provides helpful detailed guidance and requires sign language interpreters to be provided as needed during arrests, investigations, or during interrogations, regardless of where they are conducted (U.S. Department of Justice, 2015c). Additionally, where timeliness is an issue or the police officer is out in the field without immediate access to an interpreter, procedures, and guidelines for securing an interpreter must be established. These procedures differ according to the seriousness of the offense being investigated. Only when a criminal investigation involves a serious offense and time is of the essence may an investigator continue an interview with a deaf individual without an interpreter, and in that case, the investigator must document the investigation as completely as possible and notify designated police personnel. In less serious offenses, the investigator must end the interview until an interpreter is present.

Correctional Facilities

Roughly one-third of people living in correctional facilities—approximately 2.2 million people—report having at least one disability (Bureau of Justice Statistics, 2015). Needless to say, correctional facilities, such as jails and prisons, exercise vast control over their residents' lives: they dictate inmates' housing conditions; control their access to essentials like food, health care, toilets, and showers; manage their recreational, educational, and vocational opportunities; and often influence their likelihood of reentering free society. Given this tremendous power, a prison that discriminates on the basis of disability has the potential to have a particularly destructive, pervasive, and enduring impact on its inmates.

In 1998, the U.S. Supreme Court confirmed in *Pennsylvania Department of Corrections v. Yeskey* (1998) that Title II of the ADA applies to "any department, agency . . . or other instrumentality of a State," including state prisons. Accordingly, for nearly 2 decades, it has been clear that correctional facilities are barred from discriminating against inmates on the basis of their disabilities.

Put another way, people with disabilities do not lose their rights under the ADA simply because they are incarcerated.[10]

In spite of *Yeskey*, prisoners with disabilities still face significant challenges, and instances of discrimination remain common, including the provision of effective communication for deaf prisoners.

Deaf prisoners require communication access in all aspects of prison life—everything from educational programs to disciplinary hearings to religious services to medical appointments. Issues also arise because many prisons communicate announcements aurally over a loudspeaker, which is inaccessible to deaf inmates. Similarly, commands are typically given aurally, and deaf inmates are frequently punished for not following directions. They can also be put in harm's way when alarms, indicating some type of emergency within the correctional facility, do not have a visual component. Furthermore, many prisons do not have videophones and do not offer TTYs on an equal basis with those who use a voice telephone. These are just some of the many communication barriers faced by deaf prisoners.

OVERVIEW OF CASES AND SETTLEMENTS

There have been a host of lawsuits and settlements across the country on issues related to individuals who are deaf in prison. This is an issue that has been litigated for over 2 decades and shows no signs of slowing down.

Given the nature of prison incarceration, individuals who are deaf require auxiliary aids and services to participate in a wide range of prison programs. It comes as no surprise, then, that cases brought on behalf of deaf inmates in prison challenge the facility's failure to provide access in a number of ways. For example, cases challenge a correctional department's failure to provide ASL interpreters or other auxiliary aids and services to have equal access to prison programs, such as educational and vocational programs, medical appointments, and disciplinary hearings; appropriate equipment to access telephones and television; and methods to understand prison notifications and alerts.

For that reason, many cases against correctional facilities encompass a wide range of issues. And, unfortunately, these issues are not new. In an early case about the rights of deaf prisoners, *Clarkson v. Coughlin* (1995), the court granted summary judgment to the plaintiffs, deaf inmates, finding that the defendant, the commissioner of the New York State Department of Correction Services, had violated Section 504 and the ADA by failing to provide interpretive services during reception and classification, through the absence or inadequacy of assistive communication devices for telephone and television, by their failure to provide visual safety alarms, and their failure to make reasonable accommodations to participate fully in educational, vocational, and rehabilitative contexts (*Clarkson v. Coughlin*, 1995).

In 2010, the Virginia Department of Corrections settled the case *Minnis v. Johnson* (2010) (*Minnis Settlement*), which similarly addressed a broad range of issues. The settlement addresses policies, initial classification, assessment, assignment, housing, provision of auxiliary aids and services, qualifications and use of sign language interpreters, additional communications, disciplinary matters, visual alert notifications, telecommunication devices, and staff training. Notably, this case settled within 1 year of its filing.

More recently, on the 28th anniversary of the ADA, a federal judge approved a settlement in a class action affecting all Illinois deaf prisoners, *Holmes et al. v. Baldwin (2018) (Holmes Settlement)*. The class action alleged that the Illinois Department of Corrections (IDOC) systematically failed to provide ASL interpreters and other forms of communication, thus depriving deaf inmates of meaningful access to health care, religious services, educational programs, and prerelease programs. The settlement revised IDOC's process for identifying deaf inmates, as well as assessing their communication-related needs. Under the agreement, IDOC will provide enhanced screening to identify which prisoners are deaf; provide hearing aids when recommended by an audiologist; provide sign language interpreters for prisoners who communicate in ASL; ensure every Illinois prison with a deaf prisoner has at least one videophone, two TTYs, and two amplified telephones; and establish a safe way to provide accessible notifications about emergencies, evacuations, meals, showers, yard time, doctor and counselor appointments, and visitors to deaf prisoners. Some of these key terms will be examined more closely further on. This case settled 4 years after the court issued an opinion certifying the plaintiff class and denying, in large part, the defendant's motion for summary judgment (*Holmes v. Godinez*, 2015).

SIGN LANGUAGE INTERPRETERS

When plaintiffs bring cases for failure to provide ASL interpreters, one important question is under what circumstances an interpreter must be provided, as opposed to another auxiliary aid or service. There is a trend in cases and settlements that concludes that individuals whose primary language is ASL must be provided ASL interpreters for all "High Stakes Interactions." See *McBride v. Michigan Department of Corrections* (2018).

This concept was applied in the *Holmes Settlement* as well (*Holmes et al. v. Baldwin*, 2018). In this settlement agreement, High Stakes Interactions were defined as "those in which the risks of miscommunication or misunderstanding are high and the consequences of miscommunications may have serious repercussions for inmates." Such interactions include most medical care and appointments, including dental, vision, audiological, mental health care and appointments, disciplinary investigations and disciplinary hearings; educational programs, specific training sessions, and general educational opportunities that include a verbal component; vocational programs that include a verbal component; and transfer and classification meetings. The agreement also requires the provision of interpreters for religious services.

Without characterizing these important meetings as "High Stakes Interactions," other settlement agreements have included similar requirements. In *Disability Rights Florida, Inc. v. Jones* (2017), the plaintiffs asserted that Florida Department of Corrections (FDC), the third-largest state prison system in the country, had systematically failed to comply with the ADA in terms of providing deaf inmates with qualified interpreters and other auxiliary aids and services during interactions such as medical appointments and disciplinary hearings (*Disability Rights Florida v. Jones*, 2017). The settlement gives the FDC up to 4 years to come into compliance with the ADA and includes a list of programs that require the provision of ASL interpreters.

Similarly, in 2018, the United States entered into a settlement agreement with the South Carolina Department of Corrections to ensure that deaf inmates receive appropriate auxiliary aids and services (*Settlement Agreement Between the United States of America and South Carolina Department of Corrections Under the Americans With Disabilities Act*, 2018).[11] The agreement lists the programs where auxiliary aids and services, especially ASL interpreters, must be provided, including critical communication, complex information, lengthy exchanges, or anything involving legal due process; intake; orientation; classification; medical care and health programs and services, including physicals, medical screenings, treatment, dental, visual, and/or mental health examinations or treatment, and drug and alcohol recovery services; counseling or psychological services; educational and vocational programming, including any programming required for parole or early release; due process hearings, including disciplinary hearings, and hearings in which the inmate is a witness; classification review interviews; grievance interviews or processes; religious services; noncriminal investigations; and prerelease instructions.

In *Heyer v. U.S. Bureau of Prisons* (2017), the Fourth Circuit Court of Appeals concluded that there was a genuine issue of material fact as to whether the prison's failure to provide the plaintiff with ASL interpreters for medical interactions amounted to "deliberate indifference" and thus violated Heyer's Fifth Amendment rights (*Heyer v. U.S. Bureau of Prisons*, 2017). Heyer presented sufficient evidence that the prison officials knew that he was deaf and needed ASL interpreters to communicate and that he needed accurate communication for his medical treatment to be effective and yet failed to appropriately address Heyer's multiple requests for interpreters.

When correctional facilities use VRI, they must ensure that the technology meets the regulatory requirements and is not used if it would be ineffective in light of any individual circumstances. For example, in the *Minnis Settlement*, the settlement explains that if VRI is not appropriate for the situation, personnel will work to secure a qualified in-person interpreter as soon as possible. In the agreement, the parties included a list of situations where VRI would not be appropriate.

However, unlike some other contexts, given the unique nature of corrections, in some of the settlement agreements with correctional facilities, the agreements require the facilities to have a working VRI in the event of medical emergencies. See *Minnis Settlement* and *Holmes Settlement* (requiring the use of VRI during medical emergencies).

TELEPHONE ACCESS: VIDEOPHONES (VP) AND TELETYPEWRITERS (TTY)

One important legal issue is what type of telephone technology must be provided by correctional facilities for deaf inmates. Advocates argue that the goal of effective communication cannot be fully realized until prisons are required to provide VP, not just TTYs, for inmates who communicate with ASL. The National Disability Rights Network and the National Association of the Deaf have pointed out that "American Sign Language, not English, is the primary language for many people who are deaf and hard of hearing," and, because ASL is its own unique language that is distinct from English, "videophones, not TTYs, are the functional equivalent of telephones for this group of prisoners" (National Disability Rights Network and National Association of the Deaf, 2016).

This issue was addressed in *McBride v. Michigan Department of Corrections*, (2018), where the court granted the plaintiffs' motion for summary judgment in a class action filed by deaf inmates held in the custody of Michigan Department of Corrections (MDOC) alleging agency administrators and prison wardens denied them auxiliary aids and services, in violation of the ADA. Specifically, the court found that MDOC's failure to provide VP was not justified by its asserted defense of "possible safety concerns" because MDOC "failed to explain why the safety policies applied to telephone conversations 'would not be as effective at addressing risks associated with video transmissions'" (*McBride v. Michigan Department of Corrections*, 2018). The court held that MDOC must provide deaf inmates with means of communication that are "as effective as those of hearing prisoners," noting that the inmates' "desire for equally effective means of communication is not just an aspiration—it is the law." VP are necessary for effective communication and TTYs alone are insufficient because they are increasingly becoming obsolete, given their requirement that communication be in typed English, the second language for many deaf people, and TTY conversations take significantly longer than video calls (*McBride v. Michigan Department of Corrections*, 2018). MDOC's own witness compared TTYs to "sending someone a fax to their homes versus an email to communicate" (*McBride v. Michigan Department of Corrections*). The court ordered MDOC to make VP available to all deaf prisoners. See also *Rogers et al. v. Colorado Department of Corrections* (2019) (ordering the Colorado Department of Corrections to make VP available to all deaf inmates and all inmates communicating with deaf friends, family members, and others, as well as adopt effective and comprehensive policies and procedures about the use and implementation of VP, including for appropriate compliance monitoring, maintenance, and repair); *Yeh v. United States Bureau of Prisons* (2019) (the court "instituted a rigorous program of reporting and case management, designed to ensure that the preliminary injunctive relief sought by Yeh, installation of a videophone, would be accomplished in a timely fashion").

Other state correctional centers have also seen improved communication access as a result of settlement agreements by private litigants. Settlement agreements from Maryland (*Jarboe v. Maryland Department of Public Safety and Correctional Services*) and Kentucky (*Adams v. Commonwealth of Kentucky*) resulted in settlements that aim to remedy some of the barriers to effective communication in the prison system.[12] Under these settlements, deaf inmates will have access to VP to communicate with people outside of prison; adequate visual notification of oral announcements concerning emergencies; access to sign language interpreters and other auxiliary aids and services; and a broad scheme of policy implementation, training, outreach, and monitoring to ensure equal treatment of deaf individuals by prison officials. Similarly, the *Holmes Settlement* requires all facilities that house a deaf inmate to have at least one VP (*Holmes v. Baldwin*, 2018).

In addition to a claim under the ADA and Section 504, the issue of access to VP has also been viewed as constitutional in nature. In *Heyer v. U.S. Bureau of Prisons* (2017), the prison refused to acquire a VP for prisoners who were deaf, citing security concerns (*Heyer v. United States Bureau of Prisons*, 2017). The Fourth Circuit Court of Appeals held that a reasonable factfinder could find that the prison's TTY-only policy was an exaggerated response to the perceived security concerns and remanded the issue to determine whether the prison's failure to provide access to VP improperly restricted inmates' first amendment rights.

ACCESSIBLE ALERTS

It is common for communications to be done aurally through a loudspeaker. This type of alert system is not accessible to individuals who are deaf, so this has also been the subject of litigation. In *Bearden v. Clark County* (2016), the court found that the plaintiff established, as a matter of law, that the jail's communication system was inaccessible (*Bearden v. Clark County*, 2016). The plaintiff testified that "they would call my name to give me the dose [of medication] in the middle of the night when I was asleep, and I couldn't hear them calling my name" (*Bearden v. Clark County*, 2016). The court concluded that the county had failed to provide an accessible notification system so that the plaintiff had access to medication.

The issue of accessible notifications has also been part of recent settlement agreements. For example, in the *Holmes Settlement*, IDOC will provide deaf inmates with a tactile notification system so that they can receive notification of alerts, such as meal times, showers, yard, and visitors (*Holmes v. Baldwin*, 2018). In the *South Carolina Settlement*, the state will "provide an effective visual or other notification system so that inmates who have a hearing disability do not miss announcements, alarms, or other auditory information, including times for meals, recreation, education, work assignments, and other events" (*United States of America v. South Carolina Department of Corrections*, 2018).

ASSESSMENTS OF NEEDS

Courts have recently acknowledged that prisons have an affirmative obligation to evaluate the communication needs of deaf inmates. In *Pierce v. District of Columbia* (2015), although it was obvious to the prison that an inmate was deaf, the prison did not evaluate how it could enable him to communicate effectively while in prison or provide him with any accommodations (*Pierce v. District of Columbia*, 2015). In its defense, the prison argued that it was not required to accommodate the inmate because he had not specifically requested any accommodations in order to communicate effectively. The court rejected that argument and found that

> prison officials have an affirmative duty to assess the potential accommodation needs of inmates with known disabilities who are taken into custody and to provide the accommodations that are necessary . . . without regard to whether or not the disabled individual has made a specific request for accommodation. (*Pierce v. District of Columbia*, 2015)

The *Holmes Settlement* requires prison officials to proactively assess whether inmates need accommodations for communications (*Holmes et al. v. Baldwin*, 2018). The settlement agreement provides that IDOC must adopt a policy and procedure that requires routine hearing screenings of all new inmates and all current inmates who self-report as deaf. The procedure must also facilitate inmate requests for a hearing screening and conduct a hearing screening of the inmate within 30 days of making the request. Furthermore, once an inmate has been identified as deaf, IDOC must conduct an audiological evaluation every 3 years to monitor any changes in the inmate's hearing.

When prisoners first enter the IDOC system, they undergo an intake process where IDOC staff evaluate, among other things, their physical and mental health and their educational level as well as whether they are in need of protection. This information is used to determine which facility the prisoner would be sent to and what privileges they would have (*Holmes v. Godinez*, 2015). However, IDOC failed to provide deaf inmates with any assistance to effectively communicate during this intake process. Instead, prisoners were not properly identified as being deaf, and IDOC was unable to properly assess the needs of those prisoners. IDOC's failure to communicate with them effectively had far-reaching implications because it also meant that those prisoners' health care needs were not properly assessed, they were regularly given improper security classifications, and many did not receive the same types of programming opportunities available to hearing prisoners (*Holmes v. Godinez*, 2015).

ACCESS FOR COMPANIONS

As noted previously, the requirement to provide effective communication applies to companions as well. This has been applied in the criminal justice context, where courts have required prisons to make accommodations for visitors who themselves are deaf and are seeking to communicate with prison inmates. In *Durrenberger v. Texas Department of Criminal Justice* (2010), a man who was deaf visited an inmate held at a publicly funded Texas prison facility. On arrival, he told the commanding officer that he had hearing limitations and asked to be placed in an accessible phone booth to speak with the inmate.

The commanding officer informed the visitor that the prison was not equipped with any booths that had accessible communication features. He was then placed in a standard booth and was unable to hear the inmate over the telephone. On subsequent visits, he requested other accommodations, such as the use of the attorney/client booth or the use of an amplifying device to increase the volume of the telephone receiver, but to no avail. Instead, the prison occasionally placed him in a phone booth at the end because it was sometimes less noisy than other phone booths and offered him a pen and paper. He sued the prison for violating the ADA. The court held that the prison failed to show that they provided the visitor with any accommodation that allowed him to participate in the inmate visitation program and issued a permanent injunction enjoining the prison from future violations.

CRIMINAL PROCEEDINGS

A discussion of criminal justice would not be complete without a reference to accessibility within criminal court proceedings. Similarly to other aspects of the criminal justice system, disagreements and misunderstandings about when and to whom Title II applies have existed, preventing individuals with disabilities from participating fully in judicial proceedings and accessing judicial services.

Communication barriers affect not only criminal defendants but also their families, witnesses, members of the public, and court employees. Recent case law analyzing these issues reveal common barriers to accessibility, including misunderstandings about sovereign immunity, confusion about what circumstances require courts to provide accommodations, and, in some instances, indifference toward or even intentional discrimination against people with disabilities during criminal justice proceedings.

In 2004, the U.S. Supreme Court addressed the issue of sovereign immunity under Title II of the ADA in *Tennessee v. Lane* (2004). In that case, two plaintiffs, both of whom had paraplegia and used wheelchairs, brought an action against the state of Tennessee for failing to provide physically accessible courtrooms and facilities. The first plaintiff was compelled to appear on the second floor of a courthouse to answer criminal charges against him. Because there were no elevators or ramps at the courthouse, he was forced to crawl up the stairs to reach the courtroom. On his second visit, he refused to crawl up the stairs and was then arrested and jailed for failure to appear. The second plaintiff was a court reporter who had been unable to enter several county courtrooms because they were not accessible by wheelchair. As a result, she was denied several opportunities to work and participate in the judicial process.

The state argued that its Eleventh Amendment immunity, also referred to as sovereign immunity, prevented the plaintiffs from taking any action against it for monetary damages. When considering this claim, the Supreme Court first pointed out that Congress had clearly intended to abrogate or nullify states' Eleventh Amendment immunity when it enacted Title II of the ADA and that, thus, the real issue was whether Congress had the authority to abrogate sovereign immunity. The Supreme Court held that Congress had unquestionably acted within its scope of powers when it enacted Title II because Section 5 of the Fourteenth Amendment gives Congress the power to take appropriate steps to protect the public's constitutional rights. This includes the first amendment right to access criminal proceedings and the sixth amendment right for a criminal defendant to be present at all stages of his or her trial. The court underscored the validity of Title II as a response to a long history of discrimination against people with disabilities in the criminal justice system. However, the court stopped short of holding that sovereign immunity is never a valid defense to a claim brought under Title II of the ADA. Instead, the court limited its holding to only the "class of cases implicating the accessibility of judicial services" (*Tennessee v. Lane*, 2004).

Since *Lane*, the right of individuals in both criminal and civil cases to bring an action against states or government entities for ADA violations has been widely acknowledged. However, because the *Lane* holding was limited to the class of the cases involving the accessibility *of* judicial services, it sparked a new debate among individuals and government entities over which proceedings fall into that category. In *Prakel v. Indiana* (2015), a criminal defendant's son brought an action against the state of Indiana for denying him access to his mother's criminal proceedings (*Prakel v. Indiana*, 2015). The plaintiff was deaf and used ASL as his primary language. In order to participate in and understand his mother's pretrial hearings, he made multiple requests for interpreters in advance of the hearings. All of his requests were denied, and as a result, he was forced to choose between being absent from the proceedings or personally paying for an interpreter. The proceedings included a fact-finding hearing, a sentencing hearing, and a hearing to address his request for a sign language interpreter. The defendants argued that the hearings Prakel wanted to attend did not fall into the category of "judicial services" because they were not part of formal trial proceedings. The court disagreed, noting that Section 504's definition of "services, programs, and activities" as "all of the operations of . . . a local government" has also been applied to the ADA (*Prakel v. Indiana,* 2015). Accordingly, the Prakel court held that any public judicial proceeding or trial falls under the category of judicial service and must be accessible to people with disabilities.

Moreover, because the plaintiff in *Prakel* was a spectator rather than a criminal defendant, the case also raises the question of exactly whose rights are protected by the ADA. Title II states that "[a] public entity shall take appropriate steps to ensure that communications with applicants, participants, *members of the public,* and *companions with disabilities* [emphasis in original] are as effective as communications with others" (*Prakel v. Indiana,* 2015). Still, the *Prakel* defendants denied Prakel's request for a sign language interpreter partly on the basis that it was their court's practice to provide interpreters exclusively for witnesses and defendants during criminal proceedings. When determining whether the plaintiff was a qualified individual under the ADA, the court relied again on the U.S. Supreme Court's holding in *Lane,* recognizing that all members of the public have the right to participate in criminal proceedings. It also pointed out that the plain language of Title II extends the right to fully participate in public services, programs, and activities to members of the public, including spectators at criminal proceedings. While members of the public continue to face problems accessing judicial proceedings, cases like *Lane* and *Prakel* have helped to firmly establish the right of *all* people to participate in *every* stage of criminal proceedings. See also *Duvall v. County of Kitsap* (2001) (County failed to provide video-text display, which, if the county had done any investigation, would have been able to be provided through the court reporting service).

DEFENSES: UNDUE BURDEN AND FUNDAMENTAL ALTERATION

Under the ADA and Section 504, exceptions exist to the effective communication requirement. Covered entities do not need to provide auxiliary aids or services if doing so would either "fundamentally alter the nature of the goods, services, facilities, privileges, advantages, or accommodations being offered" or "would result in an undue burden, i.e., significant difficulty or expense" (ADA, 2016q; Judicial Administration, 1991c).

Further, if providing one particular auxiliary aid or service would result in a fundamental alteration or undue burden, the covered entity must provide an alternative, if one exists, so that effective communication is achieved to the maximum extent possible (ADA, 2016q; Judicial Administration, 1991c).

> Public entities with obligations under Title II have additional requirements before they can rely on the fundamental alteration or undue burden defenses. According to Title II regulations, the decision that compliance would result in such alteration or burdens must be made by the head of the public entity or his or her designee after considering all resources available for use in the funding and operation of the service, program, or activity and must be accompanied by a written statement of the reasons for reaching that conclusion (ADA, 2016q; Judicial Administration, 1991c).

For instance, in *Chisolm v. McManimon* (2001), the county detention center argued that providing the plaintiff with an ASL interpreter and a TTY would cause either an undue burden or a fundamental alteration (*Chisolm v. McManimon,* 2001). Citing the Title II regulations noted previously, the court found that the Mercer County Detention Center could not demonstrate that they had issued written statements explaining why they denied Chisolm's requests and therefore rejected this defense.

In general, defendants have a difficult time establishing undue burden and fundamental alteration in the effective communication context. Defendants sometimes use a slippery-slope argument when asserting undue burden, concerned about the potential for having to provide additional auxiliary aids or services in the future. It is important for defendants to remember to analyze the case at hand. In the *Prakel v. Indiana* (2015) case discussed previously, the defendants argued that they were not obligated to provide an ASL interpreter to the plaintiff because providing interpreters for spectators would unduly burden the court system by straining already limited financial resources (*Prakel v. Indiana,* 2015). The court rejected this argument and explained that the question at issue in this lawsuit was whether interpreting services needed to be provided to this plaintiff on a limited number of occasions, "not whether the statute requires state courts to provide interpreters for the entire deaf population throughout the Indiana court system" (*Prakel v. Indiana,* 2015). With respect to the question of whether providing interpreting services would be an undue burden to this one plaintiff, the court found that it would not.

REMEDIES

Under both Title II and Section 504, plaintiffs may seek both injunctive relief and compensatory damages. Punitive damages are not available under either law. Compensatory damages are recoverable; however, only if the plaintiff can show intentional discrimination. When deciding whether to award compensatory damages for intentional discrimination, the majority of courts require a showing of "deliberate indifference" (*Liese v. Indian River County Hospital District,* 2012). This standard does not require "personal animosity or ill will"; instead, "intentional discrimination may be inferred when a 'policymaker acted with at least deliberate indifference to the strong likelihood that a violation of federally protected rights will result from the implementation of the [challenged] policy . . . [or] custom'" (*Loeffler v. Staten Island University Hospital,* 2009).

Incarcerated people face an additional challenge in getting monetary damages for discrimination they face while they are incarcerated: the Prison Litigation Reform Act's (2012) (PLRA) personal injury requirement. The PLRA was enacted in response to what was perceived as an explosion of frivolous lawsuits brought by prisoners against prison officials.[13] To limit prisoners' ability to file lawsuits against prison officials, the PLRA includes a number of burdens and restrictions that frequently make it difficult for a lawsuit to survive, let alone result in any monetary damages. For instance, prisoners must pay all of their filing fees, even if they are indigent (Forma Pauperis, 1915), and they must first exhaust all administrative remedies within the prison system before seeking adjudication by the court (Prison Litigation Reform Act, 1995a).

The requirement to exhaust administrative remedies is particularly troublesome because if a prisoner fails to comply with even a single technical requirement, "his right to sue may be lost forever" (Fathi, 2009). Particularly problematic in the context of deaf prisoners seeking damages for violations of their rights under the ADA and Section 504 is PLRA Section 1997e's physical injury requirement. It states that "[n]o Federal civil action may be brought by a prisoner confined in a jail, prison, or other correctional facility, for mental or emotional injury suffered while in custody without a prior showing of physical injury" (Prison Litigation Reform Act, 1995b). Courts have interpreted Section 1997e as applying to claims brought under the ADA where the prisoner seeks mental or emotional damages for violation of their rights (*Cassidy v. Indiana Department of Corrections*, 2000; *Douglas v. Gusman*, 2008).

Plaintiffs are more likely to establish intentional discrimination when they clearly request an auxiliary aid or service, when the covered entity clearly disregards the request, and when the plaintiffs advise that they cannot understand the communication. For example, in *Pierce v. District of Columbia*, the jury awarded the plaintiff $70,000 (*Pierce v. District of Columbia*, 2016) where prison staff was "indisputably aware that Pierce was deaf" but failed to provide him with any accommodation (*Pierce v. District of Columbia*, 2015). Pierce had spent his 51 days in custody in "abject isolation" because prison staff "ignored his repeated requests to an interpreter" (*Pierce v. District of Columbia*, 2015). Besides ignoring Pierce's clear requests, the court was equally struck by the prison's failure to assess Pierce's accommodation needs, stating that in failing to do so, the prison staff

> figuratively shrugged and effectively sat on their hands with respect to this plainly hearing-disabled person in their custody, presumably content to rely on their own uninformed beliefs about how best to handle him and certainly failing to engage in any meaningful assessment of his needs. (*Pierce v. District of Columbia*, 2016)

Compare that case with the situation in *Rylee v. Chapman* (2009). There, the plaintiff's wife told the police before he was arrested that Rylee was deaf but was able to read lips, read, and write. He was arrested in his home, booked in jail, and spent one night in jail. Throughout the communications, Rylee presented no evidence that the police officers knew or believed that Rylee could not read lips or that he requested an interpreter. He did ask a police officer to write questions, and the officer agreed to do so. Furthermore, when asked if he could read lips, he said yes and offered that he could also read and write. All of the police procedure was by the book. As a result, the court granted the county's motion for summary judgment, and the Eleventh Circuit affirmed the decision.

When analyzing a plaintiff's request for only injunctive (nonmonetary) relief, courts consider whether there is evidence that a plaintiff is likely to return in the future such that the plaintiff has standing to seek this type of relief.

One issue that sometimes arises in these cases is whether the plaintiffs' request for injunctive relief is moot or no longer necessary, given the correctional facility's actions toward greater compliance during the pendency of the litigation (see, e.g., *McBride v. Michigan Department of Corrections* [2018]; "absent appropriate injunctive relief, the MDOC's deaf and hard of hearing inmates face a very real risk of not timely receiving the accommodations they need to effectively communicate during 'high stakes' interactions such as medical appointments").

TELECOMMUNICATIONS ACT AND HEARING AID COMPATIBILITY ACT

Prior to the passage of ADA, Congress passed amendments to the Communications Act of 1934, including the Telecommunications Act of 1996. These amendments (specifically, Section 255 of the Communications Act) required telecommunications products and services to be accessible to and usable by people with disabilities if readily achievable. These products were to be designed to be compatible with adaptive equipment. The Hearing Aid Compatibility Act of 1988 also required that telephones made in the United States or imported into the country to be compatible with hearing aids. These laws are also important to the rights of deaf individuals in the criminal justice system.

CONCLUSION

Freedom from discrimination in the field of criminal justice is crucially important to all individuals, especially those who are deaf. The power of the criminal justice system is great, and the impact of an individual's exposure to the criminal justice system is long-lasting. Although various legal remedies exist, it is important for people with disabilities and their advocates to understand their rights under the ADA and Section 504, just as it is critical for those working within the criminal justice system to understand and fulfill their responsibilities.

ACKNOWLEDGMENTS

The authors would like to thank Michelle Smit for her valuable assistance, as well as Sarah Dobrofsky, Jennifer James, Brian Phelps, Lauren Latterell Powell, and James Naughton. Funding was generously provided by the Great Lakes ADA Center and the National Institute on Disability Independent Living and Rehabilitation Research.

NOTES

1. Title II of the ADA, 42 U.S.C. § 12132 (2016) states: "No qualified individual with a disability shall, by reason of such disability, be excluded from participation in or be denied the benefits of the services, programs, or activities of a public entity, or be subjected to discrimination by any such entity."

2. Section 504 of the Rehabilitation Act, 29 U.S.C. § 794(a) (2016) states: "No otherwise qualified individual with a disability in the United States . . . shall, solely by reason of her or his disability, be excluded from the participation in, be denied the benefits of, or be subjected to discrimination under any program or activity receiving Federal financial assistance."

3. Judicial Administration, 28 C.F.R. § 35.130(b)(7)(i) ("A public entity shall make reasonable modifications in policies, practices, or procedures when the modifications are necessary to avoid discrimination on the basis of disability, unless the public entity can demonstrate that making the modifications would fundamentally alter the nature of the service, program, or activity.")

4. Judicial Administration, 28 C.F.R. § 35.130(d) ("A public entity shall administer services, programs, and activities in the most integrated setting appropriate to the needs of qualified individuals with disabilities.")

5. Judicial Administration 28 C.F.R. § 35.160(b)(1) ("A public entity shall furnish appropriate auxiliary aids and services where necessary to afford individuals with disabilities, including applicants, participants, companions, and members of the public, an equal opportunity to participate in, and enjoy the benefits of, a service, program, or activity of a public entity.")

6. *Settlement Agreement with The City of Philadelphia and The Philadelphia Police Department*, ADA.Gov. www.ada.gov/ppd_sa.html. In addition, under the terms of the settlement agreement, the City and the Police Department agreed to pay $97,500 to be distributed among individuals identified by and in amounts determined by the United States and to develop a communication card for use by law enforcement personnel to communicate with the Deaf community during routine interactions, to maintain contracts with qualified oral/sign language interpreter agencies, to update its electronic detainee tracing system to notify enforcement personnel of a detainee's disability and preferred auxiliary aids, and to develop a training program for personnel.

7. *Settlement Agreement between the United States of America and Elizabeth F. Arthur*, ADA.Gov, (2016, November 17). www.ada.gov/arlington_co_sheriff_sa.html. In addition, under the terms of the settlement agreement, the complainant was awarded $250,000, and the Sheriff agreed to implement substantial changes, including having an ADA coordinator, revising its policies to provide auxiliary aids and services promptly, ensure telephone access via VP, and provide hearing aid and cochlear implant batteries.

8. An oral interpreter facilitates communication for persons who are deaf and use speech and lipreading as their primary mode of communication. Oral interpreters silently mouth sentences to the person who is deaf. If a word is difficult to lipread, the oral interpreter may rephrase the word or sentence as needed.

9. Separately, it should be noted that ASL and English are not the same; thus some people who are deaf may be fluent in ASL but unable to read English, making passing notes ineffective even for simple communications.

10. However, it is worth noting that inmates' opportunities for recovery are limited by the PLRA, which requires prisoners to exhaust administrative remedies before filing in federal court. *See* 42 U.S.C. § 1997e.

11. The DOJ reached a settlement agreement with the South Carolina Department of Corrections (SCDC) to similarly ensure that inmates with hearing disabilities are provided with auxiliary aids and services. See *Settlement Agreement Between the United States of America and South Carolina Department of Corrections Under the Americans With Disabilities Act*. https:// www.ada.gov/south_carolina_doc_sa.html

12. For an overview of these settlements, see National Association of the Deaf's *Landmark Settlements Reached in Maryland and Kentucky for Deaf Prisoners*. https://www.nad.org/2015/06/08/landmark-settlements-reached-in-maryland-and-kentucky-for-deaf-prisoners/

13. See, e.g., Letter from National Association of Attorneys General to Senator Bob Dole (Sept. 19, 1995), 141 Cong. Rec. S14, 417-18 (daily ed. Sept. 27, 1995). (In discussing the increase in prisoner litigation, noting that "while all of these cases are not frivolous, more than 95 percent of inmate civil rights suits are dismissed without the inmate receiving anything.")

REFERENCES

Americans With Disabilities Act of 1990, 42 U.S.C. §§ 12131–12134 (2016a).
Americans With Disabilities Act of 1990, 42 U.S.C. §§ 12131–12134 (2016b).
Americans With Disabilities Act of 1990, 42 U.S.C. § 12132 (2016c).
Americans With Disabilities Act of 1990, 42 U.S.C. § 12132 (2016d).
Americans With Disabilities Act of 1990, 42 U.S.C. § 12132 (2016e).
Americans With Disabilities Act of 1990, 42 U.S.C. § 12132 (2016f).
Americans With Disabilities Act of 1990, 42 U.S.C. § 12132 (2016g).
Americans With Disabilities Act of 1990, 42 U.S.C. § 12132 (2016h).
Americans With Disabilities Act of 1990, 42 U.S.C. § 12132 (2016i).
Americans With Disabilities Act of 1990, 42 U.S.C. § 12132 (2016j).
Americans With Disabilities Act of 1990, 42 U.S.C. § 12132 (2016k).
Americans With Disabilities Act of 1990, 42 U.S.C. § 12132 (2016l).
Americans With Disabilities Act of 1990, 42 U.S.C. § 12132 (2016m).
Americans With Disabilities Act of 1990, 42 U.S.C. § 12132 (2016n).
Americans With Disabilities Act of 1990, 42 U.S.C. § 12132 (2016o).
Americans With Disabilities Act of 1990, 42 U.S.C. § 12132 (2016p).
Americans With Disabilities Act of 1990, 42 U.S.C. § 12132 (2016q).
Bahl v. County of Ramsey, 695 F.3d 778, 785 (8th Cir. 2012).
Bearden v. Clark County, 2016 WL 1158693 (W.D. Wash. Mar. 24, 2016).
Bircoll v. Miami-Dade County, 480 F.3d 1072 (11th Cir. 2007).
Bronson, J., Maruschak, L., & Berzofsky, M. (2015, December). *Disabilities among prison and jail inmates, 2011–2012*. Bureau of Statistics, Dec. 2015. www.bjs.gov/content/pub/pdf/dpji1112.pdf
Bureau of Justice Statistics. (2015). *About a third of prison and jail inmates reported a disability in 2011*. www.bjs.gov/content/pub/press/dpji1112pr.cfm
Cassidy v. Indiana Department of Corrections, 199 F.3d 374 (7th Cir. 2000).
C.V. v. Dudek, 209 F. Supp. 3d 1279 (2016) (holding, *sua sponte*, that the DOJ lacks authority to bring claims under Title II of the ADA), *appeal filed, A.R. v. Secretary Health Care Administration*, No. 17-13595, 2018 WL 1242190 (11th Cir. Aug. 8, 2017).
Chisolm v. McManimon, 275 F.3d 315 (3d Cir. 2001).
Clarkson v. Coughlin, 898 F. Supp. 1019 (S.D.N.Y. 1995).
The Communications Act of 1934, 47 U.S.C. § 151 et seq.
Disability Rights Florida, Inc. v. Jones, No. 4:16-cv-47-RS-CAS (N.D. Fla. 2017). www.floridajusticeinstitute.org/wp-content/uploads/2017/08/Settlement-Agreement-no-exhibits-searchable-07148878xB3B17.pdf
Douglas v. Gusman, 567 F. Supp. 2d 877 (E.D. La. 2008).

Durrenberger v. Texas Department of Criminal Justice, 757 F. Supp. 2d 640 (S.D. Tex. 2010).
Fathi, D. (2009). *No equal justice: The Prison Litigation Reform Act in the United States*. www.hrw.org/report/2009/06/16/no-equal-justice/prison-litigation-reform-act-united-states
Forma Pauperis. (1915). 28 U.S.C. §§ 1915(a)-(b) (2012).
Gohier v. Enright, 186 F.3d 1216, 1221 (10th Cir. 1999).
Hainze v. Richards, 207 F.3d 795, 801 (5th Cir. 2000).
Hearing Aid Compatability Act of 1988, Public Law 100-39, 102 Stat. 976 (1988).
Heyer v. United States Bureau of Prisons, 849 F.3d 202 (4th Cir. 2017).
Hoffman v. Marion County, Tex., 592 F. App'x 256 (5th Cir. 2014).
Holmes et al. v. Baldwin, 11-cv-2961, N.D. Illinois, Stipulation of Settlement, approved July 26, 2018. www.equipforequality.org/wp-content/uploads/2018/07/Holmes-Stipulation-of-Settlement.pdf
Holmes v. Godinez, 311 F.R.D. 177, 228 (N.D. Ill. 2015).
Jarboe et al. v. Maryland Department of Public Safety and Correctional Services (DPSCS), et al., U.S. District Court of Maryland Case No. 1:12-(cv-00572-ELH (2015). http://www.washlaw.org/pdf/signed_jarboe_settlement_agreement.PDF
Judicial Administration, 28 C.F.R. § 35.104 (2010).
Judicial Administration, 28 C.F.R. § 35.130(b)(7)(i) (1991a).
Judicial Administration, 28 C.F.R. § 35.130(d) (1991b).
Judicial Administration, 28 C.F.R. § 35.160(a)(1) (2010b).
Judicial Administration, 28 C.F.R. § 35.160(b)(1) (2010c).
Judicial Administration, 28 C.F.R. § 35.160(b)(2) (2010d).
Judicial Administration, 28 C.F.R. § 35.160(d) (2010e).
Judicial Administration, 28 C.F.R. § 35.164 (1991c).
Liese v. Indian River County Hosp. Dist., 701 F.3d 334 (11th Cir. 2012) (collecting cases, including cases from the Second, Eighth, Ninth, and Tenth Circuit, applying a deliberate indifference standard).
Loeffler v. Staten Island University Hosp., 582 F.3d 268, 275 (2d Cir. 2009).
Loye v. County of Dakota, 625 F.3d 494 (8th Cir. 2010).
McBride v. Michigan Department of Corrections, 294 F. Supp. 3d 695 (E.D. Mich. 2018).
Minnis v. Johnson, 10-cv-0096 (E.D. Va. filed 2010). https://www.clearinghouse.net/detailDocument.php?id=69410
Morales v. Saint Barnabas Medical Center, 13-cv-06363 (D.N.J. Consent Order, Feb. 14, 2017).
National Association of the Deaf. (2018). *Minimum standards for video remote interpreting services in medical settings*. http://nad.org/issues/technology/vri/position-statement-hospitals
National Disability Rights Network and National Association of the Deaf. (2016, January 19). *Second report and order and third further notice of proposed rulemaking*. www.ndrn.org/images/Documents/Issues/Juvenile_Justice/FCC_Comment_NDRN_NAD_FINAL_FOR_FILING.pdf
Pennsylvania Department of Corrections. Yeskey, 524 U.S. 206, 213 (1998).
Pierce v. District of Columbia, 128 F. Supp. 3d 250 (D.D.C. 2015).
Pierce v. District of Columbia, Judgment on the Verdict for Plaintiff, 2016 WL 3571562 (D.D.C. 2016).
Prakel v. Indiana, 100 F. Supp. 3d 661 (S.D. Ind. 2015).
Prison Litigation Reform Act of 1995a, Pub. L. No. 104–134, 110 Stat. 1321–66 (codified at 42 U.S.C. § 1997e (2012)).

Prison Litigation Reform Act of 1995b, Pub. L. No. 104–134, 110 Stat. 1321–66 (codified at 42 U.S.C. § 1997e (2012), 42 U.S.C. § 1997e(e) (2000)).
Rehabilitation Act of 2016, Section 504, 29 U.S.C. § 794 (2016).
Rehabilitation Act of 2016, Section 504, 29 U.S.C. § 794(a) (2016a).
Rogers et al. v. Colorado Department of Corrections, 2019 WL 4464036 (D. Colo. Sept. 19, 2019).
Rylee v. Chapman, 316 F. App'x. 901 (11th Cir. 2009).
Seremeth v. Board of County Commissioners Frederick County, 673 F.3d 333, 338–339 (4th Cir. 2012).
Settlement Agreement Between the United States of America and Mountain States Health Alliance Under the Americans With Disabilities Act. (2016). https://www.ada.gov/mountain_state_sa.html
Settlement Agreement Between the United States of America and South Carolina Department of Corrections Under the Americans With Disabilities Act. (2018). https://www.ada.gov/south_carolina_doc_sa.html
Silva v. Baptist Health South Florida, 856 F.3d 824, 832 (11th Cir. 2017).
Statement of Interest of the United States, *Robinson v. Farley*, 15-cv-00803 (2016, June 20). www.ada.gov/briefs/robinson_soi.pdf (last visited Sept. 6, 2018).
Taylor v. City of Mason, 970 F.Supp.2d 776 (S.D. Ohio 2013).
Telecommunications Act of 1996, 47 U.S.C. 609.
Tennessee v. Lane, 541 U.S. 509 (2004).
Telecommunications Act of 1996, Pub. L. No. 104-104, 110 Stat. 56, codified throughout Title 47 of the U.S.C.
Tucker v. Tennessee, 539 F.3d 526, 534 (6th Cir. 2008).
U.S. Department of Justice. (2015a). *Agreement between the United States of America and City of Rochester, New York.* www.justice.gov/crt/foia/readingroom/frequent_requests/ada_settlements/ny/ny10.txt
U.S. Department of Justice. (2015b, May 15). *Justice Department settles effective communication case with Wallingford Police Department.* www.justice.gov/usao-ct/pr/justice-department-settles-effective-communication-case-wallingford-police-department
U.S. Department of Justice. (2015c, July 29). *Rochester Police Department reaches settlement to ensure effective communication for deaf and hard of hearing individuals.* www.justice.gov/usao-edmi/pr/rochester-police-department-reaches-settlement-ensure-effective-communication-deaf
U.S. Department of Justice. (2015d, April 28). *Ware Police Department enters into agreement to guarantee effective communication for hearing impaired.* www.justice.gov/usao-ma/pr/ware-police-department-enters-agreement-guarantee-effective-communication-hearing
U.S. Department of Justice. (2016). *Office for Civil Rights letter of finding.* www.ada.gov/briefs/philadelphia_pd_lof.pdf
U.S. Department of Justice, Civil Rights Division, Disability Rights Section. (2014, January 31). *Effective communication.* www.ada.gov/effective-comm.htm
United States v. City of Columbia Police. (2016).
United States v. City of Philadelphia Police. (2016).
United States v. Elizabeth F. Arthur. (2016).
Valanzuolo v. City of New Haven, 972 F. Supp. 2d 263 (D. Conn. 2013).
Waller ex rel. Estate of Hunt v. City of Danville, 556 F.3d 171, 175 (4th Cir. 2009).
Williams v. City of New York, 121 F.Supp.3d 354 (S.D.N.Y. 2015).
Yeh v. United States Bureau of Prisons, 2019 WL 1330446 (M.D. Pa. March 25, 2019).

10

The Attorney–Client Relationship

Amber D. Farrelly

One of the most important professional relationships is between the attorney and their client. The relationship typically begins as strangers, is solidified via a contractual agreement, and is maintained through trust at will. The relationship is based on either a selective choice, as in civil cases or a necessity and right, as in criminal cases. The relationship is most often formed before the attorney has any knowledge of the case and certainly without reviewing any evidence. The client meets with the lawyer with a story. Often, the client does not know what is important, and the lawyer must direct the conversation and ask questions to ascertain relevant information. Regardless of how the relationship is formed, it is the relationship that is vital to the outcome of the case. This relationship can present unique challenges when an attorney is representing a deaf client and may be unaware of how best to work with the individual.

The attorney–client relationship is formed when either

> a person manifests to a lawyer the person's intent that the lawyer provide legal services for the person; and either (a) the lawyer manifests to the person consent to do so; or (b) the lawyer fails to manifest lack of consent to do so, and the lawyer knows or reasonably should know that the person reasonably relies on the lawyer to provide the services; or a tribunal with power to do so appoints the lawyer to provide the services. (American Law Institute, 2000)

This relationship can be strained or even fail when representing a deaf client if certain things are not taken into consideration. Aspects such as language, culture, prior knowledge, experience, use of interpreters, and other factors can impact the relationship and the case. These difficulties may be obvious if the attorney has little to no prior knowledge or awareness, but it can also affect the relationship even if the attorney is well versed in working with deaf individuals and fluent in American Sign Language (ASL). In most states, there are few attorneys who are deaf or hearing and fluent in ASL. There are some attorneys who can fingerspell or know minimal signs. In some cases, they have told the judge that interpreters may not be needed and that they can sign well enough to communicate with the client, whereas their sign language is, in fact, limited, and judges may be led to believe that they do not need to hire interpreters. This can be detrimental to the representation that the client receives. These attorneys perpetuate the myth that it is permissible to write back and forth for communication. Often, the attorneys do not realize their transgression and believe they are doing the right thing. These attorneys are saving the court money, and some judges may believe that adequate communication is happening. It is important for a deaf client to have a competent attorney who provides them with excellent communication access.

THE RIGHT TO COUNSEL

This right to an attorney in criminal cases is guaranteed by and found in the Bill of Rights. The right to counsel is a fundamental right that, until it is needed, is not given much thought. Most hearing people understand the right to an attorney on the basis of *Miranda* warnings seen repeatedly in television shows and movies and may be able to recite part of it from memory. However, to a deaf individual, this may be a vague concept that is not clearly or easily understood. Some attempts have been made to make an ASL version of the *Miranda* rights, but even so, the information can be complex and confusing. One must have extensive knowledge of legal terminology and the U.S. Constitution.

The Sixth Amendment of the Constitution provides that

> [i]n all criminal prosecutions, the accused shall enjoy the right to a speedy and public trial, by an impartial jury of the State and district wherein the crime shall have been committed, to be confronted with the witnesses against him; to have compulsory process for obtaining witnesses in his favor, and to have the Assistance of Counsel for his defense.

Although it is clear that the Sixth Amendment captures the fundamental rights to a lawyer, a trial by jury, and the confrontation of witnesses against the accused, the right to counsel has not always been so evident. It was not until 1932 when nine young Black boys charged with sexually assaulting a White girl were expeditiously tried and sentenced to death, that the law changed (*Powell et al. v. Alabama*, 1932).

Gideon v. Wainwright

Gideon v. Wainwright (1963) is perhaps one of the most important U.S. Supreme Court cases that have impacted the criminal justice system. In *Gideon*, the

Supreme Court recognized that defense lawyers "are necessities, not luxuries." The court held that the Sixth Amendment provides that "[i]n our adversary system of criminal justice, any person hauled into court, who is too poor to hire a lawyer, cannot be assured a fair trial unless counsel is provided for him."

The right to counsel is a fundamental right applied to the states via the Fourteenth Amendment of the U.S. Constitution's due process clause (U.S. Const. amend. XIV, § 1) and the Sixth Amendment. Approximately 97% of all criminal cases plead guilty (Del Valle, 2017). This leaves very few cases that make it to trial. The defense attorney must rely on the prosecution to provide them with evidence. They must rely on experts employed by the defense to assist in areas where the attorney may not be competently skilled, including experts with deaf clients. If these attorneys do not know or understand Deaf culture and other related issues, they are at a disadvantage. This is particularly relevant because most of these attorneys do not realize they are at a disadvantage. Most often, sign language interpreters are the ones with the knowledge and ability to point out some of the issues and then make them known to the attorney. For example, interpreters who often work in legal settings are familiar with how a court functions and how interpreting services are requested. Many interpreters who work in these settings may have acquired knowledge concerning social services that routinely affect deaf people, such as Social Security, rehabilitative agencies that provide services and equipment, various rules and statutes that determine which entity is responsible for paying for interpreting services as well as language and cultural nuances that may affect communication, and so forth.

It is not difficult to understand the evolution from *Powell* to today. It is a given in our current system that indigent or impoverished people, who cannot afford an attorney, are entitled to have one appointed in criminal cases. Those individuals who are wealthy enough to afford legal counsel can search for and interview potential attorneys and hire whomever they choose. People who have money and are affluent have endless potential resources. On the other hand, the indigent person who cannot afford to retain private counsel is at a disadvantage. The Supreme Court recognized that "[t]here can be no equal justice where the kind of trial a man gets depends on the amount of money he has" (*Griffin v. Illinois*, 1956). Many deaf people cannot afford representation and must rely on appointed counsel. Many cases that involve deaf clients can be even more costly because they require additional experts that focus on language, culture, and other professionals that may be unique to deaf persons.

In a criminal matter, regardless of whether the attorney is appointed or retained, the client has a right to access and communication with their attorney. In criminal cases, an interpreter is a constitutional right in order for attorney–client communication to occur. This right is guaranteed under the Sixth Amendment. In civil matters, the right to counsel is not guaranteed and provided for as in a criminal case. A party in a civil suit must retain their attorney by other means. Civil attorneys may decide to accept the case or decline it. If an interpreter is needed for attorney–client communication outside of the courtroom, then the costs are generally the responsibility of the attorney. However, in a courtroom, regardless of whether the proceedings are criminal or civil, the court is responsible for providing the interpreters.

Perhaps the most famous and memorable example of this was the 1995 OJ Simpson trial. Mr. Simpson had what was called the "Dream Team." These attorneys were some of the most influential, talented lawyers available. Initially led by Robert Shapiro, it was Johnny Cochran who would become nationally renowned for his phrase, "if it doesn't fit, you must acquit." Barry Scheck, who would later become a cofounder of the Innocence Project, guided the defense team in, what was at the time, cutting edge technology—DNA. Scheck was able to undermine the prosecution's forensic evidence. In view of the unlimited resources at their disposal, in just a short time, the Dream Team was able to successfully defend Mr. Simpson, securing an acquittal. This kind of situation would rarely happen with a deaf person because it is unusual for most people to have these kinds of monetary resources.

There is a fundamental and recognizable imbalance in resources and funds between the defendant and the prosecution. In a criminal case, it is the mighty, powerful government versus the citizen accused. The government, be it federal or state, has an ample budget at its disposal. It has unlimited resources and sole access to almost all of the evidence in the case.

This is in contrast to the typical defendant. If money and wealth are abundant, there are no bounds to the defense that can be mounted. Attorneys can invest considerable time and employ investigators and experts to inquire into every facet of the defensive theory. When representing deaf clients, it is important to have investigators who sign or have an interpreter with them to interpret for witnesses, experts who can advise about Deaf culture and education, and linguistic experts who can testify and evaluate deaf defendants for language and comprehension. It is not only costly to hire these kinds of experts but also challenging to find people with these skills.

The citizen accused has a clear limit to their financial resources. Often the choice for a defendant is to request a court-appointed/public defender or represent oneself pro se, which is often not really a "choice." Deaf people have historically been underemployed for many reasons, including discrimination, lack of employers' willingness or ability to provide accommodations, and accessibility related to training and resources. As the economy fluctuates and the government restricts household assistance, many deaf people may have limited income means.

The right to appointed counsel is applied differently across the states and does not necessarily mean a "free" lawyer. When the indigent defendant is appointed an attorney, it often leaves little time to meet and discuss the case—fears and patience then test the attorney–client relationship. The maintenance of the relationship is ultimately the responsibility of the attorney and requires absolute and complete trust and honesty. The relationship is often precarious owing to the perception and imbalance of power and request of absolute trust upon meeting. Imagine being a deaf person who is accused of a crime that they may not have committed and being appointed an attorney that they have never met before. The legal process can be slow, and the attorney and client have limited time to meet and talk about the case. An attorney may schedule an appointment and is not aware that the client requires an interpreter for the appointment, or the scheduled interpreter does not show or is unavailable. These situations can make the deaf client even more anxious and fearful about the potential outcome of the case. Additionally, the client may not realize that the attorney has many other clients and may not be as available as they think they need them to be.

Asking someone to have blind faith in a stranger with their finances, their children, or their life, is extremely demanding. Yet trust is required. The role of trust in the relationship is interdependent. If the client does not trust their attorney, they will not follow their advice. Likewise, the attorney must have the faith and confidence in their client that they have provided accurate and full information. Linguistic challenges with deaf clients may impede the confidence that the facts given to the attorney are completely accurate. This includes the lack of familiarity with legal terminology or a general misunderstanding of what the legal issues are. Clients often have the misconception that interpreters are required in every situation, although they are not (e.g., traffic violation stops typically do not warrant an interpreter on the scene by law). Additionally, deaf clients may be under the misconception that law enforcement is required to handcuff them in front of their body. These and other misconceptions are frequent. If a deaf client is diagnosed with anxiety, attention deficit disorder, autism, and so on, it can impact, or interfere with, how the attorney relays information to the deaf client. If the attorney feels that the client is withholding information, the attorney cannot adequately represent the client, in the end negatively impacting the client. It is either equally stable or equally fragile.

The client must be able to openly discuss their case regardless of their actions and what the accusations are. They must be able to confide the most intimate of details without hesitation. This can be especially challenging in assaultive cases such as sexual accusations, which can be sensitive in nature. This is made more challenging if the attorney and client are of the opposite sex. Having a female attorney asking intimate details about the nature of their client's relationship or specifics about possible sexual acts or intercourse are difficult to discuss. The challenge is compounded by adding a third person, such as an interpreter, in the room. The presence of an interpreter affects the dynamics of the interaction. Having an interpreter present impacts the relationship between the client and the attorney. Additionally, it is important to keep in mind that when the attorney is representing a deaf male client accused of a sexual crime, having a female interpreter can hinder the interaction and openness between the attorney and the client.

THE DUTY OF AN ATTORNEY

Attorneys have a variety of different roles. A lawyer acts not only as an advisor and advocate but also as a negotiator, an intermediary, and often a social worker. Attorneys assist clients by providing legal advice and guiding them through the legal process. It is the attorney's duty to investigate the allegations in the case, interview witnesses, review evidence, acquire experts if needed, look at the applicable law and ensure there have been no violations, investigate mitigation aspects, negotiate with the prosecution, cross-examine witnesses, make objections, and present legal and strategic defenses. The American Bar Association (ABA) Model Rules of Professional Conduct states that "[a] lawyer shall provide competent representation to a client. Competent representation requires the legal knowledge, skill, thoroughness and preparation reasonably necessary for the representation" (ABA Center for Professional Responsibility, 2014a, Rule 1.1). When this obligation cannot be fulfilled, the defense attorney has a duty to decline representation. This includes attorneys who are not adequately skilled in legal issues or able to effectively represent deaf clients (ABA Center for Professional Responsibility, 2014a).

In order to successfully represent any client, the attorney must be able to "understand their situation, evaluate the legal rights and duties, and give accurate legal advice as to the best course of action to pursue" (Compton, 2018). It is the duty of the attorney to present to the client their rights and to give advice. The Constitution provides that the client has the absolute right to testify and to determine whether they want to accept an offer and plea or go to trial. "Because clients often make important decisions based on the information produced by their lawyers' specialized legal evaluations, lawyers must communicate that information to clients regularly and effectively" (Compton, 2018). When attorneys do not effectively communicate with deaf clients, the information relayed to them may be inaccurate, and the decision of the client is not freely and voluntarily given.

Under *Gonzalez v. United States* (2008), trial management is up to the trial attorney, who assists by making decisions such as what arguments to pursue, objections to raise, and agreements to conclude regarding the admission of evidence. However, some decisions are reserved for the client: whether to plead guilty, waive the right to a jury trial, testify on one's own behalf, and forgo an appeal (*Jones v. Barnes*, 1983). The Supreme Court held in *United States v. Mullins* (2002) that a defendant's right to testify (or not to) is personal to the defendant, who alone may make the choice and must do so knowingly and voluntarily. "Because attorney-client communication is crucial to diligent representation, an attorney has a professional responsibility to ensure, particularly for a deaf client, that the attorney–client communication and the client–court proceeding communication are meaningful and effective throughout that legal represent" (Compton, 2018). It is imperative that the attorney listens to the client. First impressions are lasting and can often be misleading. Clients that are hesitant in their answers may be mistakenly assumed to be untruthful or hiding something. Clients who are inattentive may be masking a mental illness. Clients who are lethargic may be mistaken to be under the influence of drugs. Quiet clients may be masking misunderstanding or covering deprivation language or cognitive delay. The attorney must often elicit the true information from a client over time. It is essential to have a competent, highly skilled legal interpreter who can effectively communicate between attorney and client and be able to culturally mediate these situations. Cultural mediation is imperative because it helps to facilitate full and effective communication by filling in the gaps and supplying information to all parties, bridging the gap between the hearing and the deaf world.

Another duty of the defense attorney is to educate the client about the legal process and their options. Although television has aided the modern citizen in a superficial understanding of the processes of the criminal justice system, those who do not watch *Law and Order* and various other television crime shows are often left behind. Most deaf defendants have never heard the word "prosecutor," "burden of proof," or "presumption of innocence," and these concepts have to be explained. The attorney has a duty to educate the client about the basics of the criminal justice system, and this education must be clearly communicated. If accommodations are not provided, there can be a misunderstanding, with detrimental consequences to the defendant and all parties involved.

INTERPRETERS

For an attorney and the court to fulfill their duties, appropriate accommodations must be made for deaf clients if needed. The most common accommodation is an ASL interpreter. There are also diverse other accommodations that some clients may require.[1] It is important to defer to the client as to which accommodation best fits their needs. Although particular statutes discussing accessibility to interpreters vary among states and jurisdictions, the right to an interpreter in criminal cases is guaranteed by the U.S. Constitution. The Supreme Court held that "[t]he right of an accused in a criminal trial to due process is, in essence, the right to a fair opportunity to defend against the State's accusations" (*Chambers v. Mississippi*, 1973). This right stems from the Sixth Amendment's Compulsory Process and Confrontation Clauses and guarantees that a criminal defendant is provided with "a meaningful opportunity to present a complete defense" (*Hawkins v. Costello*, 2006). "The right to confrontation includes the right to trial proceedings interpreted in a language that a defendant can understand" (*Vasquez v. State*, 1991). "This is necessary because unless the defendant ha[s] knowledge of the testimony of the witnesses against him, he [can] not exercise his right of cross-examination" (*Garcia v. State*, 1948). Thus, when it is made known to the trial court that a defendant does not understand the English language, an interpreter must be provided to translate the proceedings for the defendant (*Baltierra v. State*, 1979). Additionally, "the Sixth Amendment right to participate in one's own trial encompasses the right to reasonable accommodations for impairments to that participation, including hearing impairments" (*United States ex Rel. Negron v. State of N.Y.*, 1970), and "that such accommodations must be commensurate with the severity of the hearing impairment" (*United States v. Crandall*, 2014). However, if the court is not made aware of the need for adequate accommodations, then the defendant will receive only those that are asserted or plainly obvious to the court. Assertion of this right must be made timely and from the outset of the case before the court. Delay may risk proper accommodations or may waive the right. This is particularly relevant in cases involving deaf clients. Although many courts will try to improvise what is thought to be accommodations by having the deaf person try to read over the court reporter's shoulder, giving a summary of the case during breaks, or using a noncertified/unqualified interpreter, these measures do not meet the requirements of due process or the law. These ad hoc measures reduce the experience to the equivalent of the client's absence from the courtroom.

The U.S. Supreme Court has long held that "[c]onsiderations of fairness, the integrity of the fact-finding process, and the potency of our adversary system of justice forbid that the state should prosecute a defendant who is not present at his own trial" (*Lewis v. United States*, 1892). In *United States v. Crandall* (2014), the Supreme Court held that a defendant who spoke no English and "s[a]t in total incomprehension as the trial proceeded" was not sufficiently "present" to satisfy the dictates of the Sixth Amendment.

> The right to be present at one's criminal trial is a fundamental right. To be 'present' requires that a defendant be more than just physically present. It assumes that a defendant will be informed about the proceedings so he or she can assist in the defense. (*State v. Calderon*, 2000)

"The accused's right to have the trial proceedings accurately interpreted in a language they understand is also a matter of due process" (*Pate v. Robinson*, 1966). Once a court is "put on notice of a defendant's severe language difficulty, make unmistakably clear to him that he has a right to have a competent translator assist him, at state expense if need be, throughout his trial" (*United States ex Rel. Negron v. State of N.Y.*, 1970) When the accessibility to interpreters is not recognized by the attorney or the court, the client's due process rights are violated, and the case is severely obstructed. Attorneys must be aware of specific laws and accommodations if challenged by the court when requesting an interpreter or other access means.

Too often, deaf clients, even with an attorney, go through the entire criminal process without an interpreter. And those who do utilize one do not do so until the final day in court, a plea that takes as little as 15 minutes, or until the decision to go to trial. And practically every entity—the court, the prosecution, and the defense attorney—may believe this is "good enough" and acceptable. Without being sure that the information was made clear to the client and that they completely understood their rights and any rights waived were made freely and voluntarily, there is a clear violation of due process.

It is imperative that when an attorney meets with a deaf client, they provide a certified, qualified interpreter or other accommodation to facilitate a meaningful conversation about the client's needs, goals, and objectives. Equally important are any additional meetings, the review of documents, and relayed information with regard to choices and rights of the client. Having a friend or family member "interpret" client meetings with the attorney is not best practice.

Additionally, and equally integral to the right to be present is that the criminal defendant "possess sufficient ability to consult with his lawyer with a reasonable degree of rational understanding" (*United States ex Rel. Negron v. State of N.Y.*, 1970). It is crucial to the attorney–client relationship that those working with the attorney are complementary to the team. This applies especially to sign language interpreters. Interpreters who work with an attorney to interpret confidential and privileged conversations for a client are considered as both experts and members of that client's case team. There is a clear alliance. The interpreter who participates as the intermediary between the attorney and the client and who is there in the capacity for communication, information, and cultural mediation sits as the interpreter for counsel (IFC). The IFC is an expert aiding the client and attorney in mediating between the hearing and deaf worlds. To fulfill this responsibility, the interpreter must be qualified and, in most instances, legally certified. Certification requirements for a legal interpreter vary from state to state. Some statutes require specific certification or licensure, whereas others do not require any. It is important to check the jurisdiction to ensure compliance with the law. Regardless of jurisdiction, as a general rule, the courts have held that the interpreter must be competent and qualified.

To utilize an unqualified interpreter would be an error. The court in *Watson v. State* (1980) held that "the trial court's appointment of an interpreter who was unqualified to 'translate' the witness's testimony and who was something less than neutral and detached vis a vis the outcome of the proceedings." Qualified "includes having an interpreter considered to possess adequate interpreting skills for the particular situation and familiar with the use of slang" (*Leal v. State*, 1989). "Translation of the proceedings in the native language of the accused ensures that the accused understands the full ramifications and proceedings against him" (*Shu Guo Kan v. State*, 1999). Both competency and adequacy of the interpreter affect the case and may be challenged.

> Where an interpreter has been appointed, the standard of review depends on the nature of the complaint made. An attack on the competency of an interpreter is distinct from an attack on the accuracy of a translation. The former is a question of law and so reviewable by an appellate court. (*Garcia v. State*, 1994)

"The competence of an interpreter is for the trial court's determination, however, and an appellate court may only reverse for an abuse of discretion" (*Mendiola v. State*, 1995; *Montoya v. State*, 1991; *Martins v. State*, 2001). In a criminal case, "the court-appointed interpreter's incomplete and inaccurate translation denied [the defendant] his right of confrontation and prevented him from adequately understanding the trial proceedings" (*Shu Guo Kan v. State*, 1999).

Likewise, the client must be made comfortable enough to share their feelings and concerns about the competency and adequacy of the interpreter with the attorney. It is the attorney's duty to prepare with the interpreter prior to any meeting or court setting. Conversely, it is equally the responsibility of the interpreter to inform the attorney of any information that is known to the interpreter and necessary to the case. This includes a concern of competency of their skill and language concerns. The interpreter must inform the attorney of any previous legal or investigative interactions with the client or any other party to the case, including prior interpreting for the complaining witness, the adverse party, any witness to the case, law enforcement, immigration officials, Child Protective Services, sexual assault exams, etc. These situations naturally provide for a clear conflict.

Conflicts, if not spotted and resolved early in a case, negatively affect the case and the parties involved. It can become a source for appeal, grievances, loss of certification, adverse action by the court, criminal charges, fines, civil liability, and, most importantly, the loss of life or liberty to the client. Any potential conflicts should be disclosed to the proper authority immediately. Who that is depends on the role the interpreter plays. To reduce the probability of a potential conflict, it is a good practice for interpreters to maintain a clear, confidential log of clients in legal and quasilegal matters for their own personal use. Confidentiality and privilege prevent an interpreter from divulging details of a legal assignment; however, preemptive avoidance of conflicts and carefulness will resolve the issue when subpoenaed in future assignments.

When working with deaf clients and interpreters, unique conflicts may arise. For example, if a family member of a deaf defendant interprets a meeting between the lawyer and the defendant and the issue is an assault involving that person's brother, there is a clear conflict of interest. The family member may influence the story, change the person's loyalties while the case is pending, or taint the interpretation of what happened with their own opinions. Interpreters must always be vigilant about conflicts and the potential for becoming involved as witnesses in the case. Uncertified and nonlegal interpreters are especially at risk for becoming a witness to the case. Should their interpretation later be questioned, the case may be appealed and/or civil action could be brought. Furthermore, there is serious question as to whether that person's knowledge of the case is protected under attorney–client privilege. Previous involvement in legal situations with the client can produce severe harm to a case. For example, an interpreter who previously interpreted proceedings in a child custody case, even years before, may affect the attorney–client relationship. Should a deaf client recognize an interpreter from a previous encounter, there may be an automatic distrust of the interpreter. The client may well remember the interpreter as then associated with the outcome of the case. The ability of the client to focus and concentrate on the case at hand and the willingness to be open and trust their attorney is diminished. If the interpreter is unaware, then the effect of distrust can ruin a case without anyone but the client knowing. Even worse is the knowledge of the situation by the interpreter without informing the attorney. Both situations are unknown to the attorney and may be mistakenly thought as permissible by the interpreter. Any prior contact between the interpreter and the client may affect the attorney–client relationship. It is ultimately the attorney's responsibility to ensure that the client is comfortable with the IFC. When trust breaks down between the attorney and the client, it is difficult to rebuild.

CONFIDENTIALITY VERSUS PRIVILEGE

There are certain ethical obligations that lawyers must meet in all cases. The most well-known is that of confidentiality and privilege between the attorney and the client. There is an assumption by most that confidentiality and privilege are interchangeable terms and concepts. And although there is a great deal of overlap, there are differences in obligation between information and communication. The purpose of attorney–client privilege is to ensure openness and trust between the lawyer and the client. It is considered to be as sacred as the penitent–priest relationship.[2] Without the insurance of confidentiality and privilege, the client, being uncomfortable or fearful that the lawyer will relay the information discussed, will not disclose everything to the lawyer. When this happens, trust is not established, and representation cannot be effective.

Confidentiality

Confidentiality applies to all lawyers representing clients and is based on ethical principles. Confidential information is any information that an attorney has learned from the representation of the client. There is an ethical duty of confidentiality that prevents the attorney from voluntarily disclosing or misusing the confidential information, and it applies in every context where the attorney–client privilege does not apply. It is thus broader than privilege. Confidentiality includes third-party information as well as the client's information. For example, when a defense attorney interviews a witness in a case, confidentiality prevents the attorney from disclosing that person's name to other entities. Even though that witness is not protected by attorney–client privilege, they are protected by confidentiality. Likewise, if an attorney is holding a press conference, confidentiality prevents the attorney from mentioning a witness's name unless the client agrees to have their name publicized. This concept of confidentiality is similar to that associated with a journalist protecting a source's name and their identity. Confidentiality applies to a certain extent to prosecutors; however, it is limited and there is no privilege. Prosecutors represent the community at large. They represent the government—the city, municipality, county/parish, state, or federal government. If there is a complainant or victim in a case, the prosecutor does not represent that person, and therefore there is no privilege. In fact, typically, the prosecution must call the complainant to the stand to testify and, under the U.S. Supreme Court case *Brady v. Maryland* (1963), is required to inform opposing counsel of inconsistencies, mitigating evidence, exculpatory evidence (evidence that tends to prove that it was not the defendant/accused that committed the crime), or any nonwork product information, including what the complainant says to law enforcement or anyone working for the prosecution, including interpreters.

Attorney–Client Privilege

Privilege, on the other hand, is based in evidentiary rules. Privilege extends beyond confidentiality. Lawyers are ethically bound to keep all communications private. Privilege is based on the Rules of Evidence and the ABA Rules and Standards of Professional Conduct and Responsibility. "The attorney-client privilege exempts from discovery and production at trial confidential communications from client to lawyer, and confidential communications from lawyer to client that may expose a client's confidential communication, if made for the purpose of securing legal advice" (Wigmore, 1905). Privilege is between the attorney and the client. It is broken by third parties being involved or present during attorney–client discussions. For example, if a client brings their friend, parent, or spouse to an attorney–client meeting, that person's attendance during attorney-client conversations breaks the attorney–client privilege. However, there are times when the presence of friends or family members of a deaf client during a general meeting with their attorney can be beneficial. When discussing what to expect concerning the case, such as how long it may take for resolution and other generalities of the system, having supportive people present during the meeting between the deaf client and the attorney may help to alleviate some anxiety and help the client to recall information that was explained by the attorney. However, when the discussion moves to the specifics of the case, that is when people other than the client need to leave the room because their continued presence means that the conversation between attorney and client is not protected by the privilege. That person is therefore a witness to the conversations and could potentially be subpoenaed by the prosecution to testify against the defendant. Attorney–client privilege extends to all members of the attorney's staff and defense team. This includes private investigators, experts, interpreters, and so on, working with the attorney and the client, regardless of the entity responsible for paying for those individuals' services, that is appointed or retained. The attorney–client privilege also applies to an individual charged with a criminal offense and appointed counsel by the court as well as an interpreter for privileged communications who also cannot reveal any communications to anyone. This makes sense because the attorney cannot be expected to zealously defend the client and simultaneously hide facts about the client and case from anyone working for them. This includes the paralegal researching case law, additional attorneys assisting in the case, as well as the investigator and interpreter. Precluding those that work for the defense attorney from gaining pertinent information about the case while working on it is ineffectual.

The attorney–client privilege is held by the client, meaning that client is the only person who can waive the right. So if the client's spouse, relative, or other asks the attorney what is going on in the case, the attorney is prevented from speaking to them without the client's approval. And the privilege extends beyond the client's and/or the attorney's death. Neither the lawyer nor any member of the defense team can break privilege and report information without suffering the consequences of disbarment, professional disciplinary sanctions, and a possible lawsuit. So although Tenet 1.0 of the NAD-RID Code of Professional Conduct, titled "Confidentiality," makes exceptions such as federal and state laws requiring mandatory reporting of abuse or threats of suicide, or responding to subpoenas,[3] this clearly does not apply to the IFC interpreting communications between the attorney and the client. For example, if the client is charged with sexual assault and during conversations with the attorney admits to abusing the child, the interpreter conveying those conversations cannot disclose that information because they are under the attorney–client privilege. Likewise, if a client in an unrelated case discloses a murder or other crime not yet investigated or known, the interpreter is also prevented, like the attorney in most situations, from reporting that crime. Anything discussed with the interpreter as a member of the defense team, whether it be between the attorney, the client, or another member of the team, is protected under attorney–client privilege. Information included in privileged communications includes dates and times that the attorney, client, and interpreter met, whom they met with, and the nature of the conversation.

Confidentiality is paramount for interpreters. The Deaf community is small, and there is a constant fear that one interpreter will tell someone else about their interpreting assignment. Deaf people use interpreters frequently in their daily lives. This includes medical, legal, and mental health assignments. If interpreters share information about the specifics of their assignments, this will not only violate the code of ethics but can also cause chaos within the Deaf and interpreting communities. However, reiterating to deaf clients that all assignments are confidential and maintaining that confidentiality helps to ensure that the community at large continues to be served.

> The attorney-client privilege may well be the pivotal element of the modern American lawyer's professional functions. It is considered indispensable to the lawyer's function as advocate on the theory that the advocate can adequately prepare a case only if the client is free to disclose everything, bad as well as good. The privilege is also considered necessary to the lawyer's function as confidential counselor in law on the similar theory that the legal counselor can properly advise the client what to do only if the client is free to make full disclosure. (Hazard, 1978, p. 1061)

Often, there is an admission of conduct that, if shared, may cause significant harm.

Most attorneys do not ask the question that is often on the public's and juries' minds: "Did you do it?" The point of not asking is sound. What impression is given of someone who asks such an accusatory question? This inquiry does not support a climate of trust. Clients are often unaware of affirmative defenses. They are not skilled in determining the applicable legal defenses. Deaf and hearing clients are usually most concerned with the outcome of the case—"what is going to happen to me?" They want a lawyer who will fight for them regardless of personal feelings, and the fear of admitting to any aspect of an allegation, regardless of how slight, means they will have relinquished the only card they have. The deaf or hearing client may think that if they make an admission, the lawyer may not fight for them. Just as it is the prosecutor's job to seek justice, it is the defense attorney's job to *zealously* represent their client within the limits of the law.

[T]he lawyer is bound by all fair and honorable means to present every defense that the law of the land permits, to the end that no person may be deprived of life or liberty, but by due process of law" (ABA Center for Professional Responsibility, 2014b).

Furthermore, "it is the duty of the lawyer to do whatever may enable him to succeed in winning his client's cause" (ABA Center for Professional Responsibility, 2014c).

LINGUISTIC COMPETENCY AND THE LEGAL SYSTEM

In all criminal cases, the defendant must be able to understand the nature of the charges against them, assist in their own defense, and freely and voluntarily make decisions in their case (U.S. Const. amend. XI). In some cases, the defendant and their interpreter may require a certified deaf interpreter (CDI). Like hearing legal interpreters, it is imperative that the CDI be well versed in legalese and qualified for legal situations and court proceedings. Likewise, if the statute requires legal/court certification for interpreters in a state, the statute also applies to CDIs, unless specifically stated otherwise. CDIs are additionally responsible for informing counsel if communication is not effective or if there are any other suspected cognitive issues hindering the client's ability to understand the situation at hand. Even with the best of interpreters and CDIs, if the defendant does not meet the legal requirements laid out in the Sixth Amendment and freely and voluntarily waives or invokes their rights to a trial, then the client and the case cannot proceed.

The issue of competency when representing deaf clients is frequently overlooked or discounted. In the legal system, competency is primarily related to mental cognition impaired by either a mental health condition or a cognitive issue. Ethically, it is the duty of counsel and the court to investigate any signs or indications that competency may be an issue. Although in some instances, there is an overt indication that the client may not be mentally competent, most often the issue of competency is hidden by other factors. Typically, the issue of competency is not immediately recognized with deaf clients. There may be a lack of language competence, fluency, or an additional physical or cognitive disability that masks the inability of the client to be competent to stand trial. The ABA

Standards for Criminal Justice suggests that attorneys seek an expert evaluation from a mental health professional within the protection of confidentiality and privilege rules where the attorney has a good faith doubt regarding the client's competence (Criminal Justice Standards on Mental Health, 2016). When determining whether the client has the ability to assist in their own defense, effective communication must be established.

For example, a deaf client who is meeting with an attorney for the first time may be extremely anxious and fearful in regard to their case. They may also anticipate that communication will be difficult. The client may therefore tell their story in a way that makes little to no sense to the attorney. Anxiety may cause them to give too much information. Likewise, the client may also leave out pertinent information because of stress or thinking that specific information is not necessary. The client may also withhold information that is important to the case because of the fear of being judged or embarrassed.

Although the client may or may not be guilty, it is possible that they have language dysfluency or other issues that could have implications for how the case is handled. Often, when deaf clients first meet with their attorney, they do not understand privilege versus communication. The client often thinks they must "sell" their story to the attorney, explaining why they are innocent and, in this process, may give too much superfluous information. The client may be agitated and communicate with the attorney in a frantic tone, needing to be reminded that guilty and not guilty are legal issues and have no bearing on what people think did or did not happen. The client may be so worried about defending themselves and making people understand what they are trying to say that they are often not clear in their communication. They are obsessed with not wanting the attorney to think negatively about them. Clients often do not understand that the legal situation is usually quite narrow, and not as broad is they believe it is. They often think they are giving the attorney information that is helpful, but frequently it does not bear on the legal situation at hand.

CONCLUSION

The attorney–client relationship is a complicated and valued one. Although there are many issues that are shared in all legal cases, there are some that are unique when working with deaf clients. There are no shortcuts. The attorney working on the case must explore these issues. Some issues are strategic in nature, whereas others are legal issues that require research, possibly necessitating the advice and assistance of experienced colleagues and experts. Regardless, the effectiveness and outcome are dependent on trust and the fulfillment of the duties of the attorney. Accommodations for the deaf client are crucial. Cases turn on the Constitutional rights of the defendant to effective communication with the attorney; the right to be linguistically present at all proceedings, confrontation, and due process; and the right to a qualified and certified interpreter.

All these issues are underlined by trust. If there is to be effective representation, there must be total reliance on the relationship between the attorney and the client. This relationship is *always* affected by the accommodations used or lack thereof. Denial of necessary accommodations ensures due process violations. Prudence in acquiring accommodations still requires vigilance. Although most often the appropriate accommodation for a deaf client is an ASL interpreter, due diligence is required. A qualified, certified interpreter who is well-versed and fulfills the full role of language and cultural mediator is invaluable. This interpreter is an expert that if appropriately utilized, ensures the success of the attorney–client relationship.

NOTES

1. Other accommodations may include Seeing Essential English (SEE), Signing Exact English (SEE 2), multimedia messaging service (MMS), Communication Access Realtime Translation (CART), and video remote interpreting.
2. Spousal privilege is not as encompassing as attorney–client and priest–penitent privileges. There are exceptions that, in general, vary based on the Federal Rules of Evidence and, of course, from state to state.
3. NAD-RID CPC.

REFERENCES

ABA Center for Professional Responsibility. (2014a). *ABA compendium of professional responsibility rules and standards.* American Bar Association.

ABA Center for Professional Responsibility. (2014b). Canon 5. In *ABA canons of center for professional ethics* (p. 425). American Bar Association.

ABA Center for Professional Responsibility. (2014c). Canon 15. In *ABA canons of center for professional ethics* (p. 427). American Bar Association.

American Law Institute. (1998). Section 14: Formation of a client-lawyer. In *Restatement of law governing lawyers third* (Vols. 1–5).

American Law Institute. (2000). Section 14. Formation of a client-lawyer relationship. In *Restatement of the law governing lawyers.*

Argersinger v. Hamlin, 407 US 25 (1972).

Baltierra v. State, 586 S.W.2d 553, 559 (Tex. Crim. App. 1979).

Boyett v. State, No. PD-0672–17, 2018 Tex. Crim. App. LEXIS 126 (Tex. Crim. App. April 25, 2018) (designated for publication).

Brady v. Maryland, 373 US 83 (1963).

California Law Review, 66 Cal. L. Rev. 1061 (1978).

Chambers v. Mississippi, 410 U.S. 284, 294, 93 S.Ct. 1038, 35 L.Ed.2d 297 (1973).

Compton, M. S. (2008). Fulfilling your professional responsibilities: Representing a deaf client in Texas. *St. Mary's Law Journal, 39,* 819.

Compton, P. (2018). Preamble. In *Texas disciplinary rules of professional conduct.* https://www.legalethicstexas.com/Ethics-Resources/Rules/Texas-Disciplinary-Rules-of-Professional-Conduct.aspx

Criminal Justice Standards on Mental Health [adopted August 8, 2016, to supplant the 3rd ed., (August 1984) of the ABA Criminal Justice Mental Health Standards]. https://www.americanbar.org/groups/criminaljustice/standards/

Del Valle, G. (2017, August 7). *Most criminal cases end in plea bargains, not trials.* https://theoutline.com/post/2066/most-criminal-cases-end-in-plea-bargains-not-trials

Developments in the law: Privileged communications. (1985). *Harvard Law Review, 98*(7), 1450–1666. https://doi.org/10.2307/1340953

Garcia v. State, 151 Tex.Crim. 593, 601, 210 S.W.2d 574 (1948).

Garcia v. State, 887 S.W.2d 862, 875 (Tex. Crim. App. 1994).

Gideon v. Wainwright, 372 U.S. 335, 344 (1963).

Gonzalez v. United States, 553 U.S. 242, 248 (2008).

Griffin v. Illinois, 351 U.S. 12, 19 (1956).

Hatfield, L. (2012, Spring). The Alton Logan case and attorney–client confidentiality: Does the rules strike the right balance? *Public Legal Decisions*, 8.

Hawkins v. Costello, 460 F.3d 238, 243 (2d Cir. 2006) (quoting Crane v. Kentucky, 476 U.S. 683, 690, 106 S.Ct. 2142, 90 L.Ed.2d 636 (1986)). United States v. Crandall, 748 F.3d 476, 481 (2d Cir. 2014).

Hazard, G. C., Jr. (1978). An historical perspective on the attorney–client privilege. *California, Law Review, 66*, 1061. https://doi.org/10.2307/3479905

Jones v. Barnes, 463 U.S. 745, 751 (1983).

Leal v. State, 782 S.W.2d 844, 849 (Tex. Crim. App. 1989).

Lewis v. United States, 146 U.S. 370, 372, 13 S.Ct. 136, 36 L.Ed. 1011 (1892).

Mendiola v. State, 924 S.W.2d 157, 162 (Tex.App.—Corpus Christi 1995, pet. ref'd, untimely filed); Montoya v. State, 811 S.W. 2d 671, 673 (Tex. App. Corpus Christi 1991, no pet). Martins v. State, 52 SW3d 459, 470 (2001).

Miner, M. (2008, January 31). The greater of two evils. *The Chicago Reader 37*(19). https://www.chicagoreader.com/chicago/the-greater-of-two-evils/Content?oid=1212988

Miranda v. Arizona, 384 U.S. 436, 440 (1966).

National Registry of Exonerations. (2016, December). *Alton Logan. Other Chicago exonerations with mistaken identifications.* https://www.law.umich.edu/special/exoneration/Pages/casedetail.aspx?caseid=3389

Pate v. Robinson, 383 U.S. 375, 378 (1966).

Powell et al. v. Alabama, 287 U.S. 45, 52 (1932).

R. Prof'l Conduct preamble ¶2, reprinted in Tex. Gov't Code Ann., tit. 2, subtit. G ap. A (Vernon 2005) (Tex. State Bar R. art. X, §9).

Shu Guo Kan v. State, 4 S.W.3d 38, 41 (Tex. App. 1999).

State v. Calderon, 13 P.3d 871, 270 Kan. 241, 253 (Kan. 2000).

Texas Disciplinary R. Prof. Conduct (1989) reprinted in Tex. Govt. Code Ann., tit.2, subtit. G, app. (Vernon Supp. 1995) (State Bar Rules Part X ([section]]9)).

U.S. Const. amend. XI.

U.S. Const. amend. XIV, § 1.

United States ex Rel. Negron v. State of N.Y., 434 F.2d 386, 390, 391 (1970).

United States v. Crandall, 748 F.3d 476, 478 (2d Cir. 2014).

United States v. Mullins, 315 F.3d 449, 452 (5th Cir. 2002).

Vasquez v. State, 819 S.W.2d 932, 937 (Tex. App.—Corpus Christi 1991, pet. ref'd).

Watson v. State, 596 S.W.2d 867, 868 (Tex. Crim. App. 1980).

Wigmore, J. H., 4 Evidence §§ 2285–92 (1905).

11

Disability Justice in the Age of Mass Incarceration

Talila A. Lewis

Racism, classism, ableism, and other oppressions intersect to create and shape how marginalized people are made vulnerable to surveillance, criminalization, police violence, and all forms of incarceration (Gibson & Lewis, 2018; Kaba, 2018; Kinna & Gordon, 2019; Lewis, 2017a, 2017b, 2017c, 2020). In this chapter, I highlight how different regimes within the criminal legal system[1] effectively collaborate to produce and exploit these vulnerabilities. Consider the following:

- Disabled people represent more than half of those killed by U.S. law enforcement annually (McNamara, 2016).
- Of 15 documented fatal police encounters with deaf[2] people in the past 20 years, all victims had at least one other marginalized identity, the most common being that victims were negatively racialized (i.e., ostensibly Black, Indigenous, Latinx) and/or had or were perceived to have other disabilities (Helping Educate to Advance the Rights of Deaf Communities [HEARD], 2020).
- Children with disabilities are four times more likely to end up in the juvenile legal system than children without disabilities—again, with percentages increasing exponentially with racially marginalized disabled children (Shaban et al., 2017).[3]
- People with disabilities represent the largest "minority" population in U.S. jails and prisons nationwide (U.S. Department of Justice, Bureau of Justice Statistics, 2006).

The story is about intersectionality at the level of both social category and structural systems (Crenshaw, 1989, 1991; Kinna & Gordon, 2019), especially because within disability communities, ableism, racism, classism, and other forms of systemic oppression abound (refer to note 2). As such, my effort is not just to bring to the fore experiences of a group that has been largely invisibilized in debates about the criminal legal system; it is also to examine and critique current trends in advocacy by and for disabled people and organizations as they attempt to respond to the criminal legal system. Innovative and intersectional advocacy approaches that are guided by and rooted in antiracist, antiableist, anticapitalist, abolitionist principles are essential to stemming the tide of mass incarceration of all people. The issue of injustice embedded in the criminal legal system has been documented for generations and it is not an abstract matter. These injustices continue to harm actual people, entire families, and whole communities, not to mention the broader harms to public health and safety. The criminal legal system so profoundly harms marginalized people—including especially negatively racialized deaf and other disabled people—that the system *must* be dismantled and marginalized communities allowed to lead the efforts to redefine justice, reimagine how true justice can be realized and restore and rebuild communities in the wake of immense harm experienced due to the current "justice" system. There are many layered issues that contribute to this injustice and harm, but this chapter will only focus on a few of these issues to illustrate the larger point.

I begin with a brief account of the phenomenon of mass incarceration. My analysis here is decidedly truncated because this chapter is part of a much larger project. But it provides context to my examination of how mass incarceration responds to and interacts with disability generally and deafness specifically.

MASS INCARCERATION

The United States imprisons more people than does any other nation in the world—and the burdens of our incarceration nation are not borne equally (Mensah & Kaufman-Mthimkhulu, 2020; Schenwar & Law, 2020). Incarceration statistics for Black, Indigenous, Latinx, and low- and no-income people are grossly disproportionately high. Black and Latinx people make up less than one-third of the U.S. population but represent nearly 60% of the incarcerated population (National Association for the Advancement of Colored People, 2018). Moreover, in 2014, incarcerated people had a median annual income of $19,185 prior to their incarceration, which is 41% less than that of nonincarcerated people of similar age (Rabuy & Kopf, 2015). Significantly, this gap in income is

> not solely the product of the well-documented disproportionate incarceration of [Black and Hispanic people], who generally earn less than [white people], . . . incarcerated people in all gender, race, and ethnicity groups earned substantially less prior to their incarceration than their non-incarcerated counterparts of similar ages. (Rabuy & Kopf, 2015)

Changes in crime rates do not explain the unprecedented increase in the U.S. jail and prison populations—from less than 200,000 in 1972 (U.S. Department of Justice, Bureau of Justice Statistics, 1982) to 2.2 million today (U.S. Department of Justice, Bureau of Justice Statistics, 2015). Instead, empirical evidence suggests that the phenomenon of mass incarceration is a function of socioeconomic and racial inequities and a range of "law and order" legal regimes (Balko, 2018, updated 2020). These regimes include drastic increases in size, scope, investments in, and reliance on what abolitionist, activist, public intellectual Angela Y. Davis has popularized as the "prison industrial complex" (Schenwar & Law, 2020), shifts in sentencing law in the direction of mandatory minimums and "three strikes" laws (Butterfield, 1998; The Sentencing Project, 2018), a weakening of already limited constitutional criminal procedural protections, and an expansion of police power and resources to surveil, stop and frisk, and arrest (Carbado, 2017). Indeed, the normative weight of carefully crafted and selectively enforced "law and order" imperatives on the criminal legal system has substantively erased notions of due process, equality, and justice, often not leaving even a veneer of fairness.

Although disparities in the treatment of and outcomes for marginalized communities have long been a hallmark of the U.S. legal system (Alexander, 2010; Blackmon, 2008; Davis, 2003; Stevenson, 2015), the sheer number of people trapped by the clutch of mass incarceration has both exacerbated "the ordinary injustices" of the criminal legal system and helped illuminate sweeping inequities inherent within it (Cooper, 2017). Ironically, mass incarceration has aided researchers, attorneys, policymakers, and advocates in tracking trends of inequity within the criminal legal system and identifying the subtle and not so subtle ways in which other spaces of state governance, such as schools, foster programs, child and family regulation agencies, and medical, mental health, and substance use programs, serve as gateways to the criminal legal system and as sites of criminalization, pathologization, and criminal enforcement (Cloud, 2019; Lewis, 2020; Mensah & Kaufman-Mthimkhulu, 2020; Roberts, 1997).

Notwithstanding a growing consensus that the criminal legal system has had—and continues to have—devastating effects on marginalized communities, by and large, opponents of mass incarceration articulate their opposition to that system regarding the harms the criminal legal system visits on negatively racialized communities; low- and no-income communities; women; lesbian, gay, bisexual, transgender, queer or questioning, intersex (LGBTQI); and other marginalized communities in silos (Center for American Progress & Movement Advanced Project, 2016; Coates, 2015; Kajstura, 2017). Most analyses wholly disregard the inextricable links between disability identities and other marginalized social categories (Kinna & Gordon, 2019; Lewis, 2020). That is to say, contestation of the criminal legal system—whether from the right or the left, whether through an abolitionist frame or a harm reduction approach—have elided the ways in which the criminal legal system decimates disabled communities.

With very few exceptions, the research (Morgan, 2017) and advocacy (Gibson & Lewis, 2018) that do focus on disability in legal and carceral systems focus almost exclusively on mental health disparities. Consequently, other disabled people—including people with mental disabilities who have other disabilities—are being funneled into courts, jails, prisons and other carceral facilities across the United States with practically no public awareness, scrutiny, or outcry (HEARD, 2018a; Lewis, 2014). I call this problem the "disability consciousness gap"—and it pervades just about every form of social justice advocacy, from organizing and litigating against police violence and ending the school-to-prison pipeline to welfare benefits interventions and LGBTQI political organizing. Consider, for example, the following empirical findings that are all but absent from mainstream discussions about social justice, in general, and policing and incarceration, in particular:

- Disability is more prevalent in marginalized communities, with disabled people being disproportionately represented among economically and racially disenfranchised communities (Berne, 2017; Vallas, 2014).
- Children with disabilities, including deaf children, are three times more likely to be placed in the foster system (National Council on Disability, 2008), and children in the foster system are at increased risk of incarceration (Cloud, 2019).
- People with disabilities experience rape and sexual assault at more than twice the rate at which persons without disabilities do and experience non-fatal violent crime at 1.5 times the rate at which persons without disabilities do (Rand & Harrell, 2007).
- Deaf children experience trauma more frequently than their hearing peers, with approximately 50% of deaf girls having been sexually abused compared with approximately 25% of hearing girls. Approximately 54% of deaf boys have been sexually abused as compared with approximately 10% of hearing boys (National Child Traumatic Stress Network, 2006).
- Young adults with disabilities are three times more likely to live in poverty as adults than their peers without disabilities (National Collaborative for Workforce & Disability for Youth, 2016).
- One study indicates that 65% of boys and 75% of girls in juvenile prisons have at least one mental health disability (Teplin et al., 2002), and up to 85% of children in juvenile prisons have at least one disability (National Council on Disability, 2015).

These data reveal that being a low- or no-income negatively racialized person with a disability is a profound "risk factor" for the very problems with the criminal legal system that scholars, policymakers, community organizers, and advocates decry. Case studies across disabilities indicate that people with disabilities have worse outcomes throughout the criminal legal system (HEARD, 2020; Nelson, 2010). Researchers have also found that "deaf people are actually overrepresented in the criminal and quasi-criminal [legal] system" (Ekes, 2007). Although some researchers suggest that a general "lack of communication and resulting knowledge deprivation makes [some deaf people] susceptible to. . . getting involved with the police" (Andrews et al., 2007), history, research, and narratives indicate that disabled people—including deaf people—are chief among the intended targets of a calculated and complex mass incarceration machine (Lewis, 2020).

Studies also indicate that people with disabilities living at the intersection of disability and other marginalities often have vastly different experiences with the system than a person who only has one marginalized identity (HEARD, 2020;

Nelson, 2010). Even still, racial justice advocates rarely view the crisis of mass incarceration through a disability justice lens or approach reform, decarceration, or abolition from a truly intersectional framework (Gibson, 2016; Lewis, 2017a, 2017b, 2017c, 2020). The converse is also true. Disability rights advocates, more often than not, fail to develop and integrate a genuinely intersectional (i.e., antiracist, anticapitalist, etc.) lens or approach to advocacy. Although single-identity advocacy approaches are most commonly employed, they are the least successful in challenging injustices within the current criminal legal system and often do more harm than good.

When well-intentioned advocates are blithely unaware of how high the stakes and how deep the injustice visited on marginalized and multiply marginalized people overcome by the criminal legal system, disabled defendants and survivors end up with the worst that mass incarceration has to offer. Indeed, the legal system's regular and casual failure to provide even the most basic access to disabled people has led to and perpetuated death by law enforcement, decades stolen from families due to wrongful convictions, and unmitigated terror behind the walls of every jail and prison in the United States. There is much that we still do not know about how people with disabilities experience the criminal legal system. One reason for the lack of information is the willful neglect of the government to track police violence or to adequately track and disaggregate disability-related data on jails, prisons, other carceral facilities, and reentry (Lee & Samee, 2016).

The failure of the government to track and disaggregate these data hurts marginalized and multiply marginalized people who have fewer resources to track this information on their own; whose stories are rarely believed without empirical evidence and published sources; and who have less economic, social and political capital to find a way to be heard (Brown et al., 2018; Gibson, 2016). Marginalized people and multiply marginalized people who cannot "provide a source or citation to verify and validate their lived experiences often never obtain resources to address the root causes of the problems" (Brown et al., 2018). Therefore, many people in positions of power, including academics, researchers, media, policymakers, politicians, law enforcement, and resourced organizations and foundations funding these organizations, reinforce violence through erasure or dilution of the narratives of marginalized people (Brown et al., 2018). In this way, cycles of violence are actively perpetuated and invited to continue.

Currently, data collection about police violence against deaf people and about deaf people in jail, prison, detention, civil commitment, and on parole and probation is being crowdsourced—mostly by the volunteer-dependent nonprofit organization, Helping Educate to Advance the Rights of Deaf Communities (HEARD). HEARD's findings to date are bleak. An alarming number of deaf people across the country are incarcerated because law enforcement, courts, court-mandated programs, and parole and probation programs refuse to provide interpreters and other reasonable accommodations (*Harris v. Georgia Department of Corrections*, 2018; *Cobb v. Georgia Department of Community Corrections*, 2019; Lewis, 2018; Nović, 2018). Instead, these systems surveil, pathologize, criminalize, incarcerate, and punish. Notably, even if the criminal legal system provided mandated access, systemic and structural inequity in the U.S. social service and criminal legal systems would all but guarantee disparate outcomes for disabled people compared to nondisabled people (Tastrom, 2020).

The narratives in this chapter illustrate the real-life consequences of systemic injustices and illuminate how even one biased, discriminatory, inaccessible, or violent law enforcement encounter leads to an irreversible cascade of injustice—especially for marginalized people. Many decades on, the carceral system still employs policies and practices that criminalize and further marginalize perpetually oppressed peoples, including those who are Black, Indigenous, Disabled, and LGBTQI. Over a very long time, the system has still not "corrected" itself (Lewis, 2019). Although law enforcement often serves as the entry point into the criminal legal system, they are not alone in their lack of disability consciousness.

TRACKING AND ACCOMMODATING

On the whole, local, state, and federal governments are not tracking disaggregated data on or about the incidence of deafness or other specific disability categories in foster systems or juvenile and adult legal or carceral systems (Gibson, 2016; Nović, 2017). On the rare occasion that deafness or disability is acknowledged within police use of force or carceral system statistics, for example, either there is no specific disability/deaf index or filter ("The counted," 2016) or people with specific disabilities such as deafness are placed into the broad and amorphous category of "disability." Other crowdsourced databases track mental health disabilities/diagnoses to the exclusion of all other disabilities ("Fatal force," 2018). Alternatively, and more commonly, disability is simply not tracked at all (Smith, 2016). Omission, as well as overly broad and overly narrow categorizations of disability, are unhelpful to courts, prisons, advocates, attorneys, incarcerated people, and society because they do not tell the story of which disabilities are present or what accommodations should be—or should have been, in the case of fatal police, jail, prison, and reentry incidents—provided by the government.

Importantly, it is nearly impossible to arrive at reliable figures on how many people with disabilities exist (Stein, 2003). This difficulty is attributable to myriad factors, including "differing operational definitions of disability, divergent sources of data, and inconsistent survey methodologies" (Stein, 2003). Difficulty in tracking disability also arises because of racialization and other societal constructions and structural inequities and perspectives that inform and mediate who can be understood to be "disabled" and what behavior is indicative of "disability" at both individual and community levels (Artiles, 2014; Ribet, 2011; Withers et al., 2019).

In any case, the failure to disaggregate and appropriately categorize various disabilities found within people and communities affected by mass incarceration leaves critical gaps in society's understanding of the full breadth and scope of the crisis of mass incarceration. Moreover, this failure to accurately disaggregate and classify various disabilities ignores the fluid and spectral nature of disability (here, spectral is used as a double entendre, mainly to connote "of or related to a spectrum" and, secondarily, to denote the incorporeal, intangible, imperceptible nature of many disabilities—especially to the outsider). Indeed, the class of disability is so expansive, and each disability so unique to each disabled person that the acknowledgment of disability *always* requires further inquiry and analysis. For example, one person with a chronic illness will differ in ability and disability from the next person with a chronic illness—even if the chronic illness is the same. A person with a chronic illness has different abilities and disabilities from a person with a different kind of disability—a DeafBlind person who does not have a chronic illness, for instance. There are also people who live with multiple disabilities—having chronic illnesses and posttraumatic stress disorder, or being DeafBlind and having complex posttraumatic stress disorder, and so forth.

Taking this analysis a step further, and honoring the ways disabilities arise, exist, and articulate themselves in and through different bodies and minds, we must not take for granted the fluidity and complexity of disability. Disabilities respond to the body, mind, family, and community they inhabit and the attention they receive. Thus, the same disability can be experienced by and expressed through people in different social, racial, gender, class, and other categories quite differently. *And* the same disabled person may express disabilities or symptoms of their disabilities differently depending on myriad factors, including what is going on with or around them, what supports they have access to, and who they are around. In short, disability is both overrepresented and often goes undiagnosed, misdiagnosed, and unaccommodated in Black/Indigenous, low-income, and other marginalized communities largely because of how structural inequities work to create, perpetuate, and erase disabilities in the *most* marginalized communities (*Peter P. v. Compton Unified School District*, 2014; *Stephen C. v. Bureau of Indian Education*, 2018; see also Smith, 2012; Tastrom, 2020). For these reasons and more, it is imperative to note that safe and holistic culturally responsive and adaptive practices for addressing and reducing harm and violence are available, attainable, broadly implementable, and necessary (Gilmore & Kilgore, 2019; Lewis, 2020). Policing is *not* such a practice.

Deaf identities are a prime example of how disability exists on a spectrum; some deaf people use hearing aids, whereas others use implants; others still do not want, use, or need any auxiliary aids—often identifying as culturally Deaf, DeafBlind, or DeafDisabled. Yet all of these people are, in fact, deaf. In terms of communication, the spectrum is even more diverse. Some deaf people use sign language, whereas others do not; some deaf people speak orally, whereas others do not; some use tactile sign language or augmentative and alternative communication; and others still rely on written communication or other communication systems, such as cued speech. Many deaf people use a fusion of several of these and other methods. Significantly, regardless of a deaf person's language or communication and auxiliary aid use, deafness falls squarely within the legal definition of disability.

A Primer: Disability, Policing, and Legal Considerations

Federal law enforcement is governed by Section 504 of the Rehabilitation Act, which prohibits disability discrimination by any federal agency or by any federally funded program or activity. The law states:

> No otherwise qualified individual with a disability in the United States . . . shall, solely by reason of her or his disability, be excluded from the participation in, be denied the benefits of, or be subjected to discrimination under any program or activity receiving federal financial assistance or under any program or activity conducted by any Executive agency. (Rehabilitation Act of 1973, 2012)

State and local law enforcement fall under Section 504 and Title II of the Americans With Disabilities Act (ADA). The ADA defines "disability" with respect to an individual, in part, as "a physical or mental impairment that substantially limits one or more major life activities" (42 U.S.C. §§ 12131 *et seq.*; 28 C.F.R. §§ 35.101–35.190). Title II of the ADA applies to "any [s]tate or local government" and "any department, agency . . . or other instrumentality of a [s]tate . . . or local government" (42 U.S.C. § 12131(1)) and applies to all police activities (28 C.F.R. § 35, App. B, Subpart A). Police departments and prison systems must "furnish appropriate auxiliary aids and services where necessary to afford individuals with disabilities . . . an equal opportunity to participate in and enjoy the benefits of [these agencies'] service, program, or activity" (28 C.F.R. § 25.160(b)). Importantly, police and prison systems must give primary consideration to the disabled person's request for a particular auxiliary aid or service (28 C.F.R. § 35.160(b)(2)). Courts have also long since established that state and local law enforcement and carceral systems are subject to the ADA (*Pennsylvania Department of Corrections v. Yeskey,* 1998). Under Section 504 and the ADA, police and prison systems have affirmative obligations to provide meaningful access and effective communication, among other things.

Sworn and civilian law enforcement personnel may not exclude or segregate deaf people from services or deny services to or otherwise discriminate against deaf people (U.S. Department of Justice, 2006). This is an affirmative obligation, and it survives regardless of where a person exists on the spectrum of disability and regardless of communication, language, and accommodation or auxiliary aid need. Accordingly, deafness should trigger the compulsory provision of auxiliary aids, reasonable accommodations, or modifications by law enforcement if law enforcement continues to be called on during sensitive and critical interactions (American Civil Liberties Union, 2016; Mizner, 2015). Data and narratives from disabled people indicate that law enforcement continues to disregard these laws (HEARD, 2020). This is another reason law enforcement should not be called for sensitive or critical interactions with disabled people or people experiencing emotional or mental disruption or distress (Çevik, 2019; Lewis, 2019).

Federal disability rights laws explicitly recognize the reality of disability being fluid by (1) demanding an individual analysis of each person's disability and support needs such that the reasonable accommodations or modification adequately suits each qualified person with a disability, and (2) insisting that primary consideration be given to the accommodation requested by the disabled person. Put plainly, federal law mandates that every qualified disabled person be provided with equal—not the same—access to programs, services, and activities by law enforcement and in courts, diversion programming, jails, prisons, and parole and probation situations, and so forth. In law and in actuality, two deaf people participating in the same prison reentry program may have different accommodations if one communicates best with the support of Deaf interpreters and the other relies on real-time captioning, for example. These federal laws are often disregarded by power holders within the criminal legal system.

In the uncommon incidences where law enforcement and related systems track disability, haphazard mass categorization of people with all manner of disability persists. This mass categorization is most harmful to people with disabilities who are deemed by the dominant majority to be particularly "nonnormative" and whose disabilities are often difficult to perceive—those who have disabilities or cultural or communicative characteristics that are not in line with the dominant majority. This group includes at least deaf people; autistic people; people with mental health disabilities/diagnoses; people with intellectual/developmental disabilities; people with traumatic brain injuries; people with auditory or visual processing or expression disabilities; people with cerebral palsy, epilepsy, and diabetes; and people experiencing strokes and other medical emergencies, among others—especially those living at the margins of the margins (e.g., Black/Indigenous, houseless, trans people with these disabilities or disability labels or symptoms).

The application of this mosaic of thought (e.g., intersectionality, disability consciousness, fluidity, spectrality) is particularly important when considering authority and carceral systems precisely because society, generally, and "authority," specifically, perceives and responds to disability differently depending on the body/mind that the disability inhabits (Nelson, 2010; Lewis, 2020). This mosaic of thought helps explain why a struggling low-income Indigenous student diagnosed with attention deficit hyperactive disorder (ADHD) is more likely to be labeled "defiant" and in need of restraint, seclusion, suspension, expulsion, or arrest, whereas a struggling upper-middle-class white student diagnosed with ADHD and precisely the same behaviors is more likely to be identified as needing additional supports, modification of their individualized education program (IEP), a little bit of grace, a few more chances, and other nonpunitive approaches (Garvey, 2018; Mizner, 2017). The next part expands this analysis by focusing specifically on policing [disability].

Policing [Disability]

Law enforcement interactions with deaf people and people with communication, intellectual, and mental disabilities and diagnoses, among others, are often unnecessarily fraught and perilous (Center, 2016). The following scenarios seem to be among the most common during law enforcement interactions and "investigations" with respect to deaf people.

Scenario No. 1

In the first scenario, a deaf person might be walking down the street using sign language or otherwise engaging in their daily life activities when an officer spots them and perceives their language or mannerisms as "unlawful," "unruly," "gang-related," or questionable for some other reason. After verbally ordering the person to follow commands, the officer either fails to recognize or refuses to believe that the person is deaf. When the deaf person does not respond, the officer frequently escalates the situation raising their voice and trying to restrain or incapacitate the deaf person—often by grabbing, tackling, beating, tasing, or shooting the person. The officer determines that the deaf person is refusing to comply with orders. Once a mistaken use of force has commenced or is complete, officers tend to double down instead of simply admitting that they made a mistake (AJ+, "Deaf Oklahoma man Pearl Pearson wins $195,000," 2018; Halsne, 2012). In furtherance of the officer's narrative, the deaf person is almost always charged with one or more of the catch-all charges of "resisting arrest," "obstructing," or "disorderly conduct," even where all other charges are dropped (AJ+, 2018; "Deaf Oklahoma man Pearl Pearson wins $195,000," 2018; Halsne, 2012; HEARD, 2020). As seen in almost every example provided in this chapter, there is a prevailing idea within police departments that people pretend to be disabled or exaggerate the extent of their disability to give officers a hard time, to challenge officers' authority, to get out of trouble, etc. However, it is exceedingly rare for people to pretend to have disabilities during interactions with law enforcement.

Examples of this first scenario play out in the cases of Esther Valdez, a young Latinx Deaf woman tackled on a busy street by an Austin Police Department officer (Smith, 2010), and of John T. Williams, a 50-year-old seventh-generation Nitinaht carver of the Nuu-chah-nulth First Nations, who was fatally shot by a Seattle Police Department officer while walking down the street (Renville, 2011). Like most deaf victims and survivors found in HEARD's database, both of these people are ostensibly negatively racialized and have other marginalized identities.

Video shows Officer Steven Willis shouting commands, then running behind Valdez, roughly grabbing Valdez, and shouting "Did you hear me?" (Smith, 2010). Valdez's partner immediately and continuously informs Willis that Valdez is deaf (Smith, 2010). The officer retorts, "No! She can comprehend what I am trying to tell her." The officer continues shouting orders at Valdez, who tries to call her mother for communication support, saying to the officer, "I'm calling my mom so she can talk to you" (Smith, 2010). This only further enrages the officer, who shouts, "You can call your mom when I'm done! You aren't in charge of this call! I'm in charge of this call!" Valdez walks away, upset and confused when Willis tackles her to the ground. She begins crying and becomes short of breath while the officer continues shouting orders (Smith, 2010). After being tackled and handcuffed, Valdez is distraught, injured, and inconsolable. Video shows her in handcuffs limping to the police cruiser, crying. The police had already ordered Valdez's partner to stay back. When the officer puts Valdez into the cruiser, the partner asks the officer again, "What is the matter with you? Don't you understand that she is deaf?" The officer responds, "Yeah, I know that, but she understands enough that she can hear you." The second officer, who arrived with a mace stick at the ready, responds with a supportive, "Yeah" (Smith, 2010).

This incident occurred in Austin, Texas, a city with one of the largest deaf populations per capita in the country, with a police department that had, a decade earlier, instituted formal protocols for interacting with deaf people and had begun training officers on Deaf culture and communication (in accordance with a settlement following a lawsuit by a DeafBlind man and his deaf wife for violating their rights during an arrest). Amber Farrelly, attorney for Esther Valdez and hundreds of other deaf defendants in Texas, stated that in just over a year, she had been appointed or hired to represent roughly 50 deaf clients. All but a very few have eventually had the charges against them dismissed by county prosecutors because "the majority of the charges filed by police have been based on misunderstanding or miscommunications" (Smith, 2010). This encounter is not exceptional (HEARD, 2020).

Video of John T. Williams's final moments are captured on dashcam (Miletich, 2011). On a sunny fall afternoon, Williams, a woodcarver who was deaf in one ear and hard of hearing in the other, calmly walked across the street in the crosswalk (Miletich, 2011). Williams was focused on the small piece of wood he was whittling with a legal three-inch carving knife (Miletich, 2011). The video shows Officer Ian Birk exiting his cruiser, walking behind Williams and, out of sight of the dashcam, shouting at William's back to stop and drop the knife (Miletich, 2011). Within 4 seconds of the first command, five gunshots are heard in rapid succession, and people walking down the busy street stop in their tracks, appearing shocked and confused (Miletich, 2011). One witness immediately confronts Birk, saying, "Did you just shoot him? He didn't do anything!" The officer shouts back, "Ma'am, he had a knife, and he wouldn't drop it!"

Birk's report stated that Williams was "brandishing" a knife in a "very confrontational posture" despite other officers finding the knife in a closed position and multiple witnesses saying Williams did nothing threatening before being fired upon. As is customary following lethal use of force by law enforcement, law enforcement, in concert with news media, dredged up and publicized Williams's history of arrests and mental health disabilities/diagnoses and drug use history in an attempt to portray the victim in a negative light (Renville, 2011). King County prosecutors declined to file charges against this officer, and the state's taxpayers paid $1.5 million to settle claims brought by Williams's family (McNerthney, 2011; Miletich, 2011).

Scenario No. 2

In the second common scenario, a call is made or a complaint lodged, and law enforcement shows up at the scene for a "welfare check" or investigation that results in injury to or death of the deaf/disabled person. Ironically, in many of these incidents, the deaf person called law enforcement for aid or protection through a video relay service or via text.

In 2012, Robert Kim, a deaf man with Type 1 diabetes, pulled over to fix a flat tire when he began slipping into a life-threatening diabetic episode (Harris, 2014). Kim was seated on the grass when the first officer from the Bridgeton Police Department (Missouri) arrived (Harris, 2014). Kim informed the officer that he was deaf, that he had trouble speaking, and that he was going into diabetic shock. This officer called for backup instead of calling emergency medical services (Harris, 2014). The second officer arrived either unaware of or unconcerned about his disabilities. Kim's complaint notes that the second officer showed up angry, screaming verbal orders that Kim could not comprehend. Then the second officer drew and fired a taser, hitting Kim in the chest, shocking Kim at least three times (Harris, 2014). Both officers also struck Kim multiple times. Doctors at the hospital where Kim was subsequently taken and assessed noted that his blood glucose level was life-threatening. In 2014, Kim filed suit against the two officers and the city of Bridgeton (Harris, 2014). Kim was the second deaf person within 30 days to sue this police department for tasing them (Harris, 2014).

Another case that exemplifies this second scenario is that of Pearl Pearson Jr., a 64-year-old Black deaf man who was pulled over by Oklahoma Highway Patrol (OHP) troopers after allegedly bumping another car while steering a large SUV ("Graphic," 2014). The driver of the other car called 911 and tailed Pearson until OHP (together with a civilian ride-along) caught up. Dashcam video shows Pearson pulling over as soon as the troopers activated their lights to indicate that he should pull over. Trooper Eric Foster springs out of his cruiser and quickly approaches Pearson's SUV, shouting commands in rapid succession ("Graphic," 2014). Pearson attempts to communicate his disability to the troopers but never has an opportunity to do so (AJ+, 2018; "Deaf Oklahoma man Pearl Pearson wins $195,000," 2018). As Pearson attempts to hand his driver's license to the troopers and inform them that he is deaf, Trooper Foster hits him directly in the eye, making communication literally impossible (AJ+, 2018; "Deaf Oklahoma man Pearl Pearson wins $195,000," 2018). Troopers Eric Foster and Kelton Hayes dragged Pearson from the vehicle and pummeled him for nearly six minutes (Thompson, 2018). Hayes, who weighed nearly 300 pounds, and Foster put their full weight on Pearson, making it difficult for him to breathe. With no pause in the violence and with blows to his face continuing, Pearson was unable to see, sign, or figure out what was going on (AJ+, 2018; "Deaf Oklahoma man Pearl Pearson wins $195,000," 2018). After the beating, Pearson's eyes were black, bloodied, and swollen shut, and his shoulder dislocated, among other injuries (AJ+, 2018; "Deaf Oklahoma man Pearl Pearson wins $195,000," 2018). Still, troopers did not call emergency medical responders or move quickly to provide immediate first aid to the elderly man they had severely injured. The hospital, at the troopers' request, ran blood work on Pearson. Pearson had no alcohol or other substances in his blood. Instead, doctors reported that Pearson, who also had diabetes, had dangerously high blood sugar levels (AJ+, 2018; "Deaf Oklahoma man Pearl Pearson wins $195,000," 2018). At least two of the troopers who beat Pearson are caught on the dashboard camera immediately afterward, cursing when they run a check of his license and find out that he is deaf (Thompson, 2018). Then, they quickly double down:

Trooper Foster: [types information while holding Pearson's driver's license and looks at the computer screen] It says hearing-impaired on the thing.
Trooper Two: It says hearing impaired!
Trooper Three: Oh, shit!
Trooper Foster: Like deaf.
[brief pause, then an inaudible comment from a trooper off dashcam, which is cut short by Trooper Foster]
Trooper Foster: It doesn't matter when we're trying to get his hands, and he's fighting. The dude was strong, man.

After that, troopers are seen and heard joking and laughing about the incident and about Pearson's badly battered face while they develop their narrative and coach one another on what to write in their reports. During the following conversation, Pearl Pearson is seated in the police cruiser with two black eyes and a dislocated shoulder, in obvious need of immediate medical attention:

Trooper One: Good job, man!
Trooper Two: [inaudible] . . . I woulda shot him.
[laughter followed by a few seconds of inaudible banter and more laughing]
Trooper Three: Hey, you know why he was resisting you? Cuz he was trying to grab this fucking card.
Trooper Foster: Ooohhhh! That's what it was! [The tone here is as if he was just learning this information, and it sounds like a good idea.]
Trooper Three: That's what it was!
Trooper Foster: I knew it!
Trooper unknown: His face is jacked up! [intense laughter from multiple troopers]

Trooper Three: Hey, make sure you record that . . . that thing was not on the outside or inside. That was in the fucking side pocket. And he never even . . .
Trooper Foster: Right. Yeah.
Trooper Three: He never said shit about it!
Trooper Foster: Yeah.
[more laughter]

Pearson, a Black deaf man, who keeps a "deaf driver" placard in his truck, and who has two sons who work as police officers, maintains that he knows precisely what to do when approached by police officers (AJ+, 2018; "Deaf Oklahoma man Pearl Pearson wins $195,000," 2018; Thompson, 2018). He asserts that he was attempting to inform the troopers that he was deaf so they could communicate effectively, and he could comply with whatever they wanted him to do (AJ+, 2018; "Deaf Oklahoma man Pearl Pearson wins $195,000," 2018; Thompson, 2018). He says he never had a chance to comply because troopers punched him in the face and assaulted him before he had an opportunity to communicate or comply (2018). Video verifies Pearson's account.

Despite these videos, District Attorney David Prater declined to charge the troopers ("Graphic," 2014). Instead, Prater praised these troopers, stating that

> Trooper Foster and Trooper Hayes demonstrated commendable restraint and judgment throughout the incident. Only minimal necessary force was employed by the troopers to defend themselves and civilians at the arrest scene from physical harm and to affect the arrest of Pearson. ("Graphic," 2014)

Prater further stated that Pearson's was a "textbook case of police restraint." As is typical in these scenarios, Prater charged Pearson with resisting arrest ("Graphic," 2014). In January 2017, after 3 years of legal battles, and with Pearson's legal team ready to go to trial the very next week, Prater dismissed the charge against Pearson, citing the "cost to taxpayers" ("Graphic," 2014).

Pearson was relieved that charges against him were dismissed after *years* of court battles. But Pearson was fearful that something similar or worse would happen to others if no meaningful steps were taken to address local law enforcement's race and disability consciousness and sensitivity issues that nearly led to his death (Thompson, 2018). After District Attorney Prater dropped the charges, Pearson sued the OHP and the troopers involved in his beating. A federal judge approved a settlement between Pearson and the State of Oklahoma (Oklahoma Department of Public Safety) and the Oklahoma County Board of County Commissioners for $175,000 and $20,000, respectively, attorney's fees not included (Stipulated Judgment, 5:15-cv-00574-W; Order and Judgment, 5:15-cv-00575-W). In the end,

Oklahoma taxpayers paid at least five times as much as they would have had Prater gone forward with prosecution, and many more times as much had no violence been used or charges been brought against Pearl Pearson in the first place (Thompson, 2018). The troopers are still working. None received any reprimand, disciplinary records, or other consequences for the extended physical beating of Pearson or their lack of candor, professionalism, courtesy, and consideration for human life in the aftermath of the incident (Thompson, 2018).

Police departments and district attorneys' responses to law enforcement's "use of force" incidents against disabled people have the potential to either decrease their frequency or to enable law enforcement to continue this behavior. District attorneys can use their platform and authority either to share accurate information about deaf and disability cultures and hold law enforcement accountable or to peddle misinformation and perpetuate stereotypes about disability while permitting and excusing violence.

Fewer than 3 years later, the Oklahoma City Police Department—also under the purview of District Attorney Prater—killed a low-income, brown-skinned DeafDisabled man named Magdiel Sanchez (Chuck, 2017). In September 2017, officers arrived at Sanchez's house at nighttime, searching for his father, who was alleged to have left the scene of a car accident. Sanchez, who used a walking stick whenever he was out in his neighborhood, saw the lights and came out to see what was going on. A home security camera shows Sanchez retreating from police officers and heading back to his home. According to neighbors, this is when officers began to shout commands at him (Chuck, 2017). Two officers simultaneously tased and shot Sanchez, killing him. Neighbors repeatedly informed officers that Sanchez was deaf and could not hear them before they tased and shot him. During the press conference where District Attorney David Prater announced his decision not to charge the officers responsible for Sanchez's death, Prater stated that "you don't need to hear to know what these officers are saying to you" (Chuck, 2017).

The next scenario relates to police investigations involving deaf people and criminal procedures that further disadvantage disabled/deaf people.

Scenario No. 3

In the third scenario, officers conduct an "investigation" without ever hearing from the deaf or disabled suspect or witnesses, or the officer bypasses an investigation altogether (Bernstein, 2012). This is especially true of deaf suspects as opposed to deaf complainants and witnesses but happens quite frequently to deaf complainants who are otherwise marginalized (Bekiempis, 2016 [Black woman]; Bernstein, 2012 [white gay man]; Matter & Heath, 2017 [white deaf androgynous person alleged to have mental illness by roommates]; Ogunyipe, 2012 [Black queer-presenting woman]). In this scenario, a deaf/disabled person is arrested, booked, jailed, sent to psychiatric detention, charged, or has their children taken, usually based solely on the word of a hearing/abled person. Similar to the preceding scenarios, once an arrest is made or charges recommended or levied, there is more pressure on law enforcement and prosecutors to continue prosecution even when there is less than adequate evidence tending to prove this deaf/disabled person's culpability. This is especially true if the person is held in jail.

The profound lack of understanding of and deeply ableist response to disability across the entire criminal legal system means that deaf people are more likely to be jailed for offenses that hearing people would not be and to spend more time in jail once they arrive (HEARD, 2020). While in jail, deaf people usually have no contact with counsel for extended periods of time even when they have requested the presence of counsel largely because of the pace of the criminal legal system in light of mass incarceration, and also because of the failure of most law enforcement, jails, and defense attorneys to appreciate the need for or provide access to qualified interpreters, accessible telecommunication, and other accommodations or auxiliary aids.

Sometimes, law enforcement does obtain *some* information from the deaf person but through unqualified people attempting to "interpret" (e.g., police officers, complainants, children) or through technology that may not be suitable for high-stress or high-stakes legal situations (e.g., cell phone note or text exchange, video remote interpreting, note pads). In many cases, deaf people who have experienced extreme physical violence and trauma are left to try to develop their own transcript of what occurred without the support of qualified interpreters (or with interpreters they have contacted and paid for on their own due to the failure of law enforcement and their own defense attorneys to follow the law). Police officers, as recently as 2020, have used or attempted to use family members, police officers, and even the alleged suspect (e.g., person alleged to have harmed a deaf person) to serve as a conduit for communication between officers and deaf people (HEARD, 2020). Each of these methods directly violates federal disability rights laws. Although all wrongful arrest and conviction cases are difficult to challenge, cases in which law enforcement, attorneys, or the courts have relied on unqualified people to interpret in cases involving deaf/disabled suspects are among the most difficult.

The following case illustrates some of these practices and is in line with policing trends related to deaf people—especially deaf people with other disabilities—across the country. This case will be referenced throughout this chapter to illustrate and challenge common law enforcement, attorney, social service agency, and advocacy practices.

Scenario No. 4

In August 2011, the Carterville Police Department (Illinois) was called to the home of a deaf mother and her upset hearing teenager. The mother communicates only through ASL—which she was introduced to particularly late in life, during college. Before learning ASL, she struggled to communicate in any language. She emphasized that English was not a language she was comfortable using. Her written and signed communication indicated that she knew her language capacities and access needs well. HEARD collected the following information from the mother. She had collected dozens of pages of documentation from the police, public defender, court, Child Protective Services (CPS), and others involved in this case.

On the evening in question, the teenager became upset when the mother picked the teenager up from a friend's house. There had been a miscommunication via text about how long the teenager would stay at the friend's home—the mother thought she was to pick up her teenager at 8:00 in the evening, whereas the teenager thought she would be picked up at 8:00 the next morning. On the way home, with hopes of a sleepover dashed, the teenager became upset, which led to a heated sign language exchange in the car. The teenager then placed a call to 911 while in the car without the mother realizing it. When the family of two arrived home, a police officer from the Carterville Police Department met them there. The officer urged the upset teenager to interpret between the officer and the mother, and the mother told the teenager to let the officer know that she would talk to him only through a qualified sign language interpreter. The officer then wrote questions down on a piece of paper. Again, the mother told the teenager to tell the officer that a qualified sign language interpreter was necessary. At this point, the mother showed the officer her personalized deaf identification card, which indicated that she was deaf and that the accommodation required for this situation was a qualified sign language interpreter (Figure 1).

The officer, feeling slighted by the mother's persistence, called the precinct to ask for advisement from the chief. Specifically, the officer's notes state that he called the chief "to ask what to do about the circumstances surrounding the difficulties in communicating with [the mother] and her demands of a Signed English Translator." The chief responded that "we would not get

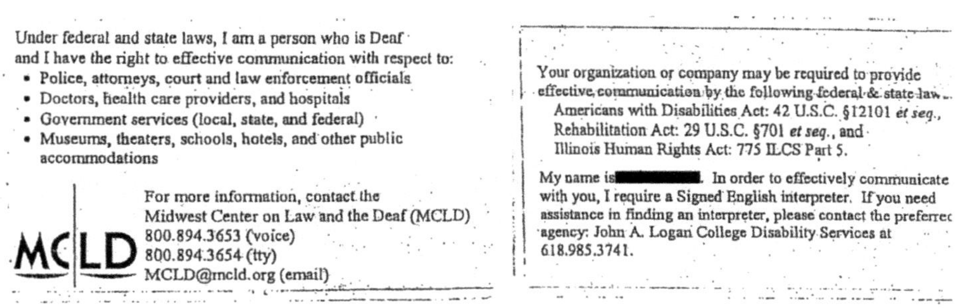
Under federal and state laws, I am a person who is Deaf and I have the right to effective communication with respect to:
- Police, attorneys, court and law enforcement officials
- Doctors, health care providers, and hospitals
- Government services (local, state, and federal)
- Museums, theaters, schools, hotels, and other public accommodations

MCLD

For more information, contact the Midwest Center on Law and the Deaf (MCLD)
800.894.3653 (voice)
800.894.3654 (tty)
MCLD@mcld.org (email)

Your organization or company may be required to provide effective communication by the following federal & state law:
Americans with Disabilities Act: 42 U.S.C. §12101 *et seq.*,
Rehabilitation Act: 29 U.S.C. §701 *et seq.*, and
Illinois Human Rights Act: 775 ILCS Part 5.

My name is [redacted]. In order to effectively communicate with you, I require a Signed English interpreter. If you need assistance in finding an interpreter, please contact the preferrec agency: John A. Logan College Disability Services at 618.985.3741.

FIGURE 1. Personalized "Deaf Card" shown to the police officer, attorneys, and the court by the mother whose name is redacted on the card.

a Signed English Translator and to only attempt to make effective communication through writing our questions and responses on paper." The chief also advised that "if it was okay with [the child] an arrest would not be made on [the mother] for Domestic Battery, due to [the mother's] failure to communicate with law enforcement on the scene effectively." The hearing teenager was then taken by the police officers and given to the hearing father, and charges were recommended against the mother. The Carterville Police Department admits in its own documentation that the mother was *never* consulted about the alleged incident, specifically because she requested an interpreter and that they did not think an interpreter was needed for communication or believe that they were required to provide one (Figure 2a and 2b).

When the mother went to the precinct on the same evening to figure out where her child had been taken, she was threatened with arrest. Confused, afraid, angry, and without her child, she returned home. The mother, while still in shock, contacted an ASL/English interpreter and asked them to support her in developing a written explanation of what occurred so she could share that information with the police department in hopes of getting her child returned. If our legal system worked as it should, this story would end with an officer returning later that night or early the next morning with an interpreter to parse

Contact with Chief of the Carterville Police Department, Carterville, Illinois

Due to the circumstances surrounding the difficulties in communicating with Mother and her demands of a Signed English Translator, I called Chief of Carterville PD for his advisement. He stated that we would not get a Signed English Translator and to only attempt to make effective communication through writing our questions and responses on paper. He also stated that if it were okay with Child, an arrest would not be made on Mother, for Domestic Battery, due to Mother's failure to effectively communicate with law enforcement on scene.

FIGURE 2a. Redacted Excerpts from the responding officer's notes, Carterville Police Department, Carterville, Illinois, dated July 9, 2011.

Interview with Mother

Child stated that her mother was deaf. Upon attempting to communicate with mother, she initially refused to make any type of response to me or even acknowledge my presence and only continued signing with child, which only caused child to cry more. Child stated that their mother was saying that she would only talk to me through a Signed English Interpreter. I next began writing my questions on paper and again child stated that their mother was saying that she was refusing to effectively communicate with me through writing our responses on paper. Mother continued to deny my presence and failed to even make eye contact with me.

FIGURE 2b. Redacted excerpts from the responding officer's notes, Carterville Police Department, Carterville, Illinois, dated July 9, 2011.

things out. This, however, would not be the case. The mother was charged with misdemeanor domestic battery, and so began the avalanche of injustice for this mother.

The fact that this Carterville police officer recorded his and his chief's refusal to provide an interpreter and the removal of a child from their mother without ever having taken a statement from the mother (though they took a statement from the hearing teenager who was the complainant) seems to indicate that the officers believed they were doing the right thing. They, in fact, thought they were doing the mother a favor by not arresting her. The mother was using sign language with her child, and the police interpreted her signing as threatening—with some parts of the police statement indicating that the "domestic situation" was "ongoing" when he arrived, whereas the mother was merely communicating in sign language with her child. Sign language is not dangerous, but law enforcement often misunderstands sign language and its attendant body language and classifiers (Smith, 2010), especially for those whose body language is decidedly exaggerated (often Black people and other negatively racialized people; deaf people with other disabilities; and people who are in pain or fear, or who are upset) or those who are seen as particularly atypical by authority figures in other ways, for example, owing to traumatic brain injury, cerebral palsy, or other disabilities.

Finally, even though the mother was cooperating with law enforcement and rationally and responsibly educating them about what was required for effective communication (which they should already have known), officers wrote the police report such that it portrays the mother as irrational and obstinate. The report states that the mother was "*unwilling* to communicate with law enforcement by writing on paper" and that she was "*unwilling* to cooperate with law enforcement's requests" (emphasis added). Evidence shows that time and again, when a deaf person asserts their right to communication access, law enforcement interprets the mere request as disrespect, intransigence, or evasion (HEARD, 2020). In the mind of police officers, any refusal to communicate in the officer's requested method is noncompliance, which, to them, points to possible culpability. Deaf people are often forced to accept less than adequate communication with law enforcement because law enforcement makes it patently clear that the mere assertion of communication access rights is a "threat" to law enforcement's authority (HEARD, 2020).

Obviously, the truth in this case and in others is innocuous and straightforward: A deaf person is the expert on their own abilities, disabilities, and communication access needs.

This mother refused to write back and forth with law enforcement, as is her right under federal disability rights laws. Federal law was on her side. It likely never crossed her mind that her request for a reasonable accommodation would not be met and her child taken. Many deaf people in her situation resort to using writing (in a language they do not use or fully understand) or to accepting less-than-qualified "interpreters" to communicate with police out of fear of retaliation or worse punishment for the continued assertion of their rights.

In this case, the mother struggles mightily with English. She assessed the serious nature of this situation and knew that her teenage child of deaf adults (Coda) was in no position to attempt to mediate between herself and law enforcement when the child had called law enforcement and was still upset with the mother. Here, the mother was correct in all of her assessments. Law enforcement was wrong. Right does not prevail in these scenarios, however. As a matter of fact, marginalized people who are in the right are often wronged by the criminal legal system. This story, like others involving law enforcement misjudgments, missteps, and mistakes, does not end here. Just one error anywhere in the criminal legal system can lead to a lifetime of consequences. In the case of deaf suspects in the criminal legal system, errors are often made at *every* step. In that regard, this mother's ordeal is particularly informative and tragic.

In October 2011, the Illinois Department of Children & Family Services (DCFS), in conjunction with domestic battery allegations against the mother, sent two letters stating that the agency had completed its investigation and determined the allegations to be "unfounded." Both letters also state that the recipient has exactly 10 days to request a report that states that the report against the recipient was falsely filed. For a person who does not read English, these letters are completely inaccessible. The mother could not understand these letters, yet she gave the letters to her appointed public defender in the hope that her attorney could help decipher them. She attached her own handwritten letter with the two DCFS letters when she shared them with her attorney. Her note read:

> I got two letters from Department of Child and Family Services (DCFS) in mail last October 28, 2011.pm. I never meet someone from IL DCFS and got those letters from them . . . I had very hard tried to understand those letters and never understood why those letters??? Words. Lack of accessibility to the justice system.

By now, the mother had been making multiple visits to the court for nearly three months, with no sign of getting her child back and no effective communication with her attorney—still not understanding what she was accused of or why her child had been removed from her home. Unable to secure an interpreter, the court reset her case numerous times. On at least two occasions, despite requests for interpreters, the court told the mother that she did not need interpreters. Finally, in December, the court provided an interpreter. The mother had now been away from her child for a full 5 months—including 2 full months since CPS sent a letter indicating that the allegations against her were unfounded. Unfortunately, this was too little, too late. Mass incarceration was not done with this mother yet.

Mass incarceration has left the most marginalized and least resourced people with little or no option other than to plead guilty. Deaf people are no exception. Jail conditions and the "trial penalty" and "bail trap," coupled with "tough on crime" policies that mandate longer sentences, has led to over 90% of people in state and federal cases pleading guilty (Rakoff, 2014). That is to say, of the 2.3 million people imprisoned, over 2 million are there because they accepted guilty pleas. Thus, innocent people plead guilty to crimes they did not commit (Rakoff, 2014). The likelihood of an accused person pleading guilty goes up exponentially if they are low- or no-income, disabled, otherwise marginalized, or at risk for losing their house, job, children, etc. Possible collateral and social consequences of pleading guilty to a crime—even one that you did not commit—are not often thoroughly explained to defendants. Notably, the implications of a guilty plea cannot be anticipated or explained by counsel who fails to follow federal disability rights laws to ensure that they can communicate effectively with their client. Defendants certainly cannot participate in their own defense in these situations. Yet most attorneys are not providing qualified sign language interpreters to communicate with deaf clients.

With no communication access to understand the letters, and no meaningful access to her own attorney, the mother, like over 90% of defendants, pled guilty to a lesser offense. She felt coerced to take the guilty plea because she thought by pleading guilty, she would be able to be with her child, whom she had now been separated from for 8 months. Her handwritten notes from this visit to court paint a clear picture of the coercion, confusion, and rights violations:

> public defender talked that state atty and walked to the room with me and same interpreter and had a supervision contact ready and explained to the interpreter that 12 months supervision is better than probation and what was on that contact and left quickly to go back to court room. The same interpreter helped telling me what I should do on that contact to sign my name on it. After signing my name on it, we went back to court room . . . I standed up to the judge to sign his name on it. I went back to work. After work at night I was thinking about court contact and was very shocked and re-read about "no initiated contact with [child]" I felt very bad about "no contact" with [child]. How very upset I was.
>
> My mental health counselor [counselor's name] read it and handed it back to me without knowing "no initiated contact with [child]." So I had to discuss what "no initiated contact with [child]" meant!! I was very upset . . . . I am not allowed to see be with back home.[child] is my only family in IL state [child] til end of 12 months supervision on [date] 2013!

Notably, the mother and her counselor communicate through an ASL interpreter. It was only with the counselor, where there was adequate time and access to process the plea agreement and effective communication, that the mother finally gained a full understanding of what she had signed. Also important to note is that the sentence was rendered almost a full year after initial contact with law enforcement (largely because of the attorney and court's failures to request and provide interpreters for several proceedings). The supervision condition lasted a full 12 months, although the mother had already spent nearly a year away from her child while the case wound its way through the criminal legal system, often delayed solely on account of the system's accommodation failures. This is another example of deaf people being unjustly accused and receiving disproportionately harsher punishments or longer sentences because of systemic failures.

In addition to not adequately explaining what the conditions of this agreement meant, no one adequately explained that this plea could be used against her by the child's other parent to help them gain custody of the child. The other parent did just that, and the mother permanently lost custody of her child. When the mother communicated with HEARD after already having pled guilty, it was patently clear that no one had taken the time to explain even the most basic information to her. She could not explain the meaning of the words "innocent" or "guilty." Specifically, when asked whether she was guilty or innocent, she responded in written English via email: "I was told that I was guilty of the crime. I don't know difference between innocent and guilt for that crime I pled guilty, but I think I am innocent of that crime." After all was said and done, this mother was ordered to pay more than $500 in fines and fees to the court, attorneys, and attendant social service agencies.

In the perfect world, someone along the long and winding trail of "justice"—CPS, the mother's defense attorney, the prosecutor, the judge, an interpreter—would have noticed and cared that this mother was not participating in her own defense or understanding what was going on or the consequences of her plea. Instead, the mother requested and was denied interpreters at every step of the criminal legal process until the very last legal proceeding, where an interpreter was provided.

Another profoundly concerning and all too common pattern with cases involving deaf people is interpreters being provided at formal court proceedings but not being at the stages prior to formal proceedings. Red flags immediately go up when interpreters are required for court proceedings but not provided during police interrogations, attorney-client meetings, and other critical steps toward this penultimate stage of the legal process. In some cases, courts provide hearing interpreters *and* certified/deaf interpreters for communication with deaf people who were provided no accommodations at all during the arrest, interrogation, or for attorney-client communication. Yet the system regularly claims that due process has been satisfied even where accommodations—inefficient though they might be—are provided for trial but disregarded for all other contacts with the system and case development.

By all accounts, this mother did everything right. She put the police, public defender, and court on notice of her disability with a personalized card provided by disability rights attorneys. The card clearly denoted the laws implicated, entities covered, and accommodations required for effective communication and provided attorneys' numbers should they require additional information. She asserted her right to an interpreter multiple times and documented every interaction with police, attorneys, and the courts. Her notes reveal clear disability rights and constitutional violations at every stage of her interaction with the system. And yet she never regained custody of her child, still has a domestic violence charge on her record, and has been permanently traumatized by the very system that claims to mete out justice.

It is also worth noting that it is practically impossible for many deaf people to file formal complaints about these persistent violations and inequities, in part because of the very inaccessibility that caused the deprivation of their rights in the first instance. In this case, even with the support of committed advocates and attorneys from nonprofits across the United States, she could not find an attorney licensed in her state who was willing and able to support her in appealing her criminal conviction or filing a civil action for disability rights violations. No one was held accountable. In this case, as in most of these cases, apart from the story the mother has and the information HEARD saved, there would be no record of the incident at all.

This case is not exceptional but for the fact that the mother was not arrested, that she was charged with just two alleged offenses as opposed to multiple charges, that the charge was relatively low-level, and that she was able to plead to a low-level charge and receive relative leniency on pleading. If she had other marginalized identities, this tragedy might have been even more tragic.

Scenario No. 5

The final scenario discussed in this section is that of signing police officers and other coercive and confusing interview and interrogation practices, namely, those practices rooted in the Reid technique (Starr, 2013; Trainum, 2016). Although many countries have banned this interrogation technique altogether because of the high risk of eliciting false confessions and misinformation, this deliberately manipulative method of questioning suspects has been used widely by law enforcement agencies in the United States for half a century (Hager, 2017; Trainum, 2016). In 2012, a Canadian provincial court judge ruled that "stripped to its bare essentials, the Reid technique is a guilt-presumptive, confrontational, psychologically manipulative procedure whose purpose is to extract a confession" (Quan, 2012). In 2017, one of the largest law enforcement consulting firms in the United States announced that it would no longer train detectives in this method, citing academic research that showed other interrogation styles to be "much less risky" (Hager, 2017).

The Reid technique is a three-phase process that begins with factual analysis, followed by a behavior analysis interview and then a nine-step interrogation (Jayne & Buckley, n.d.). Reid trainers claim to be able to determine whether a suspect is lying based on attitude, verbal and nonverbal cues, paralinguistics, and responses to interview and interrogation questions (Jayne & Buckley, n.d.). Reid trainers advise that particular behaviors are indicative of untruthfulness and others indicative of honesty (Jayne & Buckley, n.d.). Trainees are advised to interview people only when the information developed from the interview and investigation indicates that the subject is involved in the commission of the crime (Jayne & Buckley, n.d.).

Critics of the Reid technique note numerous concerns with the process (Starr, 2013; Trainum, 2016). The approach is subject to confirmation bias (i.e., likely to reinforce inaccurate beliefs and assumptions) (Starr, 2013; Trainum, 2016). The interrogation is intentionally confrontational, guilt-presumptive, and psychologically taxing, and officers are instructed to lie to make suspects believe they have evidence against them (Starr, 2013; Trainum, 2016). Ironically, the interrogation that gained the creator of the Reid technique wide acclaim actually elicited a false confession that spurred the wrongful conviction of a man whose wife had been murdered (Starr, 2013; Trainum, 2016).

The Reid technique is an example of a common practice employed by the criminal legal system that makes historically marginalized people more vulnerable because of a centering of and deeming "normal" a particular way of existing, thinking, and responding. Much of what Reid practitioners label as "deceptive" behavior is quite ordinary for many people and particularly common for many marginalized and multiply marginalized people interacting with police. The most common Reid interview and interrogation techniques and behavior evaluation criteria will achieve many more false positives and false confessions.

For example, the Reid technique teaches that someone who does not make or maintain eye contact is likely being deceptive—that truthful subjects usually maintain direct eye contact when answering key questions (Jayne & Buckley, n.d.). However, many people, including those with disabilities, either struggle with eye contact generally, are particularly averse to making eye contact when interacting with authority figures or look away when processing or expressing information, or during emotionally tinged or stressful situations. Many people from different cultures are taught not to make eye contact for culturally appropriate reasons. Although this is no indication of their untruthfulness or guilt, the Reid technique's behavior symptom analysis training offers that nonverbal behavior is harder to control than verbal behavior and that the meaning of the verbal answer is either supported or contradicted by the corresponding nonverbal behaviors (Jayne & Buckley, n.d.). Specifically, the training tells law enforcement to believe a subject's nonverbal behavior if it contradicts their nonverbal behavior—to believe the head nodding yes despite a subject saying "no," and vice versa (Jayne & Buckley, n.d.). This contradicts basic principles of human information processing and leads to misinterpretation and miscommunication with disabled people who use head nods and other movements very differently than hearing nonsigning, abled people. Despite studies having proven these theories and practices to be unreliable, law enforcement leave Reid technique trainings believing that they can distinguish between honest and dishonest people on the basis of body language, verbal and nonverbal cues, attitude, the timing of responses, lenience toward wrongdoers, etc.

During an interrogation, typical deceptive behavioral attitudes include being apologetic/accepting or quiet. Typical behavioral attitudes include being unyielding or persistent.

Figures 3a and 3b depict just some of the ways that, under the Reid praxis, many marginalized people's responses to policing systems and interactions with law enforcement are deemed "deceitful," although they are typically privileged (i.e., hearing, abled, white, wealthy, cisgender, masculine, etc.) ways of thinking, responding, behaving during police encounters deemed evidence of "truthfulness."

phase of the process	typical deceptive behavioral attitudes	typical truthful behavioral attitudes
during an interview	• overly anxious • unconcerned/unrealistic • uncooperative/defensive • guarded/evasive/hesitant • rationalizing/unhelpful • insincere • defeated	• composed • concerned/realistic • cooperative • direct/spontaneous • open/helpful • sincere • confident
during interrogation	• apologetic/accepting • quiet	• unyielding • persistent

FIGURE 3a. The chart lists two phases of the process: the interview and interrogation.

typically deceptive nonverbal behavior symptoms during interview or interrogation	• retreating from investigator • slouching • frozen • non-frontal alignment • barriered posture • erratic and rapid posture changes • head and body slump
typically truthful nonverbal behavior symptoms during interview or interrogation	• upright • open and relaxed • lean forward on occasion • frontally aligned with the interviewer • casual posture changes

FIGURE 3b. Examples of typically deceptive nonverbal behavior symptoms.

It is well settled that youth and people with mental disabilities are known to be especially susceptible to false confessions (Crane et al., 2016; Rogal, 2017). Less acknowledged and discussed is deaf and other disabled people's extreme susceptibility to the same false confession-inducing jeopardies as other marginalized populations. These jeopardies include coercive and confusing psychological interrogation techniques; vulnerability to suggestive questions and pressures to please and accommodate authority; being deferential to and trusting of authority (e.g., believing detectives who assert that they have extensive evidence proving culpability; or who say "we already know you did it, you just need to tell us exactly what happened"; or "this will be better for you if you tell us now," etc.); and cross-cultural miscommunication.

Intentional dishonesty coupled with the system's failure to provide effective communication also further impairs disabled people's ability to fully comprehend the gravity of law enforcement situations. All of this coupled with the general lack of accessible information about the dangers of the legal system; constitutional rights; and the importance of every person, regardless of disability, to immediately invoke the right to counsel and to remain silent during police questioning only contributes to the likelihood of deaf people being misunderstood, presumed guilty, and falsely confessing or providing statements that will be used against them in legal proceedings. Furthermore, many deaf suspects and defendants have other disabilities, although they are rarely discussed or accommodated. Presumptions about deaf suspects' language, literacy, mannerisms, and the tendency among officers who "know" sign language to insert themselves into this already fraught interview and interrogation calculus have disastrous and irreversible consequences. The criminal legal system has continued to churn, largely oblivious or indifferent to these dangers and injustices.

The Reid technique, coupled with disability, is the perfect storm for wrongful convictions, but an in-depth analysis of problems inherent to the Reid technique is beyond the scope of this chapter. However, it is worth noting that "more training" does not address, remedy, or end policies and practices, like the Reid technique, that create and exacerbate structural and systemic inequity—whether such trainings are related to race, ethnicity, gender, sexuality, class, age, disability, religion, or other identities. Moreover, in many cases involving wrongfully convicted disabled people, law enforcement exploits suspects' vulnerabilities and disabilities.

DEAF WRONGFUL CONVICTION CASES

Decisions about accommodations cannot be left to law enforcement at the expense of disabled people whose lives and liberty depend on having access guaranteed by federal disability rights laws, the Constitution, and basic principles of fairness and decency. The narratives below prove that under current law enforcement regimes, it is not only possible, but *highly probable* that an innocent deaf person who is being truthful, when not provided with reasonable accommodations (especially while under great pressure, operating on very little sleep, and being misled about the weight of evidence against them) can "look guilty"; be persuaded to sign documents they cannot comprehend; and even confess to crimes they did not commit. Notably, while Black people represent just 13% of the American population, they also represent the majority of innocent defendants who are wrongfully convicted in all major crime categories—accounting for 47% of the 1,900 exonerations listed in the National Registry of Exonerations as of October 2016 (Gross et al., 2017). The risk of wrongful conviction for Black disabled people is therefore exponentially increased.

Case Study No. 1: Stephen Brodie

Stephen Brodie's case illustrates what happens when a deaf person is subjected to customary police interview and interrogation practices and the whim of what law enforcement believes to be "effective communication." Stephen Brodie was a white Deaf teenager who had been through the foster system as a child (Denzel, 2016). Brodie, who uses ASL as his only language, was arrested for stealing coins from a soda machine, then subjected to a grueling interrogation about the rape of a small child, a crime he knew nothing about. The interrogation lasted 18 hours over the course of 8 days (Denzel, 2016). Officers conducted this interrogation without an interpreter for *at least* half of the time (Denzel, 2016). Transcripts from the interrogation both with and without an "interpreter" illustrate endless miscommunication and misunderstanding.

Brodie made his best attempts to understand and provide responses to officers, but their failure to provide adequate accommodations made communication impossible. Officers here likely believed that they were communicating effectively. Not only that, but applying the Reid behavior analysis framework, Brodie's responses would be deemed telltale signs of deception, evasion, and lack of cooperation. The Reid technique instructs officers to continue interrogations until the suspect is ready to confess (Jayne & Buckley, n.d.). The result in cases like this is prolonged and more intensified interrogation tactics as opposed to reprieve, reassessment, and regrouping. In command-and-control settings, "failure to comply"—even when this perceived failure results from the inability to comply—is taken as a form of defiance or resistance necessitating reprisal (Lowery, 2017). So a Deaf teenager like Stephen Brodie who responds "incorrectly" to what law enforcement deems straightforward interview and interrogation questions is presumed to be untruthful or attempting to conceal guilt as opposed to being completely disoriented and, in Brodie's own words, feeling "intimidated and scared" (Miller, 2010).

Stephen Brodie succumbed to this pressure and "confessed" to a crime he had not committed, getting many of the details of the crime wrong (Denzel, 2016). Brodie also "confessed" to many other crimes fabricated by the police (Denzel, 2016). His trial attorney attempted to suppress Brodie's false confession, to no avail (Miller, 2010). Facing a 99-year sentence, Brodie pled guilty to rape and received a 5-year sentence (Denzel, 2016). After serving his term for a crime he did not commit, Brodie refused to register on the sex offender registry, so he was incarcerated for more than ten additional years (Denzel, 2016).

In 2010, Brodie's father persuaded the Dallas County District Attorney's Conviction Integrity Unit to review Brodie's case (Denzel, 2016). It was the Integrity Unit that argued for Brodie's release (Denzel, 2016). It was discovered that the police had withheld evidence from Brodie's trial counsel, namely, that a hair found on the victim's blanket did not match Brodie and that the bloody fingerprint found on the window screen matched a man convicted of child rape who was suspected in other assaults in the area (Denzel, 2016). In 2010, a Texas district court judge vacated Brodie's conviction on the grounds of actual innocence (Denzel, 2016). By then, Stephen Brodie had spent 17 years in prison for a crime he did not commit (Denzel, 2016). Taxpayers paid for this injustice to the tune of millions of dollars between his near twenty year incarceration (wherein he was deprived of accommodations) and through a state compensation package of nearly $900,000 and monthly annuity—a pittance compared with what he needlessly endured. These injustices are only magnified and compounded for multiply marginalized deaf people.

Case Study No. 2: John H. L. Wilson Jr.

John Wilson Jr., a Black, DeafDisabled, low-income man from the District of Columbia, spent 25 years in prison after being convicted of second-degree murder in 1996 and receiving a life sentence ("Deaf man who was incarcerated," 2019). He returned home in March 2019 only after more than a decade of advocacy from HEARD and the Public Defender Service for the District of Columbia ("Deaf man who was incarcerated," 2019).

In 1994, the DC Metropolitan Police Department (MPD) interrogated John Wilson and other Black deaf/disabled witnesses—all of whom used ASL as their only or primary language and worked with ASL interpreters during subsequent grand jury testimony and trial[4]—without sign language interpreters. MPD instead used written notes and a police officer who knew how to fingerspell, Officer Myra Wheeler. One witness worked with deaf and hearing interpreter teams during Wilson's 1996 trial but received no accommodations during police interviews. The trial transcript from this witness depicts confusion during police interviews and illustrates how after advising the lead detective (Baylor) that she could not understand the fingerspelling officer (Wheeler), that Officer Baylor continued the interview. The witness admits to signing (i.e., adding her signature to a document) a statement that she could not read or understand (Figures 4a–d).

Monday, June 10, 1996.pdf

Detective Baylor at this time?

A Oh, it was very brief, it was not long.

Q During the interview you never said to Detective Baylor that you were not able to communicate well with or through the female police officer who was using sign.

THE INTERPRETER: The interpreter needs to ask the witness to repeat the answer.

THE WITNESS: I did tell the police that I did not understand, this officer was just finger spelling not signing and I did tell them.

BY MR. KIERSH:

Q Who did you say it to?

A The black male that was there, the black man.

Q Now you're able to read something that's typed up, aren't you?

A Well, I can read some; I don't read very well.

Q Do you read the newspaper ever?

A I can read some of it. Most of it is very hard for me to understand. It's very hard for me to understand, I really don't read very much.

Q After you gave the statement to Detective Baylor he gave you the chance to sign the statement, isn't that right?

THE COURT: Put her signature on it?

MR. KIERSH: Yes.

FIGURE 4a. Trial transcript, June 10, 1996, *United States v. John H.L. Wilson, Jr.*, F-9188–94.

Monday, June 10, 1996.pdf

Q Now that woman is Officer --

A Just, there was just one woman officer who was there.

Q That woman officer was Officer Wheeler, is that right?

A Who was Officer Wheeler.

Q Did that police officer, the woman police officer sign to you?

A Was that a black female?

Q The question is the woman officer who was present, did she use sign language in your presence?

A Yes.

Q Is that how you communicated with Detective Baylor using that person and her abilities to sign?

A Yes, that's how it was, that's right, the woman was there. and she helped with the signing, yes.

Q Do you recall whether or not there was a third police officer present during this interview?

A No, it was just three of us who were in that room.

Q So your testimony is that you are certain that during this interview it was just yourself and two other police officers.

A Yes, I'm sure of that answer.

Q For how long were you being questioned by

FIGURE 4b. Trial transcript, June 10, 1996, *United States v. John H.L. Wilson, Jr.*, F-9188–94.

Monday, June 10, 1996.pdf

BY MR. KIERSH:

Q And before you put your signature on the paper, Detective Baylor gave you the chance to read what it is that he typed up --

THE COURT: Sorry to do this to you, Mr. Kiersh, but you can't stand --

MR. KIERSH: I appreciate that, Your Honor.

BY MR. KIRSH:

Q Before the detective gave it to you to put your signature on it, he gave you the chance to read what he had typed up, isn't that right?

A Right, I was given the time to read them. I read it and then I signed it.

Q And before he asked you to put your signature on it, he gave you the chance to make any corrections to what was contained in the statement that he had typed up, isn't that right?

A Really I read it and I didn't understand all of it. I can't read that well but I signed it.

Q You did sign the statement after you had the chance to read it and after you had the chance to make any corrections, isn't that right?

A Right, I read through it. It was not real fast. I read through it and then I signed it.

FIGURE 4c. Trial transcript, June 10, 1996, *United States v. John H.L.Wilson, Jr.*, F-9188–94.

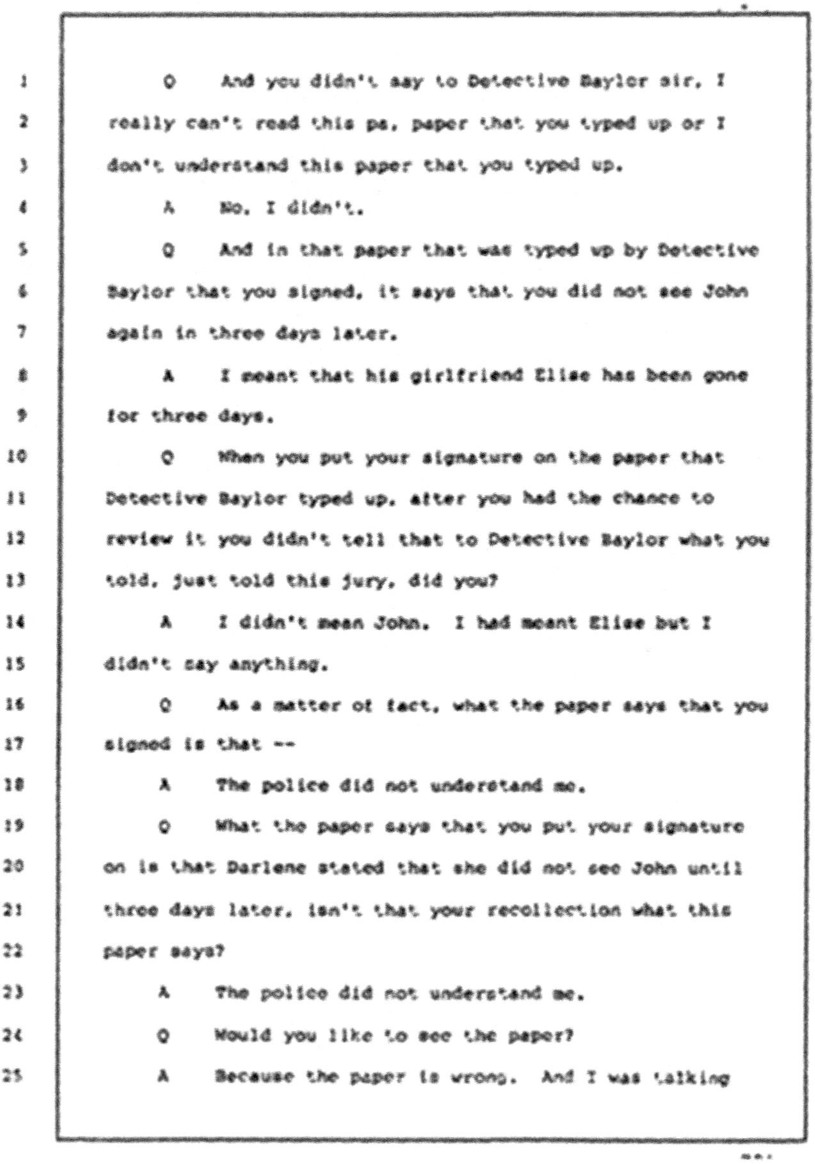

Q And you didn't say to Detective Baylor sir, I really can't read this pa, paper that you typed up or I don't understand this paper that you typed up.

A No, I didn't.

Q And in that paper that was typed up by Detective Baylor that you signed, it says that you did not see John again in three days later.

A I meant that his girlfriend Elise has been gone for three days.

Q When you put your signature on the paper that Detective Baylor typed up, after you had the chance to review it you didn't tell that to Detective Baylor what you told, just told this jury, did you?

A I didn't mean John. I had meant Elise but I didn't say anything.

Q As a matter of fact, what the paper says that you signed is that --

A The police did not understand me.

Q What the paper says that you put your signature on is that Darlene stated that she did not see John until three days later, isn't that your recollection what this paper says?

A The police did not understand me.

Q Would you like to see the paper?

A Because the paper is wrong. And I was talking

FIGURE 4d. Trial transcript, June 10, 1996, *United States v. John H.L. Wilson, Jr.*, F-9188–94.

MPD also did not provide accommodations for communication with John Wilson. Information from these grossly deficient interviews and interrogations led to Wilson's wrongful arrest and conviction. Interrogation notes and Wilson's Miranda waiver cards illustrate Wilson's earnest attempts to communicate without accommodation and ensuing frustration, confusion, and desperation (Figures 5 and 6).

The Reid technique trains law enforcement to perceive as deceptive people who are overly emphatic or repetitious about their innocence or truthfulness and those who struggle to respond clearly and directly to key questions (Jayne & Buckley, n.d.). Wilson's desperate attempts to communicate his truthfulness and innocence together with other cross-cultural miscommunications were taken as indicia of deceit and guilt as opposed to overcompensation for and confusion from MPD's failure to provide reasonable accommodations. These are just a few of countless misunderstandings. Cultural and linguistic differences between Wilson and the government's deaf/disabled witnesses, and the police officers, attorneys, and judges with whom they interacted, played a significant role in Wilson's wrongful conviction. Three of Wilson's four children were sent to the foster system following his arrest—their lives irrevocably altered by the injustice visited upon their father. This scenario continues to play out decades later.

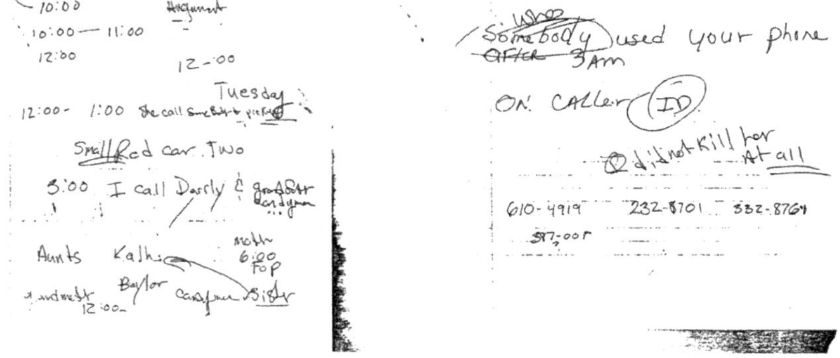

FIGURE 5. John Wilson Jr.'s interview.

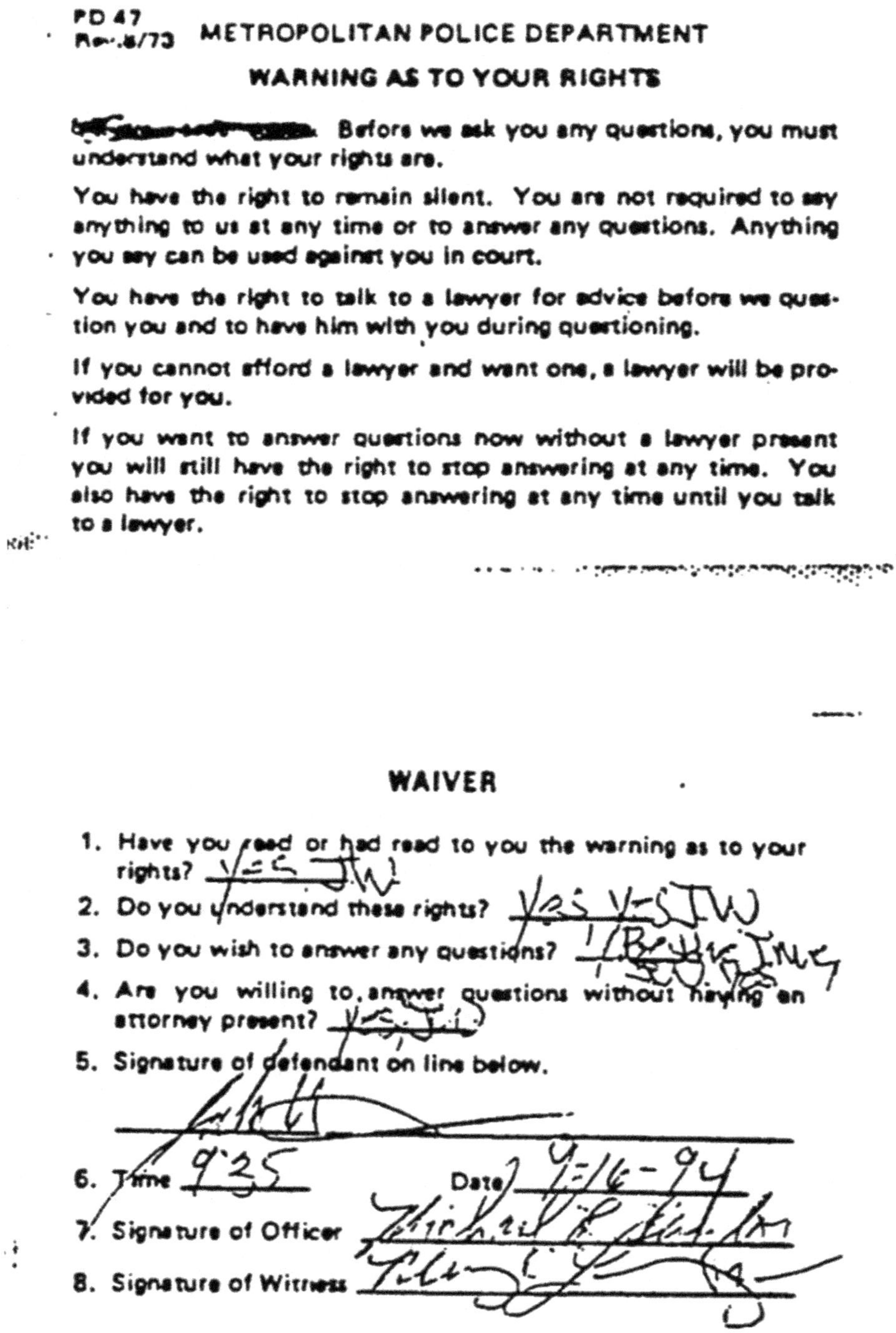

PD 47
Rev. 6/73

METROPOLITAN POLICE DEPARTMENT

WARNING AS TO YOUR RIGHTS

[redacted] Before we ask you any questions, you must understand what your rights are.

You have the right to remain silent. You are not required to say anything to us at any time or to answer any questions. Anything you say can be used against you in court.

You have the right to talk to a lawyer for advice before we question you and to have him with you during questioning.

If you cannot afford a lawyer and want one, a lawyer will be provided for you.

If you want to answer questions now without a lawyer present you will still have the right to stop answering at any time. You also have the right to stop answering at any time until you talk to a lawyer.

WAIVER

1. Have you read or had read to you the warning as to your rights? Yes JW
2. Do you understand these rights? Yes Yes JW
3. Do you wish to answer any questions?
4. Are you willing to answer questions without having an attorney present? Yes JW
5. Signature of defendant on line below.
6. Time 9:25 Date 9-16-94
7. Signature of Officer
8. Signature of Witness

FIGURE 6a. Miranda cards from John Wilson's interviews and interrogations.

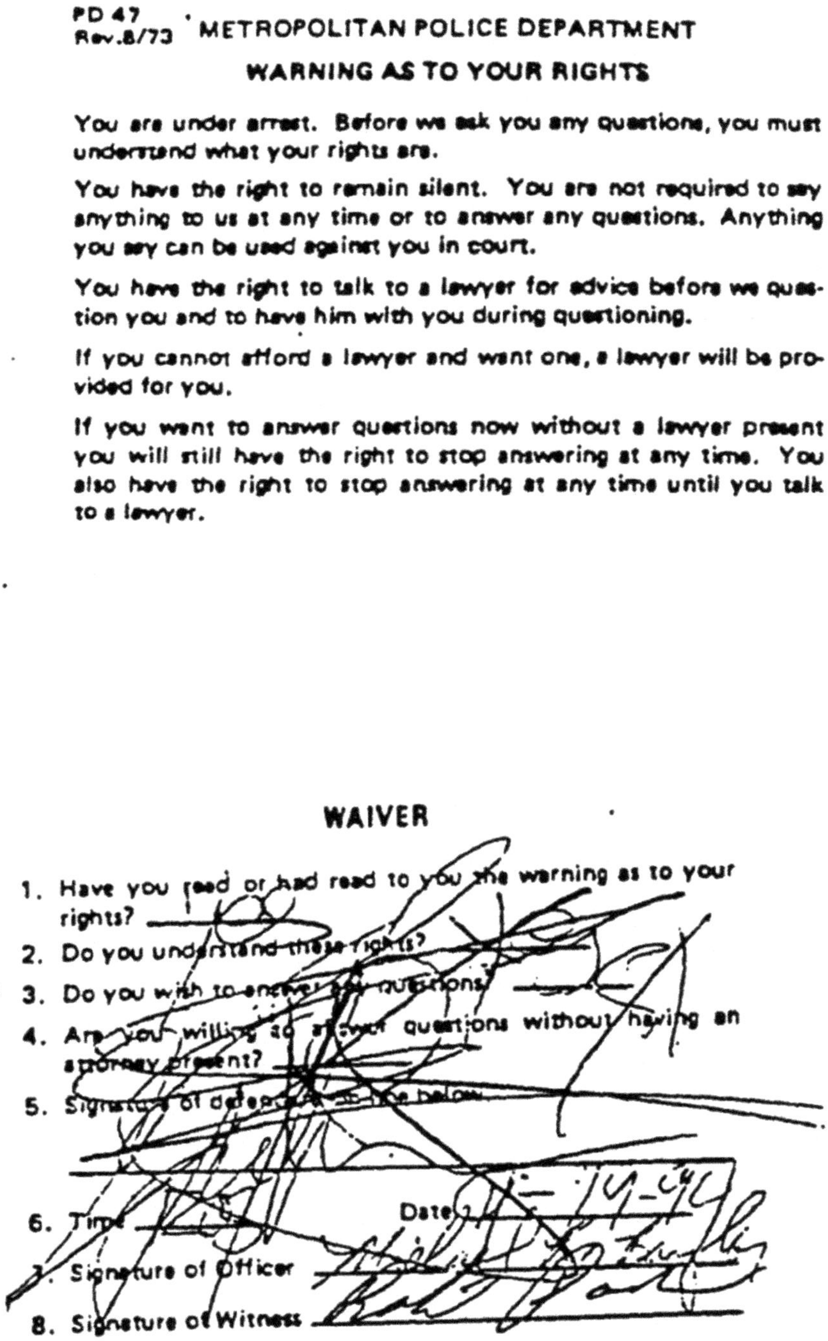

PD 47
Rev.8/73

METROPOLITAN POLICE DEPARTMENT

WARNING AS TO YOUR RIGHTS

You are under arrest. Before we ask you any questions, you must understand what your rights are.

You have the right to remain silent. You are not required to say anything to us at any time or to answer any questions. Anything you say can be used against you in court.

You have the right to talk to a lawyer for advice before we question you and to have him with you during questioning.

If you cannot afford a lawyer and want one, a lawyer will be provided for you.

If you want to answer questions now without a lawyer present you will still have the right to stop answering at any time. You also have the right to stop answering at any time until you talk to a lawyer.

WAIVER

1. Have you read or had read to you the warning as to your rights? ______
2. Do you understand these rights? ______
3. Do you wish to answer any questions? ______
4. Are you willing to answer questions without having an attorney present? ______
5. Signature of defendant on line below.

______

6. Time ______ Date ______
7. Signature of Officer ______
8. Signature of Witness ______

FIGURE 6.b Miranda cards from John Wilson's interviews and interrogations.

PD 47
Rev.8/73 METROPOLITAN POLICE DEPARTMENT

WARNING AS TO YOUR RIGHTS

You are under arrest. Before we ask you any questions, you must understand what your rights are.

You have the right to remain silent. You are not required to say anything to us at any time or to answer any questions. Anything you say can be used against you in court.

You have the right to talk to a lawyer for advice before we question you and to have him with you during questioning.

If you cannot afford a lawyer and want one, a lawyer will be provided for you.

If you want to answer questions now without a lawyer present you will still have the right to stop answering at any time. You also have the right to stop answering at any time until you talk to a lawyer.

WAIVER

1. Have you read or had read to you the warning as to your rights? Yes JW
2. Do you understand these rights? Yes, JW.
3. Do you wish to answer any questions? Yes, JW.
4. Are you willing to answer questions without having an attorney present? Yes JW
5. Signature of defendant on line below.
6. Time 12:15 Date 4-20-94
7. Signature of Officer
8. Signature of Witness

FIGURE 6.c Miranda cards from John Wilson's interviews and interrogations.

Case Study No. 2: Ricardo Harris

We see this scenario play out in the 2013 case of Ricardo Harris, a Black deaf student visiting the South for winter break from university and who is presently serving a life sentence for murder after almost precisely the same situation as occurred in John Wilson's case 20 years earlier ("Black deaf man," 2020; Lewis, 2018). Police detained and interrogated Harris about a murder using an unqualified, uncertified police dispatcher, Barbara Bell, who had a basic grasp of some signed English. Bell relied mainly on fingerspelling for expressive communication, and she could not understand Harris's ASL ("Black deaf man," 2020; Lewis, 2018).

Detectives strategically used techniques designed to gain Harris's trust prior to the interview (Jayne & Buckley, n.d.). Detectives brought food for Harris and informed him that they had called an interpreter. Officers did not put handcuffs on Harris while he waited at the precinct, so he had no reason to know that he was suspected of any crime, much less murder. Bell, a police dispatcher, arrived in all-black plain clothes to "interpret," so Harris thought Bell was an interpreter. When she signed, Harris recalls being surprised to find that she did not know ASL. Harris recalls asking if she was certified, and Bell indicated that she was certified and that no one else was available. Harris continued with the interrogation, despite not being able to fully understand Bell because he had already spent half a day waiting for an interpreter and wanted to simply share what he knew about the incident and go home. At one point, Harris diplomatically informed the detective and his attorney that he could not understand Bell because he "did not use spelling," and his sign language was from "a different state." The response to Harris's missive was to offer yet another inaccessible method of communication: "If you have any trouble, let me know? Ask for paper and a pen!"

Harris followed these instructions and attempted to aid the fingerspelling dispatcher by supplementing fingerspelling with writing and voicing. After witnessing and experiencing a traumatic event and spending almost a full day awake and on edge—a good many hours in the small windowless interrogation room with no communication—Harris spent several more hours in the same interrogation room trying to decode fingerspelling and attempting to express himself through a mix of spelling, writing, and speaking—all of which are inaccessible to him (Figure 7).

Neither the detective nor his own attorney appreciated that Harris uses ASL as his primary language or that Harris had just informed them that he could not understand the person being called to and relied upon to interpret. Harris is used to being in a position of accommodating the dominant hearing, white majority. He intuits that it is best to keep additional requests to a minimum because further requests could lead to more long hours of waiting for another interpreter. Harris does not realize that he is in danger of being charged with a serious crime. Hearing police officers and attorneys often presume and assert

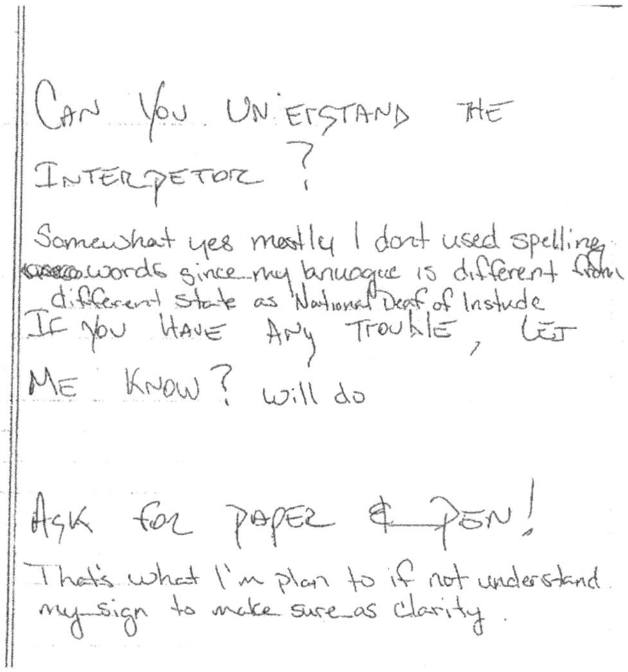
CAN YOU UN'ERSTAND THE INTERPETOR ?
Somewhat yes mostly I dont used spelling words since my lanuague is different from different state as National Deaf of Instude
IF YOU HAVE ANY TROUBLE, LET ME KNOW? will do
ASK FOR PAPER & PEN!
That's what I'm plan to if not understand my sign to make sure as clarity.

FIGURE 7. Handwritten note from the police interrogation of a Black deaf student, 2013.

that effective communication is occurring when it is not. It is also particularly difficult for police and attorneys to understand that a person who uses a signed language, whether or not they have attended university, might not be able to use or understand English or language of their home country.

Notably, even if Bell had been fluent or certified in ASL, she would still have been unqualified to interpret for this interrogation. Using officers and other law enforcement personnel as ASL interpreters raises grave concerns over confidentiality, impartiality, and conflicts of interest. An inherent imbalance of power is created by using law enforcement as interpreters with deaf suspects that makes it even more difficult for the deaf person to admit when communication is not effective. The ADA requires the use of "qualified interpreters," 42 U.S.C. § 12141 *et seq*. The implementing regulations define a qualified interpreter as one "who is able to interpret effectively, accurately, and *impartially* both receptively and expressively, using any necessary specialized vocabulary," 28 C.F.R. § 35.104 (emphasis added). Signing police officers are not neutral and therefore are never "qualified" to interpret with deaf suspects.

Harris succumbed to systemic pressure to accept less than adequate accommodations. Detectives cited "inconsistencies" in his story as it was written in English, told through the fingerspelling police dispatcher, and how it was told through a qualified interpreter some days later. In the end, Harris was charged with and convicted of murder, receiving a life sentence. Harris's defense attorney, Tom Ford, not only failed to provide interpreters for confidential attorney-client communications but also allowed his client to share information with detectives through a police employee in a language that the attorney could not understand. Ford encouraged his client to handwrite a statement in English when the detectives complained that they were unable to understand Harris through Bell and failed to hire an expert to challenge this police employee's qualifications or interpretation, among numerous other errors.

Videos of the interrogation clearly show that the communication was anything but clear. Bell repeated signs; did not share a good amount of information spoken by detectives and Tom Ford or signed by Harris; made up signs and gestures; fingerspelled; and used incorrect signs throughout grueling hours of interviews. Meanwhile, Harris politely "deaf nodded" and tried to accommodate her to the best of his ability ("Black Deaf man Ricardo Harris says he was wrongfully convicted," 2020).

These cases are generally not corrected on appeal for myriad reasons that are beyond the scope of this chapter. Ricardo Harris's case was no exception. He lost his appeals. In January 2020, the Georgia Supreme Court issued an opinion affirming his conviction. The opinion illustrated an unfortunately typical, yet still jarring, ignorance of Deaf culture and communication, specifically, and disability, generally, by the courts. The opinion stated, in part, that despite the fact that "[t]he record contains no evidence establishing Bell's professional qualifications as a sign language interpreter," Bell communicated effectively because

> the prosecutor stated that Bell was 'capable of signing, though much of her signing is by spelling out words . . . [and] . . . she was capable of communicating with the defendant, but a lot of it was slow because she was having to spell things out.' The video-recordings of the interviews in which Bell participated show her signing with Harris, and the trial court could draw inferences from those interviews about whether they were able to effectively communicate with each other. (*Harris v. Georgia*, 2020)

Obviously, people with no background on Deaf culture and who do not know sign language would be unable to determine whether the communication was effective by watching this video. The Georgia Supreme Court went on to state that "[t]he video recording of this interview shows that [Detective] Erion read the entire Miranda waiver-of-rights form to Harris and that Bell interpreted it in sign language. Harris nodded affirmatively as Bell signed to him, indicating that he understood." The criminal legal system is as fallible as the humans driving it. In far too many cases, especially those involving disabled defendants, efficiency and finality trump truth and justice. In 2020, after years of attempting to support Harris's trial and appellate attorneys, HEARD began working with the National Habeas Institute to support Harris who has now been incarcerated for nearly a decade. Harris's children and family have been harmed mentally, emotionally, physically, financially, and more.

The next section *very briefly* touches on just a few concerns related to judges, attorneys, and interpreters. Because this is an ongoing project, more in-depth treatment of these and other criminal legal system actors, practices, oversights, and errors related to deaf and other disabled people is forthcoming.

SYSTEM, PROCESS, AND ACCOUNTABILITY FAILURES: INTERPRETERS, ATTORNEYS, JUDGES, AND THE COURTS

People often assume that because prosecutors, defense attorneys, and most judges are attorneys, they are fully aware of and in compliance with their obligations pursuant to federal disability rights laws. Unfortunately, legal professionals and the courts are also lacking in deaf and disability cultural competencies. This leads to technical errors as well as outright constitutional violations in cases involving disabled defendants (Alfisi, 2013).

As noted above, federal disability rights laws require attorneys and courts to provide "qualified interpreters" and other reasonable accommodations for deaf and other disabled defendants, witnesses, 42 U.S.C. § 12141 et seq. The implementing regulations define a qualified interpreter as one "who is able to interpret effectively, accurately, and impartially both receptively and expressively, using any necessary specialized vocabulary," 28 C.F.R. § 35.104. To begin with, many courts are not following this most basic mandate (see examples below). In addition, however, the provision of interpreters is often still insufficient (LaVigne & Vernon, 2003).

Deaf people represent a relatively small minority of defendants in criminal cases, so judges, attorneys, and others who regularly participate in "the administration of justice" rarely come into contact with or make legal decisions concerning deaf people (OCIS, 2013). For instance, in 2011, 19,593 felony and misdemeanor cases were presented in the DC Superior Court (OCIS, 2013). During that same year, the DC Superior Court's Office of Court Interpreting Services dispatched 206 ASL interpreters and 16 ASL relay teams. Deaf defendants who required communication in a tactile or visual signed language therefore represented far less than one-half of 1% of all felony and misdemeanor cases in the District of Columbia, which boasts one of the largest deaf populations per capita (OCIS, 2013). This relatively low incidence contributes to gaps in disability (here, specifically deaf) consciousness in criminal law, procedure, and practice. This, coupled with the pace of proceedings, and other systemic inequity factors discussed throughout this chapter, only further thwarts a fair administration of "justice" for deaf people.

So, while in theory the criminal legal system has many people in positions of power who *should* serve as checks on errors and abuse of power, and many laws that *should* ensure that disabled people are treated with decency, reality in the era of mass incarceration is quite different.

Judges and the Courts

Courtrooms are often one of the very few places where deaf defendants may receive access to accommodations, including interpreters, transliterators, and CART. However, the provision of accommodations in the penultimate or ultimate phases of the criminal legal process does nothing to remedy the preceding accommodation failures. Additionally, when courts do provide accommodations, defendants still do not necessarily have full and equitable access. And many courts still refuse to provide accommodations. For instance, family members are still being tasked with trying to interpret during court proceedings (*see* 2016 court transcript later), and as recently as 2016, attorneys were threatened with contempt and jail time for reminding judges of their obligation to provide and pay for accommodations pursuant to federal disability rights laws and state law and court procedures ("Interview with Amber Farrelly, Esq.," 2016).

In 2016, one Black Deaf family in Mississippi requested interpreters for a court proceeding involving a young Black Deaf member of the family and his Deaf mother who planned to attend the proceeding to support her son. Multiple members of the family called the clerk of the court during the several months leading up to this proceeding to explain that the defendant was deaf and required qualified interpreters to participate in this proceeding. During this time, the defendant, like many other deaf defendants, was being held in a local jail with no access to telecommunication, accommodations, or counsel.

On the day of the hearing, no interpreters were present. Appointed counsel discussed plea agreements with his deaf client without the support of a qualified interpreter. The public defender, judge, and prosecutor then coerced the defendant's Coda sibling to attempt to interpret for her brother's proceeding. The Coda made clear to the judge that she was not an interpreter and that she was "not skilled in English." The judge responded that she did not have to worry because if she missed a word, they would just slow down and spell it for her so that she could then spell it for her brother (Figure 8).

The 43-page transcript paints the picture of coercion and confusion for the defendant and Coda. Both siblings and the Deaf mother knew that what was occurring was improper but felt as though they had no choice but to comply with the demands of those in positions of authority who held the son's life in their hands. The transcript also paints a picture of complete obliviousness of or disregard for Deaf culture and communication and for decades-old federal disability rights laws. Importantly, this case took place in the Deep South, and everyone in the courtroom except the family was white—the judge, prosecutor, defense attorney, clerk, and court reporter. There are complex and layered power dynamics and cost-benefit analyses (e.g., the harm of allowing a young Black Deaf person to be held in an adult jail with no accommodations), involving at least race, class, and disability, that led this family to feel that they had no option but to comply. The same is true in other courts across the United States.

This defendant, despite receiving no access, was ordered to pay more than $3,000 in fees to the court, public defender, and prosecutor—with each individual charge costing the defendant $451.50 in "court costs." The system continues to incentivize attaching more charges to each defendant, making it harder for the defendant to beat their case, pay mandatory fees, get jobs, and more (Romo, 2018). Then the system punishes low-income people by making payment of fines, fees, drug testing and treatment, electronic monitors, and so on, a condition for probation and arresting people who simply cannot afford to pay these fees (Romo, 2018). Mass incarceration and the criminalization of poverty

THE COURT: Okay. And are you related to Mr. Doe?

MS. Doe: My brother.

THE COURT: Okay. And I noticed that you are doing sign language; is that correct?

MS. Doe: Yes, sir.

THE COURT: And is Mr. Doe, he has a hearing impairment, correct?

MS. Doe: Yes, sir.

THE COURT: And can he understand your sign language?

(Ms. Doe signing to defendant.)

MS. Doe: He can understand some.

THE COURT: Mr. Doe, can you answer out loud at all?

(Ms. Doe signing to defendant.)

THE DEFENDANT: (Affirmative response).

THE COURT: Okay. Does he have any voice?

(Ms. Doe signing to defendant.)

THE DEFENDANT: (Affirmative response)

FIGURE 8. Transcript from a 2016 hearing where a Coda was forced to interpret for her brother's hearing.

disproportionately affect negatively racialized people and disabled people (Gibson & Lewis, 2018).

Courts and attorneys also discriminate against deaf jurors, making it difficult for deaf people to have deaf people on their juries if their case goes to trial (Montemayor, 2017). This discrimination also makes it less likely that court officials have interacted with deaf people. Relatedly, juries are provided with no information or instruction about deaf or disability cultures and communication or about what considerations exist concerning deaf/disabled defendants or witnesses, for example. As a result, deaf/disabled defendants and witness behaviors such as nodding or, particularly, emotive signing or voicing can be misunderstood and used against them during the legal process (*see* Georgia Supreme Court Opinion in Ricardo Harris case above).

Attorneys

Most attorneys representing deaf clients have never met or interacted with a deaf person, and they often make elementary communication mistakes (Alfisi, 2013). Attorneys are also unable to catch communication-related errors made by law enforcement or between law enforcement and their clients. Often, courts and bar associations do not discipline attorneys who fail to satisfy their obligations pursuant to federal disability rights laws (grievance processes are often inaccessible to disabled people) (Alfisi, 2013). In 2017, a HEARD advocate-attorney contacted Mississippi's Consumer Assistance Program (CAP), which purports to "help people with questions or problems with Mississippi's attorneys" to find out complaint options for the Black Deaf family whose Coda was forced to pose as an interpreter. This state bar association is tasked with handling complaints and discipline of its attorneys. The call lasted four minutes and ended with the attorney in charge of CAP shouting at HEARD's advocate-attorney. The bar association attorney's response to the scenario was, "if the court allowed it, then it is up to the court's discretion." HEARD informed this attorney about federal disability rights laws requiring accommodations be provided by the court and attorney. The CAP attorney responded, "I don't think that's what the law says." Upon the HEARD advocate confirming that is, in fact, what the law says, the attorney shouted, "Are you trying to dictate the law to me?"

In yet another state, a judge issued an order acknowledging that a privately retained attorney for a deaf defendant was unable to communicate with their client. Instead of ordering the attorney to hire a qualified interpreter at their own expense, as required by federal law, the judge issued an order to the sheriff requesting that the defendant's father be permitted to enter the county jail with the private attorney to attempt to mediate between the defendant and the privately retained attorney. The father only knew home signs. However, again, even if the father had been a certified interpreter, he would have been unqualified to interpret for reasons similar to the Coda and the fingerspelling police officer in the preceding scenarios (Figure 9). These and other errors frequently occur in cases involving deaf people.

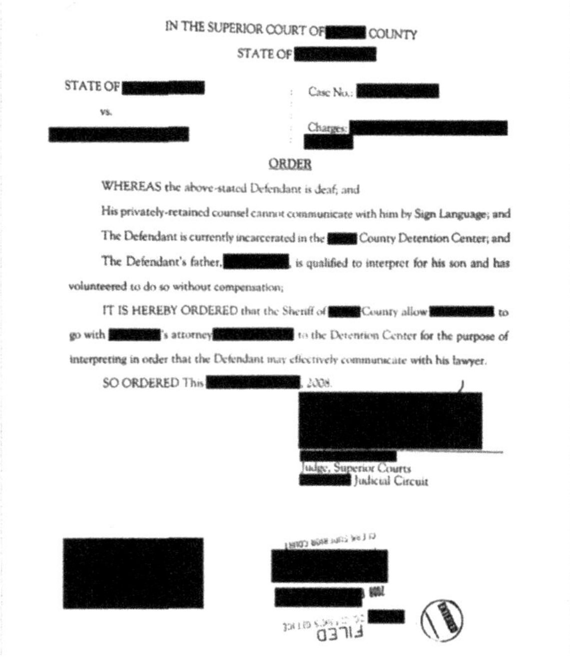

IN THE SUPERIOR COURT OF [redacted] COUNTY
STATE OF [redacted]

STATE OF [redacted] : Case No.: [redacted]
vs.
[redacted] : Charges: [redacted]

ORDER

WHEREAS the above-stated Defendant is deaf; and

His privately-retained counsel cannot communicate with him by Sign Language; and

The Defendant is currently incarcerated in the [redacted] County Detention Center; and

The Defendant's father, [redacted], is qualified to interpret for his son and has volunteered to do so without compensation;

IT IS HEREBY ORDERED that the Sheriff of [redacted] County allow [redacted] to go with [redacted]'s attorney [redacted] to the Detention Center for the purpose of interpreting in order that the Defendant may effectively communicate with his lawyer.

SO ORDERED This [redacted], 2008.

[redacted]
Judge, Superior Courts
[redacted] Judicial Circuit

[redacted]

[redacted]

FILED

FIGURE 9. Official 2008 court order.

Attorneys rarely challenge qualifications of purported interpreters or other communication-related errors at pretrial or trial phases, so the record is not preserved for appeal. Even the sharpest appellate attorneys struggle to resurrect a worthy argument if it was not properly preserved for appellate review. Many cases will ultimately have to be addressed on appeal, so it is imperative that trial counsel adequately preserve the record. Successful appeals often hinge on the record developed by defense counsel during trial. Appellate attorneys' petitions on behalf of deaf people are often unsuccessful for the same reasons trial attorneys' efforts fail deaf people.

Interpreters

The legal system does not understand or honor even the most basic tenets of language justice or cross-modal and cross-cultural communication and interpretation: language justice requires time, patience, innovation, and humility; interpreters make mistakes all the time; certifications do not make an interpreter qualified, and a qualified interpreter may still be unqualified for portions of even the same meeting or proceeding; having a team of long-time certified interpreters present *does not* mean that a disabled person has full access. The harmful hallmarks of the criminal legal system (i.e., efficiency, expediency, and finality) also elicit the worst in communication access and interpretation.

As evidenced in the preceding narratives, law enforcement, attorneys, and judges often cannot ascertain whether interpreters are qualified or whether the information is being successfully rendered or understood. To further trouble the interpretation issue, certified interpreters are sometimes not qualified (LaVigne & Vernon, 2003). Research and narratives show that an alarming number of hearing interpreters are not qualified to interpret in situations involving marginalized deaf people within the criminal legal system (Bryant, 2017) and very few interpreters understand systemic oppressions and the criminal legal system. Interpreters should come into the criminal legal system assuming mistakes have been made by police, prosecutors, defense attorneys, other interpreters, and others, and be on guard for red flags that may be indicative of wrongful arrest, coerced confessions, or other access or rights violations.

Because disabled people in stressful legal predicaments often do a cost-benefit analysis and decide against raising communication issues, interpreters in legal settings often get a pass (see previous scenarios). Faith in the legal system; the urgency of a dangerous situation; fear of and trust in power holders (including interpreters); as well as the exclusion of access to culturally competent advocates, and other cultural and sociolinguistic factors, hinder disabled people from being able to make informed decisions about whether to raise access and communication issues. Instead, disabled people overcompensate for law enforcement, attorney, and interpreter shortcomings by working even harder, extending themselves well beyond the range of their own language, communication, and fatigue capacities (Bernstein, 2012). Thereafter, misinformation and misunderstandings are attributed to the deaf person, *not* to hearing officers, attorneys, judges, or interpreters. If a deaf person raises communication concerns after spending considerable time trying to work with insufficient or improper accommodations, they are often not believed because everything *seemed* fine at the outset to the hearing power holders involved (HEARD, 2020).

Again, because many of these interactions are either not recorded or not fully recorded (e.g., recorded on body camera, which does not capture the "signing" officer's rendition of the message) or are memorialized only via audio or text, and because the criminal legal system is led by hearing/abled people who do not understand Deaf culture or communication, legal challenges to communication failures are difficult, if not impossible. Because sign language fluencies can change over time, even if an interpreter's qualifications are challenged, it is difficult to determine what level of proficiency the individual had in months or years past without an accurate and clear recording. Strict procedural time bars and the lack of disability consciousness of appellate attorneys makes it difficult to remedy cases even where a clear recording depicts jarring misinterpretations and miscommunications (see wrongful conviction cases mentioned previously).

Hearing interpreters and officers who can sign are often unable to assess whether a deaf person is fully comprehending the message. Interpreters and signing officers are often concerned about expediency and maintaining their careers and reputations, so they can be hesitant to share with their employers or colleagues their inability to communicate with a deaf person. Some unqualified interpreters and police officers and family members who have served as "interpreters" have expressed that they are "better than nothing" or "better than other local interpreters," or that they "knew the police would not provide an interpreter" (HEARD, 2020). As a result, unqualified people, including certified interpreters, have themselves reported and been reported as having continued "interpreting" despite their own recognition of being unqualified for the interaction.

ASL interpreter credentialing bodies and processes are inherently structurally and systemically inequitable (Bryant, 2017). This only compounds systemic inequity faced disabled/deaf people swept into the criminal legal system. Ironically, interpreters with the highest levels of certification are often least able to meet the communication, culture, and access needs of those trapped in the criminal legal system. In addition, the pool of court-certified interpreters is further limited due to these and other factors:

- Systemic and structural barriers to joining the interpreting profession, obtaining legal certification, and staying in the interpreting profession experienced by negatively racialized and low-income people, and disabled/deaf people and heritage signers (Bryant, 2017; Project CLIMB, 2017; Registry of Interpreters for the Deaf [RID], 2016)
- an indefinite moratorium on legal certification by the nationally recognized organization that issued legal certifications from 1998 through 2016 such that many jurisdictions require this particular certification to interpret in their courts (RID, 2018)

- conflicting out of certified legal interpreters once they have worked on different aspects of the same case (e.g., interpreters should not work as an interpreter with a complainant and a defendant in the same case; the Proceedings Interpreter should not serve as Interpreter for Counsel, although many interpreters continue to violate these and similar rules often asserting that the court, attorneys, or others have "waived" these conflicts, etc.)
- court and legal interpreter certification entities' discrimination against people with criminal records (RID, 2016b; Md. Rule 1–333 [2015]).

Some interpreters with legal certification are not "court ready." Many interpreters with legal certification are not fully bilingual, multilingual, or qualified to work with deaf people in the criminal legal system (Bryant, 2017). Importantly, *all* interpreters will have at least some people for whom they cannot interpret. Not being qualified to interpret for one or several deaf people does not necessarily call into question an interpreter's qualifications more broadly. It is actually *likely* that hearing interpreters—especially those who are not accustomed to a particular deaf person's culture, sign language, dialect, accents, or jargon—will struggle to communicate with people trapped in the carceral web. This is, in part, a testament to the spectral and intersectional qualities of deaf people, together with interconnected identities and attendant sociolinguistic expression.

The RID (2016b) membership demographics indicate that more than 87% of self-identified members identify as white, whereas Black, Latinx, and Hispanic interpreters make up less than 10% of self-identified members; and Indigenous, Native, Asian, and Pacific Islander interpreters together represent just 3% of self-identified interpreters (RID, 2018). Cross-cultural mismatching is therefore intensified in the criminal legal system, where divergence between the pool of interpreters with legal certification and deaf people they are attempting to work with is even more glaring because the criminal legal system disproportionately targets low income, negatively racialized, disabled and otherwise marginalized people, and systemic and structural barriers to certification ensure that the pool of legally certified interpreters is even less able to meet the needs of multiply marginalized people trapped in the legal system.

The interpreting profession has a white and hearing/abled supremacy problem and is long overdue for a dismantling or at least a radical shift in many areas, including increasing its number of multiply marginalized interpreters. That said, there is a common misconception that having deaf and/or negatively racialized interpreters and others who "match" the identities of targeted populations makes the criminal legal system fair. This is patently false. The legal system and interpreting industry often exploit marginalized interpreters at the expense of some of the most marginalized people in deaf communities (e.g., legal decisions are even harder to challenge if there are four interpreters—especially if two are deaf—than if there are two hearing interpreters). Unfortunately, "diversity and inclusion" models as related to the entire carceral system often only make decisions more final and cause a fundamentally unjust system to become more expensive, inordinate, palatable, and intractable.

TROUBLING "SOLUTIONS": CONTESTING THE DOMINANT RECOMMENDATIONS

In the past few decades, in the wake of dozens of lawsuits against cities and counties nationwide for their police departments' failures to follow long-standing federal disability rights laws, a flurry of "solutions" have been proposed by law enforcement, judges, and hearing/abled and deaf/disability rights groups alike (Gottfriend, 2018). When hastily adopted with no consideration of the larger machinery of policing and mass incarceration, these solutions operate as a bandage on a gaping, infected wound (Lewis, 2019).

There is a dangerously optimistic notion that lawsuits and settlements, policy adoption, police registries of deaf/disabled people, police trainings, and community policing are the remedies for injustice experienced by communities subject to policing systems (Kaba, 2014). After each tragedy, one or more of these "solutions" are used to pacify affected communities. Then, notwithstanding the application of said "solution," another tragic incident occurs, and we see the next iteration of yet another quick, feel-good solution that also fails to resolve the issues that lie at the heart of these tragedies (Schenwar & Law, 2020).

This section briefly explains some of the most commonly proposed and adopted "solutions" and advocacy strategies, offering critical intersectional analysis and recommendations based on over a decade of data and narrative collection from hundreds of disabled people and of direct support and trainings for thousands of criminal, appellate, and parole attorneys and judges.

Single-Issue Advocacy, Erasure of Intersectionality

Interactions with law enforcement are multifaceted and even more treacherous for people who exist at the intersections of marginalities (Çevik, 2019; Tastrom, 2020). The best way to tackle a collossus of a system that has so many intersecting prejudices—short of abolition—is to ensure that proposed reforms are not "reformist reforms" and to ensure that these proposals center on people living at the margins of the margins. Those in positions of influence must be accountable to and constantly centering multiply marginalized communities in conversation and negotiations with powerholders. For instance, one study found that

> discrimination and harassment by law enforcement based on sexual orientation and gender identity is an ongoing and pervasive problem in LGBT communities . . . with police abuse, neglect and misconduct consistently reported at higher frequencies by respondents of color and transgender and gender-nonconforming respondents. (Mallory et al., 2015)

Forty percent of the respondents in this study who identified as gay or bisexual men believed that contacting the police in response to a violent incident from an intimate partner would be unhelpful or very unhelpful, and 59% believed that the police would be less helpful to a gay or bisexual man than to a heterosexual woman in the same situation (Mallory, 2015). Countless stories from deaf LGBTQI people have also borne this out.

Take the case of a queer white Deaf man who survived a spate of domestic violence with a domestic partner in Portland (Bernstein, 2012). The alleged perpetrator in his case was his partner, who happened to be a hearing man. In 2012, while in the midst of one physically violent altercation, the Deaf man texted a deaf friend to ask them to contact 911 (Bernstein, 2012). The deaf friend called 911 through VRS and requested that police *and interpreters* show up to support the deaf man (Bernstein, 2012). Officers from the Portland Police Bureau arrived without interpreters (Bernstein, 2012). Police could not communicate effectively with the Deaf complainant. Instead, officers spoke to the hearing partner, who was the alleged perpetrator (Bernstein, 2012). The Deaf man showed officers his bruises and tried to communicate while "overwhelmed, disoriented, and hurt," but officers still did not provide an interpreter, making effective communication impossible (Bernstein, 2012). He did not understand that he could request that the alleged perpetrator be arrested, and police admit that they thought the Deaf man simply wanted to get back into his apartment. Once the Deaf man was back in the apartment, the police left, leaving him at risk (Bernstein, 2012).

Later that evening, the hearing partner kicked in the Deaf man's locked bedroom door and allegedly assaulted the Deaf man yet again (Bernstein, 2012). The Deaf man texted his deaf friend, who again contacted the police, requesting police and a sign language interpreter (Bernstein, 2012). Some of the same officers who responded to the earlier call showed up, again with no interpreter (Bernstein, 2012). Police reports stated that the Deaf complainant could communicate with police through writing and gestures, yet one officer called dispatch and asked for someone who knew ASL (Bernstein, 2012). A "signing" officer arrived who had basic signing skills (Bernstein, 2012). The officer apologized for her lack of fluency but also failed to call an interpreter to the scene (Bernstein, 2012). An arrest was made on the hearing partner but no statement was taken from the Deaf complainant (Bernstein, 2012). The Deaf man, who has used ASL as his primary language all his life, wrote a statement in English on his own after what could only be described as a long and traumatic day. Police finalized their report before receiving a written statement from the Deaf complainant. Charges were brought against the hearing partner and were dropped after the hearing partner died by suicide just three months after this incident.

Other recent episodes of police violence also highlight an alarming pattern of multiply marginalized disabled people being more likely to be caught in police crosshairs. Advocates and organizations who erase the racial, economic, LGBTQI, and disability status of deaf victims of police violence are unwittingly perpetuating this violence and making all communities more susceptible to this harm because it becomes increasingly more difficult to identify the underlying and interconnected causes of such violence (Lewis, 2017c, 2019; Tastrom, 2020). For instance, in the weeks following Magdiel Sanchez's murder, the National Association of the Deaf and the Oklahoma Association of the Deaf developed a joint response that failed to adequately place his murder within the context of the broader trend of police violence against marginalized people or even to mention race, class, or disability (National Association of the Deaf, 2017)—this when Sanchez existed at the margins of multiple identities, including but not limited to intellectually disabled, negatively racialized immigrants (e.g., dark-skinned Mexican man) living in a lower-income community. His existence at the intersections of these identities is precisely what caused police officers to view him as more of a "threat" than if he had been a white, abled, deaf upper- or middle-class man. This kind of erasure by resourced and influential organizations and advocates exposes all marginalized communities to further risk of police violence.

Relatedly, these organizations announced a "partnership" with the Oklahoma Police Department when deaf/disabled people from multiply marginalized groups had neither been consulted nor been invited to be involved in determining how to proceed in dealing with accountability measures. This concession and acquiescence stifled the righteous indignation of local Deaf communities, who, prior to this announcement, were out protesting the killing together with other nondeaf marginalized communities. These organizations' misguided actions chilled protest and removed the spotlight and pressure from the city and district attorney, making it that much easier for District Attorney Prater to weeks later declare Sanchez's murder to be "justified" and boldly announce that "you don't need to be able to hear to know what these officers are saying to you" (Chuck & Connor, 2017).

One example of an intersectional response to police violence is the 2016 HEARD statement on police brutality in the wake of two police killings of multiply marginalized deaf men. In August 2016, two deaf men were killed by police officers in the United States within 10 days of each other. Daniel Harris, a young white DeafDisabled man with a history of confusing and scary encounters with law enforcement and medicalized carceral systems, and Darnell Wicker, a Black, hard of hearing military veteran, were both shot within minutes of encountering law enforcement in Kentucky and North Carolina, respectively (Bailey, 2016; Helsel, 2016). Compounding the tragedy, both men were killed in front of their own homes in the presence of their loved ones (Bailey, 2016; Helsel, 2016). HEARD's letter highlighted the history of police violence against all marginalized people and placed deaf people and multiply marginalized deaf people in the larger context of policing. It states, in part:

> Already this year, over 750 people have been killed by law enforcement. Studies show that no less than 60–80% of these victims are people with disabilities. Notably, Black people and other people of color are disproportionately represented among these victims. Similarly, HEARD's multi-year investigation into police brutality against deaf people illustrates

> a clear pattern of police violence against deaf people with more than one marginalized identity. So, DeafDisabled, Deaf Black, Latinx, Indigenous, and deaf people who live in low/no-income communities, for example, are disproportionately represented in the narratives we have collected. Although many are just now taking notice, police brutality against marginalized and multiply-marginalized communities has long-since demonstrated the need for honest discussions about the very real connections between racism, classism, and ableism (e.g., audism, vidism, sanism, linguicism, etc.)—each of which are deeply embedded in police culture, policies and practices. (HEARD, 2016)

HEARD's statement goes on to caution organizations calling for more training and deaf driver cards, and encouraged solidarity across communities and movements to help end police violence through and through. This statement was shared in ASL, Spanish, and English and drafted and translated by people on three continents. Negatively racialized disabled people who are marginalized in other ways (e.g., youth, queer, migrant, undocumented, low-/no-income) led this action. This is a good example of how organizations can work toward connecting with marginalized groups and uplifting the most marginalized people within already marginalized communities to advance the rights and causes of all people. Influential, powerful, and resourced organizations must be particularly mindful of their comments about and actions in response to policing and other state violence. Their proposed solutions should be informed by those at the margins of their and other oppressed communities. Proposed solutions should make it easier, not harder, to disentangle our communities from the ever-expanding net of law enforcement.

Deaf Driver/Identification Cards and Police Registries of Disabled People

Since these and other incidents of police violence against deaf people, over a dozen police departments across the nation have begun to heavily invest in deaf driver identification placards (several of which are dangerously confusing, like those of Massachusetts and Michigan showing a picture of a gun to inquire about whether a person has a firearm license). These departments urge deaf drivers to use "the new communication tool [which is] designed to store on a sun visor, in a bag or backpack, or on a passenger seat for easy access" (DeLamielleure-Scott, 2016). According to police departments, these placards will improve safety for deaf people as well as for law enforcement (DeLamielleure-Scott, 2016). Several recent settlement agreements with police departments require the adoption of placards while other police departments are uncritically mimicking other departments (DOJ, 2016).

New York Police Department (NYPD), which has paid nearly $1 million in settlements to deaf plaintiffs in recent years, just rolled out its own version of the cards in 2018, complete with a ceremony honoring the hearing officer who "convinced the department to use these cards" (Siff, 2018). NYPD planned to send cards to 12,000 people who registered as deaf with the Department of Motor Vehicles (DMV) for such a designation to appear on their driver's license (Siff, 2018) (Figures 10 and 11).

Another concerning proposal that will allegedly address police violence against disabled people includes the formation of police and DMV registries for disabled people. In the months following the deaths of Daniel Harris and

FIGURE 10. Michigan's Deaf Driver Visor Placard.

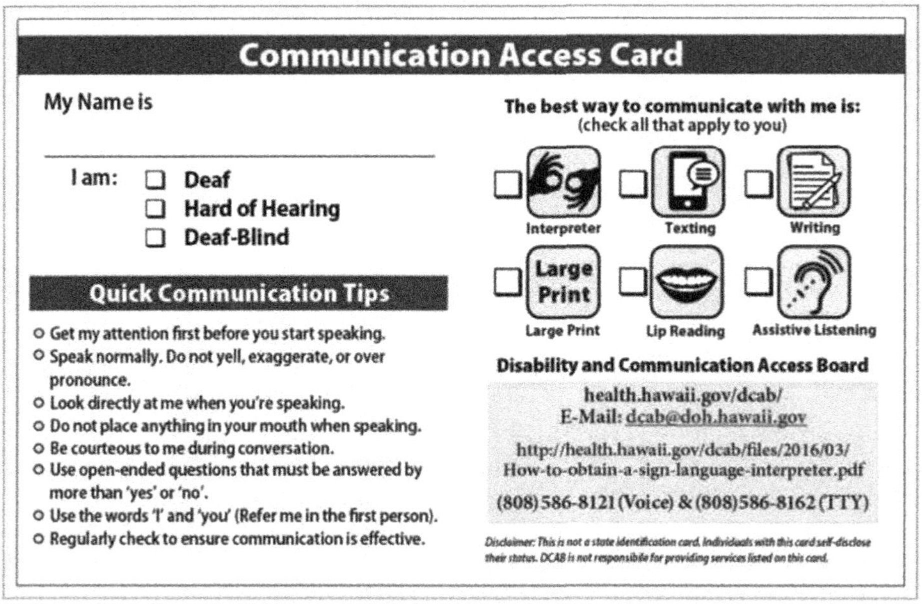

FIGURE 11. Hawaii's Deaf Driver Visor Placard.

Darnell Wicker, some people within deaf and disability communities in North Carolina, Kentucky, California, and other states have agreed to have police registries for deaf/disabled people (Molina, 2017). Articles and dialogue around these proposed measures by privileged people within deaf communities include statements like "Deaf people who get pulled over by police would no longer have to fear miscommunications with officers if [the bill] . . . becomes law" and "The symbol [on the driver's license] helps ensure mutually safe interactions during traffic stops and other situations between drivers who are deaf or hard of hearing and law enforcement officers" (Molina, 2017). But officers themselves warn that DMV registries alone may not be successful because an officer making a traffic stop gives the license plate to dispatch. Nondisabled advocates and parents of autistic children have been supporting autistic child registries and wristbands despite calls from autistic adults not to provide information to or allow tracking of autistic children by law enforcement (Biscobing, 2017).

The foregoing approaches—placards, registries, identification bands, and cards—have not proven effective in mitigating or eliminating police violence against people with disabilities (Lewis, 2019). With respect to placards, for example, there is evidence and reason to believe that they may cause police officers to behave more aggressively toward deaf people. To the extent that a person with disabilities reaches for their placard, police frequently assume or assert that they were not following instructions or are reaching for a weapon, as with Pearl Pearson (Çevik, 2019; "Graphic," 2014; Lewis, 2014; Lewis, 2019). This is particularly risky if the person with disabilities is also a negatively racialized person for whom assumptions about criminality and dangerousness presumptively attach or if the disabled person has other marginalized identities (Kindy, 2015; Lee, 2014; Tastrom, 2020; Voigt et al., 2017).

With respect to registries and placards, there is no evidence that they work, and they have the negative effect of siphoning massive amounts of funds that might otherwise be directed into social services, community-based resources that help keep Deaf communities healthy and safe and decrease reliance on police. Both approaches ignore race and class and create a false sense of safety, making disabled people less attentive during interactions with law enforcement. Moreover, registries—inside and outside of the criminal legal system—have been a basis for targeting, surveilling, and criminalizing already marginalized communities (Matter & Heath, 2017). From the internment of Japanese Americans to the use of gang databases to the arguments in favor of Muslim registries, the end result is that registries put the state in a stronger position to surveil, police, and incarcerate vulnerable communities.

Assertions that cards or registries will prevent violence and improve communication run counter to what continues to play out in police interactions with disabled people nationwide. People who show these and other cards to law enforcement are often laughed at or ridiculed, with the information on the card being completely disregarded and officers becoming agitated (HEARD, 2020; *see also* case of the Illinois mother, *supra*). People like Pearl Pearson who have a card but are beaten before having an opportunity to show them are blamed after the fact for not properly using the card or for allegedly reaching for it. People who do not have cards or who are not registered are post facto blamed for not putting the police on notice of their disability status (AJ+, 2018). These cards and registries put the onus on disabled people while requiring nothing of the hearing, abled dominant majority who hold all the power in these situations. They place the burden (and the blame when situations go awry) on individual disabled people for a systemic and structural problem. They lead to yet more money going into "reforms" that will not end criminalization, police violence, or the other myriad harms of the criminal legal system.

As for deaf communities specifically, there are additional problems with the employment of registries. For one thing, there are significant barriers to deaf people actually utilizing registries. Deaf people who are most susceptible to police violence do not often use English as a primary language. Ironically, not one state that has launched deaf/disabled registries has created an accessible ASL (or other signed language), captioned and transcribed video explanation of the rationale behind these registries; what data will be taken and what such data will be used for; who will have access to this data and how privacy will be guaranteed; what the consequence of not registering might be; or even provided basic instruction on how to get through the registration process for those who choose to do so.

Additionally, many deaf people are survivors of domestic or sexual violence or are undocumented or formerly incarcerated who are already targeted for surveillance and violence, so they may be unable to register. Others still are low- or no-income, houseless, or unable to afford costs associated with having a fixed address and other proof associated with these registries. Many registries and placards are tied to the possession of a vehicle, so those who do not drive or who cannot afford vehicles are automatically unable to register or make use of a placard. Many negatively racialized disabled people who are already skeptical and untrusting of policing systems assert that they would never register with law enforcement. Negatively racialized people are then placed in even more peril where some from their disability community (privileged people) register and they do not.

Law enforcement may presume that these ideas are fully supported by disability communities and expect all disabled people to have these verifications of their identity when only privileged and powerful people within disability communities can or will utilize these instruments. In this way, police departments can decry the failure to register as the cause or explanation of police violence against disabled people. They could also employ the presence of registries as defenses against subsequent lawsuits when they injure or kill disabled people. Arguably most important is that none of the aforementioned approaches directly engage racism, classism, or ableism as related to systems of policing.

Yet "More Training"

The demand for police training has been a particularly common and strong refrain of disabled communities. For many who have not been engaged in anti-police violence work or who have not studied the work of activists who have been engaged in decades of work to end police violence, the knee jerk reaction to police violence is to call for "more training" (NAD, 2017). Yet, despite over 50 years of police training related to disability, police violence against people with disabilities has not decreased, resources for training continue to increase, and officers who have received extensive training are themselves responsible for violence against—including the death of—disabled people (Çevik, 2014, 2019; Lewis, 2019). Of course, one can argue that perhaps the problem is not with training per se but the nature of the training and the trainers. In other places, I argue both. My view is that whether police training is helpful or not, it cannot solve the broader structural problems of policing, including the concentration of broken windows policing in low- and no-income negatively racialized communities, the commodification of criminalization, and the proliferation of racism, classism, ableism, and more in police culture. If the culture of policing systems invalidates the training, the training is rendered obsolete.

There has also been a nationwide increase in "signing" police officers and "deaf and hard of hearing liaison units." Regardless of their intention, officers who can sign continue to be the cause of a great deal of miscommunication and numerous wrongful arrests and convictions for many of the reasons listed previously (and other reasons that are beyond the scope of this chapter) (Aubrecht & Lewis, 2016). These officers tend to know just enough sign language to be dangerous (Aubrecht & Lewis, 2016). Despite often having a rudimentary knowledge of sign language, many still understand very little of the cultural, sociolinguistic, and intersectional dimensions of Deaf communities (Aubrecht & Lewis, 2016). Yet they tend to be the first people called to the scene in situations that would be best served with multiple deaf and hearing qualified interpreters and deaf advocates (HEARD, 2020). When information is taken through one of these officers, usually no qualified witness is present to correct any errors or oversights (HEARD, 2020). These officers' communication proficiency and qualifications are rarely challenged. When their qualifications are challenged, jurors and judges rarely doubt police officers.

As depicted in several foregoing scenarios, the mere presence of signing officers makes it more likely that a deaf person will not request appropriate accommodations and that the deaf person feels like the officer is "on their team" when nothing could be further from the truth (HEARD, 2020). This is why law enforcement serving as "interpreters" in law enforcement settings—regardless of their deaf status, signing qualification, or certification—is a direct violation of federal disability rights laws (HEARD, 2020).

Some disability and deaf schools and organizations help encourage community members to concede constitutional rights in legal settings. Between 2016 and 2019, for example, numerous national and state disability and deaf rights organizations and schools have hosted and sponsored law enforcement-led workshops wherein law enforcement—who themselves are often ignorant of policing systems, structural and systemic oppression, and the complexities of Deaf/disability cultures and communication—have been invited to "educate" Deaf/disabled people about how to interact with law enforcement. Ironically, many of these same officers are responsible for wrongful arrests and convictions of deaf people and hold high positions on deaf liaison units within their departments.

At one session in upstate New York, for example, law enforcement told disabled/deaf people that it was "okay to touch police officers as long as it is not on the side with the weapon." At every session, officers intentionally downplayed the seriousness and dangerousness of police interactions and became defensive when disabled people challenged or were confused by what the officers shared. At every session, law enforcement withheld critical information about constitutional and other protections like the right *not* to communicate with law enforcement and the right to counsel. Those withheld rights and liberties exist as a shield against illegal search and seizures, wrongful arrests and convictions, self-incrimination, regularly practiced coercive and confusing interrogation tactics and other legal and illegal injustices. Moreover, these trainings *never* addressed issues of race, nationality, ethnicity, class, gender, LGBTQI identities, etc., nor did they consider people with more than one disability in the category of disability being addressed (e.g., deafdisabled people were not considered at deaf-specific sessions or at disability-specific sessions).

When deaf and disability organizations and universities endorse these "trainings," they put disabled and deaf people in more danger, not least because they leave with a false sense of safety and more misguided trust in police and policing systems. The result is disabled people—especially those who are negatively racialized, queer, low- or no-income, etc.—coming away *less* prepared to safely interact with police or to navigate high-risk law enforcement interactions. Arguably more important, these approaches limit disabled communities' creative capacities to prevent, repair, and address intracommunity harm outside of policing systems.

There is an idea that if a disabled person merely acquiesces to police officers, they will be fine—that if they do not have anything to hide, they can allow authority figures and officers to search or interrogate them. However, this approach fundamentally misunderstands autonomy, consent, freedom, the criminal legal system, constitutional rights, and mass incarceration. It results in disabled people waiving their constitutional right to counsel, permitting illegal searches and seizures, and waiving their rights to trial by pleading guilty although innocent.

Too often, disability and deaf schools and rights organizations simply tell deaf/disabled people to demand "equal access." There is nothing inherently wrong with equal access. But when dealing with a system of this kind, disabled people of all ages must understand the risks and know that they have a constitutional right *not* to communicate with police and that they *must* assert this right and their right to counsel to protect their "right to remain innocent" (Duane, 2016). If a particular practice is not good for hearing, abled people (e.g., talking to the police, consenting to searches, taking polygraph examinations), making it easier for police to take advantage of having access to disabled cultural–linguistically marginalized people for the same interactions without clear explanation to disabled people about risks and rights is not only unhelpful but incredibly harmful. This lack of transparency with disabled people about risks within the legal system and naïve single-issue advocacy is dangerous (Lewis, 2019). Gaining access at the expense of freedom is not justice.

Disability and deaf schools and organizations must be at the forefront of decarceration and abolition advocacy that in the interim (pre-abolition of carceral systems) foregrounds the protection of constitutional rights and decreases acquiescence to authority, including law enforcement. Disability communities' anti-incarceration efforts must also be intentionally intersectional, centering the most marginalized community members among us.

Lawsuits, Mere Policy Adoption, and Settlement Agreements

Law enforcement does not follow its own policies, training, settlement agreements, or state and federal civil or disability rights laws (*United States v. City of Portland*, 2012; *Philip Wolfe v. City of Portland*, 2012; *Philip Wolfe v. City of Portland*, 2020). There is no evidence that taxpayer-funded lawsuits or DOJ settlement agreements lead to systemic or enduring change. In fact, many of the police departments with some of the most egregious disability rights violations have been sued or agreed to settlements addressing exactly the same violation within months or years of the next incident.

The 2017 civil complaint against the Alameda County Sherriff's Office (ACSO) for the assault and arrest of Hui Jie Jin, a 76-year-old deaf Asian American grandmother, states that "this incident is especially outrageous because only years prior, Alameda County and ACSO had been sued by the Department of Justice for precisely the same failure" (*Jin v. Alameda County*, 2018). Jin's attorneys cite a 2010 U.S. Department of Justice (DOJ) agreement with the Alameda County sheriff to "Guarantee Effective Communication for Persons Who Are Deaf, Hard of Hearing or Deaf-Blind" (*Jin v. Alameda County*, 2018). The plaintiff's attorneys go on to state that "[i]n order to settle the case with the DOJ, Alameda County, and ACSO agreed to, *inter alia*, provide sign language interpreters, auxiliary aids and services to deaf individuals, and to establish nondiscriminatory policies" (*Jin v. Alameda County*, 2018). The attorneys continue: "Based on the unlawful conduct described herein, Alameda County and ACSO clearly failed to comply with, ignored, and/or forgot about their agreement with the DOJ regarding discrimination against deaf individuals" (*Jin v. Alameda County*, 2018).

In 2012, following the domestic violence incident mentioned earlier, the Deaf man sued the city of Portland for violating the ADA. More than 20 years after the enactment of the ADA, the Portland Police Bureau ("PPB")—like countless departments across the United States—did not have policies or protocol on how to interact with deaf people. In 2013, this man settled a lawsuit against the city. A federal district court judge ordered the city of Portland to pay $51,500 and ordered the city to adopt the DOJ's model policy on how to communicate with people who are deaf. His attorney stated that "the requirement for the city to adopt this policy is a win for ensuring fairness for those with hearing problems." But ending decades of systemic ableism is not so simple, and DOJ's model policy is neither up to par or followed by other jurisdictions that have adopted the policy. Case in point: This Deaf man and other disabled people spent *years* working with PPB to try to help improve their policies and practices regarding disabled people to no avail. In 2020, he joined Disability Rights Oregon and other disabled Oregonians in a lawsuit against the City of Portland seeking injunctive relief for disabled people in Portland following PPB subjecting disabled people to excessive force and crowd control policies that failed to account for or accommodate their disabilities during protests against police violence and racial injustice, no less. (*Wolfe v. City of Portland*, 2020). All this is to say nothing of the federal government having also sued Portland in 2012 for PPB's pattern and practice of unconstitutional use of force against people with or people perceived as having mental health disabilities–a consent decree that was set to run for 5 years that is now approaching its tenth year due to persistent noncompliance. In any case, DOJ's now 15-year-old model policy template was quite literally meant to be a *model* policy, not a final policy for law enforcement, with DOJ's own introduction to the document stating in part:

> This 4-page document serves as a model for law enforcement agencies when adopting a policy on effective communication with people who are deaf or hard of hearing. Agencies are encouraged to download and adapt the policy to suit their needs. (DOJ, 2016)

However, some departments adopted this policy with no revisions. Many of these departments, like the Lakewood Police Department (Colorado), are in areas populated more densely by deaf people because of their proximity to deaf schools and service providers. Other departments, including the Charlotte-Mecklenburg Police Department, responsible for the shooting death of Daniel Harris, have adopted part of DOJ's policy almost verbatim but heeded DOJ's advice and adapted the policy to "suit *their* needs" (Charlotte-Mecklenburg Police Department, 2007) (emphasis added). And the Louisville Metro Police Department had also adopted a policy that in many ways mimics the DOJ model policy prior to its officers mortally shooting Darnell Wicker (Louisville Metro Police Department, effective 2008, revised 2016, 2017). The rush to quickly adopt written policies without taking stock of policing culture or the seminal event(s) that led to the adoption of the policies does not inspire or force change. There are rarely affirmative measures to *at least* ensure that the entire department is doing the necessary work to address structural and systemic discrimination and inequities, and with the passage of just a bit of time and turnover there is almost always blanket disregard for these policies regardless of how or why they came about. Again, if the culture of policing systems invalidates policies, policies are rendered obsolete. The same is true with settlement agreements. While DOJ has settled a few cases with police departments that move beyond the model policy (DOJ, 2016), these settlements are largely short-lived or disregarded.

DOJ's attempt to standardize a policy seems to have originated vastly different policies that are often in conflict and frequently directly counter to federal disability rights laws, criminal procedure, interpreters' codes of professional conduct, and so on. In many instances, following police departments' policies would violate deaf people's rights. In addition to being considerably outdated (i.e., mentioning teletypewriters and telecommunications devices for the deaf but not videophones, video relay service, captioned telephones, real-time text, or any other modern technology), the model policy fails to make clear that ASL—along with hundreds of other sign languages—is a full and complex language, and many deaf people do not use English (or the spoken language of their home country) as a first language or at all. This is a grave omission.

Furthermore, the model policy misconstrues the ADA and is far too generous in its assessment of the ADA's deference to law enforcement's power to (1) reject requested accommodations; (2) make determinations about the significance or weight of particular interactions and conversations; (3) decide what communication is "equally effective" for a person with whom they likely cannot communicate effectively; and (4) determine what an undue administrative or financial burden is as related to a cultural–linguistically marginalized person, the likes of whom they have never interacted with. Importantly, law enforcement generally has no context as to what case law says about legal terms of art used in the policy. The model policy states in part:

> To serve each individual effectively, primary consideration should be given to providing the type of communication aid or service requested by the individual. Officers should find out from the person who is deaf or hard of hearing what type of auxiliary aid or service he or she needs. Officers should defer to those expressed choices, unless:
>
> there is another equally effective way of communicating, given the circumstances, length, complexity, and importance of the communication, as well as the communication skills of the person who is deaf or hard of hearing; or
>
> doing so would fundamentally alter the nature of the law enforcement activity in question or would cause an undue administrative or financial burden; only the Agency head or his or her designee may make this determination.
>
> The input of people who are deaf or hard of hearing who are involved in incidents is just as important to the law enforcement process as the input of others. Officers must not draw conclusions about incidents unless they fully understand—and are understood by—all those involved, including people who are deaf or hard of hearing. (DOJ, 2006)

The model policy fails to appropriately consider the hyperauthoritarian posture of law enforcement; the realities of day-to-day law enforcement operations; presumptions made by law enforcement about people with whom they interact (i.e., often, behaviors that are seen as "suspicious" or "evasive" by law enforcement are actually typical for those expressing these behaviors, especially when they are not provided with meaningful accommodations and supports); the effects of hierarchical structures, power, and oppression on the application of this and other related policies; and the complexities of communication itself. In addition, the model policy completely lacks an intersectional perspective—failing to note that many deaf people have disabilities or that deaf people from other countries may use a different sign language, for example.

DOJ's model policy first states that the primary consideration of accommodation goes to the deaf person (pursuant to the ADA). Then it can easily be misconstrued to grant law enforcement discretion to reject a deaf person's requested accommodation in place of that which the officer *thinks* is "equally effective." This, however, runs directly counter to the ADA and judicial interpretations of the ADA. Law enforcement's unchecked authority and lack of knowledge of the law and case law, and of Deaf and disability cultures and communication, make it especially important that model policies grant no leeway to law enforcement. This is a particular imperative where civil rights and liberties are at stake, and history points to disability communities showing *extreme* deference to law enforcement and other authority figures.

So why, then, after law enforcement has violated a deaf person's rights, a lawsuit has been filed or settlement agreed upon, and policies have been put in place, do we continue to see the same problems? The missing components in these "solutions" are as follows: a fundamental misunderstanding of the actual functions and practices of policing systems (versus their stated functions and practices); lack of proper individual ownership and accountability for harm; failure to address the root cause of the violation(s) and violence; and continued investment in law enforcement coupled with divestment from community-based solutions, which only serves to increase law enforcement interactions with marginalized communities. In recent years, with a greater focus on "community policing" and on these tragic incidents, police understand that community buy-in is necessary for the survival of law enforcement (Schenwar & Law, 2020). Numerous police departments have quickly and publicly met with disabled people while in the midst of litigation—likely to moot legal claims, minimize damages, and stifle public outcry and calls for defunding and abolishing the police (Gottfriend, 2018; Schenwar & Law, 2020; Tastrom, 2020).

All of the "solutions" listed in this section inure chiefly to the benefit of law enforcement and to those possessing power and privilege within the marginalized group (e.g., Deaf people who are white, nondisabled, wealthy, literacy privileged, sighted, etc.) (Çevik, 2019; Lewis, 2019). These "solutions" often operate to protect law enforcement or reduce liability should another incident occur regardless of whether there has been an actual change in how officers interact with the marginalized community in question. These approaches make it *more* difficult to identify and address the generational, legalized, structural, and systematic problems inherent in policing systems (Carbado, 2017; Schenwar & Law, 2020; Tastrom, 2020). Many of these approaches exacerbate the problems by removing accountability from law enforcement and creating a false sense of relief for people within the marginalized groups. Since the needs of those at the margins of the margins are rarely considered, multiply marginalized people within the group frequently cannot even access these "solutions."

These "fixes" end up providing cover for and legitimizing exactly what they were supposed to address, thereby making it more difficult to hold police and policing systems accountable for their violence against disabled people (Çevik, 2019; Lewis, 2019). Or, as one professor explains this point:

> The problem is not police training, police diversity, or police methods. The problem is the dramatic and unprecedented expansion and intensity of policing in the last 40 years, a fundamental shift in the role of police in society. The problem is policing itself. (Vitale, 2017)

RECOMMENDATION: PRINCIPLED STRUGGLE

The purpose of this chapter is not to provide solutions but, instead, to serve as a framework to help move advocates and others toward the development of a set of values and principles that guide our collective struggle (Lewis, 2019).

Those values and principles should guard against the entrenchment of systemic and structural inequities while people work across identities, across communities, and across movements to end *all* forms of violence, including mass criminalization and incarceration.

Mass incarceration on the scale of that which exists in the United States is unprecedented, so many of the solutions to this crisis will be novel and seemingly impossible. Some solutions may be unsuccessful or lead to unintended, unanticipated, negative consequences. Principled struggle understands "getting it wrong" as part of the work and recognizes the collective journey as part of the victory. Federal and state laws exist to protect the rights of people with disabilities, but these laws are often not followed by power holders or are not considered when it comes to multiply marginalized disabled people. Disability justice moves us beyond disability rights frameworks that focus on rights-based achievements that do not challenge systems (Lewis, 2020). Achieving true access to justice and decreasing violence against people with disabilities will require imagination, dis/investment, flexibility, oversight, and critical reflection (Duda, 2017; Gilmore & Kilgore, 2019; Schenwar & Law, 2020). Any proposed solution to police violence against disabled people should focus on decreasing the power and budgets of law enforcement and increasing the well-being, resources, opportunities, and power of disabled communities to heal, protect, and provide for themselves (e.g., self-determination). Solutions must not develop or hone more ways to help police register, monitor, surveil, control, or punish disabled people or put any nondisabled marginalized community at further risk for police violence. Here are some suggestions that may reduce ongoing harms within the criminal legal system while we continue to work to build the world we all deserve:

- In solidarity with *all* marginalized peoples, direct time, energy, and resources into dismantling white supremacy and providing marginalized communities with the knowledge, tools, and resources necessary to reduce health, education, income, and other inequities (e.g., investment in social services; clean water and healthy food; stable quality housing; harm reduction and other drug use, dependency, and addiction support; high-quality free universal medical and mental health care; high-quality free education and early access to language for all children).
- Dismantle police unions and require law enforcement and prosecutors to have personal insurance and remove procedural and other barriers to law enforcement accountability.
- Build cross-movement campaigns to vote out district attorneys who refuse to hold law enforcement accountable for discrimination and violence against any and all people—especially marginalized people.
- Track and disaggregate data about school, police, and all institutional violence by various disabilities as well as other marginalized identities (e.g., race, class, gender, incarceration history, addiction).
- Ensure that youth understand and are prepared to combat mass criminalization and incarceration at the individual, community, and systemic levels.

- Develop knowledge of systemic and structural oppression, transformative justice, healing justice, disability justice, etc., and advocacy and community organizing skills during childhood; refine those skills through adolescence; and implement them throughout life.
- Remove law enforcement from campuses with deaf/disabled students and severely restrict or curtail schools' and universities' freedom to contact law enforcement for on-campus incidents.
- Conversations about "solutions" must center disabled people who have experienced or are at the highest risk for experiencing carceral violence (e.g., youth, negatively racialized people, including Black/Indigenous deaf people, previously institutionalized and incarcerated, low- and no-income, trans- and gender-nonconforming, DeafDisabled people, and disabled people involved in informal economies).
- Multiply marginalized disabled advocates should be hired to work with attorneys to create participatory defense models[5] for disabled people trapped in the criminal legal system. A participatory defense-like strategy should be developed for disabled defendants' cases whereby advocates and attorneys who are knowledgeable about disability and deaf cultures are welcome members of the defense. This allows disabled communities to learn more about the criminal legal system and exposes defense attorneys to disabled communities' wisdom, thereby better equipping disabled and legal communities to challenge the system through and through.
- Make the study and continuing education of antiracism, antiableism, and other anti-oppression praxes a mandatory requirement for *all* interpreters. Interpreters who do not *at a minimum* understand and practice these should not be deemed qualified to interpret, especially in legal settings.
- Intensive disability and antiableism courses should be mandated for all law students, especially those interested in the criminal legal system and all attorneys and judges operating within the same.
- Challenge policies and practices within courts, interpreting programs, and professions that have discriminatory intent or impact on marginalized people (e.g., do not hold out interpreter certification as the most important determinant or qualification for legal interpreters). The people most qualified to work with those trapped in the carceral system are often unable to access or "pass" tests/requirements established by the dominant white, hearing, wealth-privileged majority who spearhead the interpreting industry. Hire deaf incarcerated and formerly incarcerated people as evaluators of interpreters seeking legal qualification and develop a pipeline of formerly incarcerated deaf interpreters and advocates to support other deaf people affected by the criminal legal system.
- Attorneys and judges must request, provide, and pay for accommodations, and defense attorneys representing deaf defendants must challenge interpretation and other access issues for disabled clients.
- Law enforcement must audiovisually record interviews and interrogations with deaf and signing people such that the signs of all signers (i.e.,

interpreters, interviewees, signing officers, etc.) are fully visible and all people speaking are clearly audible. Defense attorneys must demand access to all audiovisual footage *and* hire experts to challenge communication, culture, and interpretation issues. Where there is incomplete or no audiovisual record (e.g., body camera), attorneys should move to suppress statements purportedly made to law enforcement.

- Where interpreters or other accommodations are not provided with law enforcement or attorney–client communication, a presumption of prejudice should attach, statements should be suppressed, and complaints filed against police and attorneys, respectively. These complaints should name police departments, officers, and attorneys and should be published periodically, translated into signed languages, and remain publicly available.
- Courts must audiovisually record all proceedings with deaf/signing people such that the signs of *all* signing people can be clearly seen and all voices of people speaking can be clearly heard.
- Appellate, habeas, actual innocence, and conviction integrity communities must work in partnership with disability communities. Communication access and disability cultures must be considered for disabled people seeking postconviction support and relief. Cases involving multiply marginalized disabled people should be prioritized.
- Advocates should create a publicly accessible complaint (and accountability) process by supporting affected community members with submitting formal complaints. Create a centralized community database of complaints if it is not safe to file complaints with law enforcement in your locality because many police departments use the fact that disabled, deaf, and signing people have filed few or no complaints as evidence of these departments' success instead of proof of inaccessibility of their complaint process.

CONCLUSION

Disability rights advocates have neglected issues of racial justice for far too long, and racial justice advocates have, similarly, taken for granted the ways in which ableism interacts with racism, classism, and other oppressions to create and perpetuate systemic inequity. Ending state violence requires a deep appreciation of how disability is created and constructed and of how disability exists, arises in, and interacts with marginalized people and communities and other oppressions. Advocates must view the crisis of mass criminalization and incarceration through a disability justice lens and approach decarceration advocacy with a truly intersectional framework that recognizes that government oppression of and violence against negatively racialized and educationally and economically disenfranchised communities has *always* been deeply rooted in, *at least*, race, class, and disability (Lewis, 2020).

Successful advocacy strategies will help weave communities together by highlighting the ties between oppressions that lead to intractable structural and systemic inequity. These integrated and intersectional advocacy approaches will provide the requisite relationships, knowledge, and tools to help organizers practice accountable advocacy that builds across identities, communities, and movements.

Effective advocacy in the 21st century looks like being "in community," creating accomplices, and acting in solidarity with *all* marginalized communities—constantly learning with and from those communities. No single group can dismantle oppressive systems on its own because all oppressions and oppressive systems are linked and depend on each other to survive and thrive. Advocates must approach legal and carceral systems with a deep understanding of the past and present inequities within these systems that demand nothing less than abolition. Only when advocates are able to name racism, classism, ableism, audism, and other forms of oppression as central to the perpetuation of mass criminalization and incarceration can we begin to end generational cycles of violence and heal our communities (Duda, 2017; Gilmore & Kilgore, 2019).

NOTES

1. The author uses the term "criminal legal system" instead of "criminal justice system" because the systemic and structural injustices that pervade the legal system make it undeserving of justice-inclusive monikers. This term also serves to distinguish between the civil legal system and the criminal legal system.

2. The author uses the term "deaf" to refer to people who are Deaf, DeafBlind, DeafDisabled, Hard of Hearing, Late Deafened. The author uses precise identifiers where necessary. For example, DeafDisabled is used when a deaf person has other disabilities. The author also honors identifiers used by individuals. In this chapter, "disability" and "disabilities" include all deaf people unless otherwise noted. Disability hierarchies (e.g., "I am Deaf, not disabled," "I am Autistic, not disabled," "I can do anything except hear," etc.) are particularly harmful to disabled people, communities, and movements. This chapter very intentionally rejects this ableist rhetoric and ideology because it reinforces the dangerous myth that there is something wrong with disability or being disabled. Disability is a natural part of the human experience that should be honored and respected. Disability hierarchies within disability communities help society and systems like the legal system to continue to engage in ableism, including audism, vidism, sanism, and other forms of oppression. This kind of intracommunity ableism harms *all* deaf people, especially multiply marginalized deaf people. This chapter challenges privileged people in deaf and other disability communities to reject this kind of horizontal ableism. The author and other Black/Indigenous community builders, cultural workers, and social justice advocates have developed and presented extensive information about ableism, racism, classism, and other oppressions within disability communities, including deaf communities.

3. Investigation finding that a Black teen with disabilities is 16 times more likely to be arrested at school than white students without disabilities and four times more likely to be arrested than white students with disabilities.

4. https://www.participatorydefense.org/

REFERENCES

AJ+. (2018). *Deaf, black and a victim of police brutality.* https://www.youtube.com/watch?v=9Rkctxo_LQI

Alexander, M. (2010). *The new Jim Crow: Mass incarceration in the age of colorblindness.* The New Press.

Alfisi, K. (2013, October 1). Groups seek more access to justice for deaf, hard-of-hearing. *Washington Lawyer.* https://dcbar.org/news-events/washington-lawyer

American Civil Liberties Union. (2016). Amicus Brief, *City and County of San Francisco v. Sheehan.* https://www.aclu.org/legal-document/city-and-county-san-francisco-v-sheehan-amicus-brief

Americans With Disabilities Act, 42 U.S.C. § 12101, *et seq.*

Andrews, J., Vernon, M., & LaVigne, M. (2007). The Bill of Rights, due process and the deaf suspect/defendant. *Journal of Interpretation, 9,* 13.

Artiles, A. J. (2014, January 3). Untangling the racialization of disabilities: An intersectionality critique across disability models. *Du Bois Review: Social Science Research on Race, 10*(2), 2013. https://doi.org/10.1017/S1742058X13000271

Aubrecht, A., & Lewis, T. A. (2016, October 13). *Deaf in prison: Interacting with signing cops.* https://www.youtube.com/watch?v=NHdz5CneAeY

Bailey, P. (2016, October 5). City may say Darnell Wicker shooting justified. *Courier Journal.* https://www.courier-journal.com/story/news/politics/metro-government/2016/10/05/city-police-shooting-darnell-wicker-justified/91605708/

Balko, R. (2018, September 18; updated 2020, June 10). There's overwhelming evidence that the criminal justice system is racist. Here's the proof. *The Washington Post.* https://www.washingtonpost.com/graphics/2020/opinions/systemic-racism-police-evidence-criminal-justice-system/

Bekiempis, V. (2016, December). Deaf woman who accused NYPD cops of wrongful arrest, denying her interpreter gets $80G from city. *NY Daily News.* http://www.nydailynews.com/new-york/deaf-woman-80g-wrongful-arrest-suit-nypd-article-1.2912383

Berne, P. (2017, May 18). *Disability justice: A working draft.* http://peakmag.net/disability-justice/disability-justice-a-working-draft/

Bernstein, M. (2012, November 17). Lack of Portland police, 911 policies for interpreters discriminate against people who are deaf, lawsuit alleges. *The Oregonian.* https://www.oregonlive.com/portland/index.ssf/2012/11/portland_police_and_9–1-1_fail.html

Biscobing, D. (2017, November 20). Buckeye police create registry program for individuals with autism, other disabilities. *ABC 15.* https://www.abc15.com/news/local-news/investigations/buckeye-police-create-registry-program-for-individuals-with-autism-other-disabilities

Black deaf man Ricardo Harris says he was wrongfully convicted. (2020, June 25). *The Daily Moth.* https://www.youtube.com/watch?v=hjzOb4_gGLc

Blackmon, D. A. (2008). *Slavery by another name: The re-enslavement of black Americans from the Civil War to World War II.* Anchor Books.

Brown, L. X. Z., Lewis, T. A., & Moore, L. (2018, June 1). *Accountable reporting on disability, race, & police violence: A community response to the "Ruderman White Paper on the Media Coverage of Use of Force and Disability."* http://www.bit.ly/disjustwpresponse

Bryant, R. (2017). Pulling back the curtain: How unwritten rules impact sign language interpreters. *Street Leverage.* https://live.streetleverage.com/pulling-back-curtain-unwritten-rules-impact-sign-language-interpreters/

Butterfield, F. (1998, August 9). Prison population growing although crime rate drops. *The New York Times.* http://www.nytimes.com/1998/08/09/us/prison-population-growing-although-crime-rate-drops.html

Carbado, D. (2017). From stopping black people to killing black people: The Fourth Amendment pathways to police violence. *California Law Review, 105*(1), 125–164. https://doi.org/10.15779/Z38GK24

Carter-Conneen, M. (2016, October 10). Special MPD unit helps build trust in D.C.'s deaf community. *WJLA ABC 7.* http://wjla.com/news/local/special-mpd-unit-helps-build-trust-in-dcs-deaf-community

Center, C. (2015, March 20). How police can stop shooting people with disabilities. *ACLU.* https://www.aclu.org/blog/national-security/how-police-can-stop-shooting-people-disabilities

Center, C. (2016, March 20). Keith Lamont Scott's disability may have gotten him killed, and he's not the only one. *ACLU.* https://www.aclu.org/blog/criminal-law-reform/reforming-police-practices/keith-lamont-scotts-disability-may-have-gotten

Center for American Progress & Movement Advanced Project. (2016, February). *Unjust: How the broken criminal justice system fails LGBT people.* http://www.lgbtmap.org/file/lgbt-criminal-justice.pdf

Çevik, K. (2014, August 4). Why autism training for law enforcement doesn't work. *The Autism Wars.* http://theautismwars.blogspot.com/2014/08/why-autism-training-for-law-enforcement.html

Çevik, K. (2019, August 3). On the dangers of faux solutions to catastrophic encounters with law enforcement. *Intersected.* https://intersecteddisability.blogspot.com/2019/08/on-dangers-of-faux-solutions-to.html?spref=fb&fbclid=IwAR3G-PIQU3eARmgWyv08u4hy_D0aGsa11rnw-6bRn_EMosoyJQihmbECqKmk

Charlotte-Mecklenburg Police Department. (2007, January 26). *Directives manual: Interpreting for the deaf and hard of hearing, Addendum—Practical suggestions for communicating.* Author. http://www.aele.org/law/2009a1103/charlotte.html

Chuck, E., & Connor, T. (2017, September 21). Deaf advocates call Oklahoma police shooting "tragic but not surprising." *NBC News.* https://www.nbcnews.com/news/us-news/deaf-advocates-call-oklahoma-police-shooting-tragic-not-surprising-n803226

Cloud, E. M. (2019). *Toward the abolition of the foster system.* Scholar and Feminist Online. https://sfonline.barnard.edu/unraveling-criminalizing-webs-building-police-free-futures/toward-the-abolition-of-the-foster-system/

Coates, T. (2015, October). The Black family in the age of mass incarceration. *The Atlantic.* https://www.theatlantic.com/magazine/archive/2015/10/the-black-family-in-the-age-of-mass-incarceration/403246/

Cobb v. Georgia Department of Community Corrections. (2019). Civil Action No. 1:19-cv-03285-WMR. https://www.aclu.org/cases/cobb-v-georgia-department-community-supervision

Cooper, A. (2017, April 16). Inside NOLA public defenders' decision to refuse felony cases. *CBS News.* https://www.cbsnews.com/news/inside-new-orleans-public-defenders-decision-to-refuse-felony-cases/?authenticated=1

The counted: People killed by police in the United States. (2016). *The Guardian.* https://www.theguardian.com/us-news/series/counted-us-police-killings

Crane, M., Nirider, L., & Drizin, S. (2016, Winter). The truth about juvenile false confessions. *American Bar Association, Insights on Law and Society, 16*(2), 10–16. https://www.americanbar.org/publications/insights_on_law_andsociety/16/winter2016/JuvenileConfessions.html

Crenshaw, K. (1989). Demarginalizing the intersection of race and sex: A Black feminist critique of antidiscrimination doctrine, feminist theory and antiracist politics. *University of Chicago Legal Forum, 1989*(1), 139–167. https://chicagounbound.uchicago.edu/cgi/viewcontent.cgi?article=1052&context=uclf

Crenshaw, K. (1991, July). Mapping the margins: Intersectionality, identity politics, and violence against women of color. *Stanford Law Review, 43*(6), 1241–1299. https://doi.org/10.2307/1229039

Davis, M. (2003) *Are prisons obsolete?* Seven Stories Press.

Deaf man who was incarcerated 25 years to be released. (2019, March 5). *The Daily Moth.* https://www.facebook.com/watch/?v=2232422283447375

Deaf Oklahoma man Pearl Pearson wins $195,000. (2018, February 20). *The Daily Moth.* https://www.facebook.com/TheDailyMoth/videos/817572561777979/UzpfSTYwNDcyMTE4NjMxNTc3NzoxNTg30Tk0MTA0NjU1MTQy/

Deaf woman sues Jacksonville Sherriff's office. (2017, April 20). *The Daily Moth.* https://www.dailymoth.com/single-post/2017/04/20/The-Daily-Moth-4-20-17

DeLamielleure-Scott, C. (2016, June 22). Cards assist law enforcement, drivers with hearing loss. *West Bloomfield Beacon.* https://www.candgnews.com/news/cards-assist-law-enforcement-drivers-hearing-loss-93863

Denzel, S. (updated 2016, June 27). Stephen Brodie profile. *The National Registry of Exonerations.* https://www.law.umich.edu/special/exoneration/Pages/casedetail.aspx?caseid=3056

District of Columbia Superior Court, Office of Court Interpreting Services. *Deaf defendants' access to the courts—Calendar years 2011 and 2012.* (Prepared by request of Anita Jarman [Executive Office] for Talila Lewis, American University law student).

DPAN.TV. (2017, November 1). *The NYPD & Video Relay Service.* https://www.facebook.com/watch/?v=735060616686338

DPAN.TV. (n.d.). *Lack of deaf cultural competency in legal system.* https://dpan.tv/series/between-the-lines/episode/lack-of-deaf-cultural-competency-in-legal-system

Duane, J. (2016, September 20). *You have the right to remain innocent.* Amazon Publishing.

Duda, J. (2017, November 9). Towards the horizon of abolition: A conversation with Mariame Kaba. *The Next System Project.* https://thenextsystem.org/learn/stories/towards-horizon-abolition-conversation-mariame-kaba

Ekes, E. (2007). The incompetency of courts and legislatures: Addressing linguistically deprived deaf defendants. *University of Cincinnati Law Review, 75,* 1649.

Fatal force. (2018). *The Washington Post.* https://www.washingtonpost.com/graphics/2018/national/police-shootings-2018/?utm_term=.dffec225d48c

Franklin, D. (2018, February 19). *Deaf man given $175,000 settlement after claiming Oklahoma troopers used excessive force during arrest.* https://kfor.com/2018/02/19/deaf-man-given-175000-settlement-after-claiming-oklahoma-troopers-used-excessive-force-during-arrest/

Garcia-Leys, S., Thompson, M., & Richardson, C. (2016, April) Mislabeled: Allegations of gang membership and their immigration consequences. *University of California, Irvine, School of Law, Immigrant Rights Clinic.* https://www.law.uci.edu/academics/real-life-learning/clinics/ucilaw-irc-MislabeledReport.pdf

Garvey, M. (2018, May 15). For students of color with disabilities, equity delayed is equity denied. *ACLU.* https://www.aclu.org/blog/disability-rights/disability-rights-and-education/students-color-disabilities-equity-delayed

General Assembly of North Carolina. (2017, Session). *Session Law 2017–191, House Bill 84, An Act to Direct the Division of Motor Vehicles to Develop a Designation for Drivers*

Licenses that May be Granted Upon Request to a Person Who Is Deaf or Hard of Hearing. https://www.ncleg.net/Sessions/2017/Bills/House/PDF/H84v7.pdf

Gibson, D. (2016, December). The Woodland Hills High School-to-prison pipeline. *HuffPost*. https://www.huffingtonpost.com/entry/the-woodland-hills-high-school-to-prison-pipeline_us_58543b23e4b0d5f48e164f08

Gibson, D., & Lewis, T. (2018, September 7). The prison strike challenges Ableism and defends disability rights. *Truthout.com*. https://truthout.org/articles/the-prison-strike-is-a-disability-rights-issue/

Gilmore, R., & Kilgore, J. (2019, June 19). *The case for abolition*. https://www.themarshallproject.org/2019/06/19/the-case-for-abolition

Gottfriend, M. H. (2018, May 29). St. Kate's students help change the way St. Paul police make arrests. *Twin Cities Pioneer Press*. https://www.twincities.com/2018/05/29/letter-from-3-st-kates-students-leads-to-st-paul-pd-policy-change-for-communicating-with-deaf/

Graphic: Oklahoma troopers accused of beating deaf man. (2014, February 27). *KFOR Oklahoma's News 4*. https://www.youtube.com/watch?v=9gMutzbOVrM

Greenberg, T. (2017, November 8). Police, schools create youth autism registry. *Cranston Herald*. http://cranstononline.com/stories/cranston-police-schools-create-autism-registry,129227

Gross, S. R., Possley, M., & Stephens, K. (2017, March 7). Race and wrongful convictions in the United States. *National Registry of Exonerations*. https://www.law.umich.edu/special/exoneration/Documents/Race_and_Wrongful_Convictions.pdf

Hager, E. (2017, March 7). The seismic change in police interrogations. *The Marshall Project*. https://www.themarshallproject.org/2017/03/07/the-seismic-change-in-police-interrogations

Halsne, C. (2012, August 5). Police use taser on deaf crime victim. *Kiro 7*. https://www.kir07.com/news/crime-law/police-use-taser-deaf-crime-victim/246931400

Hamdan, L. (2018, May 25). WBEZ report finds inadequate housing options for prisoners with disabilities in Illinois. *St. Louis Public Radio*. http://news.stlpublicradio.org/post/wbez-report-finds-inadequate-housing-options-prisoners-disabilities-illinois#stream/0

Harris v. Georgia Department of Corrections. Civil Action No. 5:16-cv-353-MTT. (2018). https://www.aclu.org/legal-document/coen-v-gdoc-complaint

Harris, J. (2014, February 21). Cop's tasering doesn't help deaf man hear. *Courthouse News Service*. https://www.courthousenews.com/cops-tasering-doesnthelp-deaf-man-hear/

Helping Educate to Advance the Rights of Deaf Communities—HEARD. (2016, August 31). *Statement on the August 2016 police killings of two deaf men, Darnell Wicker and Daniel Harris*. https://www.facebook.com/HEARDDC/videos/1262694537109381/

Helping Educate to Advance the Rights of Deaf Communities—HEARD. (2018a, August 21). *Community statement on Louisiana Department of Corrections' use of hearing imprisoned people as "interpreters" for deaf imprisoned people*. bit.ly/deafprisonla

Helping Educate to Advance the Rights of Deaf Communities—HEARD. (2018b, August 21). *HEARD's concerns about NYPD's deaf driver cards and media coverage of deaf driver cards*. https://www.facebook.com/HEARDDC/videos/vb.173173689394810/1971104159601745/?type=2&theater

Helping Educate to Advance the Rights of Deaf Communities—HEARD. (2020, June). *Police brutality and discrimination against deaf people*. https://docs.google.com/spreadsheets/d/1HZ6YLtXzRNiEsu2RCfEUb1WmsCwM4Pn89ikpAwE4b-Q/edit#gid=1519942027

Helsel, P. (2016, August 23). *Daniel Harris shooting: Mourners remember deaf man killed by police—As questions remain.* https://www.nbcnews.com/news/us-news/daniel-harris-shooting-mourners-remember-deaf-man-killed-poliDiscrimination and harassment by law enforcement officers in the LGBT communitydiscriminationce-questions-n636776

House Bill 84: Driver's License/Deaf or Hard of Hearing Designation. Committee: Date: August 10, 2017 Prepared by: Giles Perry Analysis of: S.L. 2017–191 Staff Attorney. Effective January 1, 2018. https://dashboard.ncleg.net/api/Services/BillSummary/2017/H84-SMRW-94(sl)-v-2

Interview with Amber Farrelly, Esq. (2016, May 12). *The Daily Moth.* https://www.youtube.com/watch?v=SkqPrjECefg

Jackson, A. (2018, April 22). South Carolina law enforcement seek training to improve communication with deaf community. *The Post and Courier.* https://www.postandcourier.com/news/south-carolina-law-enforcement-seek-training-to-improve-communication-with/article_19e4afda-2d1f-11e8–91d2-a321c205da3a.html

Jackson, C. (2014, January 17). State troopers violently beat deaf man for not hearing. *Deaf Network.* https://deafnetwork.com/wordpress/blog/2014/01/21/state-troopers-violently-beat-deaf-man-for-not-hearing-oklahoma/

Jayne, B., & Buckley, J. (n.d.). *The investigator anthology.* https://www.reid.com/educational_info/critictechnique.html

Jin v. Alameda County et al., Case No. 3:18-cv-04885 (2018). Complaint.

Jung, H. (2013, July 16). Portland ordered to pay deaf plaintiff $51,500, adopt police policy for communicating with hard-of-hearing. *The Oregonian.* https://www.oregonlive.com/portland/index.ssf/2013/07/portland_ordered_to_pay_deaf_p.html

Kaba, M. (2014, December 7). Police "reforms" you should always oppose. *Truthout.com.* https://truthout.org/articles/police-reforms-you-should-always-oppose/

Kaba, M. (2018). Interrupting criminalization: Research in action. *Barnard University.* http://bcrw.barnard.edu/fellows/interrupting-criminalization-research-in-action/

Kajstura, A. (2017, October 9). Women's mass incarceration: The whole pie 2017. *Prison Policy Initiative.* https://www.prisonpolicy.org/reports/pie2017women.html

Kinna, R., & Gordon, U. (Eds.). (2019). *Routledge handbook of radical politics.* Routledge.

Kindy, K. (2015, April 11). Thousands dead, few prosecuted. *The Washington Post.* http://www.washingtonpost.com/sf/investigative/2015/04/11/thousands-dead-few-prosecuted

Kolliner, K. (2018, April 24). *Medford Police offers deaf or hard of hearing cards to display.* http://ktvl.com/news/local/kims-drafts

Las Vegas Metropolitan Police Department. (n.d.). *Partners with the community policy manual: 5/107.00 Public Service/Public Order, 5/107.01 interaction with the hearing impaired.* http://www.aele.org/law/2009a1103/lasvegas.html

LaVigne, M., & Vernon, M. (2003). An interpreter isn't enough: Deafness, language, and due process. *Wisconsin Law Review,* no. 843. https://papers.ssrn.com/sol3/papers.cfm?abstract_id=1744291

Lee, J. (2014, August 15). Exactly how often do police shoot unarmed black men? *Mother Jones.* http://www.motherjones.com/politics/2014/08/police-shootings-michael-brown-ferguson-black-men

Lee, T., & Samee, S. (2016, November 14). Why doesn't the government track nationwide police use of force? *NBC News.* https://www.nbcnews.com/news/us-news/why-doesn-t-government-track-nationwide-police-use-force-n682626

Leslie, L. (2017, April 6). *Deaf driver's license bill passes NC House.* https://wwwdeaf.wral.com/deaf-driver-s-license-bill-passes-nc-house-/16630229/

Lewis, T. A. (2014, March 21). Police brutality and deaf people. *ACLU.* https://www.aclu.org/blog/national-security/police-brutality-and-deaf-people

Lewis, T. A. (2015, April 20). United States Commission on Civil Rights briefing on police practices and use of force. Testimony from Helping Educate to Advance the Rights of Deaf Communities. https://www.usccr.gov/calendar/trnscrpt/Police-Practices-and-Use-of-Force_04-20-2015.pdf

Lewis, T. A. (2017a, April 6). In the fight to close Rikers, don't forget deaf and disabled people. *Truthout.com.* https://truthout.org/articles/in-the-fight-to-close-rikers-don-t-forget-deaf-and-disabled-people/

Lewis, T. A. (2017b). Honoring Arnaldo Rios-Soto and Charles Kinsey: Achieving liberation through disability solidarity. *Harvard Kennedy School Journal of African American Public Policy,* 73–78. https://hjaap.hkspublications.org/wp-content/uploads/sites/14/2019/02/HJAAP-2017-with-cover.pdf

Lewis, T. A. (2017c, January 28). Emmett Till and the pervasive erasure of disability in conversations about white supremacy and police brutality. *Medium.* https://medium.com/@talewis/emmett-till-the-pervasive-erasure-of-disability-in-conversations-about-white-supremacy-police-5eb9ad595ba2

Lewis, T. A. (2018, June 20). In Georgia, imprisoned deaf and disabled people don't stand a chance. *ACLU.* https://www.aclu.org/blog/disability-rights/disability-rights-and-criminal-legal-system/georgia-imprisoned-deaf-and.

Lewis, T. A. (2019). *Response: Concerns re disability/deaf rights communities' responses to policing systems' violence.* https://www.talilalewis.com/blog/response-concerns-re-disabilitydeaf-rights-communities-responses-to-policing-systems-violence

Lewis, T. A. (2020, October 28). Disability justice is an essential part of abolition. *LEVEL.* https://level.medium.com/disability-justice-is-an-essential-part-of-abolishing-police-and-prisons-2b4a019b5730.

Louisville Metro Police Department. (2008, revised 2016, 2017). *Standard operating procedures: Interpreter procedures* (pp. 226–229). Author. https://www.louisville-police.org/DocumentCenter/View/615/Standard-Operating-Procedures-PDF

Lowery, W. (2017, December 8). Graphic video shows Daniel Shaver sobbing and begging officer for his life before 2016 shooting. *The Washington Post.* https://www.washingtonpost.com/news/post-nation/wp/2017/12/08/graphic-video-shows-daniel-shaver-sobbing-and-begging-officer-for-his-life-before-2016-shooting/?utm_term=.9659985bc9e7

Ludwig, M. (2016, August 22). No way to call home: Incarcerated deaf people are locked in a prison inside a prison. *Truthout.com.* https://truthout.org/articles/no-way-to-call-home-incarcerated-deaf-people-are-locked-in-a-prison-inside-a-prison/

Mallory, C., Hasenbush, A., & Sears, B. (2015, March). Discrimination and harassment by law enforcement officers in the LGBTQ community. *The Williams Institute.* https://williamsinstitute.law.ucla.edu/wp-content/uploads/LGBT-Discrimination-and-Harassment-in-Law-Enforcement-March-2015.pdf

Matter, B., & Heath, C. (2017, April 13). Federal lawsuit filed against Jacksonville Sheriff's Office; deaf woman says she was denied services. *CBS Action News Jax.* https://www.actionnewsjax.com/news/local/federal-lawsuit-filed-against-jacksonville-sheriffs-office-deaf-woman-says-she-was-denied-services/512002761

McNamara, B. (2016, September 29). Up to half of people killed by police are disabled. *Teen Vogue*. http://www.teenvogue.com/story/half-of-people-killed-by-police-have-disabilities

McNerthney, C. (2011, August 30). Woodcarver's family to get $1.5 million from city. *Seattlepi.com*. https://www.seattlepi.com/local/article/Woodcarvers-family-to-get-1-5-million-from-city-1359018.php

Mensah, S., & Kaufman-Mthimkhulu, S. (2020, July 21). *Abolition must include psychiatry*. https://disabilityvisibilityproject.com/2020/07/22/abolition-must-include-psychiatry/

Metropolitan Police Department. (2016, October 3). *Meet Officers Ellis and Jordan with MPDs deaf and hard of hearing liaison unit*. https://mpdc.dc.gov/release/meet-officers-ellis-and-jordan-mpds-deaf-and-hard-hearing-liaison-unit

Metropolitan Police Department. (n.d.). *Fifth police district welcomes 6-year-old as honorary police officer*. https://mpdc.dc.gov/multimedia/fifth-police-district-welcomes-6-year-old-honorary-police-officer

Michigan Department of Civil Rights. (2016, August). *New communication tool for drivers who are deaf or hard of hearing unveiled by Michigan Department of Civil Rights*. http://www.michigan.gov/mdcr/0,4613,7-138-385570-,00.html

Miletich, S. (2011, February 15). No charges against Seattle officer who shot woodcarver. *The Seattle Times*. https://www.seattletimes.com/seattle-news/no-charges-against-seattle-officer-who-shot-woodcarver/

Miller, C. (2010, September 28). Stephen Brodie, deaf man convicted of child rape, cleared 20 years after crime. *CBS News*. https://www.cbsnews.com/news/stephen-brodie-deaf-man-convicted-of-child-rape-cleared-20-years-after-crime/

Mizner, S. (2015, October 12). The Supreme Court leaves the Americans With Disabilities Act intact. *ACLU*. https://www.aclu.org/blog/disability-rights/disability-rights-and-criminal-justice/supreme-court-leaves-americans

Mizner, S. (2017, October 12). We don't think an 8-year-old boy should be put in handcuffs. A judge finally agreed with us. *ACLU*. https://www.aclu.org/blog/juvenile-justice/school-prison-pipeline/we-dont-think-8-year-old-boy-should-be-put-handcuffs

Molina, A. (2017, June 1). Measure aims to alert police that a driver is deaf or hard of hearing. *The Press Enterprise*. https://www.pe.com/2017/06/01/measure-aims-to-alert-police-that-a-driver-is-deaf-or-hard-of-hearing/

Montemayor, S. (2017, August 10). Excluded from a Minnesota grand jury, deaf man sues for the right to serve. *Star Tribune*. http://www.startribune.com/excluded-from-a-minnesota-grand-jury-deaf-man-sues-for-the-right-to-serve/439714133/

More Evidence in Terence Crutcher Case. (2017, April 2). *CBS news*. https://www.cbsnews.com/news/more-evidence-in-the-terence-crutcher-shooting/

Morgan, J. (2017). Caged in: The devastating harms of solitary confinement on prisoners with physical disabilities. *ACLU*. https://www.aclu.org/files/caged-in/010916-ACLU-SolitaryDisabilityReport-Accessible.pdf

Musgrave, J. (2018, March 6). Bethesda settles lawsuit with deaf over use of remote interpreters. *Palm Beach Post*. https://www.mypalmbeachpost.com/news/crime—law/bethesda-settles-lawsuit-with-deaf-over-use-remote-interpreters/DnjQrAAjH1rElgL100kK80/

National Alliance on Mental Illness. (n.d.). *Facts on children's mental health in America*. https://www.alexandriava.gov/uploadedfiles/health/info/fact_sheet.pdf

National Association for the Advancement of Colored People. (2018). *Criminal justice fact sheet*. http://www.naacp.org/criminal-justice-fact-sheet/
National Association of Criminal Defense Lawyers (NACDL). *The trial penalty: The Sixth Amendment Right to Trial on the verge of extinction and how to save it*. https://www.nacdl.org/trialpenaltyreport/
National Association of the Deaf. (2017, October). *Avoidable killings by police must stop*. https://www.nad.org/2017/10/10/avoidable-killings-by-police-must-stop/
National Center for Access to Justice. *Justice index on disability assistance*. http://www.justiceindex.org/findings/disability-assistance/
National Child Traumatic Stress Network. (2006). *Facts on trauma and deaf children*. https://www.nctsn.org/sites/default/files/resources//facts_on_trauma_deaf_children.pdf
National Collaborative for Workforce & Disability for Youth. (2016). *Guideposts for success*, (2nd ed.). http://www.ncwd-youth.info/sites/default/files/Guideposts-for-Success-(English).pdf
National Council on Disability. (2008, February 26). *Youth with disabilities in the foster care system: Barriers to success and proposed policy solutions*. http://www.ncd.gov/publications/2008/02262008
National Council on Disability. (2011, October 31). *National disability policy: A progress report*. https://ncd.gov/progress_reports/Oct312011
National Council on Disability. (2015, June 18). *Breaking the school to prison pipeline*. https://www.ncd.gov/publications/2015/06182015
Nelson, C. (2010). Racializing disability, disabling race: Policing race and mental status. *Berkeley Journal of Criminal Law, 15*(1), 1–64. https://www.bjcl.org/assets/files/15_1-Nelson-1-64.pdf
Nelson, C. (2016). Frontlines: Policing at the nexus of race and mental health. *Fordham Urban Law Journal 43*(3), 615–683. https://ir.lawnet.fordham.edu/cgi/viewcontent.cgi?article=2659&context=ulj
Nović, S. (2017, March 22). The right to remain silent: Ableism, the English to prison pipeline, and the plight of deaf inmates. *The New Inquiry*. https://thenewinquiry.com/the-right-to-remain-silent/
Nović, S. (2018, June 21). Deaf prisoners are trapped in frightening isolation. *CNN News*. https://www.cnn.com/2018/06/21/opinions/aclu-georgia-deaf-abuse-lawsuit-novic/index.html
Office of Court Interpreting Services. (2013). *Deaf defendants' access to the courts—Calendar years 2011 and 2012*. [Prepared by request of Anita Jarman (executive office) for Talila Lewis, American University law student].
Ogunyipe, B. (2012, August 17). Public statement on investigation into the battery and arrest of Lashonn White. *National Black Deaf Advocates*. https://www.nbda.org/EE/files/NBDA_Statement_on_Investigation_into_Battery_and_Arrest_of_Lashonn_White.pdf
Ontario Provincial Police. (2018, May 10). Visor Card | deafontario.ca. *Facebook*. https://www.facebook.com/750109878431818/posts/1585856871523777/
Oppel Jr., R. A. (2018, March 29). His clients weren't complaining. But the judge said this lawyer worked too hard. *The New York Times*. https://mobile.nytimes.com/2018/03/29/us/indigent-defense-lawyer-texas.html?smid=fb-share
Oregon Department of Corrections. *Rules and policies*. https://www.oregon.gov/doc/rules-and-policies/Pages/home.aspx

Parker, C. B. (2016, June 15). Stanford big data study finds racial disparities in Oakland, Calif., police behavior, offers solutions. *Stanford News*. https://news.stanford.edu/2016/06/15/stanford-big-data-study-finds-racial-disparities-oakland-calif-police-behavior-offers-solutions/
Pennsylvania Department of Corrections v. Yeskey, 524 U.S. 206, 209 (1998).
Peter P. v. Compton Unified School District. 135 F. Supp. 3d 1126 (C.D. Cal. 2015). (2014). https://casetext.com/case/pp-v-compton-unified-sch-dist-3
Philip Wolfe v. City of Portland. Complaint filed 11/13/2012. http://media.oregonlive.com/portland_impact/other/philip-wolfe-lawsuit2.pdf
Philip Wolfe v. City of Portland. Complaint filed 11/1/2020. https://www.courtlistener.com/recap/gov.uscourts.ord.156442/gov.uscourts.ord.156442.1.0.pdf
Project CLIMB. (2017). *Announcement and five-year plan*. https://www.unco.edu/project-climb/
Quan, D. (2012, September 10). Judge's ruling finds widely used police interrogation technique "oppressive." *Canada.com*. http://www.canada.com/Judge+ruling+finds+widely+used+police+interrogation+technique+oppressive/7220193/story.html
Rabuy, B., & Kopf, D. (2015, July 9). Prisons of poverty: Uncovering the pre-incarceration incomes of the imprisoned. *Prison Policy Initiative*. https://www.prisonpolicy.org/reports/income.html
Rakoff, J. S. (2014, November 20). Why innocent people plead guilty. *The New York Review of Books*. http://www.nybooks.com/articles/2014/11/20/why-innocent-people-plead-guilty/
Rand, M. R., & Harrell, E. (2009, October 1). *Crime against people with disabilities, 2017*. U.S. Department of Justice, Bureau of Justice Statistics. https://www.bjs.gov/content/pub/pdf/capd07.pdf
Registry of Interpreters for the Deaf. (last updated 2016a, June 16). *Annual report, membership demographics*. https://www.rid.org/wp-content/uploads/2018/03/FY17-Annual-Report.pdf
Registry of Interpreters for the Deaf. (last updated 2016b, June 16). *Criminal conviction policy request for comments*. https://www.rid.org/2016/06/criminal-conviction-policy-request-for-comments/
Registry of Interpreters for the Deaf. (last updated 2018, April 28). *Certifications under moratorium*. https://www.rid.org/rid-certification-overview/certifications-under-moratorium/
Rehabilitation Act of 1973, Pub. L. No. 93–112, 87 Stat. 394 (1973).
Renville, F. (2011, February 21). The shooting death of John T. Williams. *Indian Country Today*. https://newsmaven.io/indiancountrytoday/archive/the-shooting-death-of-john-t-williams-XsKxgn09GkKRECYKnd70ng/
Ribet, B. (2011). Surfacing disability through a critical race theoretical paradigm. *Georgetown Journal of Modern Critical Race Perspectives 2*, 209, 218.
Roberts, D. E. (1997). *Killing the black body: Race, reproduction, and the meaning of liberty*. Pantheon.
Rogal, L. (2017, Winter). Protecting persons with mental disabilities from making false confessions: Americans with disabilities act as a safeguard. *New Mexico Law Review. 47*, 64. https://law.vanderbilt.edu/files/publications/2017-Lauren-Rogal-NMLR-Protecting-Persons-with-Mental-Disabilities.pdf
Romo, V. (2018, August 8). Federal judge rules against imprisoning those who can't pay court fees. *NPR*. https://www.npr.org/2018/08/06/636187743/federal-judge-rules-against-imprisoning-those-who-cant-pay-court-fees

Salem City Council uses police officer as ASL interpreter. (2018, June). *The Daily Moth.* https://www.facebook.com/TheDailyMoth/videos/869760889892479
Schenwar, M., & Law, V. (2020). *Prison by any other name.* The New Press.
Schenwar, M. (2018, January 14). *Beyond reform, toward the end of policing: An interview with Alex Vitale.* http://www.truth-out.org/opinion/item/43103-beyond-reform-toward-the-end-of-policing-an-interview-with-alex-vitale
Segrest, M. (2020). *Administrations of lunacy: Racism and the haunting of American psychiatry at the Milledgeville asylum.* The New Press.
Settlement Agreement between the United States of America and the New York Police Department (2009, November 18). https://www.ada.gov/nypd.htm
Shaban, B., Bott, M., Villarreal, M., & Carroll, J. (2017, February 21). California schools call police on black students with disabilities far more often than other children. *NBC News.* http://www.nbcbayarea.com/news/local/California-Schools-Call-Police-on-Black-Students-with-Disabilities-Far-More-Often-Than-Other-Children-414433353.html
Siff, A. (2018, June 13). 12,000 deaf New Yorkers to get NYPD-issued cards to help communicate with cops. *NBC New York.* https://www.nbcnewyork.com/news/local/NYPD-Issues-Cards-Deaf-Hearing-Impaired-Drivers-485416341.html
Silver-Greenberg, J., & Dewan, S. (2018, March 31). When bail feels less like freedom, more like extortion. *The New York Times.* https://www.nytimes.com/2018/03/31/us/bail-bonds-extortion.html
Sinyangwe, S. (2017). *Mapping police violence.* https://policeviolencereport.org/
Smith, J. (2010, December 3). Tone deaf: Deaf Austinites say police can't seem to listen to reason. *The Austin Chronicle.* https://www.austinchronicle.com/news/201012–03/tone-deaf/
Smith, S. E. (2012, July 2). The hidden epidemic of undiagnosed disabilities among students of color. *AlterNet.* https://www.alternet.org/story/156119/the_hidden_epidemic_of_undiagnosed_disabilities_among_students_of_color
Smith, S. E. (2016, October 4). Disability is a hidden side of the police violence epidemic. *Vox.* https://www.vox.com/2016/10/4/13161396/disability-police-officer-shooting
Starr, D. (2013, December 9). The interview: Do police interrogation techniques produce false confessions? *The New Yorker.* https://www.newyorker.com/magazine/2013/12/09/the-interview-7
Stein, J. D. (2018, January 12). How to make an innocent client plead guilty. *The Washington Post.* https://www.washingtonpost.com/opinions/why-innocent-people-plead-guilty/2018/01/12/e05d262c-b805–11e7-a908-a3470754bbb9_story.html?utm_term=.5b359240904f
Stein, K. (2003). *The difficulty of ascertaining the number of people with a disability.* Stephen C. v. Bureau of Indian Education, No. CV-17–08004-PCT-SPL. http://www.publiccounsel.org/tools/assets/files/0986.pdf
Stevenson, B. (2015, July 7). *Slavery to mass incarceration.* https://eji.org/videos/slavery-to-mass-incarceration
Tastrom, K. (2020). Disability justice and abolition. *National Lawyers Guild.* https://www.nlg.org/disability-justice-and-abolition/
Taylor, M. T. (1993). *Interpretation skills: English to American Sign Language.* Interpreting Consolidated.
Teplin, L.A., Abram, K. M., McClelland, G. M., Dulcan, M. K., & Mericle, A. A. (2002, December). Psychiatric disorders in youth in juvenile detention. *Archives of General Psychiatry, 59.* https://doi.org/10.1001/archpsyc.59.12.1133

Terence Crutcher's sister speaks to CNN [Video clip]. (2016, September 25). *CNN*. https://www.youtube.com/watch?v=h4N44qoYZPQ

The Sentencing Project. (2018, June). *Trends in U.S. corrections*. https://sentencingproject.org/wp-content/uploads/2016/01/Trends-in-US-Corrections.pdf

Thompson, R. (2018, June 17). Pearl Pearson exclusive. *KFOR Oklahoma's News 4*. https://www.youtube.com/watch?v=mm8Dt5wen3k

Trainum, J. (2016). *How the police generate false confessions: An inside look at the interrogation room*. Rowman & Littlefield.

United States v. City of Portland, Complaint filed 12/17/2012. https://www.clearinghouse.net/chDocs/public/PN-OR-0001-0001.pdf

U.S. Department of Justice, Bureau of Justice Statistics. (1982, December). *Prisoners* 1925–81. https://www.bjs.gov/content/pub/pdf/p2581.pdf

U.S. Department of Justice, Bureau of Justice Statistics. (2006, September 6). *Study finds more than half of all prison and jail inmates have mental health problems*. http://www.bjs.gov/index.cfm?ty=pbdetail&iid=789

U.S. Department of Justice, Bureau of Justice Statistics. (2015, rev. 2016, January 21). *Correctional populations in the United States*, 2014. https://www.bjs.gov/content/pub/pdf/cpus14.pdf

U.S. Department of Justice, Civil Rights Division, Disability Rights Section. (2006, January). *Communicating with people who are deaf or hard of hearing: ADA guide for law enforcement officers*. https://www.ada.gov/lawenfcomm.htm

U.S. Department of Justice, Office of Public Affairs. (2010). *Department enters agreement with Alameda County, California, Sheriff to guarantee effective communication for persons who are deaf, hard of hearing or deaf-blind*. https://www.justice.gov/opa/pr/justice-department-enters-agreement-alameda-county-california-sheriff-guarantee-effective

U.S. Department of Justice, Office of Public Affairs. (2016, May 3). *Justice Department reaches settlement with Columbia, South Carolina, police department to ensure communication access for persons with hearing disabilities*. https://www.justice.gov/opa/pr/justice-department-reaches-settlement-columbia-south-carolina-police-department-ensure

Vallas, R. (2014, September 9). *Disability is a cause and consequence of poverty*. https://talkpoverty.org/2014/09/18/scholars-activists-poverty-data/

Vetscher, T. (2017, August 11). Deaf woman sues city of St. Paul, alleging different treatment. *ABC Eyewitness News*. http://kstp.com/news/deaf-woman-sues-st-paul-alleging-different-treatment/4569713/?cat=1

Vitale, A. S. (2017). *The end of policing*. Verso.

Voigt, R., Camp, N. P., Prabhakaran, V., Hamilton, W. L., Hetey, R. C., Griffiths, C. M., Jurgens, D., Jurafsky, D., & Eberhardt, J. L. (2017, June). Language from police body camera footage shows racial disparities in officer respect. *Proceedings of the National Academy of Sciences, 114*(25), 6521–6526. https://doi.org/10.1073/pnas.1702413114

Wagner, P., & Rauby, B. (2017, January 25). Follow the money of mass incarceration. *Prison Policy Initiative*. https://www.prisonpolicy.org/reports/money.html

Withers, A. J., & Ben-Moshe, L. with Brown, L. X. Z., Erickson, L., Silva Gorman, R. da, Lewis, T. A., McLeod, L., & Mingus, M. (2019). Radical disability politics. In R. Kinna & U. Gordon (Eds.), *Routledge handbook of radical politics* (pp. 178–192). Routledge. https://stillmyrevolution.files.wordpress.com/2019/10/radical-disability-politics.pdf

Worthington, D. (2018, June 5). Two deaf Colorado women sue saying sheriffs, police fail to provide interpreters. *The Denver Post*. https://www.denverpost.com/2018/06/05/denver-jefferson-county-sheriffs-police-lawsuit/

12

Deaf People in the Criminal Justice System: Concluding Thoughts

Debra Guthmann and Gabriel I. Lomas

Throughout this book, content experts have contributed their knowledge about the relatively unexplored topic of deaf people in the criminal justice system. In light of the information shared, the following themes have emerged regarding members of the Deaf community who find themselves engaged with the legal system: accessibility needs; gaps in data collection and the need for more research; additional training for attorneys, court personnel, and prison staff; the need for more qualified sign language interpreters, including certified deaf interpreters (CDIs), who provide services in court, prison, and juvenile facilities; the school-to-prison nexus; and the need for advocacy. This final chapter includes discussion and recommendations of critical points that the contributors have discussed throughout this book.

THEME 1: ACCESSIBILITY NEEDS

At every point in the criminal justice process, deaf people are disadvantaged by the lack of access, centering primarily around communication. As discussed in all of the chapters, hearing individuals should have equal access, starting with the first interaction with law enforcement, in the courtroom, and the prison system, and including specialized programs that may be needed during incarceration and when the deaf person is released.

Issues of accessibility are underscored in Chapter 11 by Lewis, who described the case of John T. Williams, a deaf woodcarver. In this case, a police officer shot five rounds at Mr. Williams after he failed to comply with the verbal orders of the officer. The officer was unaware that Mr. Williams was deaf. Although this case resulted in a lethal outcome, most initial interactions between deaf people and police are not deadly. However, these interactions are often unnecessarily escalated when law enforcement perceives noncompliance with verbal orders.

Poor communication access is at the core of many initial interactions that result in deaf individuals' civil rights being violated.

Once a deaf person is arrested, they will require additional interactions with the legal system: representation from an attorney and possible engagement in court-ordered services (such as anger management courses, parent training, drug treatment, and other programs courts use to reduce incarceration). Challenges with communication access usually persist because there are a limited number of treatment providers who provide specialized services in American Sign Language (ASL). Attorneys and judges may not request interpreters, resulting in delayed adjudication. Often, deaf people arrested for drug crimes cannot access treatment in community-based programs (see Chapter 5). The same is true once incarcerated because treatment programs available to hearing inmates are often inaccessible to deaf inmates. Many prisons may provide deaf inmates with teletypewriters (TTYs) for use when making calls but have not set up videophones, which are most commonly used when placing calls. In fact, TTYs are becoming obsolete because they are slow and cumbersome to use. Although hearing inmates are usually permitted to make phone calls, many deaf inmates are not provided with a videophone to make calls to family or friends. However, some prisons give inmates access. Visual alerts such as flashing lights to indicate a transition time are also rarely provided. Deaf inmates who are unaware of transition times may receive punishment for failing to follow the rules. Communication access problems persist even after inmates are released and returned to their community. In Chapter 9, Taylor and Weisberg discuss the Americans With Disabilities Act (ADA) in detail. Under Title II, public entities need to give "primary consideration" to the requests of individuals with disabilities, which means staff who work within a prison setting, if it is a public entity, should consult with the deaf individual when deciding on which auxiliary aid or service will be provided.

1. **Comprehensive communication assessments.** Communication assessments (see Chapter 2) should be used and are vital when the court is trying to determine whether a deaf individual is competent or likely to gain competence in the future. Once incarcerated, communication assessments should be developed and utilized for all inmates to periodically reevaluate the assessment tools to ensure accommodations or modifications create equal access for each individual.
2. **Visual notifications.** Visual notifications should be used along with all auditory notifications in prison (e.g., flashing lights to signal different events, marquee screens to provide scheduling information for the day).
3. **Clustered inmate housing.** When possible, deaf inmates should be housed together, being careful not to violate federal disability rights law requirements not to discriminate, segregate, or isolate. Just as hearing people require communication with others, deaf people also need a critical mass of deaf peers for healthy psychological development and emotional stability. We know that placing a hearing person in an isolated prison setting (solitary confinement)

is one of the most severe penalties available to jailers. Similarly, a deaf person placed in a general prison population without any deaf peers is isolated from their peer group. It is also important to note that the severity of the crime should be a factor when determining placement in the penal system. Deaf people who are convicted of minor crimes should not be housed with people (hearing or deaf) convicted of more serious crimes.

4. **Accessible treatment.** Deaf individuals should have the opportunity to participate in accessible treatment options while incarcerated. Any services provided to hearing inmates should be available to deaf inmates. Access to addiction treatment for deaf people, who are incarcerated or not, is challenging. For inmates convicted of a crime involving drugs or alcohol, treatment may be a condition for parole but is not always available to deaf inmates. Often, it is not that deaf inmates refuse treatment but that treatment is not an option offered to them (see Chapter 5).
5. **Cognitive and linguistic development.** We must disrupt the school-to-prison nexus by ensuring that deaf children and youth have access to quality language development, especially quality ASL instruction and interpreters (see Chapter 4). Schools should focus on having trained behavior specialists to help lessen acting-out behaviors in the school setting. Additionally, trauma-informed teaching at schools is essential to prevent behavior escalation. Clear training on adverse childhood experiences (ACEs) and factors that build resiliency in deaf children should be included when training all educators, helping professionals, and school leaders.
6. **Accessible standardized tests.** Psychological evaluations should be done by skilled clinicians who are experienced in test administration and interpretation with deaf people. Many tests are inappropriate to administer to a deaf person. Some tests are appropriate, but, owing to language complexities, should be given using direct communication, that is, by someone fluent in ASL and not using a sign language interpreter. Results should be interpreted and reported by clinicians who understand the implications of hearing loss, sign language, and the culture of deaf people. When possible, video-based standardized tests that have been validated can be used as they maintain standardization. Recent grant funds have resulted in the validation of a small number of assessments and screeners related to mental health, substance use, and an interest profiler in ASL. We recommend the use of these instruments, when possible. We also recommend the continued growth of validating more assessments in ASL using internet-based portals. However, it should be noted that a video-based test administered in ASL does not replace a signing clinician with knowledge of the deaf world. ASL-fluent clinicians can use video-based tests to improve standardization and provide fair and accurate reports.
7. **Videophones in prisons and jails.** No-cost videophones should be installed in prisons and jails throughout the United States so deaf inmates have the same ability to make approved phone calls as incarcerated hearing individuals. Additionally, requests for proposals for inmate calling services should include an updated section on deaf access such that contractors' services

always include products compatible with videophones, remote video interpreting, telephones with amplification capabilities, captioned telephones, etc.

8. **Prerecorded materials in ASL.** Providing video material in ASL could help inmates better understand the admission and orientation procedures, including prison rules, expectations, and daily schedules. Prison handbooks vary in their reading levels, with some written above the 12th-grade level (Goben et al., 2009). With the average reading level of deaf adults below grade level (Moores, 2001), it is likely that many deaf inmates do not understand the printed materials given to them when incarcerated.
9. **Safety and threat assessments.** Because deaf inmates are at risk for mistreatment and/or abuse by guards, other correctional employees, and other inmates, it is critical to provide safe, appropriate, and accessible facilities and programming to ensure their safety while incarcerated and to facilitate successful reentry upon release. Prison officials and other stakeholders should assess for safety and potential threats at each stage of the legal process and make all necessary safety provisions. Inmates who experience heightened trauma during incarceration are less likely to integrate well into the community after release.
10. **Support in aftercare or after release.** Deaf people have few resources to turn to when released from prison or jail. After being released, hearing people describe life-changing treatment after "hitting bottom." At that point, they may receive treatment and return home, working to rebuild their lives. Deaf people lack access to support services during and after treatment. After being released from prison, many deaf people have nowhere to go, as there are no halfway homes or other supportive living programs in most communities. This is an additional barrier to their rehabilitation, thwarting their desire to rebuild their lives.

THEME 2: GAPS IN DATA COLLECTION AND RESEARCH

There is a considerable lack of data related to deaf individuals within the legal system. Researching this area would benefit from information about deaf individuals involved with every stage of the system, particularly the number of deaf people who go through juvenile and adult courtrooms, reasons for charges, the numbers of juvenile and adult deaf inmates, and types of services requested and provided at each stage (interpreting as well as treatment and other clinical services).

1. **Create an ADA clearinghouse for all inmates.** Having a clearinghouse of information would help to better understand and address the needs of the deaf population. It is difficult to demonstrate need when little is known about the numbers of deaf individuals being served.

   In Chapter 1, Paris and Kessler mention a study done by The Bureau of Justice Statistics (BJS) in 2011 to 2012, which was based on prison and jail inmate self-reported data from the BJS's 2011 to 2012 National Inmate Survey (Bronson et al., 2015). This report used six questions to measure disabilities that were modeled after the 2012 American Community Survey, conducted by the U.S. Census Bureau. One of the questions asked was "are you deaf, or do you have serious difficulty hearing?" They looked at the prevalence of disabilities among prison and jail inmates and found that 32% of prisoners and 40% of jail inmates reported having at least one disability. Because the survey asks the inmates if they are deaf or have serious difficulty hearing, on the basis of this information, a report could be developed that focuses only on those who would be part of this group. This kind of data is critical to federal, state, and local policymakers in combating crime and ensuring that justice is both efficient and evenhanded. Much of the current research reflects estimates of disabilities among the general population and does not include information specifically about deaf inmates.

2. **Provide data on types of crime, disability, and sentences for all inmates.** There are likely to be differences between deaf individuals' experiences within the criminal justice system and those of hearing people. Crimes that occur within the deaf population are essentially the same as those that happen within the general population, although they may stem from different experiences arising from linguistic and cultural issues. It seems once deaf people are in the criminal justice system, they may be at risk for staying there longer or leaving without having addressed their problematic behavior. Understanding the type of crime and length of stay of all prisoners will allow researchers to better examine the root causes of the prevalence of incarceration with deaf people. It will also allow prison officials to ensure accommodation and evenhandedness in probation and parole hearings.
3. **Create multidisciplinary research teams with deaf experts.** Solid research teams should include both deaf and hearing people who are experts in stakeholder groups. Teams might include scholars in law enforcement, prison management, education, prevention, mental health, medicine, child welfare, sign language interpretation, rehabilitation, substance abuse, and other related areas. Although some research from the general population may transfer over to the deaf population, most research does not address the specific experiences of subpopulations in the legal system. Including deaf and hearing experts on research teams who know the Deaf community will help significantly with trust issues between deaf people, practitioners, and academics. Researching the deaf population requires communication access with inmates who are often compromised in language development. A diverse research team of multiple experts ensures that they can assess the language used by deaf participants.
4. **Conduct research using various methodologies.** For a complete picture of the deaf experience, we recommend that both qualitative and quantitative studies be done. The collection of quantitative and qualitative data can provide the mechanism for clearly and accurately portraying the experiences of deaf prisoners and lead to changes in policies that can create conditions to enhance justice.

    Deaf experts and professionals should be included at every step of the research process. Include deaf professionals from disciplines such as linguistics, psychology, interpretation, and research and evaluation.

    Some essential points of research with deaf people in the legal system include: (a) age of onset; (b) type of hearing loss; (c) severity of loss; (d) communication mode; (e) race and ethnic group; (f) education and training (pre-K through adult); (f) employment status; (g) participation in government-supported programs, for example, vocational rehabilitation (supplemental security income [SSI], social security disability insurance [SSDI]); (h) marital status; (i) use of assistive technologies (pre-K through adult); (j) medical circumstances, including multiple disabilities; and (k) subjective levels of importance of specific life experiences, for example, preferred mode of communication, education experience (quality and type), opportunities to function within both the deaf and hearing worlds, and perhaps others. It may also be worthwhile to collect information from parents of deaf children and youth in the juvenile system. Such data could address anticipated or chosen communication, academic, social, and assistive technologies. These data points could also help identify factors that contribute to the school-to-prison nexus.

5. **Factors that affect resiliency in deaf children.** We recommend that significant research priorities be given to ACEs and deaf children. Emphasis should be placed on language deprivation and outcomes in deaf adults. Additionally, we recommend research on school practices that promote resiliency, especially social-emotional learning, and other ecological approaches to growing both empathy and self-regulation.
6. **Law enforcement and deaf people.** Training varies from jurisdiction to jurisdiction. Furthermore, law enforcement officials change jobs, take promotions, and change agencies regularly. Creating a web-based national training for law enforcement personnel is an idea worth exploring. Committees should be formed that bring together members of the Deaf community and law enforcement to grow understanding, knowledge, and skill when working with this population. Research priorities should be focused on improving early interactions between deaf people and law enforcement officers, including initial encounters. Research should also focus on effective treatment and diversionary programs and growing the workforce to support these programs. Develop and make available a database that includes encounters with deaf people and all reports of arrests as well as weapons discharged in those encounters. Gather and report data that identifies the type of accommodations provided at various stages of interaction within the criminal justice system.
7. **Courtroom considerations.** In our experience, deaf people may be held in jail while they await their trial largely because they are a marginalized population and may lack the information necessary to handle preparations for court. Many deaf people live on disability income or are unemployed or underemployed. They are unable to post bail and often do not know how to navigate the system. Furthermore, it is our experience that they are held for longer periods of time because busy court clerks and attorneys fail to request accommodations for court hearings and trials. When the deaf person appears in court, they may be remanded to jail to wait longer for want of an interpreter to facilitate communication. It may be of interest to examine the number of days held before adjudication and the accommodations provided for hearings and trials, as well as outcomes of hearings and trials. Furthermore, data could be collected on the attorneys who represent the deaf clients, how many

deaf clients have been served by the attorney, whether they have specialized training in disability law, whether they used accommodations in their pretrial meetings, and whether they felt prepared to handle the case of a deaf client.

8. **Deaf youth and schools.** Both public schools and schools for deaf students often underreport information on deaf students who are involved in the juvenile justice system. It would be of interest to know antecedents of arrests, number of arrests, total number of deaf students served, and the demographics of those arrested. Additionally, it would be helpful to know how the student was served after being taken to the juvenile detention facility or whether the school continued to serve them. Public schools are already required to report a great deal of disability-related information to government agencies, but law enforcement and prisons are often exempt from these requirements even though the juvenile is of school age and receiving educational services. Research on the various interventions attempted by the school and community would be useful because this would contribute to the body of knowledge on effective preventive and interventive programming.
9. **Recidivism and deaf people.** Data should be gathered on the types of accessible, community-based services that were available to deaf people who reoffend and those who do not reoffend. Many communities lack accessible support services such as ASL-fluent mental health providers, substance abuse treatment, peer support, and transitional housing programs, as well as other essential options.
10. **Higher education and deaf people.** A consortium of institutions of higher education should be given the authority and obligation to pool monies and personnel with the goal of establishing a clearinghouse of data collected in order to offer a more accurate and comprehensive picture of the experience of deaf people with law enforcement, in court, and during incarceration. Initially, these institutions might focus on the development and dissemination of data collection instruments to achieve mutual goals. The goal would be for these institutions to develop reports and research on trends and best practices when working with deaf people. The institutions should study the legal system, the child welfare system, the foster care system, the law enforcement system, and the school system, among other systems that overlap with law enforcement and carceral systems. However, each of these systems must be examined as they relate to deaf children and youth.
11. **Diversity among deaf people.** The heterogeneity of the deaf population makes subcategorization crucial but also challenging. Multiple variables, some within the individual's control and some not, influence the biopsychosocial development of the individual; for example, having deaf or hearing parents, literacy level, education opportunities, age of onset of hearing loss, and presence of disabilities. The differences between the experiences of deaf people compared with hearing people and risk factors must be considered. ACEs and other environmental factors can reflect the offender's engagement with society and investment in more informed or less informed standards of conduct.

12. **Prison services and deaf people.** Once deaf people are in the legal system, they appear to be at risk of staying there longer or leaving without having addressed their offending behavior. Strategic changes in respect of how deaf people are treated in prisons, with the development of specialist deaf prison services akin to those in mental health, would address this and promote desistance in deaf offenders. Further research would be supported if governments kept records of defendants' and prisoners' hearing status and language skills alongside those of their age, gender, and criminal history. This knowledge would allow a more detailed analysis of common challenges deaf people face in the legal system (see Chapter 6).
13. **The correlation between mental health and deaf individuals.** Provide more academic research on the correlation between mental health and deaf individuals. Understanding the factors that disrupt the school-to-prison nexus and how to promote resiliency is essential to disruption. Furthermore, additional academic research on the efficacy of contemporary mental health interventions with deaf youth would help to identify evidence-based practices with this population.

THEME 3: TRAINING FOR ATTORNEYS, COURT PERSONNEL, AND PRISON STAFF

Training for law enforcement, court, and prison personnel is needed to ensure that deaf individuals have equal access to the programming and services that are available to the general population. Several commentators in this volume (Lewis, Chapter 11; Guthmann & Kolvitz, Chapter 5; and Williams, Chapter 2) wrote about the need for communication access. Prison staff may wrongly believe that deaf individuals can communicate effectively and obtain information through lipreading, even though research shows that less than one-third of information given is visible on the lips (Jeffers & Barley, 1971). Additionally, prison staff may feel that any information provided in written English, such as the inmate handbook or documents during intake and booking, will be understood clearly, even though the average reading level of the majority of deaf individuals is below grade level. Prison staff may be unaware of the cultural differences as well as communication and language challenges faced by many deaf individuals. Staff may also believe that raising their voices will enable a deaf person to hear and understand them. In most situations, these are not effective ways for many deaf inmates to communicate or obtain information. Because few prison staff know anything about ASL or Deaf culture, there are situations where correctional officers may be abusive toward deaf inmates. This is especially true if the officer does not know the inmate is deaf and thinks they are not following a directive. Examples of this were offered by Guthmann and Kolvitz, Chapter 5, in their description of how deaf inmates may find themselves in these kinds of negative situations where they are treated unfairly or even injured because the officer failed to communicate effectively.

1. **Provide training for prison staff.** Training is critical for prison staff who interact with deaf people. Training staff on how to more effectively communicate and work with deaf inmates will help to de-escalate conflicts and provide more effective inmate programming. Training should be provided at the initial hire and be ongoing throughout the career of prison staff members. Additionally, incentives could be offered for staff who learn ASL. Prison staff should also receive general disability awareness training, including specific information related to deaf individuals. The training should help to break down stigmatizing attitudes and emphasize that these individuals have the same rights as all other inmates. Training should ensure not only that deaf individuals have the same access to services and benefits as other inmates but also that they are protected from discrimination, violence, or abuse by prison staff or other detainees. Staff should also be given training information on basic mental health issues and the prevention of suicide. Some states have deaf offices with staff trained and able to assist in delivering these kinds of training programs at least on an annual basis. The presence of an ADA coordinator who knows sign language in each prison across the United States would also drastically help improve conditions for deaf people in prison.
2. **Provide training for staff working with juveniles.** The school-to-prison nexus is clearly documented and exists within the deaf population (Lomas, Chapter 4). Some of the issues may be related to language dysfluency and deficits in language development as well as a poor fund of information that can lead to misunderstandings when interacting with law enforcement and the criminal justice system. There are many examples of deaf youth being placed in juvenile justice settings and not receiving access to education and other interventions that are legally mandated under the Individuals With Disabilities Education Act and other federal laws (Lomas, Chapter 4; Shaw, Chapter 8). Educators, researchers, and other practitioners working with this population need to be aware of the school-to-prison nexus and aim to identify resources that lead to improved outcomes. Scientific studies show that early intervention is critical to prevention (Felitti et al., 1998). Efforts to disrupt the school-to-prison nexus must include skill building with deaf children, healthy attachment between caregivers and children, an understanding of legal rights under disability-related laws, as well as self-advocacy skills. For staff working with deaf youth in juvenile detention, trainings similar to those who work with adults who are deaf should be ongoing. At every stage of training, deaf people should be involved in the development, delivery, and assessment of training programs.
3. **Staff training on substance use disorders considerations for deaf individuals.** Prisons should use appropriately trained health care professionals to screen, assess, and treat substance-involved inmates using comprehensive, evidence-based approaches tailored to the needs of offenders. Often, deaf people with addiction problems find themselves incarcerated for drug- or

alcohol-related offenses. Many prisons offer treatment for addicted inmates but often do not make their treatment accessible for deaf inmates (Guthmann and Kolvitz, Chapter 5). Whenever possible, deaf inmates should be housed in larger urban areas where there is a greater likelihood that qualified interpreters will be available to work with mental health and addiction providers.

4. **Considerations for training court personnel.** Court personnel must have training on the importance of having interpreters when working with deaf clients and how to use them (see Chapter 7). For all court proceedings, it is essential to have at least two interpreters, one for the court and the other for the table where the deaf person sits with their attorney. If a proceeding is expected to last more than an hour, it is recommended that a minimum of four interpreters are used so each interpreter can be relieved from the repetitive movements inherent in sign language interpreting. Many deaf people who end up in court have limited language abilities. Thus, a certified deaf interpreter should be used to facilitate communication for the ASL interpreters. Regular training should be in place for judges and attorneys to help them understand the complexity of the interpreting process, as well as the key role interpreters have in facilitating the delivery of justice. Essential to the delivery of justice is that a defendant be able to understand the charges against them and contribute to their defense. In the case of deaf people with language and learning challenges, assessments of language and cognition should be the norm to establish that they can participate in their own defense (see Chapter 2).

THEME 4: QUALIFIED SIGN LANGUAGE INTERPRETERS

Contributors identified a need to increase the number of qualified sign language interpreters.

1. **Set minimum standards.** It is recommended that the interpreter community, organizations that oversee interpreter education and certification, members of the Deaf community, and advocates develop a training program focused on improving the skills of legal interpreting for certified interpreters and CDIs. Stakeholders should introduce legislation on the federal and/or state levels to provide consistent training requirements for court interpreters. Some states have requirements for the conduct of all court interpreters, and those standards should be applied where appropriate.
2. **Establish mental health interpreter certification.** In addition to legal interpreting requirements, there is a need to develop certification for interpreters working in mental health settings and substance abuse programs, particularly since many deaf prisoners have a high prevalence of co-occurring disorders. Sign language interpreters or other sources of appropriate access should be utilized for the provision of self-help groups such as 12-step meetings for deaf individuals.

3. **Establish a commission on legal interpreting in each state.** Establish state-level commissions on interpreting issues led by an interested State Supreme Court Justice with representation from district, circuit, and municipal courts, practicing attorneys, court administrators, deaf consumers, and interpreter leaders. The development of a commission on legal interpreting will ensure more consistent standards of practice in courtrooms across the country.

THEME 5: SCHOOL-TO-PRISON NEXUS AND DEAF YOUTH

There is substantial evidence that many inmates in the general population were propelled there by school systems ill-equipped to serve them. The same is true for deaf youth, who are often isolated in public schools and receive little to no mental health treatment when needed.

Recommendations to disrupt the school-to-prison nexus include the following:

1. **Invest heavily in parent-education programs and early childhood education to improve resiliency in deaf children and youth.** Studies show that a positive parental connection is one of the greatest tools a child can have to build resiliency. Parents of deaf children should have free access to ASL classes, parent training, and other programs known to foster communication and attachment.
2. **Develop intentional practices in the child welfare system to recruit and train more deaf and ASL-fluent foster parents.** Aim to hire staff who can meet the needs of deaf parents who are struggling with parenting. When possible, find deaf parent mentors who can help parents of deaf children. Ensure that investigative and other units in state child welfare agencies can communicate in ASL.
3. **Eliminate zero-tolerance policies in public schools.** Zero-tolerance policies often assign strict punishments for infractions that may be caused by misunderstandings and should be treated on a case-by-case basis. Earlier in the book, there is an example (Lomas, Chapter 4) in which a deaf child with generally good behavior took attention deficit hyperactivity disorder medication to school and was subsequently arrested and expelled for a drug offense. The harsh punishment may not have been handed down if not for the zero-tolerance policy.
4. **Improve legal rights and civics education in schools.** Deaf people have legal protections under disability laws, but most deaf young adults have neither the knowledge nor the skills to articulate laws when necessary and advocate for themselves.
5. **Ensure language access in schools and in carceral facilities.** Language access is critical for overall psychological development. Deaf children need not only communication access but also peers with whom they can communicate. Deaf children should attend schools with significant numbers of deaf

peers so they do not suffer from greater isolation. Likewise, it is essential that deaf inmates be housed together when possible so they have a peer group with whom they can socialize and communicate.

6. **Invest in research aimed at building resilient deaf youth.** Disrupting the school-to-prison nexus will require research to improve outcomes. Although scholarship on the general population is helpful, deaf children and youth have unique language experiences that raise risk factors associated with higher rates of incarceration. To address these unique experiences, expert scholars should conduct research focused on improving resiliency, the role of language fluency (dysfluency) in the carceral population, parent–child attachment with deaf children and adult outcomes, and other areas.

THEME 6: THE NEED FOR ADVOCACY

Only in the past decade has the light begun to shine on the deaf experience in the legal system. Now that some information has surfaced, advocacy is warranted (see Lewis, Chapter 11). Helping Educate to Advance the Rights of the Deaf is one of only a few organizations that offer advocacy for deaf people in prison. The civil rights of deaf people are violated daily during interactions with law enforcement and the justice system. Considering the dire need for advocacy, we make the following recommendations:

1. **Establish an office of the special advocate in each state.** Some states have dedicated offices within their state government infrastructure to advocate for marginalized populations. These offices, staffed by ASL-fluent personnel, preferably qualified deaf people, should be in all states and should ensure that deaf people receive access in the legal system.
2. **Mandate that all inmates with disabilities have the right to an advocate at all hearings, including parole and probation.** Often, deaf people have difficulty navigating the legal system, including nuanced parts of it. Hearings are often difficult to understand, even with qualified interpreters. An advocate would be able to explain the situation, both to the judge/board and to the deaf person.
3. **Develop scholarship on advocacy that is specific to the forensic population.** Studies have shown that people with mild to moderate disabilities are often prone to false confessions. Although little hard data exists to prove that this is happening with deaf people, it is likely to be the case. It is essential to work toward disrupting false confessions by improving interrogation practices. This area will require heavy advocacy to stimulate change.

THEME 7: PLANNING FOR THE FUTURE

We hope readers have found within these pages a variety of critical tools for advocacy, education, and action in the field. Although there has been progress in some areas, there is much work ahead. There is a need to have a larger representation of deaf professionals in the criminal justice system, including judges, attorneys, experts, and CDIs. Changes must occur in how deaf people are treated during the process spanning first interactions to release from incarceration. Strategic changes are needed in the treatment of deaf people in prisons, by developing trained professionals who can work with this population in order to help address issues that have occurred with deaf people.

REFERENCES

Bronson, J., Maruschak, L., & Berzofsky, M. (2015). *Disabilities among prison and jail inmates, 2011–2012.* http://www.bjs.gov/index.cfm?ty=pbdetail&iid=5500

Felietti, V. J., Anda, R. F., Nordenberg, D., Williamson, D. F., Spitz, A. M., Edwards, V., Koss, M. P., & Marks, J. S. (1998). Relationship of child abuse and household dysfunction to many of the leading causes of death in adults. The Adverse Childhood Experiences Study. *American Journal of Preventive Medicine, 14*(4), 245–258. https://doi.org/10.1016/s0749-3797(98)00017-8

Goben, B., Enos, K., & Andrews, J. (2009). *What to do? In jail but can't read the inmate handbook: Solutions for the Deaf offender* [Unpublished manuscript]. Lamar University.

Jeffers J., & Barley, M. (1971). *Speechreading (lipreading).* Thomas.

Moores, D. (2001). *Educating the deaf: Psychology, principles, and practices* (5th ed.). Cengage Press.

Contributors

Sally Austen, BA (Hons), MSc, PhD, consultant clinical psychologist, has worked with Deaf and deafened people for over 25 years. She has two jobs. She works for the National Health Service (NHS) in specialist deaf adult mental health services. The NHS funds three such inpatient units for adults in England and a further three community services; child services have one inpatient unit and three community hubs. Austen's private work at Austen Psychology involves undertaking expert witness court reports, training and supervision of both clinicians in deafness and interpreters in mental health, and psychological consultation to the media. She is the coeditor of *Deafness in Mind* and *Deafness and Challenging Behaviour*.

Amber D. Farrelly, JD, received her undergraduate degree from the University of Oklahoma and her Juris Doctorate from Arizona State University's Sandra Day O'Connor College of Law with the highest distinction for her pro bono work. Farrelly began her legal career clerking for both defense teams in the yogurt shop murders shortly after their reversals in 2007 until both cases were dismissed in 2009. She began practicing as a criminal defense attorney in 2009 and has worked with the Innocence Project, Innocence Project of Texas, and the Texas Civil Rights Project. Farrelly is licensed in and practices throughout the state of Texas and in the U.S. Western District. She specializes in Deaf clientele and is a Board for Evaluation of Interpreters court-certified interpreter in American Sign Language (ASL). Working with the Conviction Integrity Unit in Dallas County, she testified as an expert witness on ASL and Deaf culture in the Stephen Brodie exoneration case—the only Deaf person exonerated in the United States. She has consulted and testified in numerous cases involving Deaf individuals as an expert. Farrelly is the former president and current director of the Texas School for the Deaf Foundation Board. She is dedicated to and is an advocate for the Deaf. Farrelly received the Texas Society of Interpreters for the Deaf President's Award in 2016. She was named Travis County Woman Lawyer of the Year for 2012. She has given numerous presentations and workshops on legal interpreting and Deaf rights. She has also been a guest on *48 Hours, Full*

Frontal With Samantha Bee, America's Most Wanted, Intersections Radio, and *Legal Broadcast Network.*

Debra Guthmann, EdD, NIC, is a nationally recognized lecturer, administrator, researcher, educator, and advocate with 40 years of extensive experience in service to the Deaf community. Guthmann was the lead consultant for a federal grant at Wright State University focusing on the validation of mental health, substance abuse, and career-related screening tools in ASL. She is the founding director of the Minnesota Substance Use Disorder Program for Deaf and Hard of Hearing Individuals, which opened in 1989 and was one of the first inpatient treatment programs for deaf and hard of hearing (DHH) individuals in the country. Guthmann worked 17 years as the director of student services at the California School for the Deaf in Fremont, California, where she was responsible for admissions, clinical services, individualized education program implementation, and due process. She teaches online classes focusing on substance abuse and ethical considerations within the Deaf community. Guthmann has made over 200 national and international presentations and written numerous articles and several book chapters focusing on ethical issues, substance abuse, and treatment models to use with DHH individuals. She has also been involved in the development of a number of materials specifically designed for deaf individuals, including an Anti-Tobacco and HIV Prevention Curriculum, a training DVD for clinicians, and e-cigarette prevention materials. Additionally, Guthmann has served on a number of advisory boards and is the past president of the American Deafness and Rehabilitation Association (ADARA) and the National Association on Alcohol, Drugs and Disability.

Raychelle Harris, PhD, is currently doing authoring work for TRUE+WAY ASL curriculum with her coauthors, and recently published the second edition of *Exploring Deaf Communities* with her coauthors. In the past decade, she was a full professor in the Department of American Sign Language at Gallaudet University, Washington, DC, spending most of her time directing and teaching in the Master's in Sign Language Education program. She has worked as a Deaf interpreter and translator for over a decade. Her research interests include specialized discourses in ASL, language pedagogy, digital curriculum design and development, and language assessment. She has also spoken, presented, and published about research ethics and the cultural and linguistic aspects of teaching, interpreting, and researching with Deaf communities. She holds professional certification with the American Sign Language Teachers Association (ASLTA), is certified with the Board for Evaluation of Interpreters (BEI), and is a licensed Texas Court interpreter.

E. Basil Kessler, PhD, is an assistant professor in Counselor Education at Emporia State University. He has been professionally involved in the Deaf community of Kansas since the early 1980s. He began as the director of services at the first national social service agency for the DHH, Deaf and Hard of Hearing

Counseling Services in Wichita, Kansas. Through his work at the local and state levels, he was appointed to the board of directors of the Kansas Commission for the Deaf and Hard of Hearing. He served in this capacity as the interpreter representative, the mental health representative, and, finally, as an ex-officio member representing the Kansas State Department of Education (KSDE). Kessler served as an instructor in the Rehabilitation Services Education program at Emporia State University before becoming a program consultant with the KSDE. In that position, he worked with the educational interpreting community along with audiologists and speech pathologists across the state. He was closely involved in the Kansas Deaf-Blind Project and helped develop the Usher Syndrome Screening protocol and guidelines for that state. For 12 years, he ran the Kansas Alternative Finance Program before returning to the classroom, where he is currently an assistant professor and co-coordinator of the clinical counseling program at Emporia State University.

Marcia E. Kolvitz, PhD, is a consultant who focuses on issues related to education, vocational rehabilitation, and transition services. She has over 30 years of experience addressing education and access issues for students who are deaf and hard of hearing in K–12 programs and postsecondary educational settings. She is a frequent presenter at state, regional, and national conferences related to deafness and disability issues. Kolvitz completed a doctorate at the University of Tennessee in Human Ecology (emphasis: Human Resource Development). She has a master of arts degree and a bachelor of science degree in Communication Disorders (emphasis: Counseling Individuals Who Are Deaf and Hard of Hearing) from Northern Illinois University.

Talila A. Lewis, Esq, (no gender pronouns), is a community lawyer, educator, and organizer who works to ground all social justice movements in disability justice. Lewis's current work primarily focuses on helping people understand the inextricable links between ableism, racism, classism, and all other forms of systemic oppression and structural inequity. Recognized as a White House Champion of Change and one of *Pacific Standard Magazine's* Top 30 Thinkers Under 30, Lewis cofounded and serves as the volunteer director of HEARD, a cross-disability abolitionist community organization that focuses on supporting deaf people affected by mass incarceration. Lewis created the only national database of imprisoned deaf/blind people and works with HEARD to abolish the medical-carceral industrial complex; correct wrongful convictions of deaf/disabled people; and support multiply marginalized disabled people affected by all forms of incarceration; among other things. Lewis, a founding member of the Harriet Tubman Collective and cocreator of the Disability Solidarity praxis, also serves as a consultant for social justice organizations, and as an attorney and expert on cases involving disabled people. Lewis previously served as the Givelber Public Interest Lecturer at Northeastern University School of Law and as a visiting professor at the Rochester Institute of Technology/National Technical Institute for the Deaf. A recent graduate of American University

Washington College of Law, Lewis has received awards from numerous universities, the American Association for People with Disabilities, the American Bar Association, Congresswoman Eleanor Holmes Norton, *EBONY,* National Black Deaf Advocates, and the Nation Institute, among others. Lewis is a member of the inaugural cohorts for the Roddenberry Fellowship and the Atlantic Fellowship for Racial Equity.

Gabriel I. Lomas, PhD, is a professor of counseling in the Department of Education and Educational Psychology at Western Connecticut State University. Lomas has significant experience in psychological testing and counseling with DHH people. In particular, he worked closely with victims and offenders on thousands of child welfare cases in Texas and across the nation. He has performed countless forensic evaluations for judges and lawyers. He is frequently consulted as an expert witness in cases involving DHH victims and defendants. Lomas has published and presented widely in the area of counseling, child welfare, and assessment with DHH children and adults.

Gabriel A. "Tony" Martin, EdD, was the chair of the Department of Deaf Studies and Deaf Education at Lamar University for over 20 years and, prior to his passing in October 2016, served as the executive director of the Office of Planning and Assessment and the liaison of the Southern Association of Colleges and Schools–Commission on Colleges for Lamar University. He had a total of 33 years of teaching and teacher training in the field of deaf education. Martin was fluent in ASL and taught undergraduate, graduate, and doctoral-level courses. His primary areas of interest included educational and deaf law, administration and leadership, and higher education issues. He was an active grant writer and manager.

Donna M. Mertens, PhD, is a professor emeritus at Gallaudet University, Washington, DC. Mertens taught research methods and evaluation to deaf and hearing students at the master's and doctoral levels for over 30 years. She is now an independent consultant and continues to publish a number of books on conducting research on marginalized populations, using a transformative perspective.

Sue O'Rourke, ClinPsyD, was qualified as a clinical psychologist in 1989 and specializes in mental health and deafness. She has worked in NHS mental health services for deaf people and specializes in working with deaf offenders with mental health needs in secures services. Since 2011 she has also worked as an independent practitioner, providing psychological reports to the courts. She has carried out research relating to deaf people in the criminal justice system, on behalf of the Department of Health. She has a number of publications relating to forensic mental health and deafness and has presented at national and international conferences. For over 20 years, she has carried out many medicolegal assessments and works as an expert witness in relation to criminal, personal injury, and family proceedings involving deaf people. She has particular expertise assisting the courts in relation to vulnerable witnesses and defendants. She is lead author of the *Advocates Gateway's Tool Kit on Deafness,* a publication used by legal professionals in the United Kingdom, and is a qualified sign language interpreter.

Damara Goff Paris, EdD, is an associate professor and Rehabilitation Services Administration grant director at Emporia State University's Counselor Education program. She was the doctoral program director of Lamar University's Deaf Studies/Deaf Education program for several years and taught in higher education courses part-time for over 15 years. She has worked in professional capacities for private, nonprofit, corporate, and government agencies, including counseling and managing the Connection Program (a nonprofit mental health facility for Deaf individuals), program management of the Telecommunication Access Programs at the Oregon Public Utility Commission, and national marketing director for Sprint Relay. During her tenure at the Connection program, she served as an advocate for individuals who were incarcerated or went through the criminal justice system as defendants and also as an expert witness on some cases. A lifelong advocate for Deaf individuals, particularly Deaf women and Deaf Native Americans, she has provided support to these populations and was awarded the NAD Randall McClelland Memorial Award, OAD Woman of the Year, and Deaf Women of Achievement Award. Recently awarded the ESU Teacher's College Excellence in Scholarly Activities award, she continues to research the intersectionalities of being Deaf, Native American, and female. She currently serves as the president of ADARA.

Daniel Shaw, JD, has spent years representing hundreds of children and families throughout the State of California in special education, civil rights, and personal injury cases. He began his career working as a service coordinator for the Regional Center system, serving individuals with developmental disabilities. As a parent of a child with profound hearing loss, Shaw has sat on all sides of the table. He knows firsthand what it is like to have a child with special needs and be faced with numerous obstacles to their success. His daughter helped shaped his passion for the law and the families he serves. Shaw is an expert litigator with extensive experience litigating at the administrative level, district and state court, and the Ninth Circuit Court of Appeals. He has obtained numerous successes before the Office of Administrative Hearings, the U.S. District Court, and the Ninth Circuit Court of Appeals.

Theresa Smith, PhD, has long been both a practicing interpreter and an educator of interpreters. She holds a BA in English literature and education, an MA in counseling, both from Seattle University, and a PhD in sociocultural anthropology from the University of Washington; her dissertation was titled

"Deaf People in Context." Additionally, she is certified by the Registry of Interpreters for the Deaf (RID) in legal interpreting with the Specialist Certificate: Legal (SC:L) as well as the now defunct MCSC. Being frustrated by the limits of a traditional interpreter training program, which she coordinated for 14 years, Smith and colleagues cofounded the American Sign Language Interpreting School of Seattle, which she then directed from 1989 to 2007. During this time, she was active as a key figure in the emergence of the now well-known DeafBlind community in Seattle, after which she wrote a seminal text *Guidelines for Working and Socializing With DeafBlind Adults*. In addition to writing curricula and articles, she has served on numerous professional boards and committees. Although these interests and activities may seem unrelated, the themes that emerge connecting literature, education, counseling, anthropology, and interpreting are those of human communication, social justice, and community activism.

Barry C. Taylor, JD, is the vice president for civil rights and systemic litigation at Equip for Equality (EFE), where he has worked since 1996. At EFE, he has overseen many individual and systemic disability discrimination cases, and he is currently cocounsel in six Americans With Disabilities Act (ADA) class actions, including in *Holmes v. Baldwin*, a class action on behalf of incarcerated people who are deaf and hard of hearing. Taylor has given numerous presentations on the ADA across the country to people with disabilities, family members, attorneys, employers, businesses, service providers, and advocacy organizations. Prior to coming to EFE, Taylor was the AIDS project attorney in the Midwest regional office of Lambda Legal working to advance the civil rights of people living with HIV/AIDS. From 1988 to 1993, Taylor was a litigation associate at the Chicago law firm of Peterson and Ross. He is a 1988 graduate of the University of Illinois College of Law, where he also received his undergraduate degree in 1985.

Elizabeth Wakeland, ForenClinPsyD, is a registered and chartered forensic and clinical psychologist working in the United Kingdom. She has approximately 9 years' experience within forensic, clinical, and community settings, including prison, probation, offender personality disorder pathway services and secure settings, working with both offenders and victims across the life span. Her interest in deafness began in college, where she studied British Sign Language Level 1, and she is currently completing her Level 6 studies in British Sign Language. She has an interest in the field of deaf mental health and offending, and has published a number of papers within this area. Her doctoral thesis focused on the experiences of Deaf people, as both victims and offenders, which won a "prequalification award" from the British Psychological Society Division of Forensic Clinical Psychology for its outstanding contributions to research in this area. She has previously worked in specialist deaf adult mental health services across the charitable and NHS sectors.

Rachel M. Weisberg, JD, is a staff attorney at Equip for Equality (EFE), where she has represented hundreds of clients in individual and systemic disability discrimination cases under the ADA and analogous state and local laws. Of note, Weisberg represents a class of deaf and hard of hearing individuals incarcerated in the Illinois Department of Corrections in *Holmes v. Baldwin*. She manages EFE's Employment Rights Helpline, which aims to expand employment opportunities by providing legal and practical advice to applicants and individuals with disabilities. Weisberg is a frequent trainer on the disability rights laws. Prior to EFE, Rachel worked as an assistant attorney general in the Civil Rights Bureau and the Disability Rights Bureau of the Illinois Attorney General's Office, as a labor and employment associate at Sidley Austin LLP, and as a law clerk for Chief Judge James G. Carr in the Northern District of Ohio. Before law school, Weisberg worked as an ADA technical assistance specialist at the Mid-Atlantic ADA Center and during law school interned with EFE and the Disability Rights Section of the U.S. Department of Justice. She is a graduate of Northwestern University School of Law and the University of Michigan.

Roger C. Williams, MSW, is the executive director of the Spartanburg Area Mental Health Center with the South Carolina Department of Mental Health. He received his BSW from the Rochester Institute of Technology and his MSW, specializing in community mental health, from the University of Illinois and completed coursework toward a doctorate at the University of South Carolina, College of Social Work. Williams is a South Carolina Licensed Independent Social Worker-Clinical Practice and holds a RID Certificate of Transliteration and an SCAD/NAD IAP Level 5 and has been recognized at the state and national levels for his leadership in mental health services within the Deaf community.

Index

Figures, notes, and tables are indicated by f, n, *and* t *following the page number.*

ABA (American Bar Association), 217, 223
ableism, 244, 285, 292n2
accessibility
of alerts in prison, 196, 200–201, 305
of communication in prison, 89–90, 94–95, 196, 305, 306–307
companions, rights of, 187, 202
employers' reluctance to hire deaf people, 215
laws requiring communication access, 149
needs in criminal justice system, 304–307
of notices about policies and services, 54
of prison services and programs, 96–97, 305, 306
recommendations on, 304–307
accommodations. *See also* nondiscrimination in criminal justice system; sign language interpreters
for arrests and bookings, 15–16, 96, 245–247, 250–251
for assessments, 108, 305–306
for attorney–client relationships, 218–222, 227n1
in court rooms, 49, 268–269, 309–310
data collection on, 15–17
disability justice and mass incarceration, 233–234, 236–237
for employment, 215
preferences, deaf cards to indicate, 245, 245*f*, 250–251
for prison services and programs, 88, 96–97
recommendations for, 286–287
in schools, 79
ACTFL (American Council on the Teaching of Foreign Languages), 142
ADA. *See* Americans With Disabilities Act
addiction. *See* substance use disorders
adjudicative competence testing, 29
adolescents. *See* children and adolescents
adult basic education (ABE), 107
adverse childhood experiences (ACEs), 68, 306
advocacy
of families of deaf people, 78
of HEARD, 245, 250, 251, 256, 267, 271
recommendations for, 315
single-issue advocacy, 233, 275–278, 284
success of, 291–292
training in, 105–106
age-induced hearing loss, 11
alcohol use. *See* substance use disorders
Alexander, M., 155n17
American Bar Association (ABA), 217, 223
American Civil Liberties Union, 77, 105–106
American Community Survey, 5
American Corrections Association, 94
American Council on the Teaching of Foreign Languages (ACTFL), 142
American Psychiatric Association, 24
American Sign Language (ASL). *See also* sign language interpreters
acquisition of, ix
data collection instruments, omission of ASL in, 12
English vs., 45, 134, 154n14
prerecorded materials for prisons, 307
sign language dysfluencies and, 25
survey accessibility and, 13, 306
teachers and support staff knowledgeable in, 65–66, 73, 170, 177

Americans With Disabilities Act of 1990 (ADA)
- application to correctional facilities, 195–202
- arrests and availability of interpreters during, 77, 123, 187–190, 192, 266
- clearinghouse of information on deaf inmates, 307–308
- communication barriers, 183–187, 208n6–7
- companions, communication rights of, 202
- disability, defined, 236
- DOJ model policy on treatment of deaf people and, 287
- exigent circumstances, 187–195
- financial reimbursement for treatments and, 74
- interpreter access requirements, 198
- nondiscrimination
  - in criminal justice system, 182, 208n1, 208n3–5, 236
  - in criminal proceedings, 202–204
  - by law enforcement, 87–88, 236–237
- prison programs, access to, 96
- qualified interpreters, 155n9
- remedies under, 205–206
- self-evaluation plans, 15
- undue burden and fundamental alteration defenses and, 204–205
- video phones access, 199–200, 305

Anderson, C., 155n17
Andreasen, N., 24–25
Andrews, J., 68
appeals, 221, 267, 272
Appraisal Model of Behavior, 117–121, 117*f*
arrests and bookings. *See also* interrogations
- accommodations for, 15–16, 96, 245–247, 250–251
- ADA and Rehabilitation Act on communication during, 77, 123, 187–190, 192, 226
- cognitive disabilities and, 105
- data collection on, 15–16, 310
- deaf experience of, 92–93
- faulty investigations and, 243–244
- handcuffing policies, 77, 193–195, 216
- juvenile justice system and, 77–78
- misunderstandings and, 77, 93, 239, 282–83
- resisting, 133, 238
- sign language interpreter availability and, 77, 123, 191–195, 245–246, 265–266
- sign language use perceived as threatening, 238, 247
- substance abuse and, 83
- in United Kingdom, 123
- wrongful, 282–283

Arthur, United States v. (2016), 186, 208n7
ASL. *See* American Sign Language
assessments. *See also* communication assessments
- accommodations for, 108, 305–306
- assessor qualifications, 31–32
- of cognitive functioning, 67–68
- of mental illness, 102–103
- needs assessments in prisons, 201–202
- statistics on deaf people from, 5–6

attention deficit hyperactive disorder (ADHD), 100, 120
attorney–client relationships, xii, 212–228
- attorney training and, 311–313
- confidentiality vs. privilege, 222–225
- duty of an attorney, 216–218
- failures of, 270–272, 271*f*
- interpreters and, 218–222
- linguistic competency and legal system, 225–226
- relationship formation and, 212–213
- right to counsel and, 213–216, 283–284

Austen, Sally, xi–xii, 115
autism, 25, 120
auxiliary aids and services, 183–185, 208n6–7

Bahl v. County of Ramsey (2012), 190
Balch, G., 48–49
Barrow, L., 53
Bearden v. Clark County (2016), 200
behavioral issues. *See also* juvenile justice system
- ASL abilities of teachers and support staff, 73
- defined, 116
- lax treatment of deaf individuals, 85, 92, 118–119, 122
- rewards vs. punishments for, 118–119

Beldon, J., 52, 158n82
Belmont Report (National Commission for the Protection of Human Subjects of Biomedical and Behavioral Research), 41, 43
beneficence, 41, 43
Berman, B., 84
bias, perceptions of, 152–153. *See also* discrimination

Bienvenu, M J, 144
bilingualism, 131, 142–143, 144
Bircoll v. Miami-Dade County (2007), 189
Blanck, P., 15
Board of Educ. of Hendrick Hudson Central School District, Westchester County v. Rowley (1982), 171
body language. *See* nonverbal communication
bookings. *See* arrests and bookings
boundary setting, 118–119
Brady v. Maryland (1963), 222–223
brain injuries, 8, 120
Brick, K., 52
Brodie, Stephen, 255–56
Bronson, J., 9, 83
Brown v. Board of Education (1954), 168
Brunson, J., 45–46
Bureau of Justice Statistics, 83, 307–308
Burnett, State v. (2005), 23

California Rule of Court 5.651, 172–173
California Welfare and Institutions Code, 170
Capella, M., 47
Carson, E., 83
Carter-Long, L., 15
CASA (National Center on Addiction and Substance Abuse), 82, 97, 98–99
causes of hearing loss. *See* types and causes of hearing loss
census data, x, 5, 12
Center for Substance Abuse Treatment Improvement Protocol, 97
Center for the Assessment of Sign Language Interpretation, 148, 158n82
Centers for Disease Control and Prevention (CDC), 6, 13, 68
Centers for Independent Living (CILs), 107
certification of interpreters
  barriers and inequality in, 273–274
  deaf interpreters and, 78, 148–149, 158n82, 225, 313
  legal interpreters, 158n81, 220, 225, 273–274, 313–314
  mental health interpreters, 313
  process for, 148, 313
children and adolescents. *See also* juvenile justice system
  adverse childhood experiences and juvenile delinquency, 68, 306
  causes of hearing loss in, 7–8, 167
  false confessions and, 254
  foster care and, 78, 232, 314
  language development and, ix, 24–25, 49, 68–69. *See also* language deprivation
  overprotection of, 122
  peer pressure and, 87
  protective factors for, 118
  sexual abuse, vulnerability to, 121–122, 232
  statistics on hearing loss, 5–6
  substance use disorders and, 84–87
  youth with disabilities in correctional facilities, 9
children of deaf adults (Codas), 11, 248, 269–271
Chisolm v. McManimon (2001), 184, 205
CILs (Centers for Independent Living), 107
City of Columbia Police, United States v. (2016), 191
City of Philadelphia Police, United States v. (2018), 185, 193–195, 208n6
Civil Rights Data Collection (CRDC), 16
Clarkson v. Coughlin (1995), 196
Clyne, M., 131
Code of Professional Conduct (RID-NAD), 27, 52, 224
cognitive function
  assessment of, 67–68
  cognitive disabilities and, 105
  learning and emotional disabilities, 9, 25, 67–68, 69, 105
  risk factors and protective factors, 116–121
  sign language interpreting challenges and, 140–141
Columbia City Police, United States v. (2016), 191
Committee on Identifying the Needs of the Forensic Science Community (CIDNFSC), 40–41
communication
  ADA on barriers to, 183–187, 208n6–7
  assessments for. *See* communication assessments
  attorney–client relationship and, 216–218
  companions, accessibility rights of, 187, 202
  court system, barriers in, 202–203
  for deaf prisoners, ix–x, 87–90, 94–95, 196–201, 305–307
  deprivation of. *See* language deprivation

devices for. *See* telecommunication; videophones
early childhood experiences and, 68
families, barriers within, 118
interpreters for. *See* sign language interpreters
law enforcement issues leading to violence, incarceration, or death, 10, 15, 77, 188, 229, 238–240, 243, 277–278, 304–305
lax treatment of deaf individuals resulting from lack of, 85, 92, 118–119, 122
legal system, barriers in, 93–95
literacy levels and, 73–74, 88
misunderstandings and. *See* misunderstandings
nonverbal. *See* nonverbal communication
of notices about policies and services, 54
with research participants, 47–48
with sign language. *See* American Sign Language; sign language
skills of interpreters and, 146–148
social cognition and, 70
spectrum of, 235
teachers and support staff, ASL abilities of, 65–66, 73, 170, 177
communication assessments
assessor qualifications and, 31–32
communication cards to assist in, 194
example of report, 36–39, 38*f*
for fitness to stand trial, 22–23, 25–28, 305
forms for, 194
for inmates, 108
recommendations for, 305
structure of, 28–31
communication cards, 194, 278–282, 279–280*f*
community-based services, 17, 85
community-engaged research, 51
companions, accessibility rights of, 187, 202
competence. *See* linguistic incompetence in criminal justice and mental health system
competence to stand trial, 22–23, 25–28, 225–226, 305. *See also* communication assessments
Condon, J. C., 131
conductive hearing loss, 5
confessions. *See* false confessions
confidentiality, 48, 222–223
consumer protection advocacy, 54
co-occurring disorders, 101–104
coping strategies, 117
Corrections Today, 94
court interpreters. *See* sign language interpreters
court systems
accommodations for defendants, 218–219
data collection recommendations for, 16, 309–310
drug courts, 97
failures of, 268–270, 270*f*
fitness to stand trial and. *See* communication assessments
frame and footing for, 134
juvenile offenders and, 78
nondiscrimination in communication access, 202–203
rate of deaf cases in, 268
sign language interpreter provision in, 52–53, 78, 214–215, 248–251, 267, 272–275
simultaneous interpreting for, 133, 154n13
training for personnel, 313
wrongful conviction cases, 254–267, 257–262*f*, 264*f*, 266*f*
Crandall, United States v. (2014), 219
Crenshaw, K., 54
criminal justice system. *See also* court systems; law enforcement officers; prisons and jails
communication assessments in, 22–39. *See also* linguistic incompetence in criminal justice and mental health system
disability justice and, 229–303. *See also* disability justice and mass incarceration
IDEA and, 165–180. *See also* Individuals With Disabilities Education Act
juvenile justice system and, 63–81. *See also* juvenile justice system
nondiscrimination in, 181–211. *See also* nondiscrimination in criminal justice system
recommendations for, 304–316
research methods with deaf people in, 40–59. *See also* research methods with deaf people
sign language interpreters for, 131–162. *See also* sign language interpreters

substance use disorders of deaf offenders, 82–114. *See also* Substance use disorders
in United Kingdom, 115–130. *See also* United Kingdom, deaf people in justice system in
Crump, Charlene, 25
cultural mediation, 44–45, 218, 220
culture. *See* Deaf community; Deaf culture

data collection
on arrests and bookings, 15–16, 310
government failure in, 233–234
issues with, 11–14
recommendations for, 14–19, 55, 307–311
dating, 71–72
Davis, Angela Y., 231
Davis, F. E., 7
DeafBlindness, 6, 7, 13, 55
Deaf cards
for communication with police, 278–282, 279–280*f*
for identification and required accommodations, 242, 245, 245*f*, 250–251
Deaf community. *See also* schools for deaf students
community-based services in, 85
deaf interpreters in legal settings and, 53
deaf researchers and professionals, 44–45, 55, 308
diversity within, 3–4, 48–49, 310
enculturation of children of deaf adults, 11
gathering places for, 138, 156n43
interpreters and attorney–client relationships, 224
language disorders and, 24
peer groups in schools and, 73
prevalence of offending in, 116
as protective factor, 118
terms of reference for, 43–44
Deaf culture
attorney–client relationships and, 214–215
communication issues and misunderstandings, 273, 283
disability justice and, 267, 273
eye contact and, 252
research methods with deaf people and, 43–45, 55
risk factors for offending and, 116, 127
in schools, 65
Deaf driver or identification cards. *See* Deaf cards
Deaf interpreters
certification of, 78, 148–149, 158n82, 313
deaf-hearing interpreting teams, 52–53, 141, 148–149, 152, 157n47
linguistic competency and, 225
deafness, demographics and etiology in, x–xi, 3–21
addressing, 3–4
criminal justice and, 8–9
data collection issues, 11–14
deafness defined, viii–ix, 4
deaf people in criminal justice system, 9–11
models of deafness and, 4
noise-induced/acquired hearing loss, 8
racial and ethnic groups, 6
recommendations for data collection, 14–19
rubella and, 7
statistics from assessments, 5–6
types and causes of hearing loss, 4–5, 120, 167
Usher syndrome and, 7–8
veterans and hearing loss, 8
Deaf nod, 48, 74, 144–145, 158n65, 267
death. *See* fatalities caused law enforcement officers
Department of Education, U.S., 66, 170
Department of Health and Human Services, 41
Department of Justice
on ADA, 187–188
deaf prisoners, statistics on, 10
guide for communicating with deaf people, 123, 183
on mental health disorders of inmates, 101
model policy on treatment of deaf people, 285–288
settlement agreements, 193–194
desistance, 115, 126
developmental disorders, 25
Diagnostic and Statistical Manual of Mental Disorders (5th ed., DSM-5), 23, 67
Directory of Services for the Deaf, 7
Disability Characteristics Survey, 5
disability justice, xii, 229–303
deaf driver or identification cards and registries, 278–282, 279–280*f*
deaf people not responding to law enforcement, 238–240

discrimination protections and, 236–237
domestic disputes and, 244–251, 245–246*f*, 276
fatalities of deaf people and, 10, 229, 238–240, 243, 277–278
faulty investigations and, 243–244
law enforcement interactions, common scenarios, 237–267, 253*f*, 257–264*f*
lawsuits, policy adoption, and settlement agreements, 284–288
mass incarceration overview, 230–234
police brutality resulting from calls to law enforcement, 240–243, 277
police training and, 282–284
recommendations for, 288–291
single-issue advocacy and erasure of intersectionality, 275–278
system, process, and accountability failures, 266–272, 270–271*f*
tracking and accommodations for deaf people, 233–234
wrongful conviction cases, 94, 254–267, 257–262*f*, 264*f*, 266*f*

discourse
defined, 134
organization and style, 136
pragmatics and, 134–135
of sign language, 137–139
of suspects, 139–140

discrimination. *See also* nondiscrimination in criminal justice system
in court systems, 269–70
interpreter certifications and, 274
legal protections against, 87–88, 236–237. *See also specific laws*
LGBTQI people and, 275–276
systemic, 155n17, 286
transformative paradigm and, 42
underemployment and, 215

Doctor, P. V., 7
domestic disputes, 244–251, 245–246*f*, 276
driver's licenses, 278–282, 279–280*f*
drug courts, 97
drug use. *See* substance use disorders
Duchesneau, S. M., 44
due process, 88, 89, 169, 214, 219
Dunning–Kruger effect, 32
Durrenberger v. Texas Department of Criminal Justice (2010), 202
Duvall v. County of Kitsap (2001), 204

Eckes, Eric, 26
education. *See* schools and education
Educational Interpreter Proficiency Assessment, 31
Elementary and Secondary Education Act of 1965, 168–169
Eleventh Amendment, 202–203
Emerson, E., 116
empathy, 73, 121
employment
accommodations for, 215
deaf researchers and, 45
racism and, 155n17
substance abuse and, 107
unemployment and underemployment, 24, 107, 215
vocational rehabilitation for released inmates, 106–107
Endrew F. ex rel. Joseph F. v. Douglas County School Dist. RE-1 (2017), 171
ethics
attorney–client relationships and, 222–225
communication skills assessments and, 31
interpreters and attorney–client relationships, 224
protections for prisoners as research subjects, 41
research methods with deaf people and, 40–59. *See also* research methods with deaf people
sign language interpreters and, 148, 158n72, 224
executive functioning, 70, 120
exigent circumstances, 187–195
eye contact, 252

face-saving strategies, 145
facial grammar, 50–51
false confessions, 77–78, 251–256, 315
families of deaf people
advocacy of, 78
attorney–client privilege and, 223
children of deaf adults, 11, 248, 269–271
communication barriers within, 118
heritage language use in, 143–144
as interpreters, 248, 269–271, 273
parent-education programs, 314
Farrelly, Amber D., xi, 212, 239
fatalities caused by law enforcement officers, 10, 229, 238–240, 243, 277–278
Federal Bureau of Prisons, 87
Ferrucci, L., 5
Fifth Amendment, 198

fingerspelling
of attorneys, 213
discourses of sign language and, 137–138
of interpreters, 31
lexicalized words from, 156n41
of police officers, 256, 265–267
First Amendment, 200, 203
first responders, 105–106
fitness to stand trial, 22–23, 25–28, 225–226, 305. *See also* communication assessments
Folkman, S., 117–121, 117*f*
footing, 134–135, 136
Foreign Services Administration, 142
forensic science research, 40–41
foster care, 78, 232, 314
Fourteenth Amendment, 203, 214
frames for situations, 134–135
fundamental alteration defense, 204–205
fund of information
court experience and, 78, 124
defined, 70–71
developmental environments and, 117–118
incidental learning and, 70–71, 78, 88–89, 117–118
juvenile offenders and, 70–72, 312

Gahir, M., 115
Gallaudet, Thomas Hopkins, 72, 168
Gallaudet University, 6
Geer, S., 48
gender
of attorneys and interpreters, 216
of deaf children, 6
of people with disabilities in prisons and jails, 9
General Educational Development (GED), 107
genetic diseases, 7
Gideon v. Wainwright (1963), 213–214
Glickman, N., 24, 69
Gohier v. Enright (1999), 189
Gonzalez v. United States (2008), 217
Gridley, Samuel, 168
Guba, E., 42
guilty pleas, 78, 214, 217, 249–250, 284
Gulati, S., 152
Guthmann, Debra, vii, xi, xi–xiii, 82, 302

Habashi, J., 54
Hainze v. Richards (2000), 188
Hamerdinger, Steve, 25
handcuffs, 77, 193–195, 216
Harris, Daniel, 277, 286
Harris, Raychelle L., xi, 40, 44, 54
Harris, Ricardo, 265–67, 266*f*
Haualand, H., 116
Heard, Joseph, 94
Hearing Aid Compatibility Act of 1988, 207
hearing guilt, 65
Helping Educate to Advance the Rights of the Deaf (HEARD)
advocacy of, 245, 250, 251, 256, 267, 271
on communication rights of deaf people in prisons, 94
crowdsourced data on violence of law enforcement officers, 233
on deaf prisoner numbers, 41–42, 66
on law enforcement interactions, rights during, 77, 105–106
police brutality, statement on, 277–278
hereditary diseases, 7
heritage language users, 143–144
Hewstone, M., 4
Heyer v. U.S. Bureau of Prisons (2017), 198
Hoffman, H. J., 6
Hoffman v. Marion County Texas (2014), 192
Holmes v. Baldwin (2018), 197, 200–201
House, L., 9

IDEA. *See* Individuals With Disabilities Education Act
IEPs (individualized education plans), 169, 171–172, 174
impulse control, 70
incidental learning, 70–71, 78, 88–89, 117–118
inclusive education, 73, 168
individualized education plans (IEPs), 169, 171–172, 174
Individuals With Disabilities Education Act of 2004 (IDEA), xii, 165–180
data collection through, 16
deaf youth in juvenile correction facilities and, 170–171
free and appropriate public education, right to, 171, 173–174
history of, 168–169
juvenile justice system and, 171–173, 175–178
recommendations for, 178–179
related services, right to, 171
residency laws and juvenile justice system, 173–175

information. *See* fund of information
informed consent, 48
interpreter for counsel (IFC), 220, 224
interpreters. *See* Deaf interpreters; sign language interpreters
interrogations
ADA on, 188–189
disability justice and, 251–267. *See also* Reid technique
false confessions and, 77–78, 251–256, 315
sign language interpreter availability during, 77, 123, 265–266
video recordings of, 123, 124, 153
intersectionality
demographics and etiology of deafness and, 6
disability justice lens and, 232–235
mass incarceration and, 229–230
research methods with deaf people and, 46, 54
of research teams, 55
single-issue advocacy and, 273–276
investigations, criminal, 195, 240, 243–244
isolation
of deaf juvenile offenders in treatment institutions, 75
of deaf prisoners, x, 95–96, 125, 305–306
substance use risk factors and, 87

Jaspers, J., 4
Jin, Hui Jie, 285
Jin v. Alameda County (2018), 285
Johnson, H. A., 75
Jones, United States v. (2006), 23
Joos, M., 147, 154n3
JPay, 106
juries, 78, 269
Justice Department. *See* Department of Justice
Juvenile Justice and Delinquency Prevention Act of 1974, 16, 170, 172–173
juvenile justice system, xi, 63–81
arrests and bookings, 77–78
case study, 63–65
court experiences, 78
data collection recommendations for, 16–17, 310
history of, 65–66, 170–171
IDEA and, 171–173
mental illness in juvenile correctional facilities, 170, 229
mobility of deaf youth within, 173–175
need for research in, 79
number of youths incarcerated in, 66–67, 170
path to and path beyond, 175–178
people with disabilities and, 170, 229, 232, 292n3
recommendations for, 178–179, 314–315
school-to-prison nexus factors, 67–74, 306, 312, 314–315
treatment options through, 74–76, 76–77*f*

Kaiser Permanente Health System, 68
Kannapell, B., 51, 55
Kassin, S. M., 77–78
Kendon, A., 156n40
Kessler, E. Basil, x, 3, 307
Kim, Robert, 240
Kolvitz, Marcia, xi, 82
Kushalnagar, P., 84

Ladd, P., 4
language
defined, 156n39
development of, ix, 24–25, 49, 68–69
fluency, 141–146, 148, 158n76
language deprivation
cognitive deficits resulting from, 120
court proceedings and, 49
lack of research on, 24
language dysfluency resulting from, 25
mental health outcomes and, 167
school experiences and, 29
social cognition and, 70
substance abuse risk factors and, 88
language disorder or dysfluency
arrests and bookings, 92
attorney–client relationships and, 226
communication assessments and, 30
deaf community, rates among, 24–26
defined, 23–24
juvenile offenders and, 312
Language Rating Scale, 55
law enforcement officers. *See also* arrests and bookings; interrogations; rights during law enforcement interactions
ADA and Rehabilitation Act on communication with, 187–195, 236
communication issues
police brutality resulting from, 10, 15, 77, 133, 188, 229, 237–244, 277–278
police lenience resulting from, 85, 92, 118–119, 122

crowdsourced data on violence of, 233–234
discrimination and harassment by, 275–277
DOJ on treatment of deaf people, 285–288
domestic disputes and, 244–251, 245–246*f*
sign language use of, 256, 265–267, 276, 282–283
substance use disorders and interactions with, 105–106
training on deafness and disabilities, 105, 123, 239, 282–284, 309, 311–313
lawyers. *See* attorney–client relationships
Lazarus, R., 117–121, 117*f*
learning disabilities
brain damage and, 120
diagnosis in people who are deaf, 25
of incarcerated youth, 9, 67–68
of inmates, 100–101, 105
treatment for people who are deaf, 69
Lewis, Talila A., xi, 91, 94, 229
Lewis, Victoria Ann, 155n31
LGBTQI population, 275–276
Liese v. Indian River County Hospital District (2012), 205
Lin, F. R., 5
Lincoln, Y., 42
linguistic incompetence in criminal justice and mental health system, xi, 22–39
assessor qualifications and, 31–32
attorney–client relationships and, 225–226
communication assessment structure, 28–31
example of communication assessment report, 36–39, 38*f*
language disorders and dysfluency, 23–25
rights violations and, 49
lipreading, 50, 123, 125, 208n8, 311
literacy levels, 73–74, 88
Loeffler v. Staten Island University Hospital (2009), 205
Lomas, Gabriel I., vii, xi, xi–xiii, 61, 75, 302
Long, Greg, 26
Longmore, P. K., 155n31
Loye v. County of Dakota (2010), 188–189

Martens, Elise, 168
Martin, Gabriel A. "Tony," x, 3, 51
Mass incarceration, 230–234. *See also* disability justice
Mathers, C., 52
Matlin, Marlee, 105–106
McBride v. Michigan Department of Corrections (2018), 199, 207
McCauley, E. J., 9, 15
McCullough, C. A., 44
McKee, Michael, 85
medical model of deafness, 4
mental health. *See also* isolation
appraisals of experiences and, 120–121
communication assessments and, 22–39. *See also* linguistic incompetence in criminal justice and mental health system
language disorders and, 24
language dysfluency and, 25
mental health interpreters, 313
treatment options, 74–76, 76–77*f*
mental health courts, 103
mental illness
deaf individuals in institutions for, 116
deaf offenders and, 125–126
false confessions and, 254
inmates with substance use disorders and, 82, 100–104
leading to incarceration, 167, 172, 254
misdiagnoses of, 102–103
rates among deaf individuals, 120, 167, 311
rates in juvenile correction facilities, 170, 229
rates in prisons and jails, 101, 229
stigma and, 103
Mertens, Donna M., xi, 40, 42, 48–49, 54
Michaels, Samantha, 97
Miller, Katrina, 23–24, 46–47, 49, 51–52, 96
Mills v. Board of Education of District of Columbia (1972), 169
Minnesota Substance Use Disorder Program for Deaf and Hard of Hearing Individuals, 86–87, 92
Minnis v. Johnson (2010), 196–199
Miranda rights, 78, 105, 123, 213
misunderstandings
arrests and, 77, 93, 239, 282–283
case analyses of causes, 132–136
in interrogations, 254, 255
of legal issues, 216
legal requirements for sign language interpreters and, 197–199
literacy levels and, 73–74
police
lenience resulting from communication issues, 85, 92, 118–119, 122

as sign language interpreters, 256, 265–267, 276, 282–283
violence resulting from communication issues, 10, 15, 77, 133, 188, 237–244, 277–278
sign language interpreters and, 145–146, 272–273
substance abuse treatment and, 99
video recordings of police interviews and, 123, 124
Mitchell, R., 12
mixed hearing loss, 5
Model Health Insurance Policy Language Simplification Act, 54
Model Life, 54
Model Rules on Professional Conduct of American Bar Association, 217
moderate hearing loss, 5
modified therapeutic community (MTC) program, 104
Morales v. Saint Barnabas Medical Center (2017), 187
moral reasoning, 120
Morgan, G., 51
Mullins, United States v. (2002), 217

Nathan v. Anchorage (1998), 48
National Association of School Psychologists, 170
National Association of the Deaf, 31, 199, 277
National Association of the Deaf Law Center, 54
National Center for Education Statistics, 170
National Center on Addiction and Substance Abuse (CASA), 82, 97, 98–99
National Center on Deaf-Blindness (NCDB), 6, 13
National Child Count of Children and Youth Who Are DeafBlind, 6
National Commission for the Protection of Human Subjects of Biomedical and Behavioral Research, 41, 43
National Consortium on Interpreter Education Center, 53
National Council on Disability (NCD), 9, 16
National Crime Victimization Survey, 53
National Deaf Center, viii
National Disability Rights Network, 199
National Habeas Institute, 267
National Health and Nutritional Examination Survey (NHANES), 5, 84–85
National Health Interview Survey, 6, 13
National Institute on Deafness and other Communication Disorders, 7
National Institute on Drug Abuse (NIDA), 98
National Registry of Interpreters for the Deaf, 31
National Survey on Drug Use and Health, 85
NCD (National Council on Disability), 9, 16
NCDB (National Center on Deaf-Blindness), 6, 13
Neave-DiToro, D., 10
needs assessments, 201–202
Nett, Sholeen, 144
Newmann, K., 78
NHANES (National Health and Nutritional Examination Survey), 5, 84–85
NIDA (National Institute on Drug Abuse), 98
911 calls, 188
Niparko, J. K., 5
Nippold, M. A., 141
noise-induced hearing loss (NIHL), 8, 11
nondiscrimination in criminal justice system, xii, 181–211
accessible alerts and, 200–201
ADA and Rehabilitation Act on, 182
ADA on barriers to communication, 183–187
cases and settlements, overview, 196–197
companions, access for, 202
correctional facilities and, 195–196
criminal proceedings and, 202–204
Hearing Aid Compatibility Act, 207
law enforcement and, 187–195
need assessments, 201–202
remedies, 205–207
sign language interpreters and, 197–199
Telecommunications Act, 207
telephone access and, 199–200
undue burden and fundamental alteration, 204–205
nonverbal communication
cognitive disabilities and, 105
deaf nod, 48, 74, 144–145, 158n65, 267
exaggerated body language during signing, 238, 247

facial grammar, 50–51
during interrogations, 251–254. *See also* Reid technique

Office of Human Research Protections, 41
Oklahoma Association of the Deaf, 277
oral interpreters, 50, 208n8
O'Rourke, Susan, xi–xii, 65, 115
Ortner, S. B., 131

Paijmans, R., 119, 121
Paris, Damara Goff, vii, x, 3, 307
parole, 91–92, 98, 106, 306
pathological model of deafness, 4
Pearson, Pearl, Jr., 240–243, 281
peer pressure, 87
Pennsylvania Ass'n for Retarded Children v. Commonwealth (PARC) (1971), 169
Pennsylvania Department of Corrections v. Yeskey (1998), 189, 195–196
Pennucci, A., 156n32
people with disabilities. *See also* Individuals With Disabilities Education Act
cognitive, 105
court system and power dynamics, 269–270
defined, 234, 236
disability hierarchies and, 292n2
false confessions and, 254
inclusive and mainstream education for, 73, 168
in juvenile justice system, 170, 229, 232, 292n3
killed by law enforcement officers, 229
language and learning challenged deaf people, 69
law enforcement interactions, common scenarios, 237–267, 245–246*f*, 253*f*, 257–264*f*
police training on, 282–84
in prisons and jails, 9–10, 66–67, 101, 195–196, 229, 232, 307–308
public schools, lack of adequate diagnostic services in, 69
racial and ethnic group intersectionalities, 234–235
rate of encounters with criminal justice system, 181
registries of, 279–280
social construction of, 136, 155n31
spectrum of disabilities and, 235
substance abuse and co-occurring disabilities, 100–104
Perry, D. M., 15
Philadelphia Police, United States v. (2018), 185, 193–195, 208n6
pictograms, 194, 278–282, 279–280*f*
Pierce v. District of Columbia (2015), 201, 206
plea agreements, 249–250
Poizner, H., 25
police. *See* law enforcement officers
Pollard, R. Q, 24–25
poverty, 24, 232, 269–270
power imbalances
court system and, 269–270
between criminals and victims, 53
footing and, 134–135, 136
race and ethnicity, 269
researchers and, 48
pragmatics, 134
Prakel v. Indiana (2015), 203–204, 205
prison industrial complex, 231
Prison Litigation Reform Act of 2012 (PLRA), 205–206
Prison Policy Initiative, 66
prisons and jails
abuse in, 92–93, 95
ADA and nondiscrimination in, 195–202
alerts, accessibility of, 196, 200–201, 305
cognitive deficits of inmates, 105, 120
communication access in, ix–x, 87–90, 94–95, 196–201, 305–307
companions, accessibility rights of, 202
deaf inmates housed together in, 95–96, 108, 305–306
discrimination, legal protections against, 87–88, 205–206
lack of data on deaf individuals in, 13–14
language disorder prevalence in, 24
mass incarceration and, 230–234. *See also* disability justice
mental illness rates in, 101, 229
needs assessments in, 201–202
number of deaf individuals in, 9–10, 41–42, 66–67, 115–116
people with disabilities in, 9–10, 229, 232, 307–308
race, ethnicity, and poverty of inmates, 231
recidivism rates, 9, 17, 97–99, 310
research methods with deaf people in, 40–59. *See also* research methods with deaf people
safety assessments for deaf inmates in, 307

settlement agreements for deaf people in, 94, 97, 196–201
sexual abuse and assault in, 88, 92–93, 94, 96
substance use disorders and, 82–114. *See also* substance use disorders
training for prison staff, 311–313
wrongful imprisonment in, 94, 254–267, 257–264*f*, 266*f*
privilege, 222–225, 227n2
profound hearing loss, 5
psychiatric services, 69–70, 75–76, 76*f*
psychotic disorders, 65, 102–103
public safety, 188–193

racial and ethnic groups. *See also* intersectionality
court system and power dynamics, 269–270
deaf individuals in correctional facilities, 10
deaf researchers and professionals, 55
fatalities from law enforcement and, 229
incarceration rates and, 231
institutionalized and social racism, 155n17
people with disabilities and, 234–235, 292n3
segregation in schools and, 168
sign language interpreter representation among, 274
statistics on hearing loss among, 6
youth with disabilities in correctional facilities, 9
Raifman, I. J., 65
recidivism rates, 9, 17, 97–99, 310
recommendations
on accessibility needs, 304–307
on advocacy, 315
on data collection and research, 14–19, 53–56, 307–311
on disability justice and mass incarceration, 288–291
on future planning, 315–316
on juvenile justice system, 178–179, 314–315
on sign language interpreters, 151–153, 313–314
on substance use disorder treatments, 107–108
on training, 311–312
recordings of police interviews, 123, 124, 273
refusal to hear, 137, 156n33
registries of deaf people, 278–282, 279–280*f*
Registry of Interpreters for the Deaf (RID), 27, 52, 148, 224, 274
Rehabilitation, 91–92, 125, 170, 172
Rehabilitation Act of 1973
application to prisons and jails, 87–88
discrimination by law enforcement, protections against, 236–237
on nondiscrimination in criminal justice system, 182, 208n1, 236
remedies under, 205–206
undue burden and fundamental alteration defenses and, 204–205
on video phone access, 200
Reid technique
criticism of, 251–252
deceptive behavior based on, 252–253, 253*f*, 261
defined, 251–252
false confessions and, 254
wrongful convictions and, 254–267, 257–264*f*
remedies for discrimination, 205–206
Research and Evaluation in Education and Psychology (Mertens), 54
Research Methods in Sign Language Studies: A Practical Guide (Orfanidou), 51
research methods with deaf people, xi, 40–59
challenges in, 41–42
ethics and, 43
gaps in research and, 307–311
recommendations for, 53–56, 307–311
sign language communities' terms of reference, 43–47
transformative axiological assumption and, 42–43
transformative epistemological assumption and, 50–51
transformative methodological assumption and, 51–54
transformative ontological assumption and, 47–50
research teams, 44–45, 55, 308
residential schools, 65, 73, 118, 121
respect, 43
RespectAbility, 9–10
Rich, S., 47
RID (Registry of Interpreters for the Deaf), 27, 52, 148, 224, 274
Ridgeway, J., 10

rights during law enforcement interactions
court experiences and, 78, 203, 225
disability rights and, 247–251
duties of attorneys and, 217
educating deaf people on, 105–106, 283–284, 314
Miranda rights, 78, 105, 123, 213
right to counsel, 213–216, 283–284
self-incrimination and, 145
in United Kingdom, 123
Robinson v. Farley (2016), 188
Rogers v. Colorado Dep't of Corrections (2019), 199–200
rubella, 7
Ruderman Family Foundation, 10
Rylee v. Chapman (2009), 206–207

Sanchez, Magdiel, 243, 277
Sawyer, W., 66
schools and education. *See also* Individuals With Disabilities Education Act
ASL abilities of teachers and support staff, 65–66, 73, 170, 177
deaf students in juvenile detention centers and, 171–173, 310
diagnostic services, lack of, 69
drug and alcohol prevention in, 85–86, 89
GED and ABE programs, 107
inclusive and mainstream education for people with disabilities, 73, 168
low expectations for deaf students, 144, 156n32
school-to-prison nexus and, 72–73
social-emotional learning programs in, 71–72, 73
schools for deaf students
behavioral issues and, 65
benefits of, 73
data collection recommendations for, 16
history of, 72–73, 168
people with disabilities, specialized curriculum for, 69
residential schools, 65, 73, 118, 121
rights education in, 105–106, 283–284, 314
school-to-prison pipeline. *See* juvenile justice system
"The Secret World of Deaf Prisoners" (Ridgeway), 10
Section 504. *See* Rehabilitation Act
Securities and Exchange Commission, 54
segregation, 108, 168–169, 236, 305
self-incrimination, 145, 283
self-regulation, 70, 120
self-talk, 120
semiotics, 134
sensorineural hearing loss, 5
Seremeth v. Board of County Commissioners Frederick County (2012), 189
settlement agreements. *See also specific lawsuits*
on communication access during arrests, 193–195
for deaf people in prisons and jails, 94, 97, 196–201
effectiveness of, 284–288
on exigent circumstances, 191
on VRI use, 186–187, 200
severe hearing loss, 5
sexual abuse and assault
children and risk factors for, 121–122, 232
genders of attorneys, interpreters, and clients, 216
people with disabilities and risk factors for, 232
in prisons, 88, 92–93, 94, 96
sexual offenders
case study on, 46–47
deaf people and risk factors for becoming, 70–72, 121–122
false confessions and convictions, 255–256
juvenile, in schools, 65
legal representation for, 216, 224
shame, 144–145
Shannon-Baker, P., 54
Shaw, Daniel, xi, 165
sign language. *See also* American Sign Language; fingerspelling
construction of meanings and knowledge in, 44–45
discourses of, 137–139
exaggerated body language during, 238, 247
facial grammar, 50–51
handcuffs and, 77, 193–195, 216
as language, 153n1
language development and learning challenges, 68–69
sign language communities' terms of reference (SLCTR), 43–47
sign language dysfluencies, 25

sign language interpreters, xii, 131–162
ADA on, 183–185, 208n6–7
arrests, availability during, 77, 123, 191–195, 245–246, 265–266
in attorney–client relationships, 213, 218–222, 224
attorneys acting as, 213
availability of, 149–150
bias of, 152–153
case analyses, 132–134
certification of. *See* certification of interpreters
Code of Professional Conduct, 27, 52, 224
communication assessments and, 26–27, 31–32
communication skills of, 146–148
competence of suspects, assessing, 140–41
in court rooms and legal settings, 52–53, 78, 133, 150–151, 154n13, 214–215, 219–225, 248–251, 272–275, 313
cultural mediation of, 218, 220
Deaf-hearing interpreting teams, 52–53, 141, 148–149, 152, 157n47
Deaf interpreters. *See* Deaf interpreters
disability laws and, 244
discourse and pragmatics, 134–135
discourse of sign language, 137–139
discourse of suspects, 139–140
family members acting as, 245, 248, 269–271, 273
language fluency and, 141–146
literacy level of deaf individuals and, 73–74
misunderstandings and, 145–146, 272–273
need to increase numbers of, 313–314
nondiscrimination requirements in provision of, 197–199
organization and style, 136
police officers acting as, 256, 265–267, 276, 282–283
in prisons, lack of, 96–98, 107
recommendations for, 151–153, 313–314
social construction of people with disabilities, 136–137
victims acting as, 190
video relay and remote interpreting, ix, 89–90, 185–187, 198–199, 208n7
Sign Language Proficiency Interview, 31
simultaneous interpreting, 133, 154n13
single-issue advocacy, 233, 275–278, 284
Singleton, J., 51
SIPP (Survey of Income and Program Participation), 12
Sixth Amendment, 203, 213–216, 218–219, 225
slight or mild hearing loss, 4–5
Smith, Theresa B., xi, 131
social cognition, 70
social-emotional understanding, 71–72, 73, 121
social justice, 54–55. *See also* disability justice; transformative paradigm
social skills, 121
social supports, 118
sociocultural model of deafness, 4
socioeconomic status, 24, 232, 269–270
South Carolina Department of Corrections, United States v. (2018), 198, 201, 209n11
sovereign immunity, 202–203
standardized testing, 306
State v. Burnett (2005), 23
Stein, Christine, 10
stigma, 145
substance use disorders, xi, 82–114. *See also* treatments for substance use disorders
adverse childhood experiences and, 68
communication access in prisons and jails, 87–89
communication barriers in legal system and, 93–95
deaf inmates with, 90–93, 100–105
deaf population with, 84–86
interactions with law enforcement and, 105–106
leading to incarceration, 167
postincarceration planning and services, 106–107
prevalence of, 83–84
risk factors for, 86–87
telecommunication access and, 89–90
Sullivan, P., 121
Supreme Court, U.S.
on ADA, 195–96, 202–204
on attorney–client confidentiality, 222–123

on IDEA, 172
on right to counsel, 213–214
on right to testify, 217
on school segregation, 168
on sign language interpreters in court, 218–19
Survey of Income and Program Participation (SIPP), 12
systemic discrimination and racism, 155n17, 286

Taylor, Barry C., xi, 181
Taylor v. City of Mason (2013), 190
telecommunication
ADA on, 185–187, 208n6–7
criminal justice system and access to, 89–90, 94–95
technological advances in, ix
telecommunication device for the deaf (TTY or TDD), ix, 89, 94–95, 199–200, 305
Telecommunications Act of 1996, 207
Tennessee v. Lane (2004), 202–3, 204
terms of art, 154n4
terms of reference (TOR), 43–47
Texas Board for Evaluation of Interpreters, 31
theory of mind, 70, 120, 121, 146
tinnitus, 8
training
in advocacy, 105–106
for attorneys, 311–313
for first responders and law enforcement, 105, 123, 239, 282–283, 309, 311–313
for prison staff, 108, 311–313
recommendations for, 311–312
in Reid technique, 251, 254
for sign language interpreters, 148, 313
transformative paradigm, 42–54
transformative axiological assumption and, 42–43
transformative epistemological assumption, 50–51
transformative methodological assumption, 51–54
transformative ontological assumption, 47–50
Transformative Research and Evaluation (Mertens), 54
transitional services, 17, 106–107
treatments for substance use disorders
after prison release, 307
co-occurring disorders and, 104
for deaf individuals, 82, 85, 90–92, 95–100
for inmates, 95–100, 305, 306, 312–13
for juvenile offenders, 74–76, 76–77*f*
recommendations for, 107–108
12-step meetings, 87, 91, 108, 313
Trumbetta, S. L., 25
Tucker v. Tennessee (2008), 189
types and causes of hearing loss, 4–5, 120, 167

Umansky, L., 155n31
undue burden defense, 204–5
unemployment and underemployment, 24, 107, 215
United Kingdom, deaf people in justice system in, xi–xii, 115–130
desistance, 126
prevalence of offending in deaf communities, 115–116
punishment vs. rehabilitation, 123–126
risk factors and protective factors, 116–121, 117*f*
sexual offenders and, 121–122
United States v. See name of opposing party
Urban Institute, 82
Usher syndrome, 7–8

Valanzuolo v. City of New Haven (2013), 192
Valdez, Esther, 238–239
validity of research, 43
Vallas, R., 10, 15
VanderPyl, T., 9, 17
Vernon, McCay, 23–24, 46–47, 49, 65, 69, 83
veterans, 8, 11
victims of crime, 53–54, 65
videophones (VPs), ix, 89–90, 199–200, 305, 306–307
video recordings of police interviews and court proceedings, 123, 124, 153
video relay service (VRS), ix, 89–90
video remote interpreting (VRI), 185–187, 198–199, 208n7
violent encounters
between deaf individuals and law enforcement, 10, 15, 77, 133, 188, 229, 237–244, 277–278
lack of data on, 233
people with disabilities and, 232
substance use disorders and, 83

visual notifications, 196, 200–201, 305
vocational rehabilitation, 106–107

Wagner, P., 66
Wakeland, Elizabeth, xi–xii, 115
Waller ex rel. Estate of Hunt v. City of Danville (2009), 189
Watson v. State (1980), 220
Wei, Li, 142
Weisberg, Rachel M., xi, 181
welfare checks by police officers, 240
Wicker, Darnell, 277, 286
Williams, F., 54
Williams, John T., 10, 238–239, 304
Williams, Roger C., xi, 22
Williams v. City of New York (2015), 192–193
Wilson, John H. L., Jr., 256–261, 257–264*f*, 266*f*
World Health Organization (WHO), 4–5, 13
Worley, J., 54
written communication, 123, 192, 208n9. *See also* Deaf cards
wrongful convictions, 94, 254–267, 257–264*f*, 266*f*. *See also* false confessions

Yeh v. United States Bureau of Prisons (2019), 200
Yousef, F. S., 131

Zemedagegehu, Abreham, 10